A Theory of Primitive Christian Religion

The Religion of The Earliest Churches

Creating a Symbolic World

Gerd Theissen

Translated by
John Bowden

FORTRESS PRESS
MINNEAPOLIS

THE RELIGION OF THE EARLIEST CHURCHES
Creating a Symbolic World

Translated by John Bowden from the German, *Eine Theorie der urchristlichen Religion*, copyright © 1999 Gütersloher Verlagshaus, Gütersloh, Germany.

Cover design: Joseph Bonyata
Cover art by Farinaz Taghavi. Copyright © 1998 Photodisc, Inc. Used by permission.

ISBN 0-8006-3179-X

Typeset and manufactured in Great Britain by SCM Press, a division of SCM-Canterbury Press Ltd. AF 1-3179

03 02 01 00 99 1 2 3 4 5 6 7 8 9

To the Theological Faculties of the Universities of Glasgow and St Andrews
in gratitude for the award of honorary doctorates

Contents

Part Five: The Crises and Consolidation of Primitive Christianity 207

Preface

This book is an attempt to give a scholarly description and analysis of primitive Christian religion. It seeks to describe the content of that religion in such a way that it is accessible to men and women whether or not they are religious. Granted, there are many descriptions of the history of primitive Christianity and its religion which do not presuppose any specific positions. What is lacking is a corresponding account of primitive Christian faith – i.e. of what moved people to the depths in primitive Christianity. Those who want to inform themselves about this are referred to 'theologies of the New Testament'. However, these present an internal Christian perspective. They are written for Christians, as a rule for those who are to become clergy. They are legitimate and necessary attempts to describe a religion from within. But the New Testament and primitive Christianity are too important not to be made accessible to as many people as possible in a scholarly way. Their texts and convictions are part of the basic cultural information of human history – whether one hears them as sermon texts or reads them as part of our tradition. It is not good either for society or for the churches for them to be removed from everyday discourse.

It is true that every scholar inevitably writes from his or her standpoint. I am a Christian. I teach theology in a theological faculty. I am an ordained minister. I preach. I love primitive Christianity and its texts. Some people may find that an insuperable limitation for such an enterprise. But it makes a difference whether one elevates one's standpoint to the status of a programme or accepts it and reflects on it as a context for heuristic discovery, and not as the only context in which one's own thought is valid and can be communicated. I in fact think that we can describe the things that we love in such a way that they are understandable and accessible to all – including those who have quite different attitudes to them from ours. Scholarship proves itself in making us to enter into communication with other people who are shaped differently from ourselves, governed by other convictions, and have contrary views on many things. In today's culture, and especially in theology, this view is represented only by a minority. The postmodern mentality is not at all favourable to such an attitude. But there are related efforts in exegesis: the New Testament scholar Heikki Räisänen and I had the idea of such a description of primitive Christian religion independently of each other. Our accounts will prove different. But we are both of the opinion that scholarly communication is possible and necessary beyond the frontiers of particular religious positions.

Moreover I am of the view that such an analysis and description of primitive Christian religion is also important for church and Christianity. Today we can no longer take up one tradition without entering into dialogue with others. The 'external perspective' is increasingly becoming part of the 'internal perspective'. Dialogue with others is part of a dialogue within ourselves.

This book goes back to the Speaker's Lectures given in Oxford in Spring 1998 and 1999. I am grateful to the Faculty of Theology of the University of Oxford for the invitation to deliver these lectures. It gave me the opportunity and also the challenge to work out this outline of a theory of primitive Christian religion in a short form and limited time-span, although I had really planned to work on this project very much later and as a summary of my work on primitive Christianity. The reader will sometimes detect that here an outline is being sketched out which must be filled in and differentiated further. The need to give a short summary of the basic features of the faith, ethics, rite and history of primitive Christianity – since in my view all that belongs to a 'theory of primitive Christian religion' – has necessarily led to some simplifications. Even the notes which were added to the lectures later could not always go into the necessary discussion of details, desirable though that would have been.

I am particularly grateful to Oriel College, Oxford, and its Provost Ernest Nicholson for the hospitality that I enjoyed as visiting fellow. I thank my colleagues and friends in Oxford for many conversations, especially Robert Morgan, Christopher Rowland and Christopher Tuckett – and all those who helped me in my lectures with critical questions and comments. I am also grateful to John Bowden of SCM Press. He has long been familiar with my writing; he translated the lectures and manuscripts into English and supported me in my work. In Heidelberg my thanks go to Frau Heike Goebel and especially to Frau Helga Wolf for producing the manuscript, and to Frau Friedrike Wendt and Simone Sinn for reading the proofs and checking the references. And I thank my wife for being my conversation partner in everything – and for the whole time when I was working on this book.

I dedicate the book to the two faculties in the United Kingdom which have given me honorary doctorates, in 1980 and in 1997.

Heidelberg
24 April 1999 Gerd Theissen

Translator's note

One aspect of this translation calls for comment, namely the way in which I have chosen to render the words *Urchristentum* and *urchristlich* which occur so often in this book. I recognize that many New Testament scholars regard 'primitive' as a 'taboo' adjective to apply to Christianity. However, I have discussed the question at length with friends who are expert in this field, both in Britain and in Germany, and they have confirmed me in the conviction that there is no other possible translation. '*Ur–*' does not mean 'early' or 'earliest' or 'nascent' or 'in the making', even if such terms are commonly used. It is a far richer term. 'Primitive' may not be the ideal rendering, but I hope that readers will agree that it does the job effectively.

John Bowden
May 1999

I

Introduction: The Programme of a Theory of Primitive Christian Religion

Why a theory of primitive Christian religion? Why not a 'theology of the New Testament' to give a summary description of the faith of the first Christians?

As we know, 'theology' can be spoken of in both a descriptive and a confessional sense. The term 'theology of the New Testament' is used descriptively if it means an analysis of all the statements in the New Testament which speak of God, or of the world and human beings in their relationship to God, without making a normative claim for such statements. In my view such a descriptive theology is not in a position to cover the whole dynamic of primitive Christian belief. If we are to know the innermost motivations of the first Christians we must investigate the whole of their lives and put their theological statements in semiotic, social, psychological and historical contexts which are not directly 'theological'. The dynamic of primitive Christian faith is rooted in the dynamic of life.

At first glance, a 'theology' in the confessional sense comes much closer to this dynamic. For it is 'confessional' because it begins from the premise that this faith still has normative force and power even today. It is therefore sensitive to the fact that the faith also had this power at the time of its origins. However, we must be clear that anyone who begins an account of the first Christians from the normative premise 'God has redeemed the world in Christ and brought human life to its fulfilment' runs the risk of barring the New Testament to many of our secularized contemporaries. Anyone who does this, removes the centre of primitive Christian life from general discussion and is engaged in an internal church debate.

A theory of primitive Christian religion seeks to describe in general religious categories the dynamic of primitive Christian belief which governs the whole of life.[1] It seeks to make possible a twofold reading of this faith: a view from inside and a view from outside – and above all to mediate between these two perspectives.

Now in the scholarly study of religion there is a dispute as to what religion in fact is. The following definition cannot claim to be the only possible definition, nor does it seek to be. However, it is not at the extremes of the spectrum of possible definitions.

Religion is a cultural sign language which promises a gain in life by corresponding to an ultimate reality.[2]

The first part of the definition says what religion is, namely a cultural sign language. It therefore says something about the essence of religion. The second part says what religion brings about, namely a gain in life. That says something about its function. The definition leaves open whether and in what sense there is an ultimate reality. For the statement that religion promises a gain in life by corresponding to an ultimate reality merely takes up the way in which the religions understand themselves; it does not expect anyone to adopt this understanding.

1. The 'essence' of religion: religion as a cultural sign system

Now to the first part of the definition, which concerns the essence of religion. The definition of religion as a cultural sign language contains three characteristics: religion has a semiotic, a systemic and a cultural character. We shall discuss these in turn.

Religion is first of all a *semiotic* phenomenon. In saying this we part company with other definitions of religion. We do not say that it is experience of the holy. Nor do we say that it is a human projection. We say that it is an objective sign system. What is meant by that? Human beings cannot exist in their environment as they find it. They have to change it. They do that on the one hand by work and technology, and on the other by interpretation. The interpretation of the world is carried out by systems of interpretation: by common sense in everyday life; by science, art and religion. By work and interpretation human beings make their world a habitable home. Here the transformation of the world through interpretation does not take place through causal interventions in nature as in work and technology, but through 'signs', i.e. through material elements which as signs produce semiotic relations to something signified. Such signs and sign-systems do not alter the reality signified, but our cognitive, emotional and pragmatic relationship to it: they guide our attention, bring our impressions together coherently, and link them with our actions. Only in a world interpreted in this way can we live and breathe.[3]

Now what is the special feature of the religious sign system? It can be characterized as a combination of three forms of expression which are combined in this way only in religion: myth, rites and ethics. Here is a brief explanation of each of these forms of expression.[4]

Myths explain in narrative form what fundamentally determines the world and life.[5] Usually they tell of actions of various gods in a primal time or an end time which is remote from the present world in which people live. In the biblical tradition a change took place here at a very early stage. The myth of the fundamental acts of God was extended through history to the present; it became a narrative of salvation history which also covered the present. And at the same time the narrative about many gods became the narrative about the one and only God, who has only one social partner, the people of Israel as the representative of all human beings. We find a continuation of this development in primitive Christianity: a myth links it with a concrete history in the midst of time. One individual from the people of Israel comes into the centre of all events. A theory of primitive Christian religion must explain this unique link between myth and history.

Rites are patterns of behaviour which repeat themselves, patterns with which people break up their everyday actions in order to depict the other reality that is indicated in myths.[6] According to an ancient division they comprise:

- Words of interpretation (λεγόμενα)
- Actions (δρώμενα)
- Objects (δεικνύμενα)

In the words of interpretation the myth is made present in concentrated form. Through them actions take on symbolic surplus value and as signs are related to the 'other reality'. On the basis of this 'surplus value' the objects present in the rite are removed from everyday, secular use – including the places and buildings in which the rites take place. A theory of primitive Christian religion has to deal with a great divide in the ritual forms of religious expression. At that time – in different ways in Judaism and Christianity (and also in philosophy) – the traditional ritual actions (bloody animal sacrifices) were replaced by new (bloodless) rites. Traditional holy objects like the temple lost their 'holiness'. But above all a paradoxical new relationship developed between ritual actions and their interpretations: the first Christians developed a religious sign system without temple, without sacrifice, without priests, yet in contradiction to the facts they maintained these traditional elements of religious sign systems in their interpretations – often even in an archaic form which was already obsolete at that time. They may have ceased to sacrifice animals, but in their interpretations they reactivated a form of sacrifice which was already long obsolete, namely human sacrifice – as the atoning sacrifice of Jesus.

Finally, *ethics* is part of the religious sign language. Or more precisely, in different degrees ethical behaviour can be integrated into religious sign language. In Judaism this integration was carried out consistently. All moral norms and values were summed up in the Torah. The everyday ethic of wisdom was just as much a part of the Torah as the prophets who were regarded as exponents of the Torah. And the law, too, was completely permeated by theonomous elements – precisely at those points where it became an ethic which escaped human controls and sanctions. In other words, the one and only God governed the whole of life by his will. All behaviour gained a semiotic surplus value of meaning by being related to God's commandment and history. It was not just good or bad behaviour, but it was a behaviour required by unconditional divine commandments and sanctioned by unconditional power. So a theory of primitive religion will have to occupy itself with the way in which this integration of ethics into religion is continued in primitive Christianity and heightened into an ethical radicalism – and at the same time with how to cope with the problem that this asks too much of human beings.

If we regard religion as a sign language, we are giving it not just a semiotic but also a *systemic* character:[7] we know today that 'signs' can perform their task only in relation and opposition to other signs. Together they form a 'system'. Together the signs and forms of expression of a religion also form a sign system, a unitary 'language' which is guided by particular rules, just as a language is governed by grammar and vocabulary. Those who use it may be as little aware of this grammar as we are aware of the rules of our mother tongue when we use it: we learn a language before we laboriously learn its grammar. And we always have only parts of the vocabulary in our repertoire. Like other grammars, the grammar of religious language consists of positive and negative rules of association, i.e. indications of what one may or may not combine. If, for example, we enter a church which contains no imagery whatsoever and find on the altar nothing but an open Bible, we know that we are in a Reformed church. Within the Reformed 'dialect' of Christian sign language there is a negative rule of association which says that it is forbidden to associate God with images – even more so to depict God with images. To counterbalance this there is a positive rule of association: this God shows himself throughout holy scripture. Therefore Bible and altar are linked – and there are no decorative candles on the altar in addition to them. We know from various religious grammars whether we are moving within a Jewish, Muslim or Christian sign language – or whether, as in our example, we find ourselves within a Reformed, Lutheran or Catholic 'dialect' of our Christian sign language.

A theory of primitive Christian religion will concern itself with getting to know such a 'grammar' of primitive Christian sign language. Here the grammar of the Jewish religion is a starting point. In it we find two *basic axioms*. On the one hand there is a negative rule of association: the one and only God may not be associated with other gods – all that goes with them is an abomination to him. On the other hand we find a positive rule of association: God is uniquely associated with his people in that he made a covenant with it and gave it the Torah in order to maintain this covenant. In abstract terms, monotheism and covenantal nomism are the two basic axioms of Judaism.

In addition there are many individual *basic motifs*, i.e. grammatical rules of religious sign language, which have only a limited scope. They are subordinate to the fundamental axioms and are organized in the light of these axioms: the motifs of creation, wisdom, repentance, love of neighbour, distance from God, etc.

The question is: how far have these basic axioms and motifs been changed in primitive Christianity? Would not the rule of monotheistic exclusivism be weakened if a human being appeared alongside God as his son? At least the Christians in the Gospel of John have to defend themselves against the Jewish charge that among them a human being is making himself God. Similarly, one can ask whether covenantal nomism would not be abandoned in principle if the association of God and people were extended to all peoples by belief in a redeemer. In short, in primitive Christianity, instead of the two Jewish basic axioms of monotheism and covenantal monism, we find the two basic axioms of monotheism and belief in a redeemer – and here monotheism has been modified by belief in a redeemer and covenantal nomism has been extended to all human beings by belief in a universal redeemer.

In any case, the recognition of the systemic character of religious sign languages means that we must understand their origin as the formation of a system. But what does it mean to form a system? Two properties must be recognizable. First, a system has the capacity *to organize itself* from its own centre; i.e., its conduct and development is not just guided from outside. Secondly, it has the capacity to distinguish itself from its environment – i.e. to differentiate between *reference to itself* and *reference to outsiders*. A language system (mediated by the linguistic usage of its 'inhabitants') can test successfully whether a statement is an element of its own system (e.g. the English language) or represents an alien element (e.g. is a typically German construction), even if this construction makes use of English words. So a theory of primitive Christianity will investigate from what centre the new religious sign system organizes itself and the way in which it differs from the surrounding world – and develops and establishes develops its own rules in its own sphere (in many conflicts and controversies). Therefore we shall have to follow the process of differentiation from Judaism in the direction of a self-organizing, independent sign system.

Finally, a few words about the third characteristic of religious sign languages: they are a *cultural* phenomenon, i.e. they are neither (just) a natural nor a supernatural phenomenon. 'Cultural' means that any religious sign language is produced by human beings independently of the fact that religions understand themselves as the result of divine action. The association of particular material elements with meanings and the organization of these meanings in a system of meaning is human action; above all it is social action. For only through the participation of whole groups and communities can a sign system become effective. Religions are socio-cultural sign systems. Therefore they are historical: they come into being and pass away, split up and get mixed up. They are closely bound up with the history of those groups which hand them down. The history of primitive Christianity is the history of the origin of a new religion which detaches itself from its mother religion and becomes independent. A theory of primitive Christianity will have to be concerned with an interpretation of this change.

Renewal and change in the history of religion can take place by a re-interpretation of the traditional sign systems (e.g. through the exegesis of scripture). It can take place through a selection from the elements of traditional religion: some ritual processes like circumcision were excluded from primitive Christianity, and other elements like the commandment to love one's neighbour and the metaphor of father for God came into the centre. Finally, there is the possibility of producing new developments through an exchange with neighbouring systems of religion. Primitive Christianity, too, shaped its faith in interaction with its pagan environment – even if the old history-of-religions school overestimated the extent of this 'syncretism'.

Such a change in the religious sign system is brought about above all by *charismatics* – i.e. by the influence which individuals exert on others on the basis of an irrational power of emanation – independently of pre-existing authority roles and traditions, often in the face of the vigorous hostility of the world in which they live. The stigmatizing of the charismatic by the world around can even increase his influence: if he survives rejection by social and moral contempt and negative sanctions, he puts the 'system' which repudiates him in question all the more tenaciously. This *connection between stigma and charisma*[8] emerges in a pure form in primitive Christianity: in particular the crucified Jesus – who suffered one of the cruellest kinds of death, *mors turpissima crucis* – has here become the ruler of the world and the decisive authority. The Roman officials and soldiers who condemned him and executed him between two criminals could not guess that 300 years later the Roman empire would 'convert' to him and would confess him the judge of dead and living.

In addition to the connection between charisma and stigma there is a second *connection: between charisma and crisis*. Charismatics who have an innovative effect develop in times of upheaval, when many people are ready to forsake traditional convictions and adopt new orientations. Here I need make only two obvious points: crises are not just times of impoverishment but times of change. Even times of economic boom can shake traditional values and orientations. Furthermore crises are not just experienced by the lower strata. They embrace all social strata – and here opposition between strata or classes is almost always an element in the crisis.

2. The function of religion: religion as the promise of a gain in life

In reflecting on the cultural character of religion we have already had in view the function of religion in life, to which the second half of our definition relates. Religion is a cultural sign system which promises *a gain in life by corresponding to an ultimate reality*. Here I shall limit myself to explaining what this 'gain in life' consists of. I do not want to return to further aspects of religion until the last chapter.

In religion, a gain in life is often to be understood in a very tangible way, above all as health and help. One need think only of the miracle stories and healing charisma in primitive Christianity. But often religions promise something more sublime in addition: a life in truth and love, a gain of identity in the crises and changes of life – even the promise of eternal life.

The study of religion investigates above all the psychological and social gain in life, i.e. the function of religion in individual and social life.

In the *psychological* function of religion one can distinguish cognitive, emotional and pragmatic functions.[9]

Cognitively, religions have always offered a comprehensive interpretation of the world: they assign human beings their place in the universe of things. Only with the loss of their competence to provide a world view in modern times did a tendency develop to understand religion as 'feeling' or as a call for 'decision'. But that is one-sided. Religion maintains belief in a hidden order of things – and it functions where our knowledge fails in cognitive crises (for example in the question of what lies beyond the world in which we live and what removes us from ourselves in death). At the same time, however, religion keeps alive the sense of places of cognitive vexation: it keeps offering provocation by testimonies of the irruption of a wholly other world into our world. Primitive Christianity, too, attests such 'irruptions of revelation', which break like a thief in the night into the world in which human beings live. Time and again we hear of ecstatic phenomena, of visions and revelations.

Emotionally, religion has comparable functions: it provides a feeling of security in this world and a trust that in the end all is well or could be well. But precisely because of this, it occupies itself with those boundary situations where this trust is threatened and shaken: with anxiety, mourning, guilt and failure. Here it stabilizes people in the face of the danger of emotional collapse. At the same time religion provokes such boundary situations. It is the motivation for extremes of behaviour like asceticism and martyrdom, or evokes extreme feelings of guilt: anxiety about hell is as much part of primitive Christianity as security in the love of God.

Finally, the *pragmatic* function of religion consists in the way in which it legitimates forms of life and their patterns of behaviour. Here too we find crises both surmounted and provoked. Religion indicates possibilities of dealing pragmatically with that over which we have no control: with situations in which our patterns of behaviour fail. It surmounts the crises in our actions and yet itself creates such crises by defining zones which are not under our control: realms over which human beings could have control but over which they should not have control. Thus religion veils human life at many points with an aura of untouchability: some say with irrational taboos and others with the aura of the image of God.

The three functions of religion can be illustrated in a table:

	Religion as an ordering force	Religion as a way of surmounting crises	Religion as provoking crises
Cognitive	Construction of a cognitive order: indicating the place of human beings in the cosmos	Surmounting cognitive crises: vexation caused by frontiers	Provocation of cognitive crises: the irruption of the Wholly Other
Emotional	Construction of a basic emotional trust in a legitimate order	Surmounting emotional crises: anxiety, guilt, failure, mourning	Provocation of emotional crises through anxiety, consciousness of guilt, etc.

Pragmatic	Construction of accepted forms of life, their values and norms	Coping with crises: conversion, atonement, renewal	Provocation of crises through the pathos of the unconditioned

It is important for us to rid ourselves of any one-sided definition of the function of religion. It does not just serve to stabilize thought, feeling and action; it does not just serve to surmount crises. There can also be 'a gain in life' in the exposure of people to serious upheavals, in their being purified by 'trials' and 'temptations' and achieving a new life. We will not understand primitive Christianity if we see religion only as a way of surmounting crises. Here, rather, we keep experiencing eruptions which themselves become crises. What we hear of irrational impulses, of the irruptions of alien realities, extreme modes of behaviour like asceticism and martyrdom, certainly does not fit at all into the picture of a sedative religion which soothes metaphysical unrest in society.

The *social functions* of religion are just as manifold as its psychological functions. Certainly, here too there are mono-functional interpretations of religion, for example when it is said that religion serves to legitimate the existing social order or is the opium of the people. All that is correct, but it is not the whole truth. Here, too, we will do justice to actual religious life only by identifying a multiplicity of functions.[10] Here religion proves to have a social function above all at two points, in the socialization of the individual and in settling conflicts between groups.

The aim of the *socializing function* of religion is to internalize the values and norms of society in individuals in such a way that they become loyal inhabitants of the historically contingent 'world' in which they live. Religion helps people to grow into this order of life by rites of passage, and to remain in it when they doubt the meaning and value of the existing order in 'theodicy crises'. Often individuals who risk being 'lost' as a result of crises take up religion. But often religion also has the function of motivating people to 'drop out' of life as generally lived. In that case it becomes a counter-cultural process against the world which 'lies in ruins'.

The function of religion in *regulating conflicts* between groups and classes can be clearly distinguished from its socializing function. Here it is not just the individual who stands over against society; whole groups which form as a result of economic status or ethnic adherence come into conflict with one another. Here too we find that religion has several functions: regulating conflict, blunting conflict and intensifying conflict. Religion can both build bridges by emphasizing shared fundamental values and foment aggression by fundamentalism.

The manifold nature of the social functions of religion can be illustrated in the following table.

	Legitimation of order	Surmounting of crises	Intensifying crises
Socialization of the individual	Introduction into the social order: rites of passage, communicating value	Stabilization in theodicy crises	Towards 'dropping out' of culture
Regulating conflicts between groups	Legitimation of a minimal consensus between conflicting groups	Compensation for social damage	Protest and utopia of justice

In research into primitive Christianity one arrives at a realistic result only if one keeps all these contradictory functions in view. In primitive Christianity we find a strong tendency to make Christians the best citizens, wives and slaves by the standards of the time – i.e. a markedly conformist tendency, and at the same time a tremendous counter-cultural energy which snatched people from their normal life and made them itinerant charismatics with a deviant life-style. We find indications of a 'revolution of values' in which small people appropriate values and attitudes of the upper class – but also of a conformity in values which hold back these impulses towards a revolution in values. Anyone who seeks to investigate primitive Christianity in an unprejudiced way should always see both sides.

If we are to understand the psychological and social functions of religion, finally, it is important to be clear *how* religion can exercise these functions as a cultural sign language. Here there are two very different approaches in theories of religion.[11] For many, the religious sign system is merely secondary to the functions of religion in life. For this approach, what comes first is a religious experience (say the experience of the holy as *mysterium facinosum et tremendum*) or an elemental problem in life which is articulated in religious forms (for example, grappling with an overpowering father in the Oedipus complex). The religious sign world is then regarded as a secondary expression of such primary experiences and problems. In such theories of religion the function of religion in life or a religious experience is the real essence of religion.

Here I have already taken another position in defining the essence of religion as a cultural sign system. Behind this definition is the conviction that a historically given sign language is the condition for the possibility of religious experience and functions in life. The old Protestant dogmatic theologians expressed this in their own way when they put the *verbum externum* (i.e. the objective religious sign language, the world of the Bible and preaching) before the *verbum internum*, religious experience proper. They were right.

What we now need to clarify is the question how this religious sign world can have an effect on life. How can it govern thought, feeling and action and enable people to be engaged in social co-operation and conflict?

To answer it we need to look once again at the forms of religious expression: in the myth, rites and ethic of a religion we always find those elements which also have an effect in life: roles, symbols and norms. Here myths above all contain roles; rites work with symbols; and ethics with commandments – but it is characteristic of roles, symbols and norms that they appear everywhere. They run through all forms of expression.

Roles make identification possible. To this degree religions are an 'offer of roles' to their members.[12] We now know that adopting a role also changes one's perception: we look at a wood differently depending on whether we look at it in the role of a forester, a walker or a road-builder. Therefore the adoption of religious roles makes it possible to see the world with different eyes from usual: it becomes transparent to God. One can even say that the adoption of any role brings with it a corresponding standpoint. Anyone who adopts the role of a pupil adopts a relationship to a teacher. Anyone who adopts the role of a 'child' adopts a relationship to 'parents'. Similarly, the biblical roles at the same time 'offer' the adoption of a relationship to God. Anyone who identifies with the role of Abraham also adopts a relationship to the role of the one who made Abraham leave his ancestral home. Anyone who adopts the role of the 'I' in the psalms of lament adopts a relationship to God. Such roles do not just occur in the narratives and myths of the religions which are handed down; rather, they are 'played out' in rites – and for ethics are regarded as paradigms of behaviour. Through the performance of ritual, the adopting of roles is 'internalized'. Anyone who is baptized becomes a 'child of God'; anyone who takes part in the eucharist becomes a disciple of Jesus. Through ethical behaviour these roles are 'practised'.

Symbols come into being through a symbolic perception of the world by which real things take on the character of pointers to something else.[13] They become transparent to the whole world in which we live, to its depth dimensions and to what lies beyond it. At the same time they become transparent to the deep levels within the human soul. It makes sense to distinguish between 'symbols' and 'roles', because most symbols do not allow any identification in the sense that one can identify with them through action. Such symbols can be topological places like road, sea, wilderness, field; architectural structures like temple, house and hut; or parts of the body like hand, foot, eye, ear, heart, etc. By their character as pointers to something else they make it possible to be orientated in the world (and to grapple with one's own inner being). They construct a cosmos in which one can breathe and live. The world becomes a great house, nature a temple, the body a living sacrifice, and so on.

Religion has its most direct effect in life through *norms*.[14] These need not always be imperative formulations, although 'commandments' play a role in religious life which cannot be underestimated. Maxims in the form of sentences also serve to provide orientation in life. Some of these imperatives and sentences have a high degree of abstraction. They represent the basic motives and axioms of a religion – like the first commandment or the commandment to love one's neighbour in Judaism and Christianity.

Through roles, symbols and norms a few axioms and basic motifs are communicated in ever new variations: those elements of a grammar of the religious sign languages that we internalize in, with and under religious narratives, rites and norms. We internalize them so strongly that although they are learnt culturally, they work like an *a priori* of behaviour and experience. They govern the way in which we interpret the world and react to it. 'Faith', Paul rightly says, comes from the 'word' which is handed on in history (Rom. 10.17). What this word communicates is near to the human heart (Rom. 10.8). It is 'internalized'. We see the world in the light of such internalized convictions. So those who have internalized the basic motif of 'creation' from the offer of religious roles and symbols, i.e. the conviction that everything has been created by an infinitely superior power with human beings in the midst of it all, change their perception of the world and their behaviour in it in the light of this creation faith. Thus everything becomes transparent to the creator. And his creation is said to contain all action.

Here I shall break off my sketch of a general theory of religion. The most important categories by means of which I want to analyse primitive Christianity have been developed or mentioned briefly. So in a third part, once again as a summary, I can give a first description of primitive Christianity and sketch out three basic problems which will concern us in subsequent lectures.

3. Basic problems of a theory of primitive Christian religion

If one wants to describe the distinctive feature of primitive Christian religion, it is simplest to do so by indicating the way in which it differs from its mother religion, Judaism. Here I shall proceed by means of the categories introduced above: basic axioms, basic motifs, forms of expression and questions, each time looking for common features with Judaism and differences from it.

Whereas Judaism is governed by two *basic axioms*, an exclusive monotheism[15] and a covenantal nomism,[16] which bind God to this one people and this people to the one and only God, in primitive Christianity these basic axioms are changed. Monotheism remains the first axiom, but it is modified by the second axiom, faith in a redeemer. The whole religious sign system is restructured in the light of the figure of a single redeemer. Everything is related to this centre. This redeemer comes to stand alongside God, and Jews inevitably experienced that as a questioning of a strict monotheism. At the same time, through this faith in a redeemer, Judaism is opened to all men and women. Over wide areas primitive Christianity is universalized Judaism.

Many *basic motifs* of religion remain the same in Judaism and Christianity, except that in Christianity they crystallize around a new centre. Both religions share basic motifs of their understanding of the world. On the one hand it is a creation which is irrationally given. Time and again the divine power can intervene surprisingly in history. To balance this motif of creation and miracle we find a 'wisdom motif'. This creation is the expression of the wisdom of God, the regular structures of which can be recognized. And in the understanding of history, too, we find a hidden order – despite all the emphasis on the sovereign intervention of God: the will of God for the salvation of Israel and humankind.

Similarly, both religions share the most important basic motifs of human self-understanding. In both, faith is regarded as an appropriate access to God: attaching oneself to God in thought, feeling and will. In both, repentance is regarded as an opportunity and an offer in the confrontation of human beings with God. In both, thought is permeated with an intense feeling of distance from God; this is formulated more radically in primitive Christianity (in Paul) than in Judaism elsewhere. The motifs of faith, repentance and distance structure the relationship to God.

The structuring of the relationship with other men and women by the two basic motifs of love of neighbour and humility is comparable. In primitive Christianity, love of neighbour is extended as a continuation of Jewish tendencies so that it becomes love of the enemy, the stranger and the sinner. This is supplemented by a readiness for humility: if love of neighbour is love between equals, it can be realized only by a renunciation of their superiority by those who are superior and a revaluation of the status of the lowly, in other words by humility and renunciation of status.

Even if there are differences between Judaism and primitive Christianity at the level of the deep basic motifs, they are limited. The closeness and affinity of the two religions is indisputable. The differences appear less at the deeper level than on the surface of the forms of expression.

The first form of expression of a religion is its *myth* or its basic narrative.[17] Usually this takes place in a grey primal time, when gods established the world. In Judaism this myth had become combined with history in a unique way to form a salvation history which after primal times concentrates wholly on Israel and leads beyond the legendary primal time to the present. In it, the drama between various gods and goddesses has been replaced by the drama of the one God and the people whom he has chosen. This God no longer has a social partner among gods and goddesses, but as a social partner representative of all men and women only has Israel. Israel is God's servant, God's son, God's witness, God's wife. Primitive Christianity not only continued this history but recentred it on just one man, Jesus of Nazareth. He was understood as the fulfilment of the whole biblical history hitherto; even more, in him mythical expectations of the end time were depicted as history. He embodies the rule of God. He 'historicizes' this myth of the end time. The centring of the new religious basic narrative on this one historical figure from the present and the recent past made the new religion even more 'historical' than its mother religion. The link to concrete history was intensified. But at the same time we experience in primitive Christianity an intensification of the myth, indeed a regular remythologizing, which begins with this one historical figure. In a very short time after his death Jesus was elevated to deity: he was worshipped as Son of God, exalted Kyrios and redeemer. The time of his appearance was surrounded with the mythical aura of a new time of decision and his history was dramatized mythically as a conflict between Satan and demons, between God and his son, between the Kyrios and the spiritual powers subjected by him. Thus we find two contrary tendencies in primitive Christianity: an intensification of the relationship to history and an intensification of the myth, both a rehistoricizing and a remythologizing. Or to put it another way, history and myth enter into a unique unity in tension. A concrete human being becomes deity, deity incarnates itself in a concrete human being. This unity in tension must be the first topic of a theory of primitive Christian religion, and I shall be discussing it in Chapters 2 and 3.

The second religious form of expression is the *ethic* of primitive Christianity.[18] Here already in the history of Israel and Judaism we can observe an increasing 'theologizing' of all norms.[19] Not only the cultic commandments and a minimum of fundamental ethics as this has been formulated in the Decalogue, but all norms have been derived from the will of God and legitimated by the Torah: the whole law is theologized in such a way that it is valid not as law promulgated by kings and states but as God's law. All maxims of life derived from wisdom were regarded as part of the Torah. All prophetic injunctions were regarded as its exposition. Judaism was proud of shaping the whole of life in this way in the light of the Torah. As a result, all norms were filled with the intensity of the 'unconditional'. Primitive Christianity continued this tendency. It radicalized the traditional ethic when it provided norms for human aggressiveness, sexuality and communication extending to the innermost human depths which were also beyond social control – as in the antitheses of the Sermon on the Mount. But at the same time we find a contrary tendency: a relaxation of the ritual commandments, in which circumcision and the commandments relating to food and cleanness are set aside. In a way this relativization extends to all commandments: in view of the radicalization of basic ethical commandments, we find a developed sensitivity to the impossibility of fulfilling them and a readiness for forgiveness and reconciliation which does away with morality, and which applies even to the sinner who behaves contrary to the norms. Thus we find two opposed tendencies: on the one hand a radicalization of the norms to the limits of what is psychologically and socially possible (and often even beyond), and on the other hand a radicalization of the relaxation of norms (to the limits of what is socially tolerable). The second task of a theory of primitive Christian religion is to interpret this tension. We shall be concerned with it in Chapters 4 to 6: with the basic tension between the two tendencies towards radicalization and their effect on social and psychological life.

In the third form of religious expression, the *rite*,[20] we again find a basic tension which is characteristic of primitive Christianity. Here too – despite all discontinuity – tendencies of the preceding history of biblical religion continue: in it sacrifice had increasingly become atoning sacrifice and the rites relating to cleanness had been increasingly intensified. Certainly primitive Christianity ended the centuries-long practice of sacrifice. It put new rites, above all baptism and eucharist, in the place of the old rites. Nevertheless, we recognize the continuation of existing tendencies. For the two new rites (or sacraments) are focussed on the forgiveness of sins and atonement. In this development two contrary tendencies are now interlocked. The new sacraments which have come into being are impressively 'non-violent' in their outward celebration. They elevate everyday practices – washing and eating – to the rank of symbolism. No blood is shed in them. However, in addition to this reduction of violence in outward celebration there is a increase of violence in the interpretations by which the new rites receive their symbolic surplus value of meaning: baptism is interpreted as a voluntary acceptance of death and a symbolic burial (Rom. 6.3f.). The eucharist refers to a human sacrifice and is even interpreted (by outsiders) as barbaric cannibalism, since in it the flesh and blood of the Son of Man are consumed (John 6.51ff.). These opposed tendencies have to be interpreted in a theory of primitive Christian religion. We shall be concerned with them in Chapter 7.

Of course already we are coming to wonder whether all three basic tensions in myth, ethic and rite do not belong together. On the one side we always have a movement towards history, towards human reality, towards the everyday world; and on the other a contrary movement towards myth, radicality and cruel-seeming fantasies which run counter to the everyday world. So one can ask whether in the end the two contrary tendencies are not connected with the two basic axioms of primitive Christian religion: monotheism is bound up with an affirmation of creation, an ethical realism and a nearness to everyday life, and belief in a redeemer with a mythical divinization of Jesus, a radical ethic of the new person and an archaic interpretation of redemptive rites.

At all events, we shall be concerned with the unity and autonomy[21] of the new primitive Christianity in further chapters.

In Chapters 9 and 10 I want to show how primitive Christianity differentiated itself from Judaism and constituted itself as a distinctive sign language. We shall follow its course from a renewal movement within Judaism through being a Jewish heresy to the final schism. This development finds its climax in the New Testament in the Gospel of John, where everything in the new religion is reorganized and legitimated from a single centre: from the redeemer who is sent, whose message throughout refers to himself. He makes himself the content of his preaching and dissociates himself from the 'world' in dualistic references which indicate that it is alien.

In Chapter 11 I shall investigate how this autonomy of the new sign language developed and proved itself in the two great crises of primitive Christianity. In the first century these were the Judaistic crisis over the detachment of Christianity from Judaism, and in the second century the Gnostic crisis, which was a temptation to dissolve the Christian sign language as a special instance of a universal human symbolic language. Both crises served directly or indirectly to bring about a demarcation from the surrounding world – and were governed not least by the overall political situation of primitive Christianity.

Both crises clarify the limits of what is normatively valid sign language in primitive Christianity, not only outwardly, but also inwardly. However, within this framework primitive Christianity develops an amazing multiplicity and plurality. I shall sketch out a survey of this plurality in Chapter 12 – above all in order to show that with the formation of the canon this history ends with clear demarcations and a deliberate decision for plurality. With the formation of the canon the structure of the new sign system is complete: the end of primitive Christianity has been reached. From now on all further developments justify themselves by exegesis of the canonical scriptures.

Chapter 13 will seek to work out what gave the new religion unity and coherence in this plurality: the hidden grammar of the new sign language, its basic axioms and basic motifs which permeate the most important groups of texts, forms and themes in many variants. It embodies that which has normative effect in the historical religions. No religion can exist without such 'norming' by basic axioms and basic motifs. The analysis of such a religious grammar is therefore the task of a scholarly analysis of primitive Christianity.

In the last chapter we shall return once again to the starting point. In this chapter I have given a definition of religion and by way of experiment applied it to primitive Christianity. Here part of the definition has not been discussed. Let me remind you of our definition once again: *religion is a cultural sign system which promises a gain in life by corresponding to an ultimate reality*. I have depicted the primitive Christian religion as a *sign system* and as a *gain in life*. But what is the meaning of '*corresponding to an ultimate reality*' in such a theory of religion? That brings us to the point where a theory of primitive Christianity gives men and women today freedom to decide. They can turn such a theory into a theology of the New Testament if they use the sign language developed in primitive Christianity in order to come into contact with an ultimate reality. But they also have the freedom to occupy themselves with this religion by as it were looking after a monument which seeks to preserve the roots of our culture. Who would dispute that looking after monuments is a serious concern? At all events it is a means of preventing the destruction of monuments or forgetfulness of them.

I end with a picture of the view of primitive Christian religion put forward here. This religion is a sign language – a 'semiotic cathedral' – which has been erected in the midst of history: not out of stones but out of signs of various kinds. Like all churches and cathedrals, it too has been designed throughout by human beings, built by human beings, and is used and preserved by human beings. But just as one cannot understand the Gothic cathedrals unless one hears and sees them as a hymn of praise to God in stone, so too one cannot understand this semiotic cathedral if one forgets that those who built it once erected it as a great hymn of praise and thanks for the irruption of a transcendent reality. The secularized visitors to a cathedral can and may look at it in the awareness that here is a form of human self-transcendence moulded in stone, produced not just for religious motives but also through structures and intentions of domination and intense human anxieties and longings. But the human sensitivity of such secularized visitors would be crippled if they could not see that the cathedral was a powerful witness to human life which contains a longing for more than ongoing life. Other visitors will seek the cathedral to have their thoughts guided towards an ultimate reality by the dynamic of the building made stone. They will allow themselves to be grasped by the longing for transcendence built into it. They will join in its hymn of praise. What is there against both visitors exchanging their perspectives and entering into a rational conversation about the cathedral? The sketches of a theory of primitive religion presented here seek to make such a conversation possible – a conversation about the mysterious sign world of primitive Christian religion. For some, this is part of looking after monuments, and looking after monuments is a very noble affair. But I should add that for me, a concern with primitive Christian religion involves more than being curator of a monument.

Part One: Myth and History in Primitive Christianity

2

The Significance of the Historical Jesus for the Origin of Primitive Christian Religion

The Revitalization of the Jewish Religion by Jesus

At the centre of the religious sign system in primitive Christianity stands a remarkable combination of myth and history. One fails to recognize it if one dissolves it one-sidedly, whether in the direction of 'history' or in that of 'myth'.

Thus in the interpretation of primitive Christianity, time and again there have been attempts to regard the history of Jesus of Nazareth as the real nucleus of primitive Christian religion and to regard myth only as an expression of the significance of this historical event – as an aura which adds nothing to the event but merely veils it in a light which transfigures it. To reverse the mythologization of this history was then the liberating act of historical research.[1]

Equally one-sided were the opposite attempts to dissolve the unity of myth and history. The mythical poetry of primitive Christianity was seen as the real nucleus of primitive Christian religion and there was a tendency to explain this myth almost without reference to the history of the historical Jesus. Age-old expectations of a redeemer were said simply to have waited in the history of religion, to be put on a human being like a garment. The extreme variant of this interpretation believed that it could dispense completely with the assumption of a historical Jesus; in the more moderate variant the view was expressed that we can no longer know anything about the historical Jesus, since the mythical aura has completely absorbed the memory of him. Here it became the liberating task of historical research to reverse the historicizing of the myth so that a pure version of the religious content of mythical longings and hopes could be produced. Modern theology found a somewhat obscure linguistic rule for this. The important thing was to find the kerygmatic Christ in the texts – independently of the remains of the historical Jesus which might be woven into him, and about which there were always disputes.

Against both ways of dissolving the unity of myth and history I want to assert that everything suggests that neither a myth which was historicized at a secondary stage nor a history which was mythicized at a secondary stage stood at the centre of primitive Christianity. At the beginning stood a unity in tension of both history and myth.

Here 'history' is not simply identical with the 'historical Jesus' nor is 'myth' identical with the 'proclaimed Christ' after Easter. Rather, we can establish that the historical Jesus already lived in a myth. He expected the kingdom of God to break in and as a representative of this kingdom gave himself a central place in the event between God and the world. In so doing he historicized a myth of the end-time. An expectation focussed on an uncertain time in the (near) future became a present experience in history. Thus the unity of myth and history already began with the historical Jesus.

Conversely, the kerygmatic Christ was not just a mythical being. Rather, after Easter people carefully shaped the recollections of the historical Jesus and sketched an ever more comprehensive picture of him from them. In the earliest letters of Paul we find only historical splinters: through them we would know only that Jesus was thought to be a descendant of David (Rom. 1.3), that he taught about marriage and the way in which missionaries should live (I Cor. 7.10; 9.14), that before his death he instituted a meal to commemorate his dying (I Cor. 11.23ff.), that he died on the cross and after his death appeared alive to his disciples (I Cor. 15.3ff.). From such individual reports and many others the comprehensive picture of Jesus in the Gospels was created a generation later, so that the way in which he was anchored in historical recollection became increasingly clear over the course of time. Thus the kerygmatic Christ, too, is a unity of myth and history.

In this chapter we shall turn to the historical Jesus. Our question is: what contribution did he make to the origin of a new religious sign system? My thesis is that in his case there can be no question of a new religious sign language. What we can observe is a revitalizing of the Jewish sign language. In other words: Jesus lived, thought, worked and died as a Jew. One of the most important results of 200 years of modern research into Jesus is that he belongs to two religions: to Judaism, to which he was attached with all his heart, and to Christianity, whose central point of reference he became after his death – on the basis of interpretations of his person which his Jewish followers gave.

However, it is legitimate to ask: did not Christianity begin with Jesus, at least in an 'implicit' way? In his preaching and his activity was there not a dynamic which pointed beyond the limits of Judaism? Do we not keep hearing of conflicts with his Jewish contemporaries? Did not Jewish authorities collaborate in doing away with him? Was he perhaps caught up in an exodus from Judaism without he and his disciples being aware of the fact? In order to clarify these questions methodically and to give an answer to them I shall go on to discuss Jesus' relationship to the forms of expression of Jewish religion: to its myth, ethic and rites. I shall add a section on politics, since it could be that his violent end is to be explained more from the political than from the religious conflicts of his time, though in that period it is difficult to distinguish between religion and politics. At the end we shall then (once again) return to the question of the relationship between myth and the way in which Jesus understood himself.

1. Myth in the preaching of the historical Jesus

What is a myth? Myths are narratives from a time which was decisive for the world, with supernatural agents who turn an unstable state into a stable state. They act in a world of their own with thought-structures which differ from those of our everyday world. Within myth, two things or persons which are different in our experience can be identical 'in depth': a dead person can return in a new form; Adam's fall can repeat itself in every human being; a rite can make something else really present. If one uses this definition of myth[2] as a basis, at its heart the preaching of Jesus contains a myth, a myth of the end-time as a time which is decisive for the world, in which God will establish himself against all supernatural powers, Satan and his demons, in order to change the present unstable state of disaster into a state of salvation.[3]

This myth is simply consistent Jewish monotheism: God will finally be the one and only God, alongside whom there will no longer be any other powers to limit his rule – and he will finally realize his salvation throughout creation and in Israel. The proclamation of the rule of God is a mythical dramatization of the first commandment, except that the exodus from Egypt has been replaced by an exodus from the oppressive conditions of the present – towards the dawn of the rule of God. Jesus shares this myth with other Jews. He speaks of the rule of God without having to explain the term. And that is not fortuitous: myths express the unquestioned 'dogmatics' in a group and society. In Judaism this includes the rule of the one and only God. Now Jesus combines this talk of the kingly rule of God, i.e. a political metaphor, with a second, family, metaphor: the image of God as father. Both images come from the collective store of images in Judaism. Both had already been connected before Jesus. The metaphor of father was especially associated with the Israelites, whom God tested 'like a father', but the metaphor of king was associated with the Gentiles, whom God punishes 'like a strict king' (Wisdom 11.10). It is striking that Jesus always speaks only of the kingdom of God, of God's *basileia* as an objective entity, but never of God as 'king', of *basileus* as a personal role. This produces a void for him which he fills with the metaphor of father: in God's kingly rule God comes to power not as 'king' but as 'father'. As *familia dei*, the 'family of God', his sons and daughters have a privileged relationship to him and take part in his rule. Therefore in the Our Father the central message of Jesus is summed up as 'Our *Father*, your *king*dom come . . .' In every respect this message is thus a revitalization of the Jewish sign world in the light of two basic metaphors which come into the centre. However, for Jesus this 'myth' of the coming kingly rule of the Father takes a form which is characterized by two special features. In both cases the mythical world is extended or transformed in a unique way: by a historicizing, poeticizing and 'demilitarizing' of myth.

(a) The 'historical' transformation of myth

If those living in the present are to take part in the rule of God which is dawning, this rule of God is associated with historical experiences in the present: myth is taken into history and transformed historically. So this development did not first take place in the religious imagination of primitive Christianity but already with Jesus himself. The mythical future is present in the activity of Jesus in three ways.

- It is present through the overcoming of evil. Jesus interprets his exorcisms as the establishment of the rule of God over Satan and his powers (Matt. 12.28). Satan has already been cast down from heaven (Luke 10.18). These are doubtless mythical statements, but they are associated with concrete historical experiences: here with exorcisms.
- Furthermore, the mythical future is present as a fulfilment of the past. That for which long generations have ardently waited is now taking place in the presence of eye-witnesses (Matt. 13.16f.). The time is fulfilled and the rule of God is at hand (Mark 1.14f.).
- Finally, the mythical future is present as a hidden nucleus in the present. The rule of God is 'in your midst' (or 'in you') (Luke 17.20f.). It establishes itself like a seed which in a surprisingly short time 'develops' until the harvest (Mark 4.26–29).

New Testament exegesis cannot offer a satisfying logical interpretation for this presence of the future. Basically, according to our everyday logic these are contradictory statements. What is really future cannot be there in the present at the same time. But there is nothing strange about it within a mythical framework of thought. What is clearly different can be identical at a deep level: Jesus' action in the present, too, is in this sense 'identical in depth' with the future rule of God. The historicizing of myth works with the possibilities of mythical thought itself, even if it breaks through the separation of mythical and profane time and seeks to proclaim a 'mythical' event from a qualitatively different time as a 'historical' event in the midst of this time.

(b) The 'poetic' transformation of myth

Closely bound up with the historicizing of the myth of the end-time is its poeticizing. In aesthetic experience, too, something can be present which in reality is absent. The work of art makes it appear, even if it is only a fine semblance or 'foretaste' of the beautiful. So it is not by chance that Jesus uses aesthetic forms to communicate his message. Parables – short fictional stories of great poetic quality – are characteristic of his preaching. These are not just about the kingdom of God, as the stereotyped introductions in the Gospel of Matthew suggest. They are also about people (cf. Matt. 7.24) or 'this generation' (Matt. 11.16): in short, about God and the whole of life. But beyond doubt everything becomes transparent to the one and only God, and to this degree his coming rule which is already dawning is present everywhere. However, this presence is not a 'real mythical presence', as though the rule of God is 'incarnated' (or better 'inverbalized') in the parables. If in myth a fleeing nymph turns into a tree, she is really present in it. The tree is identical 'in depth' with the nymph. But when parables speak of God and his rule, the fictional images of the parable point to something with which they are not identical. They are only an image, the meaning of which readers and hearers must illuminate for themselves. Hearers have the freedom to discover for themselves what the images mean. Whereas myths express the unquestionable axioms of a society and culture (and may be so illogical and bizarre precisely because they express what is always presumed to be 'logical' and 'matter of course'), the parables seek to offer stimuli towards thinking in a different way about God, human beings and the world – in another way from that suggested by the axioms and dogmatics of a society. Good poetry is non-conformist. The parables of Jesus, too, offer stimuli for deviant thought – as the poetic imagery of Jewish prophecy and wisdom had always done.

(c) The 'political' transformation of myth

When Jesus dramatizes the Jewish basic axiom of the 'one and only God', historicizes it and expresses it in poetic language, he remains within the traditional eschatological expectations. But at one point we find a change in content: traditionally the apocalyptic expectation of the rule of God is almost always bound up with a victory over the Gentiles, who oppress Israel in the present. According to Isa. 33 God becomes king by winning a victory over the foreign powers and entering Zion (33.17–22). According to Isa. 24.21f. he conquers the kings of the earth in order to become 'king' himself (24.23). According to Trito-Zechariah God will be 'king over the whole earth' (Zech. 14.9) after a judgment on all hostile peoples. In the book of Daniel the kingdom of God replaces the rule of the four world kingdoms symbolized by beasts (Dan. 7). Extra-canonical sources confirm this picture: according to 1QM VI. 8 the kingly rule of God comes about through a military victory over the enemies. According to AssMos 10.1ff. the coming of the kingly rule of God is associated with a victory over the Satan and the hostile Gentiles. According to Sib. 3.767 it comes after a bloody war. However, for Jesus the rule of God is already present in hidden form without the Gentiles being conquered. The rule of God and Roman rule can co-exist for a time in the present. So the temporal fusing of present and future means more than a change in formal respects. That is confirmed by the future expectation: no victory over the Gentiles is expected in the future either, but a flood of Gentiles (perhaps together with the Diaspora Jews) from all points of the compass. It is not the Gentiles who will be excluded but those who thought that the kingdom of God belonged to them (Matt. 8.11f.). Only Satan and his demons are conquered by the kingdom of God (Matt. 11.28 par). The revolution which begins with the kingly rule of God is a revolution at a metaphysical level – an end to demonic rule – and a revolution within the people: the kingdom of God belongs to the poor (Matt. 5.3) and the children (Mark 10.14); the toll collectors and prostitutes will enter it before the pious (Matt. 21.32). So a change in the expectation of the kingdom of God should not be called a 'depoliticizing' but a 'demilitarizing'. It is detached from the great (military) victory over other peoples.

Excursus: The millenarian interpretation of the Jesus movement[4]

The rise of an eschatological expectation according to which the world is soon to be changed in a miraculous way has many parallels in the so-called 'millenarian movements' in the Third World. A comparison with them is illuminating. We keep finding ourselves in the field of conflict between two cultures, one of which advances imperialistic claims and makes an indigenous culture dependent on politics. Charismatic figures keep appearing in this situation of conflict who proclaim a change in everything and mobilize supporters for this change. There are always tensions with the political authorities. But whereas in the Third World cultures encounter one another which are in quite different stages of development, at that time in Palestine there was a clash between two highly-differentiated, equal cultures, Romans and the Jews. Each was aware of a historical calling and each had a marked sense of history, a great tradition of law, writings and a financial economy. That explains some differences from the other millenarian movements of modern time.

1. Certainly the Jesus movement begins as a movement of revitalization within Judaism. But later it is successful above all outside Judaism; indeed in the course of 300 years it conquers the 'imperialistic' alien culture: Rome converts to Christianity. There is no analogy for the spread of one of the more recent millenarian movements in the sphere of European culture.
2. In keeping with this, the Jesus movement differed from 'nativisitic' reactions against foreigners by being open to them – at first in eschatological dreams of a meal shared by the Gentiles with Abraham, Isaac and Jacob, and soon also by the acceptance of Gentiles in reality.
3. Whereas the leaders of the modern millenarian movements have almost all gone through Christian mission schools and in their revitalizing of indigenous cultures adopt syncretistic features of the superior alien culture, we cannot observe a comparable syncretism in the early Jesus movement. The message of Jesus and his first disciples is rooted in Judaism.

To sum up, one can say of 'myth' in the preaching of Jesus that the historical Jesus lived in an eschatological myth which is none other than a dramatization of the monotheistic basic axiom of Judaism. He does not leave the Jewish sign world even where he connects this myth with his own history – for the combination of myth and history is characteristic of biblical religion; nor does he leave it when by poetic parables he transforms the unquestionable axioms of myth into open stimuli and impulses which without external authority build on the inner evidence of the poetic image. And it does not leave it, even when it 'demilitarizes' the expectation of the kingdom of God. We now turn to the second form of expression of a religious sign language, ethics.

2. The ethic of Judaism and the preaching of Jesus[5]

Frequently Jesus' ethic is depicted as a surpassing of the Jewish Torah ethic. His interpretation of the Torah is said to have left the Torah behind, to have transcended it in the antitheses, to have surmounted its casuistry, to have criticized its thought in terms of recompense, etc. But only from the perspective of later Christians, who had long since parted company with Judaism, can Jesus be perceived in this way as a contrast to Judaism. In the context of his own time his ethic is part of Judaism. Just as Jesus intensified the basic features of Jewish religion by historicizing its myth (of the end-time), so too he intensified them by radicalizing its ethic. Israel had already always attributed all norms to the unconditional will of God and integrated them into the Torah: the whole of law, (experiential) wisdom, politics as criticized and influenced by prophets. Through this all norms were loaded with a unconditional claim. God's will occurred throughout life – in ethical and in ritual commandments equally. This gave all norms the function of ritual commandments, intended to make it possible to get near to God and lead a life 'in his presence'. Where we find radical tendencies in the ethical preaching of Jesus, this basic tendency of Jewish religion is continued: the link with the unconditioned has an intrinsically 'radicalizing' tendency.

Now one could see the special feature of Jesus' ethic as being the combination of this radicalizing tendency with a tolerance towards offences against norms: an ethic of reconciliation, forgiveness and acceptance of the real person. Indeed this is an important feature for Jesus, but it too is rooted in Judaism: the ethic of reconciliation between brothers is also developed in an exemplary way in the Testaments of the Twelve Patriarchs. Joseph, whose life his brothers once sought, there becomes the great model of forgiveness.

It is more important to interpret the initially contradictory evidence objectively. Here it is striking that the statements which accentuate the Torah often appear in logia – i.e. in direct formulations of imperatives and rules, whereas the tendencies to relax the Torah which come nearer to reality tend more to shape narrative traditions.

The Torah says, 'You shall honour father and mother.' A logia tradition accentuates this commandment about parents by bluntly attacking the practice of Corban, i.e. the possibility of removing objects from the grasp of (old) parents by dedicating them to the temple (Mark 7.10ff.). Even an appeal to God may not be played off against parents. The commandment about parents applies unconditionally. By contrast, another attitude to the commandment about parents appears in the apophthegm about disciples. One of those who are ready become a disciple wants to bury his dead father before following Jesus on his travels. But Jesus says to him, 'Let the dead bury their dead. Follow me!' (Matt. 8.21f.). That is an impious offence against the commandment relating to parents. It can only be understood as a symbolic action. Just as Hosea was to marry an adulteress, not to legalize adultery but to communicate his message about God's love to an adulterous people, so the disciple is to express a message: with Jesus a person has appeared who imposes unconditional obligations which even revoke the commandment relating to parents. The rule of God which he embodies has absolute priority.

The Torah also says, 'You shall not kill!', but Jesus accentuates this commandment in the first antithesis of the Sermon on the Mount by also including the sphere of anger – as an impulse towards killing. Even someone who is angry at his brother incurs guilt (Matt. 5.21f.). However, over against this logion stands a narrative like that about the cleansing of the temple, in which we see Jesus act in a 'holy anger': he violently drives those selling sacrificial animals and the moneychangers from the temple! Does what was said about anger against one's 'brother' no longer apply in the case of institutions – in the case of established situations? Is that 'anger' which must be held in check towards one's concrete fellow human beings allowed and enjoined there? Or is the abstract requirement of the logion corrected by the realism of the narrative?

The Torah also says, 'You shall not commit adultery.' In the Sermon on the Mount Jesus accentuates this commandment as well. It is to apply even to inward desire of another woman. Someone who looks covetously on another woman has already committed adultery with her in his heart (Matt. 5.28)! The logion about eunuchs which praises celibacy (Matt. 19.12), is just as strict. Over against these logia stand narratives with a marked sexual tolerance. Even if these are often late, they could contain a feature of Jesus' activity: Jesus protects an adulteress from being stoned by a pack of men (John 8.2ff.). He intercedes for the 'woman who was a sinner', who approaches him in the house of a Pharisee (Luke 7.36ff.). The reason for the differentiation of statements here could lie in the different persons to whom they are addressed: the strict sexual morality in the logia is clearly addressed to males. Men are being referred to in the remark about committing adultery by looking covetously at someone else's wife. The saying about eunuchs fits only them! But the tolerant sexual morality of the narratives is protective of women. This asymmetry, too, makes good sense.

The Torah also says: 'You shall not covet the property of others.' But Jesus intensifies this commandment by requiring renunciation of mammon. One cannot serve two masters, God and mammon (Matt. 6.24). Jesus sees little chance of the rich entering the kingdom of God (Mark 10.25). But some narratives openly report that Jesus accepted an invitation and hospitality from a rich senior toll collector (Luke 19.1ff.). The negative verdict on riches does not apply to the rich as persons – especially if they commit themselves to using their wealth socially and to compensate for damage that has been done by cheating. And the narrative about the young man who is not prepared to sell his possessions shows realistically that the radical ethic of possessions comes up against limits (Mark 10.17ff.).

Finally, the Torah says: You shall love your neighbour as yourself. Jesus declares this commandment to be the greatest commandment, which is to be set alongside the first commandment – the basic axiom of Judaism (Mark 12.28ff.). In a logia tradition he accentuates it so that it becomes a command to love one's enemy – which Matthew has rightly stylized as a demand which goes beyond the tradition by making it an antithetical contrast to the command to love one's neighbour (Matt. 5.43ff.). It is interesting that in some narrative traditions the 'enemies', the aliens and sinners, do not appear as those to whom love is to be shown, but as those who show love. All these narratives appear in the Gospel of Luke. That is no coincidence. They fit Luke's picture of the humane Jesus. Thus an '*enemy*' appears in the narrative about the centurion of Capernaum: a pagan, who possibly comes from the Roman army and now serves under a Roman client prince. It is explicitly said of him that he 'loves' the Jewish people, as is shown by the way in which he has founded a synagogue (Luke 7.5). An *alien* also appears in the story of the Good Samaritan. Although the question of love of neighbour at first seems to be focussed on extending love of neighbour to this alien, the point is that this alien himself is the one who practises love in a model way. He is not the one to whom love is shown, but the one who loves (Luke 10.30ff.). Finally, a woman who is a *sinner* appears in the story of the woman at Simon's banquet. Here, too, it is not a matter of showing love to her. Rather, she is depicted as an example of one who loves: what Simon, the host, had neglected, she performs with tears, kisses and gestures (Luke 7.36ff.). Indeed she 'loved much' (7.47).

So we find a radicalized ethic (in the form of logia) and a realistic ethic (often, but not only, in narrative form) side by side. This juxtaposition could reflect the usual contrast between an ethic which is proclaimed and an ethic which is lived out. But that is not the complete explanation. Too clearly the narratives are also often full of a radicalized ethic of demand and understanding. Now and again a deeper sense seems to underlie the juxtaposition of the two forms of radicalization. Because the radicalized demands cannot be fulfilled, the awareness grows that no one is perfect – and therefore one has the right to attack behaviour by others which transgresses norms – whether in a marginal group in one's own people or among aliens outside one's own people. So it cannot be a coincidence that the radicalization of the prohibition against killing and adultery is not formulated as an imperative. We do not find 'You shall not be angry' or 'You shall not look at a woman with sexual desire.' What we find is: 'Whoever is angry *is* guilty.' 'Whoever looks covetously at another woman *has already committed* adultery with her in his heart.' The radicalized demand here potentially turns into a recognition of the inadequacy of all human beings – and this recognition is in turn the basis of a radicalized preaching of grace.

This twofold radicalization of ethics, both in the direction of a more consistent strictness and as a readiness to forgive which transcends everything, is a development of possibilities which were already present in the Jewish tradition. It is not a break with Judaism. So there remains only one more sphere in which such a break could make itself felt: ritual sign language.

3. The Jewish rites and the preaching of Jesus

Judaism is a ritual religion. Fixed symbolic sign actions penetrate everyday life, put it under God and recall God and his present. Behind this is the admirable intention of permeating everything in life with God's presence and elevating even small unassuming gestures to the rank of worship. Iconoclastic criticism of ritual has little understanding of this. But it also has no understanding of the social function of these rites. They are visible signs of belonging to Judaism, an act of confession in public. In the exilic/post-exilic period three forms of ritual behaviour increasingly become crystallized as an identity marker of Judaism: circumcision, the commandments relating to food and the hallowing of the Sabbath. Since forms of ritual behaviour say more about social proximity to or remoteness from a group than inner convictions and notions which evade social control, an investigation of the ritual sign language will decide whether Jesus is to be put at the centre of Judaism, on its edge or beyond its limits.

First of all, one observation seems to suggest that Jesus was rooted in the heart of Judaism: not a single saying of his criticizes *circumcision*. It was already argued over in the 40s, shortly after his death. But the Gospel of Thomas is the first to attribute to Jesus a saying which relativizes the significance of circumcision (53). Now of course one could say that circumcision was not a problem in the world of Jesus because it was performed on small children without their conscious decision. It was a custom that was so taken for granted that (in Palestine) it was no longer an act of confession. By contrast, there was controversy over observing the Sabbath regulations, the commandments relating to cleanness and the commandments relating to food. Must not Jesus' attitude to Judaism show itself in these spheres?

Here we find a completely different picture from that in the case of circumcision: we hear of Jesus' conflicts over the Sabbath with Jewish authorities. In the logion about cleanness in Mark 7.15 he declares all external uncleanness irrelevant – and thus demolishes the foundation of the Levitical commandments about cleanness. The commandments relating to food seem to be scorned in the mission discourse (Luke 10.8)! But above all at the end of his activity, there is a conflict with the ritual centre of the Jewish religion, the temple. Nevertheless I want to claim that in all that he said, Jesus remained within the framework of Judaism.

As for the *Sabbath conflicts*, in the Judaism of the time there was a lively discussion about what was allowed on the Sabbath and what was not. Thus from the time of the Maccabaean wars it had been permissible to defend oneself on the Sabbath – after one occasion when 1,000 Jews had been massacred on the Sabbath because they refused to defend themselves (cf. I Macc. 1.29–41). So in exceptional circumstances killing was allowed in self-defence. When Jesus says provocatively in Mark 3.4, 'Is it lawful to do good on the Sabbath or to do evil, to save life or to kill?', he is possibly alluding to the permission to kill in times of war and arguing from the lesser to the greater: if it is already permissible to do evil, how much more is it permissible to do good! In short, Jesus is merely extending the known instances of saving life on the Sabbath to cases in which life is actively furthered. In so doing he remains within the framework of Jewish discussion of the Sabbath.

Even more than the conflicts over the Sabbath, the *logion about cleanness* in Mark 7.15 is regarded as an indication that Jesus broke with the Torah: 'There is nothing outside a man which by going into him can defile him; but the things which come out of a man are what defile him.' It is important for us that no invitation to stop observing the commandments relating to cleanness is associated with this invitation. There is no imperative demand. There is merely the indicative statement that nothing is intrinsically clean or unclean. External fulfilment of the commandments relating to cleanness was quite compatible with such a statement in the indicative – not because these commandments are intrinsically convincing, but out of respect for tradition or because of outward assimilation. By contrast, when the commandments relating to cleanness were discussed in later primitive Christianity, people talked of revelations which contained a clearly imperative invitation. In Acts 10.9ff. Peter sees many unclean animals in a vision and is repeatedly invited to 'Kill and eat!' Only now has a gnomic maxim become a concrete rule of behaviour.

Even if the commandments relating to cleanness embrace more than just the distinction between permissible and forbidden food, as *commandments relating to food* they have an intense effect on everyday life. Jesus was not specially interested in commandments relating to food. In the mission discourse he tells his disciples that they are to eat (all) that which is put in front of them (Luke 10.8). Furthermore, in his vision of the eschatological feast to which people stream from all points of the compass into the kingdom of God, he pictures a meal shared by Jews (namely the patriarchs Abraham, Isaac and Jacob) with Gentiles, regardless of the commandments about food (Matt. 8.11f.). But that vision, too, can be put within Judaism. Eschatological dreams need not be transposed into present-day practice –

and the instructions in the mission discourse are addressed to itinerant charismatics who in any case may develop a more liberal attitude to the norms of the 'normal' world.

So we cannot say that Jesus fundamentally abandoned the ritual sign language. He works on shaping it in a concrete way, and interprets it more liberally than many of his contemporaries – but all this is not a break with Judaism.

That becomes even clearer if one considers Jesus' attitude to new rites. John the Baptist had required a single *baptism* from all Jews as an expression of repentance shortly before the irruption of the eschatological judgment. Really in Judaism such repentance should have been documented by a new life. However, for John the axe had already been laid to the roots of the tree: there was no time for 'fruits of repentance'. Therefore in the name of God at the last minute he offered a symbolic 'substitute action' with which one could attest the seriousness of one's repentance. With this rite John was doubtless on the way towards creating a special group within Judaism – like the Essenes, who separated themselves ritually from the other Jews by repeated washings and boycotted the temple. From all that we know, Jesus did not baptize during the time of his public activity. He certainly called for repentance, but he dispensed with a ritual act which could demonstrate it publicly. Perhaps he could dispense with it because he was convinced that God gave people time and opportunity for a repentance attested by good deeds. At all events, in the case of Jesus the ritual demarcation from the rest of Judaism is less than in John, and far less than among the Essenes. Certainly, like the Essenes, Jesus too knows a criticism of the temple. But his prophecy about the temple is indirectly a testimony to a great inner link with the centre of the ritual sign language of Judaism. He wanted to 'reform' this centre – more precisely, to replace it with a new, eschatological temple.

Just as Jesus penetrated to the centre of Judaism with the theme of the temple, so too he belongs at the centre of Judaism. Intrinsically he is no 'marginal Jew';[6] only from the perspective of other special Jewish groups like the Pharisees, Sadducees and Essenes is he a marginal figure with problematic liberal views and a mysterious charisma which undermines the traditions.

Thus we arrive at a clear conclusion: Jesus had a Jewish identity.[7] He revitalized the sign language of Judaism. He revived it in the light of its central content – belief in the one and only God. In him we observe a historicizing of the Jewish myth of the kingly rule of God, a twofold radicalization of Jewish ethics as an intensification and relaxation of norms, and a relativizing of the rites which separated Jews from other people. His conflicts with his contemporaries were conflicts within Judaism and not with Judaism. He did not represent an exodus from Judaism but a renewal movement within it. Here he belonged in a series of renewal movements within Judaism since the period of the Maccabees – in an unbroken series of attempts to revitalize the Jewish religion. Since almost always this happened directly or indirectly as a response to the challenge from the great powers which dominated Judaism, none of these renewal movements – including the Jesus movement – can be understood without this political framework. Only political factors explain why Jesus failed.

4. The political situation of Judaism and the historical Jesus

Since Hellenistic culture, represented by the alien rule of the Ptolemies, Seleucids and Romans, exposed Judaism to an intensive pull towards assimilation, time and again renewal movements had appeared in Judaism which opposed this pull by revitalizing its own traditions. The specifically Jewish norms were accentuated. So an accentuation of the Torah is not a special feature of the Jesus movement; it appears throughout these groups. Thus in the second century BCE the older renewal movements, the Essenes, the Pharisees and – in reaction to them – the Sadducees, arose in a conflict with Hellenistic culture. Around the turn of the era a militant resistance movement, the movement of John the Baptist and a series of short-term prophetic movements arose in reaction to the new Roman culture. Finally, the resistance movement tore apart the whole of Palestinian Judaism in a revolt against Rome. However, compared with the periods before and after it, the time of Jesus was relatively peaceful. *Sub Tiberio quies* is Tacitus' verdict on Palestine in this period (*Hist.* V, 9).

The outward picture is deceptive. Conflicts seethed under the surface. They were not carried on in militant forms but with the help of symbols – with a politics of symbols which could constantly turn into more militant forms of conflict, but which also offered an opportunity for more peaceful solutions.[8]

At this time the rulers in both Galilee and Judaea attempted by means of symbols to bring Judaism closer to Hellenistic culture in order to integrate it more firmly into the Roman empire.

Around 19, Herod Antipas had a new capital built in Tiberias. The city was constructed on a Jewish cemetery (Josephus, *Antt.*18, 36–38). Antipas did this deliberately. For now he could be certain that anyone who settled in this 'unclean' city would have reckoned loyalty greater to him than loyalty to the traditional Jewish rites of cleanness. In also calling his new capital 'Tiberias', i.e. dedicating it to the ruling emperor, he indicated the long-term goal of this politics of symbols: loyalty towards the emperor and the *imperium Romanum* were to be strengthened. Moreover, he had statues of animals set up in his new palace, a transgression against the prohibition of images, which at that time was still observed relatively strictly. At the beginning of the Jewish War these statues were destroyed by an angry crowd before they could be removed by an official delegation from Jerusalem (Josephus, *Life* 65f.). The indignation about them shows the high symbolic significance that they had.

It cannot be fortuitous that we also hear of a series of conflicts in this politics of symbols from the period in office of Pontius Pilate, who was ruling at the same time as Antipas. Thus Pilate attempted to bring military standards with pictures of the emperor (or only with the imperial monogram) to Jerusalem. This violation of the prohibition against images in the holy city provoked sustained protests which forced him to abandon the enterprise (Josephus, *Antt.*18, 55–59; *BJ* 2, 169–177). It is in keeping with this that Pilate was the only prefect of Judaea to mint coins bearing pagan cultic symbols: a vessel for libation and an augur's staff. Perhaps he also violated commandments relating to cleanness in building an aqueduct. At least, the building of this also provoked vigorous protests.

It was the goal of the rulers to encourage the integration of the Jewish population of Palestine into Hellenistic pagan culture by means of symbols of acculturation. But they came up against resistance. And this resistance among the people similarly made use of symbolic political actions. Three prophets appear during the rule of Pilate. All of them also communicate their message with symbolic actions, which can be understood as a protest and a defence against the acculturation symbolism enforced from above.

First, before Jesus, *John the Baptist* appeared. His baptism is a symbolic action. And implicitly it has a political significance. If all Jews have to have themselves baptized again, the whole land is threatened with uncleanness. Here the question of cleanness is pointedly blown up – against a ruler who blatantly violated the commandments relating to cleanness in building his capital. John's criticism of Antipas's marital politics also fits this picture. For Jewish marriage laws had been violated in this marriage. Here John the Baptist was merely articulating a widespread hostility to rulers who were increasingly alienating themselves from Jewish traditions.

After Jesus *a Samaritan prophet* appeared in Samaria who promised his followers that he would locate on Mount Gerizim the temple vessels which Moses had hidden (Josephus, *Antt.*18, 85). There is no mistaking the fact that here someone came forward with the claim to be a kind of 'Moses *redivivus*' and to decide the old dispute between Jews and Samaritans over the legitimacy of places of worship in favour of the Samaritan place. Here we have a revitalizing of Samaritan religion. And it may be more than coincidence that the pagan cultic vessels which Pilate had depicted on his coins are in almost direct opposition to the hidden indigenous cultic vessels. At all events, Pilate had the Samaritan and his following massacred – and was deposed because of this blood-bath.

Jesus of Nazareth appeared chronologically between John the Baptist and the anonymous Samaritan prophet. He too expressed his message with symbolic actions,[9] which indicated an opposition to the ruling classes, the Romans and the local aristocracy allied with them.

The formation of *the group of the Twelve* is a symbolic political action – an alternative scheme to the existing constitution of Israel, and one which referred back to age-old traditions still alive only in opposition groups (like the Essenes). Indeed the twelve tribes still lived on only as a memory of a great past and as a hope for the restoration of Israel. Jesus did not expect this restoration in the framework of present structures of rule – a priestly aristocracy with one high priest at its head, who was dependent on the Romans. He developed the hope of a representative popular rule in which the people would be ruled by ordinary folk from its midst, by fishermen and countrymen (Matt. 19.28ff.).

The *entry into Jerusalem* is a further symbolic political act. At every temple festival the Roman prefect and his cohorts entered Jerusalem from the west, to safeguard law and order at festival time, when there was often unrest. For Jesus to enter Jerusalem without troops and from the east, accompanied by pilgrims, and to be greeted as a representative of the 'rule of our father David' (Mark 11.10), is probably a deliberate counter-demonstration. It is hard to understand how the unmistakable symbolic political accents in this account could be as secondary as other motifs in it.

A third symbolic political action to be mentioned here is the *cleansing of the temple* – an action which clearly fits into the sequence of prophetic symbolic acts (Mark 11.15ff.). The temple prophecy communicates the message that the present temple and the aristocracy associated with it is being stripped of its religious legitimation. God's will is for a new temple. The disruption of the sacrificial trade shows that this new temple will be different from the existing one, whether because sacrifice ceases completely or because an end will be put to temple involvement in economic interests.

We could interpret yet further actions of Jesus as expressions of a politics of symbols. As he understood them, the exorcisms become signs of the beginning of the rule of God; they are the beginning of the expulsion of all that is alien, demonic and wicked from the land (Matt. 11.18 par.). His table fellowship with the marginalized among the people anticipates the great eschatological table fellowship of the restored people in which

Gentiles from all over the world will take part – contrary to nationalistic expectations (Matt. 8.11f.). The dialogue over the payment of tax demonstrates both the opposition between imperial rule and the rule of God and the intention of avoiding a militant confrontation with alien rule. It is precisely for this reason that Jesus evades the symbolic language of the images on the coins: if imagery and legend indicate that they are the property of the emperor, then one may pay taxes to the emperor in these coins, since property must be restored to its owners. But there is also an implicit message here: God's property may be restored only to God (Mark 12.13–17)!

In all these symbolic actions, unassuming actions take on a symbolic surplus meaning which points far beyond the immediate 'action'. It is always the 'myth' in which Jesus himself lived that creates this surplus meaning: the myth of the turning point towards the kingdom of God which is imminent and is already beginning now. Only in the context of this expectation do limited actions become fundamental opposition to existing circumstances. Only as a result of it do they become 'symbolic actions', and only it gives them 'symbolic political expressive force'. This myth surrounds not only the actions and words of Jesus but also his whole person with a special aura. And it becomes his fate.

According to the reports, the ruling classes accused him on two grounds. First, because of his prophecy about the temple. This charge interested only the Sanhedrin. The accounts of a hearing before Pilate say nothing of it. Here a second charge plays a decisive role: the charge that as 'king' he sought power. Both charges correspond to the two symbolic political actions reported previously: the cleansing of the temple and the entry into Jerusalem. Such actions inevitably caused political unrest. Jesus was executed as a political trouble-maker, denounced by the temple aristocracy for his attack on the temple, and killed by the Romans because of their expectation that he represented the indigenous kingdom as king of the Jews. But how did Jesus himself regard such expectations and fears? How did he understand himself?

5. Myth and Jesus' understanding of himself[10]

The question how Jesus understood himself can be clarified only within the framework of the Jewish sign language existing at that time. Jesus could express the role he attributed to himself only with the means of his religion. Before one discusses the question whether he possibly used titles to refer to himself, and if so which, one should be clear that it is not this or that title that is decisive for his understanding of himself but the 'historicizing' of the myth of the end-time throughout his activity. It surrounded his person with a supernatural aura. It gave him the decisive role in the drama between God and human beings in the present: it made the rule of God a historical experience in the present – in which on the one hand concrete present experiences became the mythical real presence of the rule of God, and on the other parables and symbolic actions became signs of a mythical reality which was not (yet) present.

This supernatural aura produced by the myth – a myth in which Jesus and his disciples themselves lived – was the cause of the charisma with which Jesus fascinated his followers and provoked his opponents. Jesus was a Jewish charismatic whose attraction derived from the fact that he gave the mythical, ethical and ritual sign language of Judaism new life from the centre of Jewish faith, namely from the basic axiom of monotheistic belief. His preaching was strictly theocentric. With this revitalization of the religious sign language of Judaism, Jesus stood in a chain of revitalizing movements from Maccabaean times, all of which were opposed to the threat of a dissolution of Jewish identity through the overwhelming power of an alien Hellenistic culture, however much their opposition, too, might be stamped by precisely this alien culture. Now it is characteristic of charismatics that they can exercise their authority (their 'charisma') even without basing themselves on existing traditions and roles – indeed, often over against them. So Jesus need not necessarily have identified himself as redeemer and bringer of salvation with a given role. Even if it is very difficult to be sure, I think it improbable that Jesus related a pre-existing role-expectation to himself. The following arguments move me to make this remark:

(*a*) John the Baptist had aroused the expectation of a *stronger one* and coming one through his preaching (Matt. 3.11 par.). This expectation must have been alive in the circles around Jesus. For like Jesus himself, many of his disciples and followers came from the group of John's sympathizers. This expectation of a stronger one got by without a title. Neither the 'stronger one' nor the 'coming one' is a fixed messianic title. Yet 'the stronger one' refers to a lofty figure who transcends all previous dimensions – so that time and again it has been argued that by it John the Baptist meant God himself.

(*b*) Other people probably applied to Jesus the expectation that he was the 'messiah'. This title seems characteristically to be used by others (cf. Mark 13.21, which warns against people who identify others as messiah). This expectation could also have been expressed in the circle of the disciples in Peter's messianic confession (Mark 8.29). The people could have confronted him with the longing for a 'son of David', a Davidide from the royal family (cf. Mark 10.47, 48). Very probably the fear that he was a messianic pretender to the throne played a role in the proceedings of the authorities against him: he is executed as 'king of the Jews' (Mark 15.26) – and the passion narrative makes it clear that this king is none other than the 'messiah' (Mark 15.32). Followers and opponents possible longed for him or feared him as the 'messiah'. But his own attitude to this expectation remains unclear. All we can say is that before Pilate he did not distance himself from these expectations sufficiently clearly.

(*c*) The only 'title' which occurs frequently on Jesus' lips is the enigmatic expression '*son of man*'. At that time, in everyday language it meant 'any man' or 'a man' and occasionally could also be a periphrasis for 'I'. Here, however, this meaning is not to be found in a lexicon but can always only arise *ad hoc*. Alongside this there is an expression from visionary language: talk of a supernatural judge at the end of days who looks '*like* a son of man' (Dan. 7.14). The visionary-language tradition also emphasizes the humanity of this figure: the one like a human being is opposed to the power of the beasts, which embody the various bestial kingdoms of the world. He embodies a humane alternative to their empires. 'Son of Man' is not a fixed title in either of the two traditions. And in neither of these traditions is it exclusively related to a person. Jesus could have used the expression. Possibly it only became an honorific title through the use that he made of it. Probably Jesus was the first to give a term for any human being the connotations of messianic dignity. However, it does not make any difference to the expressive force of this central position of the term 'son of man' if we attribute this development first to primitive Christianity. The 'man' is the only expression in the Synoptic Gospels which primitive Christian imagination regarded as a characteristic term that Jesus used of himself. However one interprets it, in this way Jesus (or primitive Christianity) expresses a 'humanizing' of the myth. A figure designated by the term for '*the* man' comes to the centre of the religious sign system. The comparative texts from elsewhere in Judaism about a lofty figure who is seen in visions always still contain a comparative particle: this figure is 'like a man' and 'like a son of man'. But here he becomes '*the* man'. He comes into the centre of religious sign language. However, possibly that is only a post-Easter development. I shall be discussing this in the next chapter.

To sum up the argument: we do not have on the one hand the historical Jesus in a world without myth – and on the other side the mythical Christ who on the basis of post-Easter interpretations is increasingly distanced from the historical world. The historical Jesus already lived in a myth which revitalized the monotheistic basic axiom of the Jewish religion. He lived in a myth of the coming kingdom of God in which what Jewish monotheism had always postulated would finally become reality: God becomes the reality that determines everything. Jesus could presuppose this myth in his preaching; he does not explain it anywhere. But he changed it by the way in which he lived in and with it. 1. He historicized it by combining it with his own history and his actions. 2. It gave him a poetic form of expressions in parables which contained impulses towards a new perception of God. 3. He combined it with symbolic-political forms of expression and thus demilitarized it, in so far as he detached the hope for victory over the Gentiles and the subjection of them from it. But he did not depoliticize it. Rather, Jesus stood in the context of the symbolic-political controversies of his time. Just as the expectation of an eschatological change in all things would not have arisen without the conflict between the superior powers of the world and the Jewish people, so too this political tension stands in the background of the eschatological preaching of Jesus. But Jesus gives the religious hope greater autonomy over against politics: loyalty to God does not compel rebellion against the emperor, but for that reason it does not compel unconditional loyalty to the emperor either. Where the two come into conflict, people have to decide: 'Render to Caesar that which is Caesar's – and to God, that which is God's' (Mark 12.17).

3

How Did Jesus Come to be Deified?

The Transformation of the Jewish Sign System by Post-Easter Belief in Christ

The historical Jesus revitalized Jewish religion. He brought its basic conviction of the one and only God into the centre of religious sign language in a new way by proclaiming the breaking in of the rule of God. But the first Christians put Jesus himself at the centre of their religious sign world: in their hymns and prayers they enthroned him at the right hand of God and thus laid the foundation for the separation of Christianity and Judaism. This way from the theocentricity of Jesus to the christocentricity of the Christians, from the Jewish charismatic Jesus to his deification, from the historicizing of the myth by Jesus to the mythologizing of his history among his followers, is a central theme of a theory of primitive Christian religion.

There is a consensus that the first Christians said far more about Jesus than Jesus ever said about himself. Moreover there is also a consensus that the impulse towards this transcending of all the sayings of the historical Jesus came from the Easter appearances. They are well attested as visionary experiences. There should be no doubt about their content as authentic subjective experience, regardless of how this experience is interpreted.

Of course one may ask: do we not come up against a limitation of any scholarly analysis here? Can one talk about the Easter event in such a way that the argument can be followed by both insiders and outsiders? At least the 'semiotic' process associated with this event which is tangible for us clearly shows that Jesus becomes the centre (or the head) of the religious sign system, as a result of which one of its basic rules seems to be abrogated: the distance between God and human beings and the exclusiveness of God who has no one alongside him – and tolerates no gods beside himself. With Jesus this logic seems to be reversed: because for the first Christians he indisputably stands alongside God, he himself must be a God! How could this exaltation of Jesus come about?

The appearances alone can hardly explain it. We have no historical analogies for someone becoming 'Messiah' or 'Son of Man' or 'Son of God' through appearances. Rather, the appearances must have been experienced in the light of particular convictions for them to be able to create the certainty that Jesus has divine status and forms the centre of the religious sign world.[1]

Such processes of the transformation of a religious sign system can be illuminated from two sides which it is impossible to separate: in the light of the experiences which shake the existing system – and in the light of the existing system which incorporates such experiences.

As far as the *experiences* are concerned, the transformation of the Jewish sign world is provoked by an experience of dissonance. The dissonance is that between the charisma of Jesus and his crucifixion. His charisma had aroused the expectation that he would play the decisive role in the eschatological event between God and human beings. The crucifixion was the failure of these expectations – indeed more: it was a deliberate mockery and humiliation of such expectations. The *titulus* on the cross which identified the one who was executed as 'king of the Jews' contained the message that all hopes for a liberator of Israel were to be crucified along with the crucified Jesus. In order to get over such an experience of dissonance, the crucified had to be given an even higher rank and value than that originally attributed to him. By overcoming death he proved himself to be finally more powerful than his judges and executioners. Thus the Easter appearances made possible an infinite heightening of the value of the person of Jesus, as a result of which the extreme dissonance between his charisma and the cross could also be overcome.

However, such experiences are not enough to explain the elevation of the person of Jesus to divine status. In addition there is a latent readiness of the religious *sign system* to employ such experiences of dissonance in a particular sense. My thesis is that the exaltation of Jesus to divine status could bring about a reduction of cognitive dissonance only because it corresponded to a dynamic contained in Jewish monotheism. Belief in the one and only God had formed in the sixth century BC through the surmounting of a similar experience of crisis: the exaltation of YHWH to be the one and only God was as much the surmounting of a crisis as was the exaltation of Jesus to unique divine status. The same 'monotheistic dynamic' is at work in both processes, so that the deification of Jesus did not contradict the Jewish sign world, but consistently 'built it up' and 'fulfilled' it. Those who enthroned Jesus at the right hand of God were not Gentiles but Jews; and they did this in the awareness not of forsaking their Jewish monotheism but rather of consummating it.

In what did this monotheistic dynamic consist in the sixth century BC?[2] Already in the pre-exilic period Israel had been required to worship only

YHWH. Regardless of whether this monolatrous movement was the concern of a radical minority or could build on a broad consensus among the people, it was decisive that monolatry did not put the existence of other gods in question. Monolatry acknowledges that other people worship other gods, but precisely because of that insists that Israel should worship only YHWH. It was the experiences of crisis in the sixth century which first led from such monolatry to a consistent monotheism that denies the existence of other gods. In the face of the destruction of Jerusalem, the deportation of the upper class and the long exile, the only possibility was either to recognize the superiority of the victorious nations and their gods – or to hold firm to belief in YHWH by compensating for the catastrophe on earth by a victory in heaven. The other gods were said not to exist. They were not the victors in battle against Israel; the one and only God, who had made use of other peoples to punish Israel, was the victor. Once judgment had been inflicted he would lead Israel again into a new future. YHWH even ruled over the victors. The more total the defeat of YHWH and his people seemed to be in earthly history, the more powerful this 'metaphysical' victory of YHWH over all other gods in heaven (and therefore in the religious sign world) had to be.

So the monotheistic dynamic has three closely associated aspects:

- First, it is the *surmounting of cognitive dissonance* in a catastrophe; it gets over the discrepancy between the expectations of salvation from YHWH and the disaster that is experienced in history.
- Secondly, it is confirmation and *intensification* of a consensus, an already-existing tendency towards monolatry which is heightened so that it becomes 'monotheism'.
- Thirdly, it is the *competitive outdoing* of the other gods and the peoples who worship them. In the face of the one and only God they all become ridiculous 'nothings'.

This monotheistic dynamic is repeated in the christological dynamic of the sign world of primitive Christianity. The *experience of crisis* here is the crucifixion as the refutation of the expectations attached to Jesus. The Easter appearances made it possible to transform this defeat into a victory of the exalted one over his judges and the world. The deepest humiliation could be compensated for only by an exaltation which outdid everything. The dissonance of the cross was got over by elevating the crucified Jesus to a status equal to God.

This exaltation confirms an already existing *conviction of faith*: God can raise the dead to new life. And conversely, wherever the dead are raised to new life, there is an act of God. Thus the Easter appearances could activate and confirm a basic motif of Jewish religion: belief in the one and only God who can create life *ex nihilo* – though this nothingness is usually imagined as a chaotic 'something'. Just as God once created the world from nothing, so too he was active in the present overcoming death by calling into being that which was not (Rom. 4.17).

The consciousness that the Jewish system of convictions was superior to all other systems of religious conviction was reinforced by the entry of Jesus into a status equal to God. The elevation of Jesus to deity set in motion a *competitive outdoing* which worked out Jesus' superiority to all other rival figures – in Judaism and paganism. Jesus is a name above all names. But this constant outdoing of other *numina* leads indirectly to assimilations. Therefore in the development of christology we find an explicit 'competitive syncretism'.[3]

So my thesis proves to be that only within a religious frame of reference in which there was a 'programme' for reinterpreting defeats as victories and extreme humiliation as exaltation could the Easter appearances be the occasion and impulse for the deification of Jesus. Since this 'programme' was already active in the formation of the monotheistic basic axiom of the Jewish religion, the deification of Jesus became possible only on the basis of a dynamic immanent in Jewish monotheism – even if it was soon experienced as a threat to this monotheism.

I shall go on to discuss the transformation of the Jewish sign system under the three aspects mentioned above: as a way of surmounting dissonance, as an intensification of monotheistic belief, and as a syncretistic outdoing of competition.

1. The exaltation of Jesus as a way of surmounting dissonance

The exaltation of Jesus to divine status served to surmount a cognitive dissonance. But it would be too easy simply to think in psychological categories – in other words to see at work here that mechanism which after we have brought a house for which we paid more than we wanted or could afford or than the house was objectively worth, makes us enthuse about the value of this house in order to make us forget that there is a discrepancy between price and result. An increase of value in the imagination is often a psychological compensation for a real reduction in value which is not conceded. A better comparison is the discrepancy between a theoretical system and provocative experiences which force us to reconstruct the theory. Such a discrepancy and its consequences in the system are more than the psychological processes in which the discrepancy is discovered and its consequences are coped with. The experiences with Jesus and his failure also tear open a deep discrepancy which necessitated the reconstruction of a religious sign system. This reconstruction gave a redeemer a central position. This *religious* discrepancy (i.e. a contradiction between sign system and experience) is the decisive thing. But the reconstruction of the sign system came about through *individual* conflicts in the lives of individuals and had consequences for the *social* life of primitive Christian groups. As a reconstruction of an objective religious sign system it is certainly more than the sum of the psychological and social changes in which this reconstruction took place. But without these psychological and social changes we can hardly understand what happened at that time. So we shall discuss the exaltation of Jesus in turn as the surmounting of religious, psychological and social dissonance.

The *religious* dissonance which had to be surmounted was the contradiction of charisma and cross, the contradiction between the expectations of a charismatic surrounded with a messianic aura and his failure on the cross. His message during his lifetime had promised that the rule of God which was breaking in would resolve the contradiction between Israel's hope of a restoration of independence and its lasting dependence on alien powers. This proclamation indicated the basic religious conflict between religious hopes and convictions and the experiences which contradicted them. But the crucifixion seemed to disseminate quite a different message, namely that the hopes for the restoration of Israel were vain and would come to grief on the resistance of the Romans. Crucifixion was the usual punishment for slaves and rebels, and it proclaimed: this is what will happen to all those who hoped for an imminent change or even sought to bring it in. And here, too, there is a general religious conflict: what promises religious hope is stranded and shattered on the rocks of hostile reality. The exaltation of Jesus through his death could surmount this 'dissonance' in a convincing way. For the exaltation of Jesus to a world beyond death in which God alone rules removed his authority from any human power. Even the strongest legions had to capitulate at the frontier of death. The close association of the crucified Jesus with God gave his authority an origin removed from all disappointments and with a superior origin. He participated in the power of the one and only God which overcomes death.[4]

The basic contradiction between a religious sign world and historical experience sketched out here had an effect on individuals in producing *personal conflicts*, so that the 'Easter event' also has a psychological dimension. Granted, we know only a little about the personal experience and behaviour of the Easter witnesses. But it is not fortuitous that the little that we do know points in this direction.[5]

Peter, the first witness, experienced the basic conflict between religious conviction and experience as a personal contradiction between his bond of discipleship to Jesus and his denial of Jesus in the night that he was betrayed. Therefore for Peter the Easter appearance did not just mean the reduction of a basic religious discrepancy between hope and experience but quite personally the overcoming of a split with himself. The few traces of his Easter experience in our sources indicate that. In John 21.15ff. the risen Jesus asks him three times 'Do you love me' – unmistakably taking up Peter's threefold denial. For Peter, Easter is a 'reacceptance' of the one who denied Jesus!

As brother of Jesus, James experienced this basic conflict as a contradiction between family ties and the distancing of the family from Jesus in his lifetime: it had attempted to show that he was mad (Mark 3.20f.). Perhaps for James (and through him also for the other members of the family) Easter was a reconciliation with their brother. Possibly Easter was also the reacceptance of a family tradition that had been suppressed or denied. If the family claimed Davidic descent, as is possible, it could now develop the messianism contained in that claim instead of suppressing it and denying it.[6]

Paul experienced the basic conflict between Israel's hopes and the historical experience in concrete terms as a conflict between his hostility to the crucified Jesus, whom he regarded as one cursed by the law, and an unconscious conflict over the law within himself which he had attempted to suppress by an ostentatious zeal for the law. In repudiating the one cursed by the law he had also repudiated something in himself, and by accepting the crucified Jesus he accepted a dark side in himself.[7]

We can demonstrate a conflict least for Mary Magdalene – who perhaps was the first to have a largely 'lost' Easter appearance. We can conjecture that the care for Jesus attributed to the women could not be expressed after his death: no woman could care for his body and see to his burial. If the Easter appearances to the women are associated with an attempt to make good this care, while the narrative may be legendary, it could point to a real motif: the crucified Jesus had been buried without the care of the women close to him.

The motives are different in all these individuals. A single psychological explanation is impossible – apart from the fact that in every case a strong positive or negative bond with the crucified Jesus is combined with an internal conflict within the witnesses to Easter. But this psychological conflict always develops within the given framework of that fundamental conflict between the axioms and motifs of Jewish faith and the experience of failure. The religious sign system precedes the personal experiences – and cannot be explained from these experiences.[8]

That is also true of the *social* dimension of Easter faith. The exaltation of the crucified Jesus to divine status had an effect on claims to authority in the primitive Christian community and its influence on the world around. The formula tradition of appearances already mentions two group appearances alongside individual experiences: one to the Twelve, with whom a claim to leadership of the restored twelve tribes is associated. Probably Peter gathered the Twelve, convinced that they (without Judas) would now be appointed to their promised leadership role. Alongside this, an enigmatic appearance to 5, 000 brothers is related – here an egalitarian element in primitive Christianity is addressed with the term 'brother' (the sisters probably included). It is even more important that all Christians could experience their outsider role as a potential authority role on the basis of the cross and Easter. Just as Jesus deliberately adopted the role of an outsider, so they too could deliberately adopt outsider roles – in the awareness that the world which rejected them was as wrong as the world which rejected and killed Jesus. In primitive Christianity we find a prime example of the connection between stigma and charisma: the stigmatized role, voluntarily accepted, becomes the foundation of charismatic influence if the charismatics have survived the repudiation of society – and now question the legitimacy of this repudiation and the norms, values and convictions that are effective in it. And where was there such an overwhelming survival of social stigmatization as in the case of Jesus, the one who had been crucified and was risen? Where was there a greater swing from rejection to exaltation than with him?

2. The exaltation of Jesus as the intensification of the basic conviction of monotheism

The Philippians hymn depicts the extreme self-humiliation and self-stigmatization of Jesus to the point of death on the cross in order to provide a foundation for the fact that God exalts him above all other powers. The hope of Deutero-Isaiah that one day all human beings will confess the one and only God is transferred to him (cf. the quotation of Isa. 45.23 in Phil. 2.10f.). Except that now the homage of those who are in heaven, on earth and under the earth is given to Jesus as Kyrios. The exaltation of Jesus to a godlike status is thus not depicted as an attack on the monotheistic conviction but as a fulfilment of the expectation of a belief in the one and only God which will establish itself all over the world.

This freedom from any tension between monotheism and christology is characteristic of the first generation of primitive Christianity. Certainly through Paul we hear a good deal about controversies with Jews and Jewish

Christians over questions of the law. But nowhere do we hear of controversies over a 'high christology' and a threat to monotheism from it as we do later in the Gospel of John. The two 'theological' writings or groups of writings preserved from the first generation – the Logia source and the authentic letters of Paul – solve the problem (which was not yet a problem) in very different ways. Only if we attempt to add their two solutions together does there arise that theological christocentricity which had to be criticized by Jews as a threat to pure monotheism.

The Logia source (perhaps in connection with its final redaction) begins with the temptation story – which is formally somewhat out of place in a collection of logia. In these temptations Jesus acquires his authority in order to be able to teach the words which follow. Monotheism is a decisive test. In exemplary fashion Jesus rejects the temptation to worship another alongside God as a satanic temptation. In short, the Jesus of the Logia source is an exemplary monotheist.

Paul takes another course. The historical Jesus interests him only in passing. For Paul, his sayings contain no absolute obligations. Otherwise he would not relativize the saying about divorce in connection with mixed marriages or as an apostle deliberately 'scorn' the prohibition in the mission discourse about earning one's own living. For Paul, the authority of Jesus is not based on the words and actions of the earthly Jesus but on the one action of God. God sent Jesus as his only son. And God raised him from the dead in a sovereign creative act. Thus the exalted one owes his divine status wholly and exclusively to God alone. Any suspicion that a human being has made himself God is excluded. For Paul is not interested in Jesus the human being. He does not want to know Christ 'after the flesh'. We can probably reverse the connection: because Paul is still deeply rooted in basic monotheistic convictions, he cannot find any positive relationship to the earthly Jesus. Paul had a fear of surrounding the earthly Jesus with a divine aura, because for him there is a great distance between any human being and the one God. For him Jesus' earthly existence is only his divesting himself so that he is bare humanity. Jesus' total failure in earthly life, the cross, shows that all his dignity is the work of God. If Paul worships him as a godlike being, what he worships in him has come into being exclusively through God's sovereign action and not through the great deeds or words of a human being.

So in the first generation we still have no balance between the tradition of the earthly Jesus on the one hand, in which Jesus as subject of his words and actions gains his status by preserving and proving his monotheistic faith through all temptations, and on the other the kergyma of the action of God in his humiliated and exalted son in which God alone is the subject and bestows all dignity – independently of the words and actions of the earthly Jesus. Only with the writing of Gospels does the second generation create a synthesis which from Mark to John increasingly fuses the earthly Jesus with the exalted one.

Only now does the dignity of the exalted Jesus already appear as the claim of the earthly Jesus. The Johannine Jesus asserts on the basis of his miracles that he is doing the works of God (John 5.17). The earthly Jesus brings the message: I and the Father are one (John 10.30). And in both cases there are attempts on the part of the Johannine Jews to kill him, since in their eyes in both cases the basic monotheistic axiom of the Jewish religion is being violated. Here Jesus apparently makes himself God. Only now does the high christology become a basis of separation between Jews and Christians.

It must be emphasized all the more that initially the exaltation of the crucified Jesus is understood as the establishment of monotheistic faith. The one and only God, alongside whom all the other gods are 'nothing', has subjected and done away with all other powers and authorities (i.e. all other gods and numinous powers) through the son whom he has sent. As the earthly one and the exalted one, Jesus had the mandate consistently to carry through and establish monotheistic faith.

3. The exaltation of Jesus as the outdoing of competition

The link between belief in Christ and the monotheistic dynamic which established the one and only God over against all the gods necessarily led to a continuous heightening of the dignity of Christ in the period after Easter. The new Kyrios Jesus had to establish himself in the face of all rival gods and outdo them. For with monotheism, primitive Christianity had inherited this sense of superiority and antisyncretistic self-understanding: it repudiated both the worship of other gods and the adoption of elements of the religious sign language associated with other cults. Precisely for that reason, time and again it had to make its claim to superiority and exclusiveness plausible – not by adopting alien views, which was impossible in view of its antisyncretistic self-understanding, but by shaping its own religious sign world in a way which made it capable of competing with other religions. Rivals in the marketplace in part resemble one another when they are struggling to meet the same needs. The same is true of religions in a pluralistic situation. They have to 'imitate' one another in order to outdo one another in the imitation. And the imitation comes about by shaping their own tradition as the counterpart of others. I call such an indirect way of reciprocal influence 'competitive syncretism'.

In Christianity this competitive syncretism works in two directions: on the one hand the power of Christ is exalted above all other authorities and powers, and on the other Christ is brought nearer to human beings than all other deities. We find side by side an increase in distance which raises the exalted one above all powers and removes him from human life and human limitations – and a reduction in distance which binds him closer to the human fate than other deities. Probably above all the interlocking of the two tendencies in one and the same figure gave the new faith its vital force. It fulfilled a secret longing of the religions of its time – both in Judaism and in the pagan religions: the longing for a deity which stood above all powers, yet at the same time associated itself closely with human living and dying.

(a) Outdoing power through exaltation

The force at work in this competitive syncretism can best be demonstrated by means of I Cor. 8.5, where with the help of a traditional formula Paul relates his monotheistic faith to pagan polytheism. There he begins by fundamentally denying the existence of pagan gods, but he adds a qualification:

For although there may be so-called
gods either in heaven — or on earth
as indeed there are many gods — and many lords
yet for us there is
only one God and Father — and one Kyrios Jesus Christ,
from whom are all things — through whom are all things
and for whom we exist — and we through him.

What is worth noting here is that Paul transfers the *heis theos* formula (a key term of strict monotheism) to christology and varies it to become the *heis kyrios* formula. This transference of divine predicates to Jesus is reinforced by the formula using 'all', which is similarly related to both God and the Kyrios. Paul clearly contrasts both with the other gods: here there is one God, there the many gods; here the one Kyrios, there the many *kyrioi*. The result is a polemical contrast between the two. Thus the other gods, who according to Paul really do not exist at all, are devalued. Later Paul explains their negative existence more closely: they exist only as demons (I Cor. 10.19f.).

In my view, the outdoing of power by a competitive contrast and the demonization of devalued 'rivals' can best be observed in the relationship between belief in Christ and the emperor cult.[9] Among Jews the repudiation of the emperor cult was accepted as an element of their tradition. Things were different with the (Gentile) Christians. Here the repudiation of the emperor cult did not seem legitimated by tradition but was based on 'decision'. This was all the less understandable when the Christians (unlike the Jews) offered worship to a human figure as to a deity (*quasi deo*) (Pliny, *Epistles* X, 96). Even the Romans nowhere took the initiative in requiring the emperor cult, but at most introduced it into trials as a 'means of proof' and an opportunity for 'conversion' from the terrible superstition of the Christians. In primitive Christianity there was a general awareness of a fundamental opposition to it.

We encounter this awareness wherever the emperor is *demonized*. He is seen as the Satan, the ruler over the demons. One of the oldest instances of this is the temptation story. The Roman emperor is probably the model for the Satan who in it requires *proskynesis* of Jesus and promises kingdoms in return, and Jesus rejects this offer as an offence against monotheism. For Gaius Caligula introduced the *proskynesis* into court ceremonial in Rome and granted client kings kingdoms (as did other emperors), but was the only emperor to come into direct opposition to Jewish monotheism through his attempt to transform the Jerusalem temple into a place of the emperor cult.[10]

In the tradition behind Mark 13, anxiety about the desecration of the temple under Caligula could have led to a prophetic summons to flee to the hills: the 'abomination of desolation' which is not to stand in the temple but which evidently already exists would then be the status of Gaius Caligula, already made and waiting to be transported to Jerusalem.[11]

The power of Rome also appears as Satan in the Gospel of John. According to John 8.44, the Johannine Jews who want to kill Jesus are not doing their own will as free children of Abraham but the will of Satan, the 'ruler of this world', as he is called at another point. This ruler becomes active through Judas: Jesus announces him in John 14.30 and he then appears as Judas, who among other things appears as the commander of a Roman cohort (John 18.3). In the end Jesus is executed because otherwise Pilate would be disloyal to the emperor: this emperor is the 'ruler of this world', whose will is done with the execution of Jesus. This ruler of the world has robbed the Jews of their freedom, so that they want to kill Jesus. For the moment power over Jesus has been granted to him and his official Pilate 'from above' (i.e. by God)!

The demonization of the emperor is clearest in the Apocalypse of John. The Satanic beast from the abyss requires the emperor cult and is the embodiment of the Roman power which is hostile to God (Rev. 13).

However, the demonization of the emperors is only one side of the 'competitive outdoing' of the emperor to whom religious worship is offered. The other side is the shaping of christology *as a contrast*: consciously or unconsciously, it sometimes becomes a counterpart to the emperor cult. The details of such references are disputed, and I can only mention them briefly here.

In Rom. 1.3f. Paul quotes a pre-Pauline formula with a two-stage christology. Jesus comes from the house of David, but through the resurrection was appointed Son of God 'in power' (i.e. in reality and effect). In using this formula in the introduction to a letter to the Romans written about 56, Paul is probably alluding to the death of the emperor Claudius on 13 October 54 and his divinization after death. Claudius came from the Julian-Claudian house and (like other emperors) was only elevated to *divus* after his death. His apotheosis was not undisputed, as is shown by Seneca's satire *Apocolocyntosis*, which appeared shortly after his death. In it the emperor asks to be received among the gods in heaven, but is rejected as unworthy and sent to the underworld.[12]

In its account of the story of Jesus, the Gospel of Mark can be read as a 'counter-Gospel' to the propaganda about the rulers of the time. The *euaggelion* of Jesus Christ stands in contradiction to the *euaggelia* of the rise of the Flavians to power (Josephus, *BJ* 4, 618, 656). Prophecies were also transferred to the Flavians. Of them, too, miracles were told which were meant to legitimate their rule. Vespasian, too, was declared to be 'son of God' (i.e. of Ammon). In the face of his rise Mark writes an anti-Gospel, relates the way of Jesus to his 'kingdom', and recounts the prophecy of John the Baptist which legitimated Jesus and the many miracles which proved his authority. The message of the Gospel of Mark is that Jesus of Nazareth, not the Flavians, has brought the fulfilment of the promise. The political and religious propaganda of the new rulers is a sign of the end time in which believers will be led astray by the powers hostile to God.[13]

The Gospel of Matthew takes this message further. It implicitly grapples with the hope which was alive in the Jewish War and bitterly disappointed, that the East would again come to rule over the West through a ruler from Judaea. Josephus bears witness that many 'wise men' were led astray by similar passages of scripture (*BJ* 6, 312f.). Against this the Gospel of Matthew says that this expected ruler has already appeared in Jesus. He is the one in whom the expectations of the Orient represented by the Magi from the East are fulfilled. He is the king in whom the expectations of the Jews and their writings have been fulfilled, even in detail. He is the son of David who will bring salvation. But unlike the expected warrior figures, this son of David appears without military power; he does not wage war, but heals the sick and enters his capital riding on an ass. He has rejected the temptation of earthly rule over the world in order after his resurrection to receive all power in heaven and on earth and to rule over all peoples through his commandments (and not through troops).[14]

A further witness to christology as a contrast to the emperor cult is the letter to the Ephesians. Here Christ is the 'peacemaker' who overcomes the hostility between Jews and Gentiles, who reconciles the two groups and in a triumphal advent 'comes' to proclaim his peace (Eph. 2.17). All the images – peacemaker, reconciler, advent to proclaim peace – have analogies in the *pax* propaganda of the Flavians. The Flavians, too attempted to integrate the Jews into the Roman empire by involving them in the building of the new temple for Jupiter Capitolinus. The former temple tax had now to be paid to this symbol of Roman rule – a kind of cultic forced integration of Judaism. The Flavians inevitably failed with such a policy, whereas the letter to the Ephesians is proud that the Christian community is creating what failed in political reality, namely the integration of Jews and Gentiles in one community and one worship.[15]

Among the gods of the ancient world the emperors were the most recent newcomers. Other gods might find new worshippers, but were themselves age-old. Yet here it was possible to experience that something was changing in the heavens. No living and personal piety was associated with the emperor but it was the expression of social integration: it was an opportunity for the dependent population to express political loyalty in a religious form and a means for the ruling class to give the *imperium romanum* a religious 'clamp'. Where the emperor was worshipped, there was a solidarity which transcended regions. The emperor cult was actively supported above all by the politically and socially successful, by the *honoratiores* in the provinces and the successful freedmen, by new client princes like Herod I, who had the emperor worshipped in the cult in both Caesarea and Sebaste, and by the military. The army bore the images of the emperor on its standards – as an expression of political loyalty and of a special relationship to the ruler. The army was the emperor's social clientele and offered limited opportunities for advancement. In other words, the supporters of the emperor cult were the upwardly mobile groups together with traditional local groups of *honoratiores* who thus indicated their arrival in an imperial aristocracy which transcended the regions.

While around the turn of the century the 'world rulers' were thus taking the place of gods, little groups in the Roman empire were elevating an alternative ruler of the world over all other deities and attributing to him the subjection of all powers and authorities in heaven and on earth. They said that no other numina existed. This 'revolution in heaven' was not attributed to any member of the ruling class but to a member of a subject people, not a victor, but one who had been crucified. He found his 'social clientele' across all provinces and peoples. He created a network of solidarity between his scattered followers which transcended the regions, above all where the Roman empire showed weaknesses in integration: among the urban groups at all levels who had been excluded by the (local and imperial) political system. Here people felt how the empire was growing together beyond the regions, but could not find any privileged part in it. Anyone who joined these followers of the crucified one had been gripped by a general mobility which did not show itself in social changes but in a religious and ethical change, in repentance and conversion, not to loyalty to emperor and empire, but to a bond with Christ and his kingdom. And like the social clientele of the emperor, the 'social clientele' of this ruler of the world embraced people of all classes, from the most powerful senators to the slaves of the *familia Caesaris*: his communities united people of all classes, though clearly more from the lower classes than from the upper classes (I Cor. 1.26).

There was thus a certain structural analogy between the emperors and their social clientele on the one hand and Christ and his followers on the other. In both connections one found forms of solidarity which transcended the regions, a promise of a change of life, a cohesion which transcended classes, and a certain privilege which others who lived without such a relationship to the 'ruler of the world' did not have. However, the social *Sitz im Leben* was different. On the one hand there were socio-political groups and processes, and on the other religious groups and changes. However, the structural similarity which was nevertheless present could make the two rivals in a society in which political and religious processes were closely interwoven. In the visions of the Apocalypse a seer has bluntly expressed this incompatibility, less on the basis of real conflicts and persecutions than on the basis of conflicts which were feared and a clear insight into the fundamental antagonism between the two.

(b) Outdoing salvation through nearness

The experience of the divine has two sides: superior power and saving nearness. In their religious imagination the first Christians put Christ above all other deities, and by this 'revolution in heaven' (in the semiotic cosmos of their convictions) stripped all others of power. However, the young faith derived its power of attraction above all from the nearness of this new deity to human beings. The incarnate Christ represents the real presence of God among human beings, in his activity and suffering to the death. The separation between God and human beings is overcome by him.

Tendencies towards such a reduction of the distance between God and humankind were present at the time. In Judaism there were certainly strong inhibitions about abolishing the distance between God and human beings. The one and only God is transcendent. No other religion of antiquity emphasizes that as much as Judaism. Precisely for that reason we find in it a longing to overcome this distance. It is echoed in primitive Christianity, and where it is expressed characteristically makes use of a language borrowed from pagan religion. This can be shown particularly at two points:

- First, in the development of the notion of a redeemer in which divinity and humanity are indissolubly combined: through the incarnation and conception of the redeemer by the Spirit, notions which go beyond Jewish traditions;
- Secondly, through the development of an understanding of a sacrament which symbolizes an identification of Christians with the human fate of the redeemer in a way which goes beyond analogies from the history of religion, but is stimulated by them.

(i) The primitive Christian notion of the redeemer as an expression of the reduction of religious distance

In Judaism, the longing for a reduction in religious distance is expressed among other things by the development of mediator figures who build a bridge from God to human beings. These mediator figures are either hypostatized divine attributes or persons in the divine world who are sent to earth: angels or pre-existent human beings.[16]

The 'attributes' of God directed towards the world are above all hypostatized: his 'wisdom' and his 'reason' (or his 'Logos'). They take on increasingly independent existence. They are the deity itself in so far as it can be experienced as being near in the world and history and among human beings. Thus in Wisdom 7.26f. we read of 'wisdom':

> She is a reflection of eternal light,
> a spotless mirror of the working of God,
> and an image of his goodness.
> Though she is but one, she can do all things,
> and while remaining in herself, she renews all things;
> in every generation she passes into holy souls
> and makes them friends of God, and prophets.

In primitive Christianity Jesus is regarded as a messenger and incarnation of Sophia (Wisdom) and the Logos (God's reason). But in the Jewish statements about Sophia and the Logos these are never incarnated exclusively in one human being. Sophia and Logos are present wherever human beings learn the Torah and follow God's will: in the souls of the pious and prophets (Wisdom 7.27). They do not become flesh and do not transform themselves into a real human existence. Therefore they can enter many souls. The New Testament notion of incarnation clearly goes beyond analogous notions of an incorporation of wisdom into many human beings; it expresses the real presence of God in an individual. The same is true of angelic figures and pre-existent human beings who mediate between God and humankind. When they are sent to earth as messengers of God they do not alter their mode of existence in any way, but merely change their location. We find no mediation between the being of God and human being, but a change of location by a figure which remains the same. Even if some statements in early christology could be interpreted to indicate that Christ is an angel (or a messenger sent to earth by God), primitive Christian christology goes beyond this: this messenger assumes real human nature and dies the death – although in the divine world he was far more than an angel. This messenger is the real presence of God among human beings.

In the Synoptic Gospels the notion of the real presence of God among human beings is expressed by the notion of the procreation of the Son of God by the Spirit, and in Paul and John by the notion of incarnation. In both cases the primitive Christian sign language makes use of pagan notions here.

Jews basically had a horror of the sexual union of divine and human beings. Genesis 6.1ff. depicts how the sons of God fathered the giants of primal times by human women – the cause of the great catastrophe of the Flood. The apocalyptic literature sees the origin of all evil in this union of the divine and the human which is contrary to nature (Ethiopian Enoch). Even Adam's sin sometimes pales by comparison with this incursion of evil.

The notion of a procreation by God could find a way into Judaism only in a very sublimated form. Philo attributes the miraculous birth of children and patriarchs to divine power in a literal interpretation of the texts (*Questions on Genesis* III 18, 56). At the same time he interprets the marriages of the patriarchs allegorically as marriages with virtues (*On the Cherubim* 41ff.). He says that the virtues are a fruit of the seed of God in human beings. What is an allegorical picture in Philo is remythicized in the infancy narratives: through his spirit and power God procreates not only virtues but a real human being. This human being owes his special nature to divine procreation. The angel proclaims to Mary in Luke 1.35:

The Holy Spirit will come upon you
and the power of the Most High will overshadow you;
therefore the child to be born will be called the holy,
the Son of God.

Even if one then relies on Old Testament passages for a basis for this procreation by the spirit, on Ps. 2.7 and Isa. 7.14 (LXX), one is initially introducing the pagan notion of the procreation of a human being by divine power into these passages. F. Bovon rightly states: 'The procreation of the Messiah by the divine Spirit is a development of Jewish messianism under foreign influences . . .'[17]

In Paul and John the notion of the real presence of God is expressed by the notion of incarnation:[18]

Who, though he was in the form of God,
did not count equality with God a thing to be grasped,
but emptied himself,
taking the form of a servant
(Phil. 2.6f.).

And the Logos became flesh
and dwelt among us,
and we saw his glory
(John 1.14).

For in him dwells the fullness of Godhead bodily
(Col. 2.9).

The incorporation of wisdom in human beings is in any case a preliminary stage of such notions. Wisdom incorporates itself in different 'souls', but not in the flesh of a singular human being. Wisdom is the Torah which all human beings are to accept into their lives. Rather, full belief in the incarnation has its closest analogies in statements about gods who appear on earth in human form. Acts offers one example of this. Because of the miraculous healing of a lame man, the inhabitants of Lystra take Paul and Barnabas to be gods: 'The gods have come down to us in the likeness of men' (Acts 14.11). This same idea can be associated elsewhere with rulers and wise men. Thus after his transportation Romulus says:

It was the will of the gods, my Proculus, that I should dwell so long among men, build a city destined to the greatest power and the highest praise, and then again inhabit the heaven whence I came (Plutarch, *Romulus* 28, 2).

So only with the aid of pagan traditions was the complete real presence of God among human beings expressed by procreation through the spirit and the notion of incarnation.

(ii) The primitive Christian understanding of the sacrament as an expression of a reduction of religious distance

In conclusion, I want to make a brief mention of the sacraments which came into being in primitive Christianity. I shall be analysing them at length later. Among other things, it is characteristic of both sacraments, baptism and eucharist, that they arise out of ritual symbolic actions which originally had no reference to the death of a deity. Baptism arises out of the baptism of John, which serves for the forgiveness of sins in the face of the coming final judgment. The eucharist arises out of the meals held by Jesus, which symbolize salvation even now in the face of the coming feast in the kingdom of God. Baptism is first interpreted as baptism into the death of Jesus and a symbolic burial with him in Rom. 6.1ff. The eucharist was interpreted in terms of Jesus' imminent death either by the historical Jesus himself at his last supper or after his death. At any rate, the Didache still knows of a eucharist with no reference to Jesus' death (Did. 9/10)! At all events, we note a tendency to concentrate the ritual sign language of primitive Christianity on the death of a deity – and to associate human beings in different ways with this death. Here, too, in my view the boundaries of Jewish tradition are left behind. For in both cases the symbol language of the sacraments violates the Jewish notions of taboo. The identification of baptism with a burial associated it with a place of uncleanness. The tomb and death were places with negative connotations. The interpretation of eating and drinking in terms of the body and blood of Christ touched on deeply rooted taboos about eating blood. However, the nearness of the deity in death has certain analogies in pagan religions, though it outdoes these on one decisive point: nowhere is the identification of human beings with the death of the deity depicted so clearly and unequivocally as in the primitive Christian sacraments.

It is certainly true that in antiquity we find belief in dying gods. Here there are always two gods: an older female deity and a younger partner deity, usually a male partner. The younger partner deity suffers death. The older one mourns this. In the conflict between life and death, death is partly abolished – but there is never a real resurrection.[19]

The following survey shows that most of these deities come from the East.[20] Only in Eleusis do we find a genuinely Greek cult:

Original area of dissemination	Older female deity	Younger partner deity
Eleusis	Demeter	Persephone
Mesopotamia	Ishtar	Tammuz
Ugarit	Anath	Baal
Phoenicia	Astarte	Adonis
Phrygia	Cybele	Attis
Egypt	Isis	Osiris

In the Greek view the gods are really immortal. They live at a distance from death. But the myth which underlies the Eleusinian and Orphic mysteries shows that even the world of the gods is not spared the intervention of death. That is even more true of the Eastern gods. The intervention of death is described in different ways. In the first three cases, with Persephone, Tammuz and Baal, the young partner deity is carried off into the underworld and kept there. In the last three cases the deity is killed violently: Osiris is struck or drowned by his brother Seth and then cut in pieces. Attis castrates himself and dies. Adonis is killed by a wild boar. The overcoming of death is not resurrection. Osiris rules as king of the world of the dead. Persephone has to spend four months of the year in the underworld. The corpse of Attis does not decay. Flowers rise from the blood of Adonis. It is therefore misleading to talk of 'dying and rising gods'. There are dying gods who wrest some 'life' from death by compromises.

Only some of these deities were worshipped in mystery cults, i.e. in cults which were not celebrated in public but into which individuals had to be initiated. Thus there were mysteries of Demeter, Cybele and Isis. At best one could see an analogy to Christian baptism as a dying with Christ in these initiation rites. But that would be to overlook an important difference: the festivals (whether public festivals or 'private' mysteries) in which the fate of the dying deities is celebrated are all associated with rites of lamentation; the adherents of the deity join the older female deity in mourning the loss of the partner deity. The adherents thus do not experience the death themselves, but lament it. They identify more with the older, mourning, deity than with the younger, dying, deity, even if there are also the beginnings of the latter identification. But in the Christian sacraments the 'adherents of Jesus' experience his death in symbolic form. They are buried with him in baptism; they eat food which is identified with his death. The longing for nearness to the deity which we find at that time in cults of dying deities is taken up and outdone here.

Now we can sum up. In the myth of primitive Christianity we find a unique combination of history and myth: a mytho-historical basic narrative. A radical historicization of the myth begins with the historical Jesus, impelled by him: his 'incarnation' in a concrete human being. At the same time a mythicization of this human being begins. On the basis of the Easter faith he shares in the status and power of the one and only God. This deification of Jesus is an expression of a way of surmounting cognitive dissonance in which the same motives are at work as in the working out of Jewish monotheism. The claim to revelation and validity of divine or human figures who fail can be maintained only if they are clearly exalted above all those powers which made them fail. In the encounter of primitive Christianity with pagan religion this genuinely monotheistic dynamic becomes a 'competitive syncretism'. The rivalry with other powerful deities (like the divinized emperors) impels the exaltation of Jesus beyond all powers and rules: all must bend their knee before Christ! The rivalry with other dying deities leads the humiliation of Jesus to be interpreted as a nearness of salvation to human beings which cannot be outdone: no other deity is so close to human beings in their transitoriness, their wretchedness and their guilt. Thus in the semiotic world of primitive Christianity, the figure of Christ does not just come into the centre but reaches the highest height and deepest depth. It rules in heaven over all powers, and descends into hell. In describing the formation of this figure as a way of surmounting dissonance, however, we have already made a presupposition: that an unconditional claim is in dissonance with experiences which contradict it. The question remains: how is it that human beings 'model' historically relative phenomena with the 'tools' of an unconditional claim? So we have not yet fully grasped the mystery of religious imagination which is at work in the deification of Jesus. I therefore want to return to this theme in the last chapter.

Part Two: The Ethics of Primitive Christianity

4

The Two Basic Values of the Primitive Christian Ethic: Love of Neighbour and Renunciation of Status

Religious myths make it possible for people to co-ordinate their behaviour with the aid of shared symbols and roles. We understand these roles and symbols correctly only when we put them in the relevant context of behaviour. This context of behaviour comprises both actual behaviour and the behaviour required by norms and values. We call the whole of the behaviour which is in fact practised and required in a group an 'ethic'.[1] Accordingly, the ethic of primitive Christianity is not something which is added to the primary significance of religious myths (their roles and symbols) only at a secondary stage, but is a constitutive part of this significance. The ethic is part of the significance of the myth.

From a historical perspective the primitive Christian ethic is located between Judaism and paganism. It is the ethic of a group which comes from Judaism but which found most of its supporters in paganism. It distinguishes itself only gradually from the Jewish ethic. It intensifies and radicalizes beginnings which are already there, but has a tendency to outdo these with a 'better righteousness' (Matt. 5.20). This competitive tendency is continued in the pagan milieu. The first Christians wanted to live up to many norms of their pagan environment in an exemplary way. But at the same time there is a qualitative transformation of the ethic here. Primitive Christianity introduces into the pagan world two values from the Jewish tradition which are new in this form: love of neighbour and humility (or renunciation of status). Therefore in addition to an assimilation to the values and norms of the pagan environment (with a claim to outdo them), we find the awareness of a conflict with it. Alongside the claim to fulfil the general norms of the surrounding world better than anyone else, we find a counter-cultural awareness which makes the primitive religion seem almost like a 'religion of drop-outs'.

In a description of the primitive Christian ethic[2] it is natural initially to concentrate on the two basic values of love of neighbour and renunciation of status. The combination of them is the novel feature of the primitive Christian ethic in the pagan world (though not in the Jewish world). Moreover they relate to two fundamental dimensions of social relationships. Love concerns above all the relationship between the insider group and the outsider group. Primitive Christian love seeks to cross this boundary. The renunciation of status concerns the relationship between those in high positions and those in low positions. The renunciation of status (or humility) requires people to renounce the display, establishment or possession of a superior status. Here the boundary between 'above' and 'below' is to be crossed.

In going on to analyse these two basic values, I want to pay attention to three questions:

1. What is the relationship between these two basic values? Is love understood as love for fellow human beings of the same status? What happens to love when there are differences in status? Is there an organic connection between love and humility? Does each have an effect on the other?

2. What is the relationship between the ethic of love and humility and the primitive Christian myth? Are myth and ethic so much one that the ethic appears to be the interpretation of the myth and the myth to be the foundation of the ethic?

3. What is the relationship between the radicalization of love and humility and the radicalization of grace? Is there a connection between the radicalization of demand and grace – the basic tension in the primitive Christian ethic – and a tension between myth and history in the basic primitive Christian narrative?

After discussing the two basic values in this chapter, in the next I shall investigate a broader spectrum of the primitive Christian ethic to show that these two basic values form the key to the understanding of many individual demands.

1. Love of neighbour as the first basic value in primitive Christianity[3]

Love of neighbour already occurs in the Old Testament and in Judaism. It is required for the first time in the Holiness Code, i.e. in the latest of the great legal corpora. What is meant in Lev. 19.18 is love of the neighbour who in principle has the same status. In part his equal status is a fact – he is a neighbour who can appear as an opponent in law and has the same rights – and in part the recognition of this equal status is a demand. For one is to love one's neighbour 'as oneself'. Now in Lev.19 this love of neighbour is combined with an ethic of mercy universal throughout the Near East, which is shown to the weak, widows and orphans, i.e. to those who have unequal or marginal status. Only in Israel is this group of the classical *personae miserabiles* enlarged by strangers. The command to love one's neighbour is explicitly extended specifically to them:

> The stranger who sojourns with you shall be to you as the native among you, and you shall love him as yourself; for you were strangers in the land of Egypt: I am the Lord your God (Lev. 19.34).

Thus the extension of the command to love one's neighbour to members of the 'outsider group' already begins in the Old Testament. Moreover the context of love of neighbour shows that it is inculcated specifically in the relationship to enemies and opponents (at law), and that those who are socially weaker are also included. In other words, the commandment to love one's neighbour already occurs in its first formulation as love of the enemy, the stranger and the weak.[4] It applies to 'neighbours' who in principle have equal rights, but it becomes acute precisely where these equal rights and this equal worth are no longer taken for granted or are no longer accepted as something to be taken for granted.

We can give only a fragmentary sketch of the further development of the commandment to love one's neighbour. It is important for us that tendencies both to extend and to limit love of neighbour stand side by side in early Judaism, as they do (later) in primitive Christianity.

The Testaments of the Twelve Patriarchs are the best example of tendencies to extend the commandment. In farewell speeches to their sons, the twelve sons of Jacob develop an impressive ethic of love of neighbour and brotherliness. In them, the great sin against brotherliness is the selling of Joseph into slavery, the deliberate annihilation of his status and his freedom. Nevertheless Joseph achieves office and high honours in Egypt. The brothers meet him as fugitives seeking help. He shows his brotherly love by forgiving them and not playing off his high status against his brothers. His love for them includes renunciation of status. 'I did not exalt myself above them arrogantly because of my worldly position of glory, but I was among them as one of the least' (TestJos 17.8). At the same time, the love of neighbour advocated in the Testaments of the Twelve Patriarchs – in addition to crossing the boundary between above and below – also has the beginnings of crossing the boundary between inside group and outside group. Love is to be shown not only to brothers but 'to all human beings' (TestIss 7.6, variant reading). Characteristically, the extended commandment to love appears as a commandment to show mercy. Thus Zebulon admonishes his sons: 'Show mercy to your neighbour, have compassion on *all*, not only on human beings but also on dumb animals' (TestZeb 5.1).

The best example of the opposite tendency, the *limitation* of love of neighbour, is given by the Qumran texts. In the Community Rule all members of their own special community are under an obligation 'to love all sons of light . . . but to hate all sons of darkness' (1QS 1.9–11). However, love of neighbour within the community is not shown to everyone as a member of equal worth; rather, everyone is to be loved 'according to his lot in God's design' (1QS 1.10). The community has a strictly hierarchical structure. The repeated admonitions to 'humility' mean that each accepts his status in this hierarchical order.

(a) Tendencies towards extension in primitive Christianity

The primitive Christian ethic of love of neighbour is a radicalization of the Jewish ethic. What is new is that the twofold commandment to love God and one's neighbour comes to the centre and is explicitly called the greatest commandment. It already exists before Jesus, but not in such a central position. It is extended further in accordance with 'tendencies' which we already found in the Old Testament.[5]

First, love of neighbour becomes *love of enemy* (Matt. 5.43ff.). Here one's enemy is not just one's personal enemy. Rather, 'enemies' are spoken of as a group which has the power of persecution and discrimination. Accordingly, the command is not addressed to individuals in the singular, but to a collective in the plural: 'Love your enemies'.[6]

Secondly, love of neighbour is extended to become *love of the stranger* (Luke 10.25ff.). In the exemplary story of the Good Samaritan, the Samaritan proves to be a 'neighbour', not on the basis of a pre-existing status but on the basis of his behaviour. He came 'near' to his neighbour, i.e., unlike the priest and the Levite he went out of his way to look after the half-dead victim of the robbers.[7]

Thirdly, love of neighbour becomes *love of the sinner* (Luke 7.36ff.). The woman who was a sinner, who is discriminated against by others, is accepted by Jesus, and she responds with her love, by moistening his feet with her tears and drying them with her hair.

In the Jesus tradition this extension of love is combined with a renunciation of love of the closest members of one's family: 'If any one comes to me and does not hate his own father and mother and wife and children and brothers and sisters, yes, and even his own life, he cannot be my disciple' (Luke 14.26). All attempts to deny or to tone down this ethic which is so critical of the family – and which is also attested in other sayings – are a vain labour of love. Whatever one understands by 'hate', it is the opposite of 'love' (cf. Matt. 6.24; Luke 16.13). There is no disputing the fact that precisely what is required to be shown to the enemy, the stranger and the despised sinner is put in question when it comes to members of the family. Now this very ethic which is critical of the family shows that here love is detaching itself from its first *Sitz im Leben* – from love in the family and between relations – and is shown to those who stand outside this narrow circle. Whereas normally those who are closest of all are preferred and loved, and the others have a more distant role (if need be, conflict with them must be risked), here the situation is reversed. Disciples may risk conflict with the family, but they are to practise love towards outsiders!

In addition, this extended love of neighbour has a second characteristic. By being extended it threatens to lose the symmetry that it has in principle: the enemies are not people of equal status. They are groups with superior power. When Matthew sets the commandment to love one's neighbour against the commandment to love one's enemy and depicts love of enemy as a radicalization of love of neighbour, in quoting Lev. 19.18 he omits the 'formula of equal value'. He does not say, 'You have heard it said, "You shall love your neighbour *as yourself*"', but only, 'You shall love your neighbour' (Matt. 5.43; 19.19 and 22.39 differ). He rightly senses that the element of equal worth must be absent from love of enemy.

Nevertheless, this tendency of love to acknowledge the equal worth of others is maintained. Luke in particular proves sensitive to this. Nor is this simply by putting at the centre of his formulation of the commandment to love one's enemy the Golden Rule (Luke 6.31), i.e. a principle of mutuality which in this context can only mean an ideal mutuality: one must do to enemies what one would in principle want of them, but in reality may not in fact expect. In other words, one should be guided by the criterion of mutuality even where this mutuality is deliberately violated by others.

Even more vivid are the concrete examples of extended love which Luke offers. The Samaritan stranger is not the one to whom love is shown but the one who shows it. After the priest and Levite have failed, in the traditional sequence an 'Israelite' should really have appeared to show the love of neighbour which is enjoined. His place is taken by a Samaritan, who takes over the role of the Israelite with equal rights; he is not the one to whom acts of mercy are shown and through this behaviour becomes the 'neighbour'.

Similarly, the woman who was a sinner is not just one who receives Jesus' love. The reason that Jesus gives for forgiving her is 'for she has loved much' (Luke 7.47). She, too, is thus the subject of love. And like the Samaritan, she is explicitly recognized as the one who shows love.

It is perhaps no coincidence that Luke also makes a representative of the national 'enemies' appear as the one who shows love. The Jewish elders expressly confirm of the pagan centurion of Capernaum that 'He loves our people' (Luke 7.5).

Love which crosses boundaries, which includes the outsider and the marginalized, proves itself in particular by recognizing outsiders as those who show love. Here the equality in principle contained in the love of neighbour establishes itself in the face of actual differences. But there is no mistaking the fact that the extension of love beyond the narrower inner group is unavoidably bound up with the fact that now great differences of rank, status and power come into play – whether it is that this extended love becomes mercy towards the one who is utterly weak (so that in the story of the Good Samaritan 'love of neighbour' and 'mercy' are fused) or that it becomes love of the overpoweringly strong enemy. With this extension, equality of status becomes improbable.

(b) Tendencies towards restriction in primitive Christianity

The development in primitive Christianity outside the Synoptic tradition, which is stamped by the influence of Jesus, tends to go in a different direction: now we find tendencies towards a certain restriction of the commandment to love, but at the same time also a heightened sensitivity to the equal worth of human beings which is intended in love.

The restrictive tendency is well known. In I Thess. 3.12 Paul still presents 'love to one another and to all men' side by side on the same level, but in Gal. 6.10 he introduces a gradation. His admonition is, 'Let us do good to all men, and especially to those who are of the household of faith.' Accordingly, the members of the community are privileged – without Paul ever having given up love of strangers and enemies (cf. Rom. 12.9–21). The Gospel of John goes still further: it seems to oppose community and world in a dualistic way. Here love is still 'mutual love' (John 13.34; 15.12, 17). In the Johannine letters it appears as 'love of the brethren', which is limited to the community (I John 2.10, etc.). However, we should not fail to recognize that this mutual love should also have an effect outside. It is to be an identity marker for the disciples of Jesus by which everyone (i.e. including outsiders) is to recognize them (John 13.35). All are potentially included in this love, because God loved the whole world and not just the elect in it (cf. John 3.16).

This tendency to restrict love is usually evaluated one-sidedly as a history of loss. But it is more than that. The rooting of love in the community as its *Sitz im Leben* also brings out more strongly its innate tendency to regard all human beings as equal in principle – especially in Paul, the letter of James and the Gospel of John. In this view of people bound together through love as equals a 'gain' can be seen.

Where *Paul* is using the obligation to love in arguments and admonitions connected with concrete problems, he certainly always presupposes a lack of equilibrium. He appeals to the superior to show love to the inferior. But it is striking that here he envisages equality as the goal. For him, love leads to an equilibrium between differences of rank and status. Thus he admonishes the strong to meet the weak in love (I Cor. 8.1; cf. Rom. 14.15). Love is the opposite of inflating oneself in a way which demonstratively asserts a higher status of knowledge and action (cf. I Cor. 8.1). He also asks the Corinthians to make a collection for the poor in Jerusalem as a proof of their love. The aim is to produce equality, so that one does not have a surplus while the other is in need (II Cor. 8.7ff.). Philemon the slave-owner is to resume relations with the slave Onesimus who has left him, no longer as a slave but as a brother. In order to make it clear that by this he does not mean a 'spiritual brotherhood' which has no consequences in everyday dealings, Paul explicitly emphasizes that from now on the former slave is to be a brother both in the flesh and in the Lord (Philemon 16).[8] Finally, the Corinthians are to forgive an evildoer, since Paul has forgiven him. He is again to become a member of the community with equal rights (II Cor 2.5–11). Certainly Paul says that love endures all things. But even for him it does not endure differences in principle between Christians. It aims at equality, whether by the superior coming down to the level of the inferior, or by a slave being elevated to become a 'brother'.

The *letter of James* formulates this tendency towards equal rights in love of neighbour almost as a programme. After emphasizing by means of a fictitious example (but one which may be representative of analogous real situations) that those who are socially superior are not to be favoured by the community and that the socially inferior are not to be humiliated, he interprets the commandment to love one's neighbour as a contradiction to the unequal treatment of people (James 2.1–11). 'If you really fulfil the royal law, according to the scripture, "You shall love your neighbour as yourself, " you do well, but if you show partiality, you commit sin, and are convicted by the law as transgressors' (James 2.8f.).

The *Gospel of John* is the culmination of this development. As is well known, on the one hand it keeps love within the community, but on the other hand, the way in which this mutual love relativizes status emerges in it all the more clearly. The first half of the Gospel depicts Jesus as the revealer of life who at the end of his public activity notes in retrospect that he has fulfilled the Father's commandment: 'And I know that his commandment is eternal life. What I say, therefore, I say as the Father has bidden me' (John 12.50). In addition, the second part depicts the revelation of love for the disciples. It is not just expressed in the fact that now Jesus realizes and hands on a 'new commandment' (in addition to the commandment to reveal life) – a commandment to love one another – but shows itself first in an action of Jesus. In the foot-washing scene, Jesus' love for his own is depicted as a model for all disciples. Jesus demonstratively renounces his status as 'lord' and 'master'. He adopts the role of the slave, the disciple and the woman. For the service of foot-washing was expected above all of these. With this renunciation of status he provokes the protest of Peter, i.e. the protest of the one who is later appointed leader of the community. The love which in the community dispenses with any demonstration or imposition of status stands in opposition not only to the world but also to tendencies in the community. It must prevail against a hierarchical consciousness. The task of Jesus is completed in the revelation of this love – in the communication of the new commandment. Only with it has Jesus revealed *everything* that he has heard from the Father. Only through the revelation of this love and this commandment to love have the disciples really become Jesus' friends instead of slaves (John 15.15).[9]

So we find two tendencies in the development of the commandment to love in primitive Christianity. On the one hand there is the crossing of the boundaries between insider group and outsider group, and on the other there is the crossing of the boundaries between 'above' and 'below'. But both these tendencies to cross boundaries cannot come into effect fully the same time. Love which embraces people even beyond their own inner groups encounters difficulties because it must accept real differences in status. Mutual love between people of equal status is limited to small groups. In them the aim of all love, the acknowledgment of the equal value of other human beings, can be realized in exemplary fashion. But such a love encounters difficulties because it has to limit itself to its own group (and even there is always under attack): differences of status can be relativized more easily within an inner group than in those spheres over which a group at any rate has little influence.

We found the first tendency in the Synoptic tradition, which has been stamped by the earthly Jesus. Here love crosses the boundaries of the inner group but comes up against differences in status. We found the second tendency in the Pauline and Johannine traditions, which are stamped by belief in the exalted Christ. Here love crosses boundaries of status, but remains tied to the sphere of the inner group.

At the same time we found a second difference: love in the Synoptic tradition is the other side of a readiness for conflict with members of the family. It is radical, and has counter-cultural tendencies in the direction of a religion of 'drop-outs', i.e. homeless itinerant charismatics. This readiness for conflict falls into the background in the Pauline and Johannine traditions, giving way to an ethic which markedly supports the family. With the revaluation of the inner group the oldest of all inner groups, the family, is revalued.

These are the two topics which will occupy us in what follows: first the renunciation of status as the second basic value of the primitive Christian ethic, and further the radical nature of this ethic, which seems to ask too much of human beings and calls for compensation.

2. Renunciation of status as the second basic value in primitive Christianity[10]

If love of neighbour in principle means that neighbours and fellow human beings have equal rights, but everywhere come up against an inequality which really exists, the relativizing and overcoming of differences of status must necessarily become the complementary value of love of neighbour, whether by the superior renouncing their status or by the status of the inferior being elevated.

There are three terms for this second basic value of the primitive Christian ethic. Traditionally it is termed '*humility*', *humilitas*. In addition to conduct it also embraces the inner disposition. It denotes both the one who has a lowly status and inwardly accepts it and the one who has a high status but does not exploit it. In this respect humility is the broadest term.

If one wants to emphasize the humility of the one who renounces what he has, the term '*renunciation of status*' is appropriate. This always indicates a movment from above downwards – including the inner disposition that goes with it. Renunciation of status can be a renunciation of displaying one's status (i.e. modesty); it can be a renunciation of using a higher status to impose one's will; or it can even be renunciation of the possession of a status, as for example when someone gives up a previous calling and follows Jesus.

A corresponding elevation of status is often associated with renunciation of status in the biblical tradition. Humiliation and exaltation go together. The term '*change of position*' is appropriate to denote this comprehensive process.

Some special features of *humilitas* in primitive Christianity already emerge from a short survey of the most important statements.

Change of position can be described in primitive Christianity either as an exchange between the first and the last (cf. Mark 10.31; Matt. 19.30; 20.16; Luke 13.30) or as an intrinsic connection between the humble and the exalted (Luke 14.11; 18.14; Matt. 23.12; Phil. 2.6ff.; II Cor. 11.7; James 4.10). One variant of a change of position is particularly characteristic: humbling oneself leads to the exalting of others. This is characteristic of the Christ event, but also of Paul, when he asks ironically, : 'Did I commit a sin in abasing myself that you might be exalted?' (II Cor. 11.7).

Renunciation of status is spoken of in logia like 'Whoever would be great among you must be your servant, and whoever would be first among you must be slave of all' (Mark 10.43f.; cf. 9.35; Matt. 23.11). It is characteristic of primitive Christianity that it makes renunciation of status the presupposition for authority within the community. 'Humility', elsewhere the disposition of slaves and dependants, becomes the characteristic of those who want to assume leadership roles in the community.

Finally, there are admonitions in primitive Christianity to *humility* (*tapeinophrosune*) – i.e. explicitly to a particular inner disposition. Here the admonition to mutual humility is characteristic. As one example which is characterisic of others mention might be made of Phil. 2.3: 'Do nothing from selfishness or conceit, but in humility count others better than yourselves' (cf. also Rom. 12.16; Eph. 4.2; I Peter 5.5). Whereas the commandment to love is firmly rooted in the Jewish tradition and converges with pagan admonitions to engage in pro-social behaviour, renunciation of status and humility as mutual social behaviour are something new. Certainly humility towards God (as a religious virtue) is firmly rooted in Jewish tradition. But humility towards one fellow human beings (as a social virtue) develops from this only at a late stage in the New Testament period (independently of primitive Christianity). This social virtue goes against a code of honour common in antiquity, according to which each is to behave in keeping with his status, and the increase in status and respect is one of the most important motives for action. Within the framework of this code of honour 'humility' *(tapeinophrosune)* is regarded as a servile, contemptible disposition. Here the new Jewish and Christian ethic of humility leads to a 'transvaluation of values'. A moral defect becomes a virtue. The novelty of the primitive Christian (and Jewish) ethic therefore becomes evident much more clearly than in the case of 'love of neighbour', or more precisely: only in the combination of the two values of love and humility does the basic structure and the novelty of the primitive Christian ethic become visible.

How did this new social virtue come to be discovered? How did it come about that the humility shown to superior gods was transformed into a constructive social attitude? The presuppositions here were new concepts of the action of God, the action of the king and behaviour in communities. Here too I can give only a brief sketch of the development.

However much people in ancient societies may have emphasized and defended their own status (as people do everywhere) or even competed for reputation and honour (as in the agonistic Graeco-Hellenistic culture), they took humility towards the gods for granted. The East emphasized the distance from the gods even more than the West. But the same numinous experience becomes evident when Chilon (c. 560 BCE) says of Zeus: 'He humbles the lofty and exalts the lowly' (Diogenes Laertius 1, 49), or Isaiah preaches: 'The haughty looks of man shall be brought low, and the pride of men shall be humbled, and the Lord alone will be exalted in that day' (Isa. 2.11).

The first step towards a positive evaluation of humbling and exalting takes place when the humbling and exalting action of God becomes an image of hope and is not just the expression of a humble fear before the superior power of destiny. Only then does it become a possible model and guideline for human behaviour. We find isolated instances of this in pagan antiquity. In Xenophon's *Anabasis* their general tells the Greeks, who are numerically inferior, that the gods are on their side, 'especially since they are in a position quickly to make the great small and to deliver the small, even in a difficult situation, if they so will' (III, 2, 10). But it is above all in Israel – among a notoriously inferior small people – that this exchange of loftiness and lowliness becomes an image of hope. One example must suffice here. In I Sam.2.6f. Hannah exults:

> The Lord kills and brings to life;
> he brings down to the pit and raises up.
> The Lord makes poor and makes rich;
> he brings low, he also exalts.

One could produce many other examples of this *axiom of a change of position* which structures the statements about divine action.

However, this is still a long way from the readiness to renounce status voluntarily. The renunciation of status is most easily possible for the one who in any case has the highest status. He loses nothing if he comes 'closer' to others. We therefore find the first beginnings of a renunciation of status (or 'humility') as a social virtue in the ideal of the king. They appear in rare sketches of a humane rule.[11] In pagan antiquity it is said of king Agesilaus that he despised those who were excessively proud, 'but was more modest (ταπεινότερος) than ordinary people' (Xenophon, *Agesilaus*, fourth century BCE). The Macedonian king Antigonos Gonatas (died 239) coined the famous statement that 'kingly rule is an honourable slavery' (an ἔνδοξος δουλεία) (Aelian, *Var.*2.20). In the biblical sphere the ideal of the future messianic king is shown in Zech. 9.9. He will ride humbly (Hebrew *ani*; Greek πραύς) into Jerusalem on an ass. It is no coincidence that the same word for 'humble' *(ani)* also appears in some 'royal psalms' as the term used by the suppliant to describe himself (cf. Ps. 18.28 [27] = II Sam.22.28; 40.18 (17) = 70.6 [5]; 86.1 and 109.22).

The third step towards *humility* was first taken in small communitarian societies. Here too the individual had nothing to lose by relativizing status and rank. In so far as all observe the rules and norms of the community, he gains from the strong solidarity of the community. Therefore 'humility' occurs clearly as a social virtue perhaps for the first time in the Qumran texts:

> No man shall move down from his place nor move up from his allotted position. For according to the holy design, they shall all of them be in a community of truth and virtuous humility, of loving-kindness and good intent towards the other, and (they shall all of them be) sons of the everlasting company (1QS 2.23–25, translation Vermes).

It is clear here that 'humility' *(anawah)* does not mean renunciation of status and rank but the affirmation of the status given one in a community with a strict hierarchical organization. Only in the idealizing view of Philo does this 'humility' become a mutual virtue with an egalitarian background. 'There are no slaves at all among them, but all are free and do services for one another' (Philo, *Good Man* 79). Here he goes far beyond the reality of the Essene communities.

The primitive Christian ethic of humility consistently develops the three presuppositions that I have mentioned. However, two different tendencies are evident here. In the Synoptic tradition, which is stamped by the earthly Jesus, the axiom of change of position works in conjunction with the requirement of renunciation of status. Renunciation of status above all is called for – in critical contrast to those who have status and power. By contrast, there are no admonitions to humility (ταπεινοφροσύνη) as a disposition which shapes the whole of action. Admonitions to 'humility' come into the foreground first in the primitive Christian epistolary literature, in the characteristic form of a 'mutual' humility, until in the later period of primitive Christianity it becomes the one-sided 'humility' of those who subordinate themselves. The critical effect of the aim of change of position and the admonitions to renounce status fades into the background.

(a) Renunciation of status in the Synoptic tradition

First let us look at the Synoptic sphere. Here we find the first presupposition for the development of humility as a social virtue: the interpretation of God's action in the light of the axiom about changing positions as saving humiliation and exaltation. We find it programmatically in the *Magnificat*. God establishes his salvation by casting down the mighty from their thrones and exalting the humble (Luke 1.52). This change of position becomes evident in the birth of the Messiah. The Messiah's birth from an ordinary woman from the people, a woman who describes her status as 'lowliness' (ταπεινότης), already conveys the message that the new ruler will usher in a comprehensive change. Exaltation and humiliation are images of hope for the great eschatological turning-point which begins in the midst of time. This image of hope is combined with critical impulses. Luke-Acts in particular often articulate criticism of the powerful. In the temptation story, the Satan who as ruler of the world claims divine status and the worship that goes with it is transparently the Roman empire (Luke 4.5–8). The Jewish king Agrippa I, who accepts an acclamation as 'God', is immediately thereafter cast down by God in misery and death (Acts 12.20–23). For Luke, that God casts down the mighty from their thrones is at the same time both a historical experience and a hope.

The second presupposition for the development of humility as a social virtue is also given in the Synoptic tradition: the ideal of a human ruler which includes the self-limitation of rule by renunciation of status. Jesus is consistently depicted as the realization of this ideal of a human ruler. He is the humble king who rides into Jerualem on an ass (Zech. 9.9 = Matt. 21.5; John 12.15). He is the sovereign son of God who could exercise all divine power, but who renounces the exercising of it in order to go his way to the utmost humiliation on the cross. As the Son of Man who has not come to be served, but to serve all with the sacrifice of his life, he is both a model for his disciples (Mark 10.45) and also the opposite of the earthly rulers who oppress their peoples and abuse their power over men and women (Mark 10.42).[12] Therefore among the disciples only the one who is ready to be the servant and slave of all is to have authority. The call to renounce status is thus formulated in deliberate contrast to the inhumane political rulers. Granted, Luke omits this pericope about the conversation with the sons of Zebedee, but he makes a decisive statement at an even more central point, at the last supper. He contrasts the political rule of kings who conceal their rule under an ideology of beneficence with humble service in the community (Luke 22.24–27).

Thus in the Synoptic tradition humility is clearly 'renunciation of status', and this renunciation of status is bound up with a critical impetus against those who have a lofty status. In the framework of this tradition humility is not a virtue of the lowly who fit into their lowly status by subordinating themselves to rule. On the contrary, humility is an imitation of the ruler of the world who voluntarily renounces his status. Humility is the virtue of the powerful.

(b) Humility focussed on mutuality in the epistolary literature

A new development begins here in the epistolary literature of primitive Christianity. The axiom of a change of position and the renunciation of status are still influential in it until they are combined with a third presupposition: the rise of humility as a social virtue. This becomes embedded in communitarian communities. Within the Christian community, humility is not a servile attitude towards rulers and the powerful but behaviour towards all fellow men and women, regardless of their social status. It is the imitation of the one who forsook his high status in pre-existence in order to bring about the salvation of human beings on earth by humbling himself.

There is a new element here compared with the Synoptic tradition. In the communities, humility and a renunciation of status focussed on mutuality is required. This element of mutuality is still not very developed even in the Jewish tradition (but cf. the offerings of mutual service by the Essenes according to Philo, *Good Man* 79). Probably this admonition to mutuality has been taken over from the commandment to love. For this clearly states 'love one another', ἀγαπᾶτε ἀλλήλους (cf. I Thess 3.12; 4.29; Rom. 13.8; I Peter 1.22; John 13.34; 15.12, etc.). The inner link between love and humility emerges from Gal. 5.13, where Paul admonishes, 'through love be servants of one another'. The loss of status (by being slaves to one another) is compensated for by the gain in fellowship, and in reality is no loss, since everyone is prepared for it. If one wants to keep the newly achieved Christian 'freedom' one should be ready for mutual 'slavery' through love (Gal. 5.12f.).

In Paul and the tradition stamped by him we also find a combination of love, humility and mutuality at other points. Since they are hardly ever noted, here are the most important instances.

In Phil. 2.2f. Paul calls for unanimity. He begins with an invitation to love and ends with an admonition to serve one another: 'In humility count others better than yourselves.' This humility is further characterized as an attitude in which 'each looks not only to his own interests but also to the interests of others' – according to I Cor. 13.5 this also applies to love. The model for this attitude is Christ himself. The Philippians hymn depicts his 'renunciation of status' – and a change of position which alters the whole world through the humiliation and exaltation of Christ.

Romans 12.9ff. contains an admonition to love. This love also includes being of one mind or seeking this 'mutually'. That is made specific in an admonition to show humility: 'Do not be haughty, but associate with the lowly' (Rom. 12.16). Again we find here a combination of humility, mutuality and love.

This combination also occurs in Eph. 4.2 in an admonition to the community to show unity. Among other things there is an admonition to 'meekness with patience, forbearing one another with love'. Here, too, humility is a form of aimed at mutuality. And as in the other passages, such a mutual readiness to recognize the other as superior reduces the conflicts in the community. It is the condition for unity.

Paul combines these admonitions to mutual humility which further fellowship with a critical use of the axiom of a change of position. He does not call for 'humility' in order to create one-sided respect for authorities within the community. On the contrary, with his apostolic authority he demonstratively puts himself under the community. The apostles belong to the community; they belong to Christ (I Cor. 3.21–23). This subordination to the community can be formulated ironically: Paul is a fool, he is weak and despised, while the community is wise, strong and respected (I Cor. 4.10). But this irony contains one of Paul's basic convictions. Otherwise he would not write to the Corinthians that he bears the death of Jesus in his life, so that the life of Jesus may be revealed among them (II Cor. 4.11); he humiliates himself so that they may be exalted (II Cor. 11.7). Thus Paul combines the ethic of mutual 'humility' with a critical view of authorities within the community. However, for that reason, in contrast to the Gospels he expresses no criticism of the 'worldly' authorities. Certainly one can note a tension between the order of love in the community (Rom. 12.9–21; 13.8ff.) and the legal order of the state (Rom. 13.1–7). But in contrast to the Synoptics that does not lead to any criticism of political authorities. Rather, Paul admonishes people to be subject to them as part of an order which encourages the good and punishes evil.

As we already saw in discussing the commandment to love, in the Gospel of John, too, we find a combination of mutual love and an attitude of mutual service. But this 'humble' attitude is (deliberately?) not described with the vocabulary of 'humility'. In the Gospel of John there are no words from the root *tapeinos*. Rather, the disciples of Jesus are called on no longer to understand themselves as slaves but to understand themselves as friends. The exploitation of humility to stabilize rule is remote in such a milieu.

However, this possibility already makes an appearance in the New

Testament. In I Peter 5.5 there is an admonition to mutual humility. But there is no immediate association with love in the context. The admonition is to be subject to leaders of the community. 'Likewise, you that are younger be subject to the elders. Clothe yourselves, all of you, with humility towards one another, for God opposes the proud, but gives grace to the humble.' Here the community leaders are certainly included in the admonition to humility, but humility also means being subject to them. I Clement goes even further. Here humility is no longer mutual but is a one-sided recognition of the authorities within the community. The rebels in Corinth are told that people will pray for them 'that meekness and humility are granted them so that they yield, not to us but to the will of God' (I Clem. 56.1). Mutual humility has become one-sided submission.[13]

Thus the investigation of the second basic value of humility has shown that it is closely bound up with the first basic value of 'love'. In the Synoptic tradition, statements about both basic values still stand side by side, with relatively little connection between them. In Paul (and to a certain degree also in John) they are combined organically: mutual humility is regarded as an expression of mutual love. Whereas the Synoptic tradition combines humility and renunciation of status with a critical impulse against the powerful, in Paul this critical impulse is lacking when it comes to authorities outside the community; instead, however, by his own example he emphasizes all the more strongly the relativity of authority within the community. That changes later: in I Clement humility has become submission to the community authorities.

3. The primitive Christian 'myth' and the two basic values of primitive Christianity

Our starting point at the beginning of this chapter was that the ethic of a religious community corresponds to its myth and interprets it. At the end we can confirm this: the shaping of the primitive Christian myth is governed throughout by the two basic values of primitive Christianity: the fate of the Son of God and revealer is an expression of the love of God for human beings. This love of God is heightened to the extreme: it becomes love of the enemy and the sinner. It is shown specifically to those who live in conflict with God (Rom. 5.6ff.). The same is true of the second basic value, humility: the way of the Son of God into the world is an expression of the greatest renunciation of status conceivable. The pre-existent one was equal to God, but he renounced this status, became human and assumed the form of a slave. Here too the renunciation of status is intensified to the extreme, to the point of voluntary martyrdom. He humbled himself to the point of death on the cross. He was executed in the way that criminals, slaves and rebels were executed (Phil. 2.6f.). It is irrelevant to our question whether the primitive Christian myth produced a corresponding ethic or the primitive Christian ethic produced a myth to go with it. Whatever the case, each reinforces the other. The narrative sign language of the myth finds its parallel in the pragmatic sign language of the ethic.

Now we saw that in reality the primitive Christian myth is a composite unity of myth and history which forms a unique religious basic narrative. Conflicting tendencies towards the historicizing of myth and the mythicizing of history combine to shape it. Similarly, we also find an immanent tension in the primitive Christian ethic: the tension between a radicalizing of demand and a radicalizing of grace.

The requirement for love and humility is radicalized in a way which asks too much of human capabilities. That happens especially where the requirement to love the enemy, the stranger and the sinner is combined with an ascetic break with the closest members of the family. It also happens where the renunciation of status called for is intensified to the point of martyrdom. Asceticism and martyrdom make the most excessive demands. But over against these and other radical demands in the primitive Christian texts, there are statements about a grace of God which is all the more radical, and the requirement of a readiness for people to forgive one another which is equally so. In conclusion I shall show how this tension is socially and psychologically necessary, and how the inner unity behind this tension becomes possible only through the basic narrative of primitive Christianity: it is occasioned by the sign system of primitive Christian faith.

1. From a sociological perspective, any group with intensified norms has to activate contrary tendencies towards the relaxation of norms so that the intensified norms do not split the group – even if only into a hierarchy of real and deficient 'members'. So it is no chance that at the centre of the Sermon on the Mount, the embodiment of a collection of radicalized demands, we have the Our Father with the petition for forgiveness. Moreover, only the petition for forgiveness is explicitly taken up in the immediate context. One can live with unfulfillable demands only if one is certain of forgiveness despite not fulfilling the norms – and one accepts those who fall short of the radicalized norms. According to the Sermon on the Mount, forgiveness by God imposes an obligation to forgive one another (Matt. 6.14).

2. From a psychological perspective there is similarly an almost necessary change of radical demand into radical acceptance. If all demands are so accentuated that they can no longer hold, then everyone is dependent on grace – and no one has a right to criticize fellow human beings in a

moralizing way. No one is any better than anyone else. If in addition, on the premise that ethical human actions have consequences in natural events, it is expected that human sins will lead to a cosmic catastrophe but this catastrophe does not take place, any moment of the world as it continues to exist can be experienced as a sign of the grace of God. Instead of bringing in the punitive judgment on the world and all the sinners in it which they deserve, God gives all a quite unmerited chance by making his sun continue to rise on the good and the evil!

3. However, the shift from an intensification of norms to a relaxation of norms has a sociological and psychological effect only if it has an objective foundation in a religious sign system. The two basic values of primitive Christianity, love and the renunciation of status, are not just radicalized as demands on human action. They are also depicted in the basic primitive Christian narrative of the action of God: God himself realizes love (without human involvement) by loving his enemies, the sinners; and God realizes humility by coming close to human beings in their finitude by renouncing his status. Those who have internalized love and humility and also experience the encounter with God in the light of these basic values will find their own failures over these basic values counterbalanced by trust that they will be realized through God's action. Here the unique combination of myth and history plays an important role. For only if the pre-existent God (who can be spoken of only in mythical form) enters real history (which must be spoken of historically) does he really come close to the sinful and finite human being. There is an analogy between God's descent in the primitive Christian myth and the acceptance of human beings by God in the primitive Christian ethic – just as there is an analogy between the transcending of history by myth and the transcending of human possibilities of behaviour by radicalized demands. Because the historical presence is a transition to a 'wholly other reality' which can only be depicted mythically, the radical demands of primitive Christianity can be formulated in it: the primitive Christian ethic is therefore an 'interim ethic',[14] except that the whole of history has become an 'interim' and not just a final phase in it. This results in an organic combination of myth and ethic: the radicalizing of grace is grounded in the historicizing of myth, and the acceptance of human beings is the descent of divine reality into history. The transcending of history in myth is in turn the basis for the transcending of human possibilities in the radical ethic. We shall also be concerned with this unity of myth and ethic in the second chapter on the ethic of primitive Christianity.

5

Dealing with Power and Possessions in Primitive Christianity. The Ethical Demands in the Light of the Two Basic Values: I

How can the basic values of an ethic be recognized? Sometimes they are emphasized as basic by the representatives of an ethic themselves. That is the case with the love of neighbour in primitive Christianity. It is explicitly put at the head of all the commandments along with the command to love one's enemies (Matt. 22.34ff. par). But we cannot indicate any comparable marking of humility and renunciation of status as a basic value. Therefore here we must add further criteria: basic values are combined with the central convictions of a group. The renunciation of status structures christology. Humiliation and exaltation become its framework (Phil. 2.6ff.). And the notion of love also finds expression here: the sending of the Son into the world and his self-surrender is an expression of love (John 3.16f.). Thirdly, one can refer to a formal criterion: basic values keep recurring in most texts of a community. Love and the renunciation of status are important themes in almost all texts in primitive Christianity – especially in the Synoptic, Pauline and Johannine literature. But a last criterion is probably decisive: basic values prove to be *basic* values by shaping other values and norms. They serve as meta-values and meta-norms for other ethical statements. I shall demonstrate that in this chapter.

We saw that in primitive Christianity, in the horizontal dimension of social relations love of neighbour crosses the boundaries between inner group and outer group. In the vertical dimension, humility crosses the boundaries between above and below, between those in high positions and those in low ones. Now in my view this twofold crossing of boundaries can be demonstrated throughout the primitive Christian ethic, even where there is no direct mention of either love or humility.

The primitive Christian ethic consists first of all in the universalization of values and norms which had hitherto been attached to a particular *ethnos*, the people chosen by God. They also become accessible to others (here this universalization corresponded to Jewish expectations and hopes).

In this way election and promise, law and wisdom, being a child of Abraham and an heir, are universalized. When at the end of the Gospel of Matthew the exalted Jesus says, 'Go and make disciples of all nations . . . and teach them to observe all that I have commanded you' (Matt. 28.19f.), the disciples are being commanded to make the Jewish ethic as presented by Jesus accessible to all peoples. This process of the universalization of Jewish values and norms is bound up with a 'counter-current', a partial acculturation to pagan values and norms (cf. Phil. 4.8). This leads to an exchange between Judaism and the pagan world.

This second process is less often noted. The primitive Christian ethic often consists of making the values and norms of the upper class accessible to all. One could speak of a 'democratization' of an ancient aristocratic ethic of rule. Here, too, this process, which takes place from above downwards, comes up against a counter-current: similarly we find an 'aristocratization' of a popular mentality. An ethic rooted in the lower classes is formulated in such a way as to be presented with an aristocratic self-confidence. The two basic values of primitive Christianity in particular are examples of this. Love of neighbour has its setting in the ethic of neighbourliness, not the ethic of rule. Humility stems from the mentality of little people. But in primitive Christianity both are formulated anew in such way that they become the sign of people who have been given a high status by God. They become sovereign love of enemy and the renunciation of status by the superior – both based on ideals of rule.

Here I shall demonstrate this exchange between upper-class and lower-class virtues in primitive Christianity in four spheres: in attitudes to power and possessions as the two fundamental material values, and in dealing with wisdom and holiness as the fundamental spiritual values in the society of that time. Such changes of ethic do not take place in a vacuum. They display a social dynamic. The very selection and distribution of the goods and values mentioned can best be elucidated by an approach based on sociology and social history.

History can be regarded as a struggle over the distribution of opportunities in life, which time and again is about four goods: the distribution of rule and possessions on the one side and the distribution of education and normative power on the other. This struggle over distribution is carried on with 'coercive' and 'economic' power, but also with 'persuasive' and 'normative' power.[1] In this view conflict appears to be the normal state of affairs; what needs to be explained is why time and again there is co-operation and consensus despite this structure of conflict. Within the framework of such a 'conflict theory' of society[2] the only explanation that can usually be given is that the stronger groups and classes force co-operation and consensus on the weaker ones. The ideological weapons they use to do this include the normative power of religion and the persuasive power of the educated. But we also find these as weapons on the other side: time and again oppressed groups and classes rebel against the rulers and the 'ruling system' which they manipulate – and also use the weapons of religion and education as legitimation. The struggle over distribution is notoriously accompanied by a struggle over legitimation.

However, one can also interpret history and society in a different way, without denying these conflicts – namely in the light of a theory of integration. Here co-operation and consensus appear as the norm. What needs explaining is how despite the great advantages of co-operation and the forming of a consensus, time and again there are conflicts which break up all possibilities of co-operation and consensus. Here history is interpreted less as a notorious struggle over distribution than as the effort to construct an order of human society which time and again has to be defended against the chaos of social crises and catastrophes. Here, therefore, not only do groups and classes stand over against one another, but the social order as a whole stands over against individuals who internalize this order or withdraw from it. From this perspective the validity of normative power and the fundamental consensus based on it is so elementary that this order can be broken up only by extreme political or social self-interest.

My concern here is not to combine both approaches to a social theory in a more comprehensive theory. That is neither necessary nor useful. For it seems that social reality itself displays that contradiction which is reflected in the two contradictory theories. That can best be observed in those societies in which conflict and integration have institutionalized themselves in different ways, with the political and the religious system, king and priest, standing over against each other. The political system is concerned with limiting and resolving conflicts by force, the religious system with maintaining the basic order and belief in it.[3]

In ancient Judaism we can observe such a tendency towards differentiation between power and religion. The political system was dominated by the Romans and their client princes. It distributed power and possessions. But the religious system had its centre in the temple and its priesthood. It distributed holiness and unholiness, cleanness and uncleanness, sin and salvation. Of course the two overlapped. But in Judaism the 'scribes', the representatives of wisdom, were largely to be assigned to the religious system. The tensions between the two systems did not just display themselves in different institutions. They also occur in the eschatological dreams: on the one hand there was the expectation of a royal Messiah, who also took on functions of holiness (PsSol 17). In the Qumran writings, however, we meet the expectation of a dyarchy of the royal and the priestly Messiah, in which the latter has the pre-eminence. As for primitive Christianity, it is certainly characteristic that the Synoptic Jesus came into conflict with both systems: his entry as the messianic king who humbly enters his capital as an antitype of the rulers who really exist signalizes a conflict with the political system. He is executed by the representatives of the political system as 'king of the Jews'. But his cleansing of the temple is a parallel symbolic act which reveals a conflict with the religious system: the temple is to be liberated from unholy activities. This puts the distribution of clean and unclean in question: it is no coincidence that Jesus is accused before the temple authorities because of his prophecy against the temple!

I shall therefore discuss in succession, first the attitude of primitive Christianity to power and possessions – as the decisive material goods which are at issue in the struggle over distribution. After that I shall discuss its attitude to wisdom and (priestly) holiness – as the decisive non-material goods with which the social order is maintained and legitimated. In each of these spheres I shall show that transfers of values and norms take place both upwards and downwards. The result is a peculiar combination of upper-class and lower-class values. But at the same time there is also an openness to the 'Gentiles', i.e. to a transcending of the boundaries between clean and unclean, holy and unholy, and thus an exchange beyond the boundaries of cultures. Primitive Christianity continues both developments, which are deeply rooted in Judaism: in it, historical events led time and again to an alliance of upper class and lower class, indeed had to do so – and from the time of the penetration of Hellenism into the East there was a lively exchange with pagan culture. Thus in its characteristic ethic, primitive Christianity is through and through a product of Jewish history.

1. A change of value in dealing with power and rule

Political rule has always surrounded itself with a religious aura.[4] The rulers of the ancient Near East understood themselves as 'sons of God', and Greek cities honoured extraordinary 'benefactions' of rulers in cultic form. In particular, the rise of empires which transcended individual peoples gave a new impetus to the ruler cult: at least after his death, the imperialism of Alexander the Great was legitimated by a ruler cult, and so was the imperialism of the Roman emperors, who had themselves worshipped as divine beings in the provinces during their lifetimes, and after their deaths also in Rome. In Israel, too, kings legitimated themselves as 'sons of God'. But a limit was set to such a religious transfiguration of power with the collapse of the monarchy. It was transformed into hope for a future king legitimated by God: the Messiah. This hope was given new life precisely in the face of the advance of alien empires. This happens in PsSol. 17 as a reaction to the Romans. The Davidic Messiah expected there has three features:

(*a*) He is a charismatic ruler over the twelve tribes and realizes pure theocracy among them: God's *basileia*.

(*b*) He achieves *peace* in the land and renounces military force.

(*c*) However, he has previously driven the *enemies* from the land and conquered them (with the force of his mouth!).

In the Jesus tradition and the later primitive Christian traditions, related expectations of a ruler are taken up and transformed. It is characteristic that the three elements mentioned – theocratic power, the creation of peace and the overcoming of enemies – are now associated not only with an individual ruler but with followers of Jesus, i.e. with small folk from the people.

(*a*) At the centre of Jesus' preaching stands the proclamation of God's *basileia*. This kingdom is usually imagined as one in which human beings will be subjects, but now under a more humane ruler than the corrupt human rulers. But there is much to suggest that Jesus also wanted to promise his followers high status in the *basileia*: participation in power or a *symbasileia*. He promised them: 'Blessed are the poor, for the *basileia* of God belongs to them' (Matt. 5.3). The parallelism between this beatitude and the promise to those who mourn and those who are hungry is decisive for understanding it. If those who mourn will be comforted and those who are hungry will be full – then the first beatitude, too, will aim at the overcoming of that deficiency which is denoted by 'poverty'. No riches are promised. Why? Linguistically, poverty is always associated with oppression by those who are more powerful. In the linguistic tradition of the Bible it is more than mere economic power. It is political impotence. Therefore 'holding power' is a positive counterpart. Accordingly we must understand the beatitude to mean that power will belong to the poor who are now oppressed by the powerful. Therefore the disciples are not 'subjects' but 'king's sons', free from special guidance (Matt. 17.24ff.). Therefore Jesus can associate them with kings. Despite their situation they are worth more than King Solomon (Matt. 6.29; 12.42). Therefore the Twelve in particular are promised that they will judge the tribes of Israel (Matt. 19.28 par.). According to PsSol.17.26, that is the task of the royal Messiah. Here it is transferred to a messianic collective. The traditional messianic expectation has been transformed into a group messiahship.[5] This notion of the *symbasileia* of Christians has a long influence: Paul knows of the promise that Christians will 'rule' with Christ in life (Rom. 5.17). They will judge angels

(I Cor. 6.3), indeed even now they have come to rule (I Cor. 4.8). As citizens of the heavenly *politeuma* they have a high rank (Phil. 3.21). They are free (Gal. 4.26). As members of the body of the Messiah they all have a charisma. A disciple of Paul sees them as already co-regents with Christ in the present. Ephesians combines republican imagery with these monarchical metaphors of enthronement: those who were originally aliens and sojourners – i.e. inhabitants of the city with lesser rights (cf. Eph. 2.6, 19) have become fellow-citizens with Christ. The *symbasileia* is present and future – future, for example, in the Pastorals: 'If we endure, we shall also reign with (him)' (II Tim.2.12) and above all in the Apocalypse, where the Messiah's throne is promised to the one who overcomes (Rev. 2.26ff.; 3.21; 20.6).

(*b*) The task of the ruler is to make *peace*. Good rulers are described as peacemakers – whether these are historical rulers like the Hasmonaean prince Simon (in I Macc. 14.1ff.) and the young Herod (Josephus, *Antt.*14, 160; cf. 15, 348), or the expected messianic son of David in PsSol 17. Jesus also promises this function of rule to his disciples: 'Blessed are the peacemakers, for they shall be called sons of God' (Matt. 5.9). The combination of the title son of God with a classic function of the ruler also prompts associations with royal power in this beatitude. The Christians enter into the role of those rulers who make peace with the claim to being 'sons of God' (or, in a rather weaker form, *divi filii*).[6] In Ephesians this peacemaking is transferred to Jews and Christians. 'Peace' is denationalized. It includes enemies. Here Christ as peacemaker and reconciler is unmistakably depicted as an antitype to the emperor. But Christians assume an important role in this 'peace process', not only as Christ's co-regents but as his fellow-fighters. They fight in the *militia Christi* against the evil numinous powers which hitherto have divided Gentiles and Jews – and all this 'for the gospel of peace' (Eph. 6.15).

(*c*) Of course the ruler ideal also includes the overcoming of *enemies*. Here what is expected of the Messiah is somewhat ambivalent. On the one hand he is to prevail against the Gentiles and drive them out (PsSol 17.21ff.); on the other he is to attract them from all points of the compass so that they stream to Zion in the great pilgrimage of the peoples (PsSol 17.31). This humane feature of the messianic king is further developed in primitive Christianity: the Gentiles hope for the Messiah (cf. Matt. 12.21 = Isa. 42.4; Rom. 15.12 = Isa. 11.10). A humane variant of the ancient ruler ideal even embraces love of enemy:

> 'When someone commended the maxim of Cleomenes, who on being asked what a good king ought to do, said, "To do good to his friends and

evil to his enemies, " Ariston said, "How much better, my good sir, to do good to our friends and to make friends of our enemies"' (Plutarch, *Moralia* 218A).

In primitive Christianity, the starting point for the radicalization of love of neighbour so that it becomes love of enemy is a lower-class ideal: characteristically the two members of the Jewish upper class, Josephus and Philo, never speak of 'love of neighbour'. They prefer the aristocratic concept of philanthropy. This is the ideal of a ruler in antiquity. By contrast, primitive Christianity continues the Jewish people's ethic of neighbourliness and combines it with an aristocratic ethic of rule. That love of neighbour becomes love of enemy accords with the principle of humane rulers that they should deal generously with their enemies.[7] The love of enemy in the Sermon on the Mount says that all Christians should practise the clemency of Caesar and the 'gentleness' of the king – not from the position of those who are outwardly superior but from the position of those who are persecuted and scorned. Precisely by doing this they will be 'sons of God', i.e. hold a position of royal dignity. Here is the democratization of an ideal of rule which was also known in Judaism. The Letter of Aristeas advocates it (cf. Aristeas 188, 207, 254). It is said of Agrippa I that he thought 'gentleness' more royal than anger (Josephus, *Antt.*19, 334). The primitive Christian love of enemy is thus a good example of the exchange of upper-class and lower-class values.

This transfer of upper-class values downwards by transferring power, peacemaking and love of enemy to ordinary people is combined with a 'transfer upwards' of lower-class values, an aristocratizing of reconciliation and love of neighbour. The two cannot be separated. Yet here no harmonious ethic of an equilibrium between lower and upper class develops. We find a clear criticism of the powerful, the sharpness of which betrays a perspective from below, even if the arguments used against the powerful often come from the upper classes: the nature of power should be transformed, and it should be based on renunciation of status. Whoever would be first should be ready to become the servant and slave of all – in deliberate contrast to political rule (Mark 10.42–44). It is expected that the powerful will be cast down from their thrones (Luke 1.52). And even where they are not openly attacked, they are attacked in a hidden way in mythical imagery – most clearly in Rev. 12 and 13, where the Roman empire plainly stands behind the satanic rule of the beasts. This underground aggressiveness against the powerful must therefore be held in check by an equally decisive obligation to be loyal to the state (Rom. 13.1–7). Therefore we find a very much more moderate ethic as a counterbalance, above all in the epistolary literature. But the more radical critical attitude is present and shows that in primitive Christianity, upper-class values were not imitated admiringly but appropriated in a revolutionary way: they were snatched from a ruling class which had been repudiated in order to be practised by ordinary people in a different form.

At the same time it has to be emphasized that the primitive Christian ethic develops not only in processes of exchange between the upper and lower classes but also by the crossing of ethnic boundaries. The transformation of notions of power, peace and the enemy does not just benefit one's own national group. On the contrary, a denationalization takes place in the primitive Christian ethic. The *basileia* of God is opened wide for the distant Gentiles, who stream in from all points of the compass (perhaps together with the Diaspora Jews, Matt. 8.11f.). God's *basileia* no longer establishes itself against the national enemies but against mythical enemies, against Satan and the demons (Matt. 12.28). The same is true of 'peace'. In Ephesians, peace is reconciliation between Jews and Gentiles. Christ, the great peacemaker, achieves precisely what the Roman emperors could not. They failed to integrate the Jewish people. Certainly after the First Jewish War, when the rebuilding of the temple of Jupiter Capitolinus in Rome was financed by the temple tax, a kind of forced cultic integration took place – but not inner reconciliation. By contrast, the Christ of Ephesians destroys the enmity between Jews and Gentiles and brings both together in the same worship: here Christ reconciles those who are near and those who are far off (Eph. 2.17; cf. Isa. 52.7). A similar formula appears in Acts, which sees the realization of the proclamation of peace to those who are near and those who are far off made in Isa. 57.19 in the acceptance of the Roman centurion Cornelius (Acts 10.36). Finally, the transcending of national boundaries is evident in the case of love of enemy: the enemies are described as persecutors and mockers in a way which also includes national enemies and the politically powerful.

In conclusion, let us look again briefly at the psychological side of this new way of dealing with power and rule. The ancient ethic of rule includes the control of anger. Those who cannot control themselves cannot control others. However, such self-control is necessary above all where the rulers can give their emotions free rein without being damaged directly – but in the long term destabilize their rule. Therefore the great theme of the upper-class ethic of the ancient world is not the control of sexuality but the control of anger or self-control in ruling over others. This requirement for anger to be controlled is radicalized in primitive Christianity. The first antithesis of the Sermon on the Mount rightly sees the close connection between killing and anger. Now the power to kill is something that above all the powerful have. Anyone who kills becomes lord over another's life. The key to coping ethically with this uncanny possibility lies within a person: in overcoming anger. In the first antithesis the aristocratic ruler's ethic of the control of anger is now transformed into an ethic of brotherhood:

> You have heard that it was said to the men of old, 'You shall not kill; and whoever kills shall be liable to judgment.' But I say to you that every one is angry with his *brother* shall be liable to judgment; whoever insults his brother shall be liable to the council; and whoever says, 'You fool', shall be liable to the hell of fire (Matt. 5.21–22).

Here controlling one's anger does not serve to control others but to be reconciled with them. It is to make life together in a community of brothers and sisters possible.

The renunciation of the will to rule over others goes even further. In the Sermon on the Mount we find the call not only to overcome aggressiveness towards others but also to endure the aggressiveness of others demonstratively. This paradoxical admonition is formulated in the fifth antithesis: one is not to resist evil but, 'If anyone strikes you on the right cheek, turn to him the other also' (Matt. 5.39). This is the classical requirement for self-stigmatization, i.e. for the demonstrative and voluntary adoption of a subordinate position which draws the aggression of others upon itself and endures it. Through this the other is not to be reinforced in his action but to be disconcerted. The many examples of self-stigmatizing behaviour in primitive Christianity with precisely this purpose – not least the central role of self-stigmatization in christology – support this interpretation, which sees in the paradoxical renunciation of resistance a call to the other to change his behaviour. The Son of God voluntarily accepts the role of the crucified one, which is despised in social morality, in order to win over God's 'enemies' to God. He seeks to change them by delivering himself over defenceless to human wickedness and violence.

2. A change of value in dealing with possessions and wealth

In primitive Christianity, in dealing with possessions and wealth, aristocratic values are also taken over by ordinary people and thus fused with their own values. We can recognize the 'benefactor mentality' which was widespread in the ruling classes and among kings as a model for the primitive Christian ethic. We find this mentality in the ancient Near East, where kings and officials propagate a solicitous attitude towards the poor and the weak. Many Egyptian officials boast in their epitaphs that, for example, they have clothed the naked and fed the hungry. We find a comparable attitude in ancient 'euergetism', the donation of private gifts to the public.[8] Here we always have forms of domination: kings, aristocrats and officials use such gifts to secure the loyalty of those over whom they rule. The ancient urban culture of the polis even lived largely on the voluntary payment of the expenses of public services by benefactors (often in order to obtain an office): the expenses of building and maintaining baths, theatres, market places, aqueducts, games and theatre performances, etc. Such 'benefactions' benefitted all the (free) citizens as citizens of their city. No one thought of giving special support to the poor. Here the East differed from the West.

It is generally recognized that with primitive Christianity a change of values took place within the pagan world (not within Judaism). Ancient euergetism was replaced by Christian mercy, which by preference turned to the poor and the weak. One could interpret this change in values as the dissemination in the West by primitive Christianity of a general oriental ethic of mercy which had already been shown to the poor and weak (thus H. Bolkestein).[9] But this would be to fail to recognize that the oriental ethic of mercy among kings and officials was already clearly changed in Israel. It was combined with the 'love of neighbour', i.e. a pro-social form of behaviour towards neighbours of equal status. An ethic of kings became an obligation on the whole people: all were to support widows, orphans and aliens – not because in principle they were superior to them, but because Israel itself had belonged among the weak and the strangers in Egypt. Therefore it is far more appropriate to follow P. Veyne in assuming that with the primitive Christian ethic of mercy a popular morality of mutual support has risen to aristocratic circles.[10] Here this popular morality fuses with submerged parts of an aristocratic benefactor mentality. This fusion can be shown at two points: first in the maxim of ancient benefactors 'It is better to give than to receive' (in Acts 20.35), and secondly in the acts of mercy listed in Matt. 25.35ff.

(*a*) Everyone knows Jesus' saying 'It is better to give than to receive' as a proverb. It does not occur in the Gospels. The Lukan Paul passes it on in his farewell speech in Miletus as a saying of Jesus – and as part of his own legacy (Acts 20.35). It is less well known that this is a general *maxim of benefactors* in antiquity and that it can first be demonstrated as a maxim for royal disposition and behaviour.[11] It can be inferred from Thucydides (II, 97, 4) as a principle of the Persian royal house and is attributed in different variants to the Persian king Artaxerxes (Plutarch, *Mor* 173D) and the Hellenistic ruler Ptolemy (Aelian, *VarHis* XIII, 13). Aristotle described the aristocratic virtue of *eleutheriotes*, i.e. generosity or *liberalitas (EthNic* IV 1, 1120a) in accord with this maxim. In primitive Christianity, for the first time this royal and aristocratic maxim was demonstrably transferred to little people. In the process its content had to be modified. For kings and rich aristocrats had an abundance of possessions from which they could give. By contrast, little people had only what they had earned by their own work. Therefore Paul only introduces the ancient maxim of benefactors after he has presented himself as a model for the community (or its elders) because he works with his own hands to feed himself and his fellow-workers. He says that he is not a burden on anyone, but rather has worked so hard that he can also support the weak. Here unmistakably an originally aristocratic maxim is 'redirected' to people who first have to earn through manual work the means of supporting others and becoming active as 'benefactors'. A further possibility of becoming a 'benefactor', even for someone without means, lies in renunciation. The great model for this is the poor widow who sacrifices her last small coin – and with this quantitatively slight sacrifice qualitatively gives more than many rich people (Mark 12.41–44). In primitive Christianity this invitation to renunciation leads to the custom of the diaconal fast, i.e. the fast in favour of others. For example, the apologist Aristides praises the primitive Christian communities: 'If among them there is some poor and needy person and they have no surplus, they fast for one or two days so that they can satisfy the need of the needy for food' (*Apol.* 15.8). Thus 'to give is better than to receive', the maxim of the ancient benefactor, could be practised in the communities only in a changed form: combined with a strict work ethic and with a readiness for renunciation and fasting. Here upper-class and lower-class values are combined in a characteristic way. However, this changes the purpose of the benefaction. It is no longer to safeguard rule or to increase public prestige. It is to provide for all in a communitarian fellowship in which all support one another.

(*b*) The 'acts of mercy' described in Matt. 25.31–46 also first appear in antiquity as the good works of senior Egyptian officials. In mentioning them on their epitaphs they do not just want to create a 'moral identity' which will get them fame after death in this world and access to the other world. At the same time they are demonstrating their status. The 'ideal biography' of the major-domo Harwa shows this with disarming openness. He also includes the bestowing of offices among his benefactions:

> I did what men love and the gods praise, a true dignitary who had no fault. I gave bread to the hungry, clothes to the naked; I was one who drove away suffering and warded off need, who buried the honourable

and cared for the old, who drove away the distress of those with nothing, a shade for the orphan, a helper for the widows, who bestowed office on one who was still in swaddling clothes . . .[12]

With Matthew the comparable acts no longer serve to demonstrate power and rule. On the contrary, the acts of mercy are summed up in the term 'serve' (Matt. 25.44), more precisely as service of the ruler of the world, who is represented in an unknown way in all sufferers. Here the sufferers have the higher status, not the helpers. Whereas elsewhere in antiquity the helpers are brought near to God – for example when Pliny the Elder says *Deus est mortali juvare mortalem* (*Natural history* II, 5, 18), here God appears in the role of the one who suffers; helping becomes serving, not ruling.

The two examples of a transfer of upper-class values upwards, to be combined with the mentality of small people, could be neglected, did not many other observations indicate that in primitive Christianity the balancing of material possessions was not just a matter between rich and poor but a task for all. Of course special demands were made on the rich. And at an early stage there were already the beginnings of legitimating this through a kind of 'circular theory' of giving.[13] This appears first in I Clem. 38.1–2 and is then developed in Shepherd of Hermas, *Sim.*II.5–10. According to this the poor are rich with God, whereas the rich have a debit balance with him. God hears the prayers of the poor. Now if the rich who do not have much to say to God support the poor, the poor pray for them – and God then sees that the wealth of the rich does not cease, so that they can continue to give to the poor. Such notions of a 'vertical solidarity' are balanced out and corrected in Christianity by notions of a 'horizontal solidarity'. This includes Paul's demand, which has already been discussed, that one should work with one's own hands to support the weak (Acts 20.35). It also includes the admonition of John the Baptist in Luke 3.11 that those who have two garments should give one to someone who has none, and should do the same with food. This admonition is not addressed to rich people, who certainly have more than two garments. Horizontal solidarity also includes the admonition in Luke's Sermon on the Plain to lend without expecting anything back. In conclusion, Luke varies this admonition when he says, 'Lend without despairing of anything' (δανίζετε μηδὲν ἀπελπίζοντες, Luke 6.35). ἀπελπίζειν always means 'despair' and not 'expect back'. Here, too, the usual meaning of the word makes good sense: anyone who does not lend out of his surplus but out of his substance can indeed despair if he is not paid back. Elsewhere, too, in this passage of Luke's Sermon on the Plain rich people are not addressed directly (rather, they are attacked in their absence in the form of harsh woes). Nor does the invitation 'Of him who takes away your goods do not ask them again' (Luke 6.30) fit the rich; they were probably well able to defend themselves if anyone wanted to take anything from them. Here ordinary people are being invited to give. Finally we might remember Paul: he praises the communities of Macedonia because despite their great poverty they have contributed to the collection for Jerusalem (II Cor. 8.2).[14]

The construction of such a horizontal solidarity prevented the primitive Christian communities from becoming the social clientele for some rich patrons. At any rate the latter had a strong position in the communities. The Christians probably gathered in their houses – as they were the only ones to have larger rooms. Their support was indispensable for the system of charity. But precisely for that reason there was the danger that they would be treated in a privileged way. The letter of James warns against this (2.1ff.). The actual importance of the rich was structurally compensated for by elements of horizontal solidarity, and morally by the sharp criticism of wealth in the Jesus tradition, which had a long influence: 'It is easier for a camel to go through the eye of a needle than for a rich man to enter the kingdom of God' (Mark 10.23). This morally aggressive condemnation of the rich must have seemed like a call to the rich to separate themselves from their dangerous wealth – so as to be able to enter the kingdom of God. It had an effect above all in limiting their moral reputation. Before God they were poor. And conversely, 'Has not God chosen those who are poor in the world to be rich in faith and heirs of the kingdom which he promises to those who love him?' (James 2.5). These criticisms of wealth probably remained alive so long because they were needed to limit the influence of the rich in the community.[15] This aggressiveness against the rich shows that in primitive Christianity people had also detached themselves in principle from euergetism. In the Gospel of Luke Jesus can attack it directly as the ideology of rule:

> The kings of the Gentiles rule over their peoples;
> and those in authority are called benefactors (εὐεργέται).
> But not so with you;
> rather let the greatest among you become as the youngest,
> and the leader as one who serves (Luke 22.25f.).

This may be sufficient evidence of the fusing of upper-class and lower class values in dealing with possessions and wealth. But what about openness to outsider groups? Is the ethic of help in primitive Christianity also open to strangers? Does it extend beyond national boundaries? There is in fact clear evidence of this. The collection made by the Antioch community for Jerusalem is an illuminating example. At the same time it illuminates in a vivid way the transference of ancient euergetism to little people. According to Acts 11.27ff., at the time of a great famine under Claudius the Antiochene community made a collection for the Jerusalem community, which was brought to Jerusalem by Barnabas and Paul. Historically there is at least a structural situation underlying this note: support which could be repeated. For Paul later organizes a collection for Jerusalem, possibly on the model of a collection by the Antiochene community which had been made previously. This collection could have been made at the time of a great famine between 46 and 48 BCE. Josephus reports this famine (*Antt.*20, 49–53), but knows nothing of the supportive action of Christian communities abroad. However, he does report a great supportive action by Queen Helena of Adiabene, who had newly gone over to Judaism. She had great masses of grain bought up and distributed in Jerusalem. In this way she is said to have saved many lives. What the queen did in great style, the Christians also did on their modest scale: they too became active as benefactors beyond a particular region. Like kings, they too practised 'benefactions' to their brothers and sisters. In so doing they too went beyond national boundaries, since according to Acts the Antioch community was the first community also to include Gentile Christians (those who had been converted to 'Judaism' – just as the royal house of Adiabene had been converted to it). When Paul later made a collection for remote Jerusalem in the communities of Asia Minor and Greece, little people with their small contributions may also have found themselves benefactors organizing gifts extending beyond their region, as otherwise only kings and aristocrats could do.

Elsewhere, too, the traditions of primitive Christianity show tendencies towards the extension of readiness to give help beyond national and cultural boundaries. This extension is the point in the exemplary story of the Good Samaritan: here love of neighbour shows itself in how one deals with the stranger (Luke 20.25ff.). The same thing is said in the great description of the judgment of the world in Matt. 25.15ff.: in it, all nations (πάντα τὰ ἔθνη) are measured by whether they have helped the suffering brothers and sisters of the judge of the world. The question is addressed to all, regardless of their nationality.

It finally remains for us to look at the psychological motivations which correspond to such an attitude to possessions and wealth. As so often, here we find more moderate and more radical demands side by side. The warning against avarice or *pleonexia* which is widespread (above all in the epistolary literature; cf. Mark 7.22; Luke 12.15; Col. 3.5; Eph. 5.3) is moderate. Avarice goes with idolatry (Col. 3.5; Eph. 5.5) and excludes people from the kingdom of God (I Cor. 6.10; Eph. 5.5). It is reprehensible because it seeks to have more than the basic needs of life. The demand in the Synoptic tradition to free oneself even from worries about elementary needs of life – and not just from seeking anything beyond them – is more radical. In Matt. 6.25ff. the disciples are required not to be anxious about food and clothing, Like the birds of the air and the lilies of the field, they are to trust that God will see to their needs. However, they are to be anxious for the 'kingdom of God' (some manuscripts write only 'for the kingdom'), since then everything else will be given to them. The logic of this admonition is that anyone who has the kingdom need not worry about food, drink and clothing. That is no longer a problem for the ruling groups. Thus seeking the 'kingdom (of God)' is seeking *symbasileia* – participation in active rule through which the disciples will be put in the position of being, like king Solomon, free of anxiety about such everyday matters as clothing. We must understand this promise to mean that just as food, drink and clothing will be given to them in addition (προστεθήσεται) – as goods which they now have in their possession – so the kingdom is given to them as a good which they now have at their disposal. In my opinion the saying is addressed to homeless itinerant charismatics, even if against the background of their life-style it draws quite general conclusions which apply to all – like the universal truth that no one can add anything to his life and that each day brings its own cares. Because this attribution to a specific *Sitz im Leben* is sometimes disputed,[16] here are just two arguments.

1. The image of the birds of the air can be evaluated quite differently from the way in which it is evaluated in this admonition by Jesus. Observation and traditional imagery make the birds in particular obvious examples of care in building nests and emphasize the great diligence with which they work on their nests and feed their young (cf. IV Macc. 14.15–17). But none of that is evaluated: they become images of freedom from anxiety and work. Here the reality which is being referred to reverses the image: namely the reality of the itinerant charismatics who in fact do not work to provide for themselves.

2. A second observation is that those who talk of everyday cares usually think of caring for others. This is the sense in which Paul speaks in I Cor. 7 of the mutual care of a married couple for each other – and therefore this care can be evaluated more positively than the anxiety about eating and drinking in Matt. 6.25ff. (cf. further the mutual care in the body of Christ in I Cor. 12.25). However, nothing of such a concern for others can be detected in Matt. 6.25ff. Those addressed care nothing for their children, their wives, their families. We hear only of one care, that for their own lives. That is more appropriate for itinerant charismatics who have separated from their families.

Now it is illuminating for the primitive Christian ethic that precisely these marginal figures are asked to show a royal awareness: unconcerned, like those who exercise 'rule', they are to liberate themselves from anxiety about elementary needs – and in so doing distinguish themselves from all other people. Here an aristocratic self-confidence is attributed to outsiders.

Looking back on the topics of the primitive Christian ethic of power and possessions which we have been discussing, in conclusion we should recall a phenomenon which we have encountered in both complexes of topics and will encounter again: the juxtaposition of a radical and a moderate ethic,[17] the former often in the Synoptic tradition and the latter often in the epistolary literature. We can easily explain this juxtaposition if we compare Jesus traditions with statements of Paul on related subjects. Here we may often wonder whether Paul is consciously or unconsciously referring to a corresponding Jesus tradition.

The logion about divorce originally seeks to exclude any possible divorce (Luke 16.17; Mark 10.12ff.). However, not only is it toned down in Mark by the *porneia* clause but it is also toned down in Paul by a kind of 'mixed-marriage' clause. Paul accepts divorce in marriages between Christians and non-Christians if it originates with the non-Christian partner (I Cor. 7.10ff.). That is doubtless a more practical, more moderate, version of the divorce rule.

The rules about equipment in the speech to missionaries who are being sent out obligates them to a demonstrative renunciation of provisions and to trust in finding support (Luke 10.3ff.). Paul turns this rule about equipment into the privilege that apostles may require support from communities – and is proud that he has renounced this privilege (I Cor. 9.1ff.).

According to a bold saying of Jesus (in Matt. 21.31), prostitutes (πόρναι in the feminine form) have an opportunity to enter the kingdom of God before the scribes and priests. In Paul, by contrast, whoremongers (πόρνοι in the masculine form) are strictly excluded from the kingdom of God (I Cor. 6.9). Here he is even 'stricter' than Jesus, but removes himself from the radicalism of Jesus in turning to the outcast and the sinners.

The statements about the rich are comparable. According to Jesus they have no chance of getting into the kingdom of God (Mark 10.25). In Paul the rich become people who are greedy for possessions: they are excluded from entering the *basileia* (I Cor. 6.10; cf. Eph. 5.5). Thus the rich who are not 'avaricious' are not affected.

The kingdom of God itself is depicted in sayings of Jesus with the image of a great feast. People from everywhere will stream into it to recline at table with the three patriarchs (Matt. 8.10f.). By contrast Paul emphasizes, almost clearly dissociating himself from such earthly notions, that 'the kingdom of God does not mean food and drink but righteousness and peace and joy in the Holy Spirit' (Rom. 14.17).

Jesus requires taxes to be paid to the emperor: there is no religious obligation to refuse to pay tax. But he adds a proviso to the expected answer: give to God what is God's (Mark 12.13ff.). In Paul there are certainly similar notions (and such traditions?), but he does not make a contrast between the emperor and God: 'Pay all of them their dues, taxes to whom taxes are due, revenue to whom revenue is due, respect to whom respect is due, honour to whom honour is due' (Rom. 13.7).

The Sermon on the Mount calls for enemies to be loved, persecutors to be blessed and for a demonstrative renunciation of resistance to evildoers (Matt. 5.38ff.). There are comparable admonitions in Rom. 12. Paul, too, does not want evil to be recompensed with evil, but he realistically adds: 'If possible, so far as depends on you, leave peaceably with all' (Rom. 12.18).

The logion about cleanness in Mark 7.15 is a bold and radical saying which denies that there is any external uncleanness and removes the foundation from the commandments about food. Paul too shares this attitude, 'All is clean,' but he adds a qualification: 'but it is wrong for anyone to make others fall by what he eats' (Rom. 14.20). For the sake of the common life and the other person it is worth not practising consistently a principle which is intrinsically correct.

Jesus requires his disciples to leave their work and family to follow him (Mark 1.16ff.). Paul tells his communities almost the opposite: each is to remain in the state in which he was called. The great change through liberation in Christ must not lead to outward changes (I Cor. 7.17, 20, 24).

There is a historical explanation for the juxtaposition of a radical and a moderate ethic, and a substantive interpretation of it can be offered. Historically, a sociological explanation is the natural one. In origin, the radical ethic derives from itinerant primitive Christian charismatics who had detached themselves from the domesticating ties of everyday life. They lived a life detached from power, possessions, work and family. At their centre stood Jesus, himself an itinerant charismatic, whose life-style was also continued after Easter. These itinerant charismatics were the first authorities in the primitive Christian communities which were gradually coming into being. Their traditions have been preserved above all in the Synoptic Gospels. Their ethic is an 'itinerant radicalism'. The development of primitive Christianity is then governed by a shift in the authority structure in the local communities. These gain in independence, orientate themselves on their own community leaders, the bishops, deacons and presbyters, and increasingly shield themselves from the itinerant charismatics who are travelling around.

However, the moderate and increasingly conservative ethic of the domestic state establishes itself with ever greater weight. Criticism of the family is replaced with an ethic which supports the family, the renunciation of possessions with a social way of dealing with possessions, the criticism of power with selective adaptation to the power structures of the world, etc. This development already begins with Paul – an itinerant charismatic whose greatness consisted in the fact that he subordinated his whole activity to the building up of local communities. This more moderate ethic has been preserved for us in the epistolary literature. It appears above all in the Deutero-Paulines as a conservative 'patriarchalism of love'.

However, this historical distinction should not lead us to overlook the substantive connection between the two forms of ethic. From the beginning the itinerant charismatics had formulated their message for groups of settled sympathizers. Of course there are many statements in their traditions which apply to everyone. Conversely, the later local communities also live by a lively exchange between one another, which was made possible by travelling Christians. One admires the charismatic authorities of the early period. Their traditions have been preserved for us in the Synoptic Gospels in a way which also makes them accessible to local communities. For the remarkable thing is that the radical traditions of the earlier period continued to be preserved later. They continued to be regarded as relevant. Here the criticism of wealth took on a new function, as did the criticism of power in the Jesus traditions. They served within the community to shape the offices which came into being in a communitarian way – to subordinate them to the community as ministries and not set them over the community by virtue of general social status. Moreover, the juxtaposition of the two forms of ethic paved the way towards seeing them both as stages of the same ethic.

In addition a second factor preserved the radical ethic. It is also at work in the mythical shaping of the Christ event.[18] It is coded in it in mythical form and thus preserved. Christ himself becomes the primal model of a renunciation of power and a criticism of the powerful. He is the power of God which revealed itself in the cross as 'weakness'. The rulers of this world crucified him, but were overcome by him. Christ himself becomes the primal model for the renunciation of possessions. He is the one who forsook his wealth in the pre-existent world. Paul writes to the Corinthians: 'Though he was rich, yet for your sake he became poor, so that by his poverty you might become rich' (II Cor. 8.9). That is also true of the next set of themes, the way in which wisdom was dealt with. Here too the Christ (interpreted in mythical terms) embodies the radical change of criteria. The one who is the wisdom of God became folly. And on the basis of this, all worldly wisdom is devalued (I Cor. 1.18ff.). Myth and ethic form a unity. Through myth a radical ethic is preserved which can continue to have an effect long after the ethic which is in fact practised has already become much more 'moderate'.

6

Dealing with Wisdom and Holiness in Primitive Christianity. Ethical Demands in the Light of the Two Basic Values: II

It is obvious that there are disputes over power and possessions in history. But there are also struggles over the distribution of education and wisdom, holiness and cleanness. Who has access to socially recognized knowledge? Who embodies the highest degree of holiness and normative power? There is a dispute over these questions, too, and this dispute is also a struggle over the distribution of power, for wisdom gives power and holiness bestows influence. Nevertheless, this struggle over distribution takes a different course from political and economic conflict. Wise men and priests have the power to define and legitimate. They define what is good and evil, clean and unclean, what is salvation and what is not. And they use their power to remove legitimation from what they regard as evil, unclean and unholy. To do so they refer to a pre-existing order, which they partly take from the structure of reality (as in wisdom) and partly infer from traditional knowledge of revelation (as in priestly knowledge). Their influence and their power is based on belief in a legitimate order. To the real struggle over the distribution of material goods they add a struggle over the legitimation of the right order of things. Therefore their power is also an opportunity to contain, to limit and to regulate the real struggles over distribution. From the perspective of the legitimate order the conflict is a a disruption, a deviation, something that has to be overcome.

Wisdom and holiness can have their *Sitz im Leben* in particular institutions and groups. Even if those who hold power and the rich will always tend to control the institutions which order wisdom and priestly knowledge, it would be wrong to see wise men and priests as mere puppets of the power elites – and their activity only as the ideological accompaniment to the power of weapons and goods. That would be to underestimate the tremendous significance of legitimacy. Once political authorities have lost their legitimacy, they soon also lose real power. In my view, with the discussion over legitimacy an independent factor enters social and political conflicts. In antiquity, too, people were already aware of this opposition of normative power and political rule. Plato dreamed of the union of wisdom and power, of the king who at the same time is the perfect sage, and of the sage who is the perfect king.[1] And this dream continued to be dreamed after him, The Jew Philo sees it fulfilled in Moses, who was the perfect king, priest and prophet, all at the same time.[2]

Because of a unique historical situation, in the Judaism of the time of Jesus power and wealth on the one hand and wisdom and holiness on the other were 'organized' in different centres – with many links between them. In the course of time wisdom had become a religious wisdom with a close link to the temple, as is shown by the enthusiastic description of the temple cult in Jesus Sirach's great wisdom book (Sir. 50.1–24). Scribes who went by the religious traditions of the people were the representatives of Jewish wisdom. On the other hand, political power was represented by the Romans and the local aristocracy which co-operated with them – the Herodians and their followers. It must be emphasized that such a differentiation is not necessary. It is absent from many societies. It established itself in European history in the opposition of state and church, but this is a special development, the roots of which lie in the period of the origin of primitive Christianity. At all events it is historically meaningful to consider separately attitudes to power and possessions and to wisdom and holiness.

1. A change of value in dealing with wisdom[3]

In antiquity there was a certain consensus that wisdom is hardly to be found among the lower classes. Philosophy, the 'love of wisdom', was largely a matter for the upper class. And if in the figure of Socrates it was combined with the life of craftsmen, and the Cynic philosophers were consciously opposed to a hierarchically divided society, we can read off their counter-cultural protest what was generally true in their culture: the great philosophers like Plato and Aristotle were members of the upper class!

Unfortunately we cannot give a clear social location to Old Testament wisdom. It is certain that there was a wisdom in the upper classes associated with the court, but this does not exclude the possibility that popular wisdom traditions in Israel were also cultivated elsewhere. However, only in the Hellenistic period do we find clear evidence of the association of wisdom with the upper class: Jesus Sirach not only tied wisdom (once international and universal) to the revealed Torah and the people of Israel, but within the Jewish people he made a distinction between upper class and lower class, between those who have to do physical work and those who are relieved of it (Sir. 38.24–39.11). As a principle he states: 'The wisdom of the scribe depends on the opportunity of leisure; and he who has little business may become wise' (Sir. 38.24). For people engaged in physical work are so caught up in their toil that they have no time or energy to set their minds on higher thoughts. As examples Sirach mentions the farmer, craftsman and master craftsman (the *tekton* and *architekton*), the cutter of seals on signets, the smith and the potter. His ironic comments on the farmer are particularly piquant: he sees him talking to his oxen and bulls instead of engaging in a wisdom dialogue:

> How can he become wise who handles the plough,
> and who glories in the shaft of a goad,
> who drives oxen and is occupied with their work,
> and whose talk is with young bulls?
> He sets his heart on ploughing furrows,
> and he is careful about fodder for the heifers (Sir. 38.25–26).

Certainly Jesus Sirach does not despise working men. He can even grant that they have a 'relative' wisdom when at the end of his remarks about builders and manual workers he writes: 'All these rely upon their hands, and each is wise in his work' (Sir. 38.31). But their great defect is that they do not play any great role in public life, in the popular assembly and the community, and do not know the legal traditions and wisdom sayings. They are wise only in their 'work' (Sir. 38.34). By contrast, the true wise man is 'wise' in dealing with the public word. And he occupies himself with the great texts of the tradition: 'other is the one who devotes himself to the study of the law of the Most High and seeks out the wisdom of all the ancients' (39.1).

Around 200 years after Jesus Sirach, Jesus appears as a wisdom teacher in Galilee and Judaea, although by origin he had no education which would qualify him in a way that others could recognize. The story of his rejection in Nazareth indicates that. There he teaches in the synagogue and causes amazement and offence: 'And many who heard him were astonished, saying, "Where did this man get all this? What is the wisdom given to him? What mighty works are wrought by his hands! Is not this the carpenter, the son of Mary and brother of James and Joses and Judas and Simon, and are not his sisters here with us?", and they took offence at him' (Mark 6.2f.). According to the criteria of Jesus Sirach, Jesus would be excluded from real wisdom because he was a craftsman, a *tekton!*

This wisdom of Jesus finds a new audience, which like the teacher of this wisdom is really excluded from it by traditional criteria. Here wisdom appears as revealed wisdom, which remains hidden from the wise and understanding, but is revealed by God to those who have not come of age. It is communicated by Jesus. Here he, Jesus, takes the place of wisdom. He, Jesus, addresses the call of wisdom to her pupils when he exclaims to the people:

> Come to me, all who labour and are heavy laden,
> and I will give you rest.
> Take my yoke upon you, and learn from me;
> for I am gentle and lowly in heart,
> and you will find rest for your souls.
> For my yoke is easy and my burden is light (Matt. 11.28f.).

What is termed the 'call of the saviour' has many parallels in Jesus Sirach. There wisdom calls, 'Come to me, you who desire me . . .' (Sirach 24.19). She woos people with the argument, 'See with your eyes that I have laboured little and found for myself much rest' (51.27 LXX). They are wooed with the words: 'Put your neck under the yoke and bear your burden' (51.26). But whereas Jesus Sirach excludes all who work from wisdom, Jesus' saying is addressed to workers. It addresses those who slave away and are burdened. It addresses people who had previously been excluded from wisdom. Here it is emphasized that Jesus thus belongs in a general tendency to combine scribal activity and earning one's living and to do away with that elitist limitation of true wisdom to the upper class which we found in Jesus Sirach.

However, the new audience of Jesus' wisdom includes not only the workers but the women. The pericope about Mary and Martha shows Jesus as a teacher. Mary finds in listening to his wisdom that rest which her sister Martha does not find. In so doing she drops out of the roles expected of women. But it is explicitly said that here she has chosen the better part (Luke 10.38–42). That the wisdom teaching of Jesus is addressed to women is also shown by a formal feature in some traditions: we often find pairs with a symmetry of gender, i.e. parallel sayings which are addressed to men and women. These include, for example the parable of the lost sheep and the lost drachma: the good shepherd is a man and the owner of the drachma a woman (Luke 15.1ff.). The birds of the heavens who do not work stand for agricultural work (according to an ancient gender stereotype, outside work is the domain of the man); the lilies of the field for spinning (according to the same stereotype, inside work is the woman's domain) (Matt. 6.25ff.), etc.[4]

The Jesus tradition clearly articulates an awareness that with such wisdom an 'upper-class value' is made accessible to ordinary people. In Matt. 12.41f. Jesus compares his audience on the one hand with the Ninevites who repented at the preaching of Jonah. The whole people is meant here. But then he adds a second comparison. They are similarly comparable to the Queen of the South, who came to Solomon to hear his wisdom. Now in Jesus there is a greater wisdom than the wisdom of Solomon!

In Paul this revaluation of wisdom is continued. For him, too, God's hidden wisdom seeks a new audience where no wisdom of this world is to be found. Wisdom finds this audience in the primitive Christian communities where, as in Corinth, 'not many were wise according to worldly standards, not many were powerful, not many were of noble birth' (I Cor. 1.26). To the world this wisdom is 'folly'. But this folly is more powerful than the wisdom of the world. The revaluation of wisdom and folly are expressed with unsurpassable sharpness.

The letter of James makes a programmatic distinction between two kinds of wisdom: an earthly wisdom which provokes envy and strife, and a wisdom 'from above' which is peaceable, generous, merciful, unpartisan and without hypocrisy (James 3.13–18). These two kinds of wisdom cannot be assigned to social classes, but they can be assigned to social attitudes: the true wisdom which comes from God is 'humble'; it is associated with a renunciation of claims to status. And to this degree it is accessible to the 'lowly'.

In fact Christianity was a wisdom for the ordinary person: wisdom not in the sense of great intellectual training but in the sense of a consistent shaping of life in accordance with a few principles. In this sense, the physician Galen in the second century CE confirms to Christians that among them men and even women lead a philosophical life. He makes explicit mention of self-discipline, self-control over food and drink and a striving for righteousness as characteristics of the philosophical life of Christians: as an expression of their love of wisdom (*De pulsum differentiis* 3, 31).

Unmistakably, in the way in which primitive Christianity deals with wisdom (in parallel to developments in Judaism) there is a transfer of upper-class education downwards, but this changes its character in the process: it increasingly becomes a paradoxical wisdom of revelation, which reveals itself precisely to those who are traditionally excluded from wisdom. This appropriation of wisdom is combined with a vehement polemic against the representatives of traditional wisdom: against the scribes and experts in the law. Even if we limit ourselves to the earliest sayings against them in Q and Mark, it is striking that the main target of the criticism is the anti-social behaviour of these experts in dealing with their wisdom. They impose burdens on others through their teaching, but do not even bend their little fingers to bear them (Luke 11.46). Indeed they have the key to knowledge, but instead of using it to make wisdom accessible to others, they prevent others from attaining it – quite regardless of the fact that they themselves remain outside (Luke 11.52). They attach importance to pre-eminence and places of honour – and at the same time enrich themselves from the possessions of poor widows (Mark 12.38–40). Thus there is criticism of precisely what is propagated in Christianity: the opening of wisdom to all, including the weary and heavy-laden, and also to those who are not honoured for their wisdom.

This wisdom does not just cross social boundaries from above downwards. It also opens up beyond traditional national boundaries. In addition, however, we must remember that wisdom is originally an international phenomenon. That is not just a discovery of modern scholars who found parts of the sayings of Amenemope in the book of Proverbs (22.17–23.12). It was also known by the ancient traditions: King Solomon exchanges his wisdom with King Hiram of Tyre (Josephus, *Antt.*8, 143). He attracts the Queen of Sheba with it (I Kings 10/II Chron. 9). But here a nationalization of wisdom had begun after the Old Testament period. After the first beginnings of it in Deut. 4.6–8 it is carried through in the book of Jesus Sirach: the wisdom which comes from God sought a dwelling-place among all peoples, but did not find it, so at God's command she settled in Israel. There she now serves God in the holy tabernacle, i.e. in the temple (Sir. 24.3–10). In this process wisdom increasingly changes from being an experiential wisdom open to all into a wisdom of revelation which is accessible only to an elect circle: according to Jesus Sirach only to the Jewish people. In the apocalyptic writings she is even limited to small groups in Israel. For according to Ethiopian Enoch 42.1–2 she found no dwelling place on earth, even in Israel.

> Wisdom could not find a place in which she could dwell, but a place was found for her in the heavens. Then wisdom went out to dwell with the children of the people, but she found no dwelling place. So wisdom returned to her place and she settled permanently among the angels.

There, in heaven, she is now accessible only to elect seers and visionaries who have written wisdom down in works which contain revelations only for small circles.

In addition, in primitive Christianity a further restriction of wisdom takes place: it is concentrated in a single person, in Jesus. He is far more than King Solomon with his wisdom (Matt. 12.42). He contains in himself all 'riches of wisdom and knowledge' (Col. 2.3). But mediated through this one person these riches are now accessible to all – in Israel and beyond.

This is already becoming evident in the Jesus tradition. When Jesus is compared with Solomon and his wisdom, this wisdom *a priori* appears as something which also attracts foreigners. Since as a parallel to this comparison with Solomon there is a comparison with the preacher Jonah, who led the foreign Ninevites to repent, Jesus' appeal to the Gentiles as well is clearly emphasized: in Jesus, Jewish wisdom takes on a form which makes it accessible to Gentiles.

In the epistolary literature we find the so-called 'scheme of revelation', i.e. the idea that God's mystery had long been hidden but became accessible in Christ and now also includes the Gentiles (cf. Rom. 16.25–27; Col. 1.26f.; Eph. 3.13). Here one could almost see a deliberate reworking of the wisdom traditions: according to the tradition, wisdom sought a dwelling among all peoples (or Gentiles) but found it only in Israel (Sir. 24). The scheme of revelation in primitive Christianity presents a far-reaching variant on this notion in that now Gentiles (instead of Israel) become the place where the wisdom of God is revealed.[5] The connection with traditional wisdom motifs becomes evident in the fact that this mystery of God which is being revealed is called 'God's manifold wisdom' (Eph. 3.10), is attributed to the 'only wise God' (Rom. 16.27), or is described as wisdom teaching (Col. 1.28). Here the Christian authors of the letters are self-confidently saying that the wisdom present in Christian teaching is a revelation accessible to all peoples.

Again we can observe those processes of the transformation of ethics which also applied to the way in which power and possessions were dealt with. Instead of being an upper-class privilege, wisdom becomes a 'knowledge' that is accessible to all. However, in so doing it changes its form by being combined with the forms of lower-class wisdom: on the one hand it becomes a paradoxical wisdom of revelation which remains hidden from the professional sages, and on the other it is combined with simple sentences, images and parables which anyone can understand. The wisdom which has been transformed in this way is accessible to all people.

The connection between myth and ethic, ethic and community, is particularly clear in the history of the 'wisdom tradition'. From the late writings in the Old Testament onwards we observe a 'rise' of wisdom. Wisdom is not just 'objectified' as a good worth striving for, nor is it poetically 'personified', but it is 'hypostatized' as an independent aspect of God. Wisdom comes to stand alongside God, and in the process is fused with the wife of God, the queen of heaven, who is suppressed by monotheistic faith. This rise of wisdom in heaven was matched by a rise of the social group of the wise on earth: new educated elites claimed to have direct access to God in the form of wisdom speculations – relatively independently of the revelation mediated in history (cf. Prov.1–8; Sir. 24; Wisdom 7–10). A contrary tendency occurs in the New Testament: wisdom is again brought down from heaven and made accessible in a concrete person on earth, in Jesus of Nazareth. However, soon (and probably also on the basis of the identification of Jesus with wisdom) wisdom is made a partner of God in heaven who acts independently. We can observe how initially (in Q) Jesus was the messenger of wisdom, and how in Matthew he is perhaps identified with 'wisdom' (cf. Matt. 11.19 with 11.2; Matt. 23.24 with Luke 11.49), but later completely enters into the role of the pre-existent divine wisdom. Above all the Gospel of John speaks of him in the framework of such a 'wisdom christology'; here feminine 'wisdom' is exchanged for the male 'Logos' (John 1.1ff.).[6] Here too we still sense that such a revelation of wisdom above all addresses members of the upper class: the 'leader' of the Jews, Nicodemus, is the first, as 'teacher of Israel' (i.e. as a professional sage), to be confronted with the Johannine kerygma of the pre-existent emissary (John 3.1ff.). And the family of Lazarus, whose life has a touch of luxury (detectable in precious unguents and a rock tomb), was one of Jesus' closest friends (John 11.1ff.; 12.3ff.). But here too a beggar born blind is first shown that human beings have to have their eyes opened by a miracle for them to come to the knowledge of truth (John 9.1ff.). The stamp that wisdom has left on the Gospel of John is further evident where Jesus as the bread of life calls for his revelation to be received (John.6.35ff.), which recalls the invitation of Wisdom to her banquet (cf. Prov.9.1ff.), or where he promises to quench thirst by communicating divine wisdom (John 4.10ff.; 7.37–39). This is reminiscent of the call of Wisdom in Jesus Sirach: 'Those who eat me will hunger for more, and those who drink me will thirst for more' (Sir. 24.22). Or where Jesus reveals himself as the true vine in which all the disciples are bound together by love. This recalls the way in which Wisdom introduces herself in Sir. 24.17f.: 'Like a vine I caused loveliness to bud . . . I am the mother of beautiful love, of fear, of knowledge, and of holy hope.' In the figure of the 'spirit of truth' Jesus can remain with his own for ever as revealed wisdom, even after his farewell (John 14.15ff., 25f., etc.).

2. A change of value in dealing with holiness and cleanness

The powerful and the rich strive to surround their power and their possessions with the aura of holiness and legitimacy. The wise men and the priests control this aura and it often seduces them into increasing their political power and their economic possessions. But their real power is the power of definition. According to Lev. 10.10f., priests have the authority

> 'to distinguish between what is holy and what is not holy, and between what is not clean and what is clean'. They are 'to teach the people of Israel all the statutes which the Lord has spoken to them by Moses'.

The two terms 'holy' and 'clean', which are used almost as synonyms, do not have the same meaning. 'Holiness' is primarily a quality of God which can be transferred secondarily to human beings, objects and rites. The opposite to 'holy' is profane, not unclean. For the holy can also be unclean or make unclean when it comes into contact with human beings who do not possess the requisite degree of holiness. Cleanness is in turn primarily a quality of people and objects. Cleanness means being fit for the cult: it makes it possible for men and women to be admitted to the cult and for vessels to be used in it. The profane can be clean and unclean. The difference between clean and clean becomes relevant to action only in a cultic approach to God.[7]

In what follows we can discuss only a few aspects of the distinction between holy and unholy, clean and unclean – namely the strategies which are used to safeguard power with the aid of categories of holiness: strategies to safeguard status, to demarcate priests from laity, to secure privileges.

Status is safeguarded through a wealth of regulations about descent and marriage. All priests have to be descended from priests and attest this descent by a genealogy (cf. Josephus, *Life* 1). A priest may not marry a prostitute, a divorced woman, a woman who has been taken prisoner of war, and of course may not marry a foreigner (Lev. 21.7–8; Josephus, *Against Apion*, 1, 31). Even stricter regulations apply in the case of the high priests.

Intensifications of taboos for priests increase their distance from the laity. Uncleanness as a taboo is bound up above all with the frontiers of life: with death and sickness, with sexuality and menstruation. Priests have to keep away from all corpses (Num. 19) and may perform rites of mourning only in the case of the very closest members of their family (Lev. 21.1–4, 11f.). The requirements for sexual control are greater in their cases than in others: the sons of Eli forfeit the right of their family to the priesthood because they sleep in the sanctuary with women who came there to worship (I Sam. 2.22–24). The encounter with the holy can require sexual abstinence: Moses and the whole people must abstain from sexual activity for three days before the revelation on Sinai (Ex. 19.15).

The *relaxation of taboos* for priests is the other side of their special 'holiness'. They have access to the holy even where others are excluded. Here hierarchical limits are drawn: the holy of holies is entered only once a year by the high priest, the temple hall is entered only by some elect priests, the court of the priests by all priests, the adjacent court by all the males of Israel; the last court in the holy precinct may also be entered by women. Outside the holy precincts Gentiles, too, may enter the grounds of the temple.

Over against this there were already always 'tendencies towards democratization'. For 'holiness' is the basis not only of differences of status within the people but also of the difference between the people of Israel and the other peoples. Of all Israel it is required that 'You shall be holy, for I the Lord your God am holy' (Lev. 19.2; cf. 22.31ff.). All Israel is promised, 'You shall become to me a kingdom of priests and a holy people' (Ex. 19.6). This consciousness that all are holy can lead to criticism of privileged priestly holiness, as is shown by the rebellion of Korah's mob (Num. 16). The 'democratizing' tendencies which are suppressed here establish themselves increasingly in the course of time: in the New Testament period in particular there are clearly many special groups in Israel which extend priestly holiness to the laity, as a way of safeguarding the demarcation of their traditions against foreigners.

The tendencies to extend holiness and requirements for holiness in the Jesus movement and in primitive Christianity are part of a change of value which extends throughout Judaism. The only difference is that in primitive Christianity notions of holiness are extended even to non-Jews if they join the Christian faith.

The *safeguarding of status* by descent, the first strategy for safeguarding priestly privileges, is done away with in primitive Christianity – not just in the case of the privileges of an elite among the people, but also in the case of the privileges of the people as a whole. The preaching of John the Baptist is already fundamental polemic against a saving status guaranteed by descent through Abraham (Matt. 3.9 par.). All Israelites must gain their saving status anew by a rite of cleansing, baptism. In primitive Christianity this baptism is associated with the Holy Spirit. The Spirit becomes the power which bestows status and takes the place of genealogical descent. This can be seen in an exemplary way in Jesus: the spirit which descends on him at baptism bestows on him the status of 'Son of God' (Mark 1.9–11) or makes it possible to proclaim this status publicly (Matt. 3.17). Similarly, in a pre-Pauline formula, the exalted Jesus is given his status as 'Son of God' by the 'spirit of holiness'. Thus the status which Jesus already had as a descendant of David is crossed through and outdone (Rom. 1.3f.). The authors of the Gospels of Matthew and Luke consciously take into account a tension between their patrilinear genealogies and the notion of the procreation of Jesus through the Spirit to show that the real basis of his messianic status is not his royal descent but his procreation through the Spirit. This procreation through the Spirit interrupts the genealogy. It is interesting that Matthew counts among the forebears of Jesus four women who contravene the exalted requirements of holiness in priestly marriages: Tamar had been widowed, Rahab was a prostitute, Ruth a foreigner and Bathsheba an adulteress.[8] Nevertheless Jesus is the Messiah, whose procreation is through the Spirit. He is thus also a model for all Christians. For regardless of descent and origin, all Christians owe their status as 'sons of God' (Rom. 8.4; Gal. 4.6) to the Spirit. All are 'saints' (cf. Rom. 1.7; I Cor. 1.2, etc.). At a very early stage 'the saints' became a term which all Christians used of themselves: all are what otherwise only priests were in an emphatic sense.

Are the *intensifications of taboos* transferred to all with the status of holiness? Intensifications of norms are indeed attested. However, the question is: to what degree are they cultically inspired? In the case of Jesus, here one comes up against an open situation. His identification of remarriage with adultery in the logion about divorce is based on an understanding of marriage according to which a marriage is valid even beyond separation and divorce. The rules for the marriage of priests, according to which a priest was forbidden to marry a divorced person (Lev. 21.7), may have been the analogy and inspiration for this intensified marriage ethic. However, that is by no means certain. At the same time, in sayings of Jesus sexual asceticism can be regarded as becoming eunuchs for the sake of the kingdom of God (Matt. 19.12). Eunuchs were excluded from the cult (cf. Deut. 23.1f.). Here requirements of holiness were deliberately done away with: what makes a person unfit for the cult brings him near to the kingdom of God. Moreover, it should be recalled that the morality of sexual asceticism in the sayings of Jesus stands over against a morality which shows marked tolerance over sex in some narratives about Jesus' dealings with women (Luke 7.3ff; John 8.2ff.).

This morality of sexual tolerance is absent from Paul. Here we still find the requirements of an intensified sexual control which are now explicitly grounded in the priestly character of the Christian life: 'Shun fornication . . . Do you not know that your body is a temple of the Holy Spirit within you . . .' (I Cor. 6.18f.). The first requirement in the hallowing of life commanded by God is to abstain from fornication (I Thess. 4.3). But not only the sexual ethic is understood by Paul as an expression of the 'hallowing' of life. If Christians' bodies are temples, then in these temples, all their lives they offer 'reasonable worship'. Christians are to offer their bodies to God as a 'living and holy sacrifice' (Rom. 12.1). This is the heading for the paraenesis which embraces the whole of Christian life: serenity in the social life of the community, mutual love which is also to be shown to outsiders, loyalty to the state, etc. Sexual ethics are touched on only right at the periphery (cf. Rom. 13.13). This 'worship in the everyday world' is not the behaviour of isolated individuals. It is behaviour in the framework of the community. For the community itself is the new temple of God (I Cor. 3.16ff.). Since the death of Christ, its life has now become a constant Passover in which the old leaven is to be done away with – i.e. its members are to separate themselves from all immorality (I Cor. 5.6f.). Since their conversion they have all been 'washed, sanctified and justified by Christ' (I Cor. 6.11). Ritual cleansing, baptism (to which the 'washing' alludes), leads to sanctification. This in turn consists in a new ethical life of righteousness. Thus in primitive Christianity cultic sanctification becomes an ethical way of life in the sphere of the community. It should be emphasized that this shows its Jewish character: the penetration of the whole of life by ritual and ethical commandments from the Torah, with no distinction being made between these in principle, is a characteristic of Jewish communities and groups. Even if the Christians gave up some ritual modes of behaviour – especially those which served as Jewish identity markers – , in hallowing the whole of life they were following a deeply Jewish pattern. And in transferring priestly notions to the whole of life here, they were corresponding to tendencies in contemporary Judaism.

I Peter is a classic example of this transference of priestly status and behaviour to all members of the community: as a community Christians form a 'spiritual temple and a holy priesthood, to offer spiritual sacrifices' (2.5). They have a high status as 'a chosen race, a royal priesthood, a holy people' (2.9), to which even those who did not originally belong to the people of God now belong (2.10). This is immediately followed by the admonition to behave in an exemplary way among the Gentiles (2.11f.) – although in one respect the Christians are acting against the consensus of the whole of their world. They have abandoned the way of life inherited from their fathers, indeed they even regard the break with tradition as redemption: 'You know that you were ransomed from the futile ways inherited from your fathers not with perishable silver or gold, but with the precious blood of Christ' (1.18f.). Only by turning from their former life, by breaking with tradition, have they attained holiness:

> As obedient children, do not be conformed to the passions of your former ignorance, but as he who called you is holy, be holy yourselves in all your conduct (I Peter 1.14–16).

Here, too, holiness is clearly a new way of life in the framework of the community, a turning away from pagan ways of life. And although I Peter is here preaching an ethic of assimilation and a willingness to stigmatize oneself by bearing suffering, it calls for this humble behaviour with the aristocratic awareness that those who suffer as slaves or Christians are in reality of royal stock!

So one can also speak of a transfer of aristocratic values downwards in dealing with priestly values. As elsewhere, this transfer downwards is also combined with a criticism of the traditional priestly elites. From them are taken over not only notions of a good life (in a modified form), but also the means of criticizing priestly exclusiveness.

The priestly *relaxations of taboos* (i.e. the right of priests to transgress some taboos which beyond question apply to laity) are themselves used as arguments against cultic norms. Already in Mark, the freedom to pluck ears of corn on the sabbath is justified by a reference to the behaviour of King David and Abiathar the priest (Mark 2.23–28), although David did not break any sabbath when he ate the shewbread and the ears of corn in the field were certainly rather different from the shewbread in the temple. The decisive point is rather that just as King David claimed a priestly privilege for himself, so now the followers of Jesus are claming a royal right when they break the sabbath. Thus they appropriate priestly privileges in order to abolish priestly cultic requirements. Matthew has further reinforced the relevant arguments (Matt. 12.1ff.): he refers to the priests serving in the temple in the sabbath. If priests work on the sabbath, so too may Christians, especially if they do so for mercy, which is to be estimated even higher than sacrifice. The way in which he justifies the second breach of the sabbath, the healing of a man with a paralysed hand on the sabbath, is illuminating. Matthew adds (going beyond Mark) the argument about the sheep which has fallen into a pit which was also current in other Jewish debates on the sabbath: 'What man of you, if he has one sheep and it falls into a pit on the sabbath, will not lay hold of it and lift it out?' (Matt. 12.11). He quite naturally presupposes people who have only one sheep. Here the thought is of poor and little people. These very people are expected to have the self-confidence of priests and kings!

This free and provocative way of dealing with cultic norms and taboos necessarily led to a conflict with the priests, especially as with his prophecy about the temple Jesus was directly attacking the cultic centre of Judaism. It was not so much the rival sages (the scribes of the Pharisees) as the Sadducean priests who were active in his death. And even after his death they remained the most important opponents of the Jesus movement in Judaism.

The attitude to the temple can also illustrate the last tendency in this change of value that we shall be discussing: the denationalization of holiness. Probably nowhere else was the power to define holiness so massively effective as in the exclusion of Gentiles from the temple. Inscriptions were set up in the inner temple precinct which threatened any foreigner with death if he entered it.[9] The threat was formulated in an obscure way: 'Anyone will be the cause of his own death.' Even spontaneous lynch justice was not completely excluded by such threats, since it was left open who would do the killing. The first Christians (perhaps on the basis of Jesus' sayings about the pilgrimage of the nations) hoped that this exclusion of the Gentiles from the temple would be done away with in the near future. In the account of the cleansing of the temple in Mark, Jesus expresses this hope in words from Isa. 56.7. The temple is to become a place of prayer for all peoples (Mark 11.17). Perhaps Stephen expressed this hope. It could underlie the charge that he expected Jesus to destroy the temple and that there would be a change in the customs of Moses (Acts 6.14) 'in the future' (!). If Stephen had prophesied that in the future the Gentiles would no longer be excluded from the temple, it would be understandable why he should be done away with by lynch justice (in an extended interpretation of the warning inscriptions). Later it is insinuated that Paul brought a Gentile into the inner precinct of the temple (Acts 21.28), and he too almost become a victim of lynch law and mob assassination. The accusation against Paul certainly contains a grain of truth, in that the opening up of the temple was in line with the hopes of Paul and other Christians. Paul himself could understand his missionary work among the Gentiles as a priestly service, 'so that the offering of the Gentiles may be acceptable, sanctified by the Holy Spirit' (Rom. 15.16). In fact he wants to bring the Gentiles to the temple. All nations are to be sanctified. There is no doubt that in primitive Christianity the commandment 'to be holy as God is holy' is extended to all nations (I Peter 1.14ff.; 2.10).

Finally, the unity of myth and ethic, ethic and community, can also be demonstrated in the way in which the priestly values of cleanness and holiness are dealt with. If priestly power consists in defining and 'distributing' salvation and damnation, holiness and unholiness, sin and righteousness, a radical change begins to take place in this distribution. The Gentiles who were previously 'unclean' become 'clean', and sinners become righteous. In the Christ myth this is matched by the way in which Christ, though innocent, takes guilt upon himself; though righteous, suffers; though blessed, bears the curse. Here, as elsewhere, Paul 'codes' the transvaluation of other values in the images of his christology and in so doing vividly conceptualizes them. The Christ event comes about in a change not just of power and weakness, riches and poverty, wisdom and folly, but also of sin and righteousness:

> For in Christ God was reconciling the world to himself . . . For our sake he made him to be sin who knew no sin, so that in him we might become the righteousness of God (II Cor. 5.19, 21).

Or,

> Christ redeemed us from the curse of the law, having become a curse for us . . . that in Christ Jesus the blessing of Abraham might come upon the Gentiles (Gal. 3.13f.).

Paul did not yet develop such a christology systematically in cultic categories. However, elements of it are already to be found in him: the notion of the vicarious atoning death, the priestly intercession of the risen Christ before God (Rom. 8.14).

We first find the consistent construction of such a christology in cultic categories in the letter to the Hebrews. It combines two basic images, on the one hand the world as a temple where Christ has entered into the holy of holies, and on the other history as the way taken by the people of God through the wilderness. The combination of the two images (distributed between the so-called dogmatic and parenetic parts of Hebrews) results in a transformation of cultic values. The high priest Christ indeed entered the holy of holies only once, but he is no longer the only one to do so; rather, he paves the way for all members of the people of God. He has become their forerunner (Heb. 6.20) and paves a new way once and for all (10.20). In the cosmic world there are no longer any priests and lay people. All find access to the holy of holies – the destination of the great journey through history: the city of the living God (12.22). This way is paved by Christ, but is followed by observing ethics. The sacrifice of the heavenly high priest takes place in order to cleanse 'our conscience from dead works' (9.9). The cult above all makes freedom from a 'bad conscience' possible (10.22). For everyone, the way to God is by proving their faith as persistence and loyalty on the journey through history. This community has given up a priestly hierarchy: beside the one high priest there is no room for a multiplicity of priests on earth. All this is part of the old world which is passing away.

I am coming to the end of my comments on the ethic of primitive Christianity. Once again I shall briefly sum up its basic notions before adding some thoughts to take us further. The ethic of primitive

Christianity is governed by two basic values: love of neighbour and humility. These two basic values cross the boundaries between the inside group and the outside group in a radicalized love of neighbour which is also shown to the stranger, the enemy and the sinner. And they cross boundaries between those above and those below in a radicalized humility which is not expected of those below but of those above, becoming the criterion for power and authority. In their vertical and horizontal dimensions these two movements which cross boundaries also shape the rest of the primitive Christian ethic, i.e. the ideas about dealing with power and possessions, with wisdom and holiness. Here there is always a 'descent' of upper-class values which crosses an 'ascent' of lower-class values; and here there is always a denationalization of ideas of values which are associated with an acculturation to the ethic of other peoples.

The social *Sitz im Leben* of such an ethic is groups in which upper class and lower class, Jews and Gentiles, are brought nearer together than elsewhere in society, not only in ethical discourse but also in real life – even if in the case of the upper class this is only its periphery, which has no political power. These groups with a social composition developed into separate entities alongside the two decisive social units of ancient society: the family and the state, or *oikos* and *polis*. Although these groups arose out of a movement of itinerant charismatics with a deviant life and a radical ethic, relatively quickly they became independent of their origins and developed a very much more moderate ethic. But the original radicality had an effect even on this moderate ethic. For the communities had to set themselves apart from the other basic social units of ancient society. The tensions with the family remained. In a counter-reaction to this ethic which was critical of the family, an ethic was even developed which provided marked support for the family (the 'patriarchalism of love' in the Christian household, the purest form of which we find in the Deutero-Paulines). But it is no coincidence that even now, the sayings of Jesus which were critical of the family continued to be handed down and used: in cases of conflict the community insisted that its convictions should be established in the face of family ties. Similarly, tensions with the state remained. In reactions to tendencies which were critical of the state an ethic was developed which showed an emphatic loyalty to the state (in Rom. 13.1–7 and I Peter 2.13–17). But here too it is no coincidence that the traditions which were critical of the state remained alive. For in cases of conflict, here too the community expected its members to refuse to obey the state because of their convictions: martyrdom was a possibility, though a rare one. And it brought great 'prestige' in the community.

The social dynamic behind the primitive Christian ethic, which has been sketched out here only in a cursory way, can perhaps explain the basic tension in this ethic: the tension between the radicalization of demand and of grace, between the intensification of norms and the relaxation of norms. This tension is ultimately suggested in its very structure: those who radicalize love of neighbour and humility towards others need only intensify these same values in their own case – and then they arrive at an ethic of accepting themselves despite all their failings. But how does this radicalization which is presupposed come about? Certainly all ethical norms have a tendency in this direction. In everyday life they are realized only with compromises. In themselves they give rise to a tension between ideal and real ethics. But there must be specific conditions for the radical ethic to establish itself.

In my view the radicalization of demands can come about when ordinary people set out to imitate and to realize aristocratic values – above all when they take over not only the substance of norms but also the aristocratic self-confidence which is associated with them: the claim to do things better than others. The first Christians in fact wanted to achieve a better righteousness (Matt. 5.20). They wanted to be the 'light of the world' and the 'salt of the earth' (Matt. 5.13–16). They wanted to outdo the consensus of their environment even where they shared it: it was their claim to be not only good but better people. One senses this even in the more 'conservative' admonitions to households. Their aim was slaves who were not only good but blameless; wives and citizens who were not only good but exemplary. Communities in which groups from the upper and lower classes come closer together than elsewhere in society offer an opportunity for this 'transfer downwards of upper-class values' and the radicalization of ethics associated with it. But the stimulus for this may have begun in the original movement of homeless itinerant charismatics. Those who stand outside all social ties can also cross the boundaries of status and hierarchy in their thought and patterns of life.

The radicalization of grace may similarly have had a *Sitz im Leben* and a function in the life of primitive Christian communities. For these newly founded communities had to develop a high degree of integration – the more so, the more they sought to bring together people of quite different origins, cultures and status. This integration would have been *a priori* doomed to failure had not the radical demands for pro-social behaviour been balanced out by an ethic which took into account the actuality of human failure and found ways of making it possible for the failures and the guilty to live together in self-respect. The primitive Christian groups could only manage to live out their radical ethic of love and humility because they had an equally radical conviction about the worth of the sinner: the sinner is loved by God. Redemption is for sinners. They have the opportunity of a new beginning.

This co-existence of a radical ethic with average normal human life was made easier by the primitive Christian ethic being inscribed in the Christ event (as a unique combination of history and myth). It was not just an ethic of human behaviour but the ethic of divine action. God himself brought about that transvaluation of values which made power weakness, possessions poverty, wisdom folly, and sin righteousness. All this took place in the fate of the Son of God – and especially through his way to the cross and the surmounting of it in the resurrection. As soon as the primitive Christian ethic was firmly inscribed on this myth, no one could remove it from the basic convictions of primitive Christianity. However far the real life of the community might be removed from it, time and again it could be renewed from this basic narrative of the Christian faith.

Here the basic tension of the primitive Christian ethic recurs in the basic mytho-historical narrative of primitive Christianity. On the one hand is all the solemnity of the entrance of a divine being into this world. This being truly became human: flesh, suffering and death. In him the deity itself assumed finite human reality, remote from God. This is matched by the radicalization of grace, the acceptance of that which is incomplete, contrary to norms and lost. On the other hand, an element in this basic mytho-historical narrative is the surmounting of this reality through the resurrection. With it, a new reality begins in the midst of the old world. With it, new possibilities of behaviour are opened up. This is matched by the radicalization of the demands which underlie the vision of a new human being who is utterly steeped in love of God and neighbour, who makes fellow human beings the object neither of sexual desire nor unbridled aggression, who in the struggle over opportunities in life disseminates peace and renounces lies and deception, and who is motivated by the beatitude 'Blessed are the pure in heart, for they shall see God' (Matt. 5.8).

A personal comment to end with. Some people may find my account of the primitive Christian ethic too 'positive'. Hasn't a modern man introduced his notions of a universalizable ethic into the analysis of primitive Christianity? Perhaps one may ask in return: is a modern ethic orientated on communicative understanding perhaps more governed by Chrsitian traditions than it realizes itself? Do we perhaps find some primitive Christian values so close to our own because we have already been shaped by them beforehand? We can leave the answer open. Primitive Christianity is not just an ethic. It is myth and rite. And here (particularly in ritual sign language) we encounter notions which offend us and are un-modern. And possibly the point of the rites of primitive Christianity lies precisely here.

Part Three: The Ritual Sign Language of Primitive Christianity

7

The Origin of the Primitive Christian Sacraments from Symbolic Actions

Religions are sign systems which point to an ultimate reality. Anyone who studies the history of primitive Christian religion can follow the origin of a new religious sign system or, to use another image, the building of a semiotic cathedral. Its building material consists of signs in three different forms: a narrative sign language consisting of myth and history; a prescriptive sign language consisting of imperatives and evaluations; and a ritual sign language consisting of the primitive Christian sacraments of baptism and eucharist. Now that I have discussed the narrative and prescriptive sign language of primitive Christianity, in the next two chapters I shall turn to ritual sign language. It is often underestimated, because only a few texts in the New Testament relate to the primitive Christian rites. But it is of great importance: the whole sign system of a religion is concentrated in its rites.

The first question is: What is a rite?

The primary context in which a religious myth is enacted is the rite, not the ethic.[1] But what is a rite? Rites are actions which become an end in themselves through the strict observance of rules. Therefore they need not in themselves have a religious character. Profane everyday life is also full of rites. However, even secularized ceremonies often have a religious aura. Why? There are two reasons for this.

First, the strict way in which rites are regulated makes them independent of space and time, so that they can be repeated as an identical sequence of actions. They are privileged means of structuring space and time by periodical festivals and of preserving or renewing human identity through changes by rites of passage. By their identity, which is independent of space and time, they make it possible to 'drop out' of the flow of transitoriness. Human beings therefore experience them time and again as an incursion of the 'eternal' into time.

Second, rites are freed from everyday purposiveness. An action which is an end in itself can become the symbolic depiction of the ultimate reality which in itself is purpose, meaning and value – and on which everything that has meaning and value depends. What is intrinsically regular is hallowed in the rite. Therefore rites are privileged means of depicting the basic rules of social life which are unconditionally binding on all – in other words, what makes possible a co-ordination of action, thought and feeling.

As a regulated action which is an end in itself, the rite is opposed to chaos, i.e. the embodiment of that which is unregulated, disordered, disruptive. Rites serve to ward off chaos. Or to put it another way: they serve to ward off anxiety that hurls people into psychological chaos[2] and aggression that hurls people into social chaos. However, this warding off of chaos or of the dissolution of the existing order does not take place by suppressing chaos but by admitting it in ritualized form. V. Turner[3] has demonstrated that rites of transition take people out of the old structures of society into a kind of counter-society in which an anti-structure to the old structures of society is built up. And they take people on from this threshold into a new order. What is true of rites of transition is also true of other rites which recur periodically. One need think only of the Saturnalia, in which social order is stood on its head and for the moment slaves become masters. So we must reckon to find in all rites elements of an anti-order which allows precisely that which is otherwise taboo. We are not to conclude from this that the group concerned wants to do away with these taboos. On the contrary. The abolition of them which is allowed by ritual (and is often indicated only symbolically) is intended to reinforce the taboos and unconditional norms in reality. Psychological and social chaos is not overcome by suppressing and displacing the chaotic but by admitting it and shaping it in ritual form.

Primitive Christian religion offers a unique opportunity to study a ritual sign language. For here it comes into being to some degree 'before our eyes'. In it we can observe a powerful transformation of traditional ritual language. At that time sacrifices were being replaced by a new ritual language – in Judaism, in some philosophical currents and in primitive Christianity. For very different reasons, the sacrificial cult was coming to an end in these three spheres.

First of all I shall describe this new, ritual sign language as a whole. After that I shall pursue its origin and change.

1. The ritual sign language of primitive Christianity as a whole

Above, I emphasized two privileged functions of the rite: the structuring of time and the co-ordination of people. Both functions are present in any rite. But sometimes they become particularly clear in special 'rites'. So too in baptism and the eucharist.[4]

Biographical time is structured by rites of passage, i.e. rites of transformation which accompany life from the cradle to the grave at the decisive points of transition. Some of these rites become detached from standardized biographical contexts. That is true of the rites of initiation into the mystery cults, which are based on a free decision to join a cult and are not attached to a particular period in life. Primitive Christian baptism is such a rite of initiation.

By contrast, in antiquity the co-ordination of life in communities took place above all through sacrifices, especially where they were connected with shared meals. The primitive Christian eucharist is beyond doubt a rite of integration (constantly repeated) which renews the cohesion of the community.

Thus the two basic functions of the rite emerge one-sidedly in each of the two sacraments of primitive Christianity. Baptism is the decisive rite of initiation; the eucharist the central rite of integration. However, it would be wrong to limit the new ritual sign language to these two rites. Rather, alongside them we find many other non-verbal gestures and actions which have ritual character. Through this sign language important parts of the body take on a semantic quality:

In the laying on of hands the *hands* take on the significance of depicting the communication of the Spirit at baptism in a symbolic way. Through this every Christian is given an exalted status. Therefore it is not surprising that the laying on of hands takes on a special function in the ordination of individual office-holders (I Tim.4.14; II Tim.1.6), quite apart from the fact that it also plays an important role in healings.

The *feet* are the centre of the rite of foot-washing (John 13.1ff.). This rite is attached to a gesture of hospitality. By washing one another's feet the followers of Jesus symbolize their 'humility', i.e. the renunciation of domination. On the other side the gesture of 'shaking off the dust' from one's feet is a rite of ritual separation and distancing when hospitality is refused (cf. Luke 10.10–12 par.).

The *head* could have played a special role in anointing (Mark 14.3). However, in principle the whole body can be anointed.

The *mouth* is incorporated into ritual sign language in the 'holy kiss' (cf. I Cor. 16.20; II Cor. 13.12; Rom. 16.16; I Peter 5.14). The gesture speaks for itself: it symbolizes the brotherly and sisterly care of Christians for one another.

The *tongue* also becomes the organ of a ritual sign language. Speaking with tongues (or glossolalia) is a ritualizing of language. The tongue is released from the burden of its specific everyday purposes and finds a new use as an emotional expression of ecstatic states (cf. I Cor. 12.10, 30; 13.1; 14.1ff.). Granted, the stream of sounds is not fixed in a ritualized way. But the appearance of glossolalia in a liturgical framework shows the way towards a fixed ritualization.

Like any language, ritual sign language in its different elements forms a 'whole' which takes on its significance through a network of oppositions, antonyms and synonyms, and in which some parts are more central than others. The ritual sign system as a whole could express the fact that in primitive Christian religion the whole body is to become a 'living sacrifice' which is to be offered in everyday life. However, the central significance of baptism and eucharist requires a special explanation, especially as both rites established themselves in the face of others. Thus in Corinth there were efforts to make glossolalia the decisive ritual of initiation: in that case only those who spoke with tongues would be Christians in the real sense. And in the Gospel of John a tendency becomes evident to deepen, if not replace, the eucharist by foot-washing. However, neither of these tendencies became established. That must be because of a special characteristic of baptism and eucharist, possibly a characteristic that both have in common. Baptism and eucharist stand out by virtue of a common semantic reference: both are (at a secondary stage) interpreted in terms of the death of Christ. Baptism originally took place for the forgiveness of sins in the face of the imminent judgment. After Romans 6 it becomes baptism into the death of Christ. The eucharist came into being from the meals that Jesus held. In remembrance of the last supper it is related to the death of Jesus. And this death of Jesus in turn takes the place of the ancient sacrifices.

If ritual sign language is a whole, one could say that as a whole it is opposed to the current traditional sign language. It replaces the traditional sacrifices. It does so in its central rites by being closely connected with the one sacrifice of Jesus on the cross. In addition it does so in a wealth of non-verbal ritual gestures, as a result of which the whole body becomes the 'sacrifice' – with hand, foot, mouth and tongue. From this one can conjecture that at least in part the ritual sign language of primitive Christianity has become functionally equivalent to the traditional sacrifices.

Unfortunately we are a long way from having a general theory of sacrifice.[5] But in my view many aspects in existing theories of sacrifice can be integrated if we see sacrificial praxis as a symbolic depiction of the fact that life lives at the expense of other life – and at the same time as an attempt to exploit this connection for oneself: one's own life is to be safeguarded and enriched by the surrender or even destruction of another life. Here it is important to remember that the conflict over opportunities in life displays itself in direct aggression only in extreme cases (therefore it is one-sided to interpret sacrifice only as an expression of aggression and a means of coping with aggression). It also shows itself in competition for the same goods. It shows itself in the one-sided exchange of goods in which one party has a disproportionate advantage. Even if sacrifice is understood only as gift and not as vicarious killing, it can thus express the universal 'law of life' that life lives at the expense of other life.

The new ritual sign language of primitive Christianity could then indicate that something has changed in the attitude to this 'struggle over life'. The replacement of the many sacrifices which repeat themselves by the one sacrifice of Christ could mean that the enhancement of life does not just take place through the surrender of other life and at the cost of other life; gain in life can also come about through the offering of one's own life in favour of other life.

If this (provisional) assumption is correct, the primitive Christian sacraments, closely connected as they were with the sacrificial death of Christ, would express a central statement of the ethics and the basic narrative of primitive Christianity. Precisely because of that, we must ask critically: How did this close connection between Christ's sacrificial death and the primitive Christian sacraments come about?

As I have said, a general theory of sacrifice is a utopia. The proponents of the various theories of sacrifice often resort to a postulated 'primal scene' at the beginning of sacrificial practice.[6] Thus reference is made to the need in hunting cultures to direct all aggression towards one goal – and to exclude it from the hunting group itself; it is also necessary to expiate the encroachment on life and to share the booty fairly. The sacrificial ritual fulfils these functions. But the motives present at the origin of sacrifice do not of themselves explain why agrarian cultures and urban societies continued to sacrifice for centuries.

In my view the end of sacrificial practice in the centuries around the beginning of our era offers an opportunity for knowledge. This has the advantage that here we do not need to postulate events in a dim prehistory, but can interpret existing sources. Of course the results for the sacrificial cult which arise from a study of its end are as limited in their way as those which begin from a postulated situation of its origin. But they too can lay claim to becoming part of a general theory of sacrifice.

In the case of primitive Christianity, a second feature has to be added: the one sacrifice of Jesus which replaces the many sacrifices was originally a unique martyrdom. Only at a secondary stage did it come to be connected with repeated ritual processes. And these rites, too, were understood only in the making. Only subsequently did symbolic actions with an eschatological orientation, namely a baptism with water as a forerunner of baptism with the Spirit and a meal as forerunner of the eschatological meal, become representations of a past saving event: a baptism into the death of

Jesus and a eucharist in memory of his death. In what follows I shall describe this process, i.e. first of all the stage of the origin of the new rites in which they are not yet related to the death of Jesus; then their transformation and reinterpretation as a result of this death – which in its interpretation as a sacrificial death contributed to the ending of the practice of sacrifice.

2. Symbolic actions as preliminary forms of the sacraments

My thesis is that the new ritual sign language of primitive Christianity arose out of prophetic symbolic actions with which John the Baptist and Jesus delivered their eschatological message (in latent opposition to the traditional rites).[7] These symbolic actions became primitive Christian sacraments only by their secondary reference to the fate of Jesus, especially his death, interpreted as a sacrifice. Only in connection with this interpretation in terms of the death of Jesus did they have the power to supersede the traditional sacrifices. Only now did they become a new ritual sign language which functionally and semiotically was the equivalent of sacrifice. Four features characterize the original symbolic actions:

1. *Their reference to history.* As a rule, rites are age-old. They have been practised from primal times. And they are practised because they have already been there since primal times. However, the two sacraments of primitive Christianity, baptism and eucharist, came into being in the midst of time – or more precisely in the historical present of Christianity, which experienced it as an end-time. With his baptism, John the Baptist creatively formed a new rite by making the repeated washings of Judaism a single baptism on the threshold of the end-time. Jesus provided the stimulus for the eucharist by associating with his person at his last supper (through words which can no longer be reconstructed clearly) meals which were held repeatedly. The primitive Christian rites are 'new' rites, the origin of which does not lie in a mythical primal time, rites which do not go back to gods, but to two charismatic figures of the recent past.

2. *Their prophetic character.* Both rites are originally prophetic symbolic actions, i.e. patterns of action focussed on a unique situation, the primary purpose of which is to convey a message. Both baptism and the meals which Jesus held contain a message in a unique situation – the last situation in the face of the imminent end. And neither can be separated from its 'founder'.

Baptism is performed only by John the Baptist. It is not self-baptism. Even John's disciple Jesus refrained from practising it. For him it is exclusively John's baptism. This exclusive attachment to a single individual can be explained only by the character of baptism as a prophetic symbolic action. For such actions are always associated with the singular message of a particular prophet.[8]

The same is true of the meals which Jesus held. They contain the message that God's salvation is present through fellowship with toll collectors and sinners – with a view to an eschatological feast in the kingdom of God to which people (including Gentiles, i.e. 'sinners') will stream from all points of the compass. Fellowship with toll collectors and sinners is bound up with the person of Jesus – and therefore Jesus causes offence by this fellowship!

3. *Their liminal character.* Both original forms of primitive Christian sacraments are threshold rituals. However, in contrast to the rites of passage they are the crossing, not of a biographical threshold, but of the threshold to a new world. John's baptism with water precedes the eschatological baptism with spirit and fire. Jesus' meals are held in anticipation of the eschatological feast in the kingdom of God. At the last supper Jesus could have deliberately looked forward to this eschatological feast: he expects that the next meal he celebrates will be in the kingdom of God (after it has dawned, Mark 14.25). As in other 'threshold rituals', here too we find a certain 'anti-structure' to the traditional forms of life. Baptism contains a latent opposition to the temple cult.[9] For the cult offered forgiveness of sins – for the individual in sacrifices of expiation for guilt, for the whole people on the Day of Atonement. In proclaiming only a few miles from the temple that all have to submit to the baptism for the forgiveness of sins, John the Baptist is implicitly passing a vote of no confidence in the effectiveness of the traditional rites of atonement. In celebrating a meal with his disciples in Passover week (in my view before the Passover feast proper), to which he gives a special significance by words of interpretation, Jesus is implicitly, perhaps even deliberately, constructing an alternative to the temple ritual.[10]

4. *Their everyday symbolism.* The original forms of the sacrament do not contain any elaborate ritual ornaments. They do not have the complicated liturgical aesthetics of established rituals.[11] Simple and everyday happenings are given symbolic content. This symbolic content can easily be picked up: it is obvious that a 'washing' in a transferred sense can also indicate a 'cleansing' from sins. It is equally obvious that an earthly meal can be anticipation of the eschatological joy at the banquet in the end time. There is an iconic relationship between everyday performance and the symbolic sense.

There may be a certain irony in the fact that symbolic actions which were associated with a unique situation and a unique prophetic figure became repeated actions which were performed by interchangeable occupants of a 'role' and became bound up with offices. A singular message became an institution. Yet this development is not quite as paradoxical as it first seems. Originally a confrontation with the imminent end was associated with the symbolic actions. Because this end no longer left any time to prove repentance by good deeds and a changed way of life, John the Baptist (or, as one must say within a religious language, God through his prophets) offered a symbolic substitute action. The earnestness of the renunciation of the old life was credibly documented by the preceding public self-accusation, and the will to a new life was equally credibly documented by the acceptance of baptism. The promise of new life was given to those who repented and was assured them through baptism. Jesus' last supper might also have been celebrated in high eschatological excitement. Jesus was probably uncertain to the last whether the conflict with the temple aristocracy would escalate to the point at which he would be removed by force or whether the kingdom of God would break in before that. So he can say that he will not drink of the fruit of the vine until he drinks it new in the kingdom of God (Mark 14.25). Both symbolic actions thus bear the traces of a confrontation with the end which is about to break in immediately – and precisely for that reason sacraments could develop from them in which, in the experience of the participants, eternity keeps breaking into 'time'. But before this development came about, the two symbolic actions had to be reinterpreted.

3. The transformation of prophetic symbolic actions into primitive Christian sacraments

The transformation of the prophetic symbolic actions of John the Baptist and Jesus into the primitive Christian sacraments is bound up with a threefold change: 1. a new interpretation of these symbolic actions in terms of the death of Jesus; 2. a dissolution of the iconic relationship between external performance and religious significance; and 3. an accentuation of the violations of liminal taboos in the ritual sphere. These three developments are closely connected, indeed are fundamentally given by the reference to the death of Jesus. With this reference, new rites which have a mysterious effect come into being, and in my view only because of this mysterious force do they have the power really to replace the old ritual sign language of sacrifice.

(a) The reference to the death of Jesus

The secondary reference of a symbolic action to the death of Jesus can be demonstrated most clearly in the case of baptism. John the Baptist baptizes in the expectation of a stronger one who will bring in a final baptism with fire and spirit. Primitive Christianity identified this stronger one with Jesus. He was the one who baptized with spirit. The experiences of the Spirit in the community were seen as living proof that he was filling his followers with divine power from heaven. The baptism associated with the bestowing of the Spirit is attached to the 'name of Jesus' (Matt. 28.19; Acts 2.38; etc.). This might have been meant as a reference to the exalted Christ whose authority was being claimed in baptism. But soon the earthly Jesus also had to be included. For baptism was associated with the promise of the forgiveness of sins, and an early consensus in primitive Christianity was that the forgiveness of sins was brought about by the expiatory death of Jesus (cf. I Cor. 15.3–5). Thus there was an intrinsic necessity for baptism for the forgiveness of sins in the name of Jesus also to be related to the death of Jesus. The salvation gained through the death of Jesus was promised to the baptized through baptism as the forgiveness of sins – through a verbal promise and the non-verbal language of the rite. For that reason, however, baptism was not yet interpreted as a symbolic dying and being buried with Christ. This last step was made possible from two directions. On the one hand, in pagan initiation rites of the time we find a symbolic dramatization of the experience of death (e.g. in the Isis cult). In analogy to that, baptism came to be interpreted as a symbolic experience of death.[12] On the other hand, at a very early stage 'baptism' became a metaphor for the danger of death and the experience of death (Mark 10.38).

However, such a traditio-historical reconstruction of the development leading up to the interpretation of baptism as death is not in itself sufficient explanation of the impact of this interpretation. This new radical interpretation of baptism must be seen in connection with a far-reaching change in the *Sitz im Leben* of baptism. John's baptism called on Israelites to repent. This repentance was a return to God the Father, not a radical new beginning. Israel was to realize what it had always been meant to be by God. In the case of Gentiles, however, baptism was something different. Gentiles were not to 'return' to the gods of their fathers but to make a radical break with them in order to serve the one and only God. For them, the break with their previous life was far deeper – as deep as the gulf between death and life. Here the association of baptism with death and (new) life immediately becomes evident, especially since in Judaism the conversion to Jewish faith was already interpreted as a new creation from death (Joseph and Asenath

8.10; 15.5). So it is no coincidence that this interpretation of baptism in terms of death first occurs with Paul, the great missionary to the Gentiles. His preaching required more than repentance of the Gentiles; it required a break with the past and a far-reaching transformation of their whole being. It required no less than for the old man to die with Christ, in order to begin a completely new life with Christ.

It is harder to demonstrate that the eucharist, too, was associated with the death of Jesus only at a secondary stage. The only thing that is certain is that Jesus' last supper was preceded by other communal meals which contained a symbolic surplus of meaning. If ever, it was only at his last supper that Jesus made a link between the supper and his death. In that case the secondary interpretation of the 'supper' in terms of death would go right back to the historical Jesus. All the words of institution contain this reference. But it could also be the case that this reference to Jesus' death was created only after Easter and on the basis of his execution which had taken place in the meantime. In support of this is the fact that forms of eucharist with no reference to Jesus' death have been preserved in the Didache (9/10), and that in the Gospel of John the foot-washing has replaced the eucharist and at the last supper there is no interpretation of the elements in terms of the death of Jesus (although John knows this, cf. 6.52–58). Finally, this could be suggested by the fact that the association of the last supper with the promise of the new covenant (thus in the Pauline variant of the words of institution) is one of the earliest interpretations of the eucharist. Now in Jeremiah the 'new covenant' is not associated with sacrifices. In Hebrews it is even deliberately opposed to the sacrifices of the Old Testament (cf. Heb. 8.7ff.; 10.16f.).

This reference to Jesus' death brings out something that had already been present in the meals which Jesus had held: the forgiveness of sins. The earthly Jesus' acceptance of the sinner at table on an equal footing now becomes possible – after his death and in his absence – by a reference to his 'dying for us' (and by the conviction of his mysterious presence at the eucharist as the risen Christ).

Thus in both symbolic actions, the reference to the death of Jesus reinforces the link with the forgiveness of sins. In this way the forgiveness of sins becomes independent of the historical John, with whom baptism had hitherto exclusively been associated; and it becomes independent of the earthly Jesus, whose presence at meals represented something of the real presence of salvation for those round the table. By being grounded in the death of Jesus, forgiveness of sins remains accessible even after his death. Only now can these rites be repeated, detached from the charismatic figures who once 'invented' them. Only now is their original reference to the future supplemented by a 'reference to the past', to the death of Jesus. They no longer look towards the future judgment (like baptism) or the future salvation (like the meals that Jesus held), but communicate salvation which has already been realized – by the death of Jesus which has taken place in the meantime. And this communication becomes something extremely mysterious. That leads to the next point.

(b) The tension between outward performance and religious significance

With the new reference to the death of Jesus the new rites lose their visible or 'iconic' character: a cleansing with water can be understood as an image of an inner cleansing, and earthly food as an image of the heavenly meal. By contrast, the primitive Christian sacraments have an aniconic character. That can be demonstrated in the case of both sacraments.

Baptism is not an image of the death of Jesus.[13] On the one hand it did not take place through the immersion of the whole person in the water, which could still have been interpreted as a symbolic death through drowning. Rather, the candidates stood in the water and had water poured over them. In an analogous way, indeed, baptism with the Spirit was expected as an 'outpouring' of the Holy Spirit. The first depictions of baptism do not have any complete immersion of the whole body. As a rule, the baptismal fonts which have been preserved are far too small for that. Moreover the reduction of baptism to a threefold sprinkling with water in the Didache (7.1–3) if there is no running or standing water in the neighbourhood is best explained if people were baptized by being sprinkled with water or having it poured on them, and not by immersion. On the other hand we have to note that a depiction of the relationship to the death of Jesus would not have arisen as a result of immersion either. For Jesus did not die by drowning. He was crucified and buried. We know of no 'water burials'. There is no visible relationship between baptism and a burial (cf. Rom. 6.4). The association between the ritual event and its religious significance here is no longer iconic, but is communicated by narrative: by telling of Jesus' death, i.e. by words. The religious imagination of believers creates the link between the external aspect of the sacrament and its inner meaning. As a result, the significance of faith increases.

The same increase in aniconic abstraction can also be noted in the case of the eucharist. There is a pictorial analogy between the earthly meal and the heavenly meal; however, there is none between the consumption of bread and wine and the crucifixion of Jesus. Bread is not flesh. When 'this is my body' is said, the semantic tension between the signifier and the signified (between the bread and the body of Christ) is unmistakable. It would already be less in the case of flesh. Therefore the words can only be meant in a transferred or 'metaphorical' sense. Indeed it is evident that bread is not 'body'. The same can be said of the wine. Nowhere in primitive Christian texts is importance attached to the wine being red, so that the colour would create an iconic relationship to the blood.[14] The eucharist, too, has an aniconic character. The link to the significance of the ritual is made by the religious imagination: through thoughts of Jesus' last supper and the passion. The passion is present through words and through the imaginative power of faith. Word and faith bridge the drifting apart of signifier and signified.

This drifting apart of outward celebration and religious meaning becomes even clearer if we use sacrifice as a comparison. By comparison with sacrifice the eucharist is 'unbloody', undramatic, close to everyday life and not at all ceremonial in its outward celebration. But things are different when we come to its religious significance. The association with the death of Jesus arouses recollections of an archaic rite: human sacrifice. The clear decrease in violence in outward celebration – no animal is slaughtered, no blood flows – is matched by an increase in violence in the narrative that goes with the eucharist, which is present in the religious imagination. That leads to a last point.

(c) The crossing of taboo thresholds in the primitive Christian sacraments

The association of symbolic actions with the death of Jesus crosses taboo thresholds in a form which has the protection of ritual: not through the external performance of the actions, since they are quite harmless – eating and drinking, washing and pouring – but in the religious imagination which is associated with them.

That is quite evident in the case of the eucharist. The association made in the 'narrative' of the eucharist with a crucified man whose death is represented ritually already crosses the great threshold of inhibitions about human sacrifice, albeit only in the imagination and not in reality. For the historical death of Jesus on the cross was not a ritual sacrifice – and what is done in eucharistic ritual is not killing. Only through the association of the death of Jesus with the eucharist did a unique martyrdom become the foundation of a rite that was repeated. But that in itself was not enough. The identification of bread and wine with the body and blood of Christ touches on one of the deepest taboos in Judaism: the prohibition against consuming blood. Blood was regarded as the seat of life (Gen. 9.4ff.). By avoiding the consumption of any blood in the way they slaughtered animals, Jews respected the life in the animals they slaughtered. The invitation to drink blood – even if this was a 'symbolic' way of drinking blood – would necessarily have been an abomination to any Jew. Sometimes this violation of the blood taboo was an argument for denying that the historical Jesus spoke the words of institution. But that is merely to shift the problem, for the words of institution were already current in Jewish Christianity. Paul, a Jewish Christian, knows them and hands them on. The Gospel of Matthew reproduces them despite its Jewish Christian stamp. Quite apart from that, there remains the scandal that as symbolic cannibalism, consuming the body and blood of Christ touches on a taboo for anyone, whether Jew or non-Jew. Nevertheless the eucharist was established precisely by these 'anti-moral' interpretations! Here we should remember that there is nothing unusual about contravening norms and taboos in a protected space which is set apart by ritual. On the contrary, if one particularly wants to reinforce order in life, one can stage the corresponding anti-order in a rite. Here a group is in no way showing its immorality. Rather, the offence against the taboo allowed in the virtual space of the rite makes it possible to observe this taboo all the better in reality. The barbarism in the rite which is allowed in the imagination is a contribution towards overcoming the barbarism in everyday life, addressing the anti-social impulses, grasping them, and transforming them into pro-social motivation. They are worked on and transformed in ritual.

An obvious objection to this interpretation of the eucharist as a ritually staged transgression of a taboo is that only to modern sensibilities is there a transgression against a taboo here. Ancient people did not experience it as such. This objection can be countered. On the one hand, outsiders charged the early Christians with celebrating 'Thyestian' banquets – secret cannibalistic orgies.[15] The charge is unjustified. But it is based on a general ritual knowledge in antiquity that breaches of taboo are staged in religious celebrations. On the other hand, already at a very early stage Christians stated that the eucharist can potentially symbolize a crime. Paul warns the Corinthians: 'Whoever eats the bread or drinks the cup of the Lord in an unworthy manner will be guilty of profaning the body and blood of the Lord' (I Cor. 11.27). If the eucharist becomes an occasion for acting out social differences, then according to Paul it in fact becomes a 'crime', as though those taking part in the eucharist had killed Jesus himself. It is only its ritual shaping in the sense of Christian faith and Christian ethics that transforms this potential crime into a sacrament which conveys salvation.

At first glance the crossing of a taboo threshold seems less evident in the case of baptism. Here too the breach of such a liminal taboo begins only with the (secondary) interpretation of baptism in terms of death: strictly speaking, Paul does not identify baptism with death but with being buried.

Just as a burial is the socially valid confirmation of a death which has already taken place, so in Romans 6.3f. baptism as being buried with Christ is the external confirmation of an inner dying with Christ which is taking place, a process of which Paul can also speak independently of baptism (e.g. in Gal. 2.19f.).

A taboo is touched on with this metaphor of grave and burial. For Jews, graves are places of concentrated uncleanness. One has to keep well away from them. Even if they are decorated outside, inside they are full of 'bones and uncleanness' (Matt. 23.27). For that reason, houses must not be built on graves. Graves must be located away from the places where life is lived. Because the dead and corpses make people unclean, priests may take part in the burial only of their very closest relatives (cf. Lev. 21.1–4). The high priest is even forbidden to join in the mourning ceremonies for his mother and father, because he may not make himself unclean by their bodies (Lev. 21.11). Now in the primitive Christian interpretation of baptism it is precisely the grave, this unclean place, which becomes the place where the old man is overcome so that the new man may attain salvation. And here, too, we may presume that the stimulating effect of this on experience and behaviour lies precisely in the transgression of a taboo staged in ritual: with their whole experience, those who have been baptized have exposed themselves to a place of horror and uncleanness. They have suffered death in symbolic form and have not only survived this danger zone but come through it to salvation. This can bring freedom from the universal human fear of death. Here this death is not just regarded as the destiny of human nature but as the consequence of sin. The symbolic anticipation of death also provokes and overcomes a heightened consciousness of sin: 'For the one who has died (in baptism) has become free from sin' (Rom. 6.7).

However, in baptism the crossing of the taboo threshold is by no means as intensive as it is in the eucharist. For the question of cleanness and uncleanness does not involve moral taboos (as in the case of cannibalism and killing), but ritual taboos, which symbolize above all separation and distance. The uncleanness of human beings and things signalizes 'Don't touch me!' So it is not surprising if baptism above all overcomes anxieties about social contact and the limitations imposed by taboos. In Galatians Paul hands on a baptismal tradition according to which those baptized have put on Christ. For them, 'There is neither Jew nor Greek, there is neither slave nor free, there is neither male nor female; for you are all one in Christ Jesus' (Gal. 3.28). If one envisages how many taboos can be imposed to maintain the social differences mentioned here, one can judge the magnitude of the step towards overcoming such social taboos which has been taken by those who have been baptized. If as a first stage they have overcome such social taboos in baptism, in a second stage they will also be admitted to the eucharist, in which even more elementary moral taboos will be touched on.

However, all this does not serve to dissolve these taboos, but to internalize a deepened certainty of salvation and morality. How are we to imagine that? Or, to put it another way, what do the two sacraments produce? And how do they work? Of course within a theory of primitive Christian religion we cannot simply resort to the dogmatic patterns of explanation in traditional theology. But these patterns are a help, especially since often acute reflection has been set down in them. According to them, sacraments communicate salvation by bringing about through the combination of word and element a *verbum visible,* a non-verbal language which, if it is heard and accepted in faith, can effectively change people. If we adopt the formal categories of this sacramental theology, we can note a drifting apart of the elements and the words that go with them. What happens with the elements, with water, bread and wine, is an everyday, undramatic event without any violence. By comparison with the ritual sacrifices of antiquity there is a consistent reduction of violence here. But what is added by the word as the inner meaning of this event represents an extraordinary increase in imagined violence: baptism is a symbolic suicide voluntarily undertaken, and the eucharist is based on the killing of another human being. In my view the effectiveness of the sacraments is grounded in precisely this tension.

Baptism ritually stimulates the anxiety about one's becoming a victim which has to die – laden with its own sins as a result of which its *own* life is forfeit. Anxiety about existence and failure are here depicted, staged and ritually overcome, because for the baptized the grave and death, places occupied by anxiety, become the gateway to salvation. In the eucharist the guilty consciousness that all life lives at the expense of *other* life is ritually stimulated. It is kept alert by the notion that another person is being sacrificed for the believers, who appropriate this life which has been surrendered for them in the most primitive way – by a symbolic cannibalism. Thus baptism is about anxiety over sin and death in respect of one's own life (which like everything else can become a victim), but the eucharist is about guilt and anxiety about death in respect of the life of another (who is destroyed as a victim in our place). The rites express in an unacknowledged way the hidden anti-social nature of human beings. But they do so in order to change this anti-social human nature into motivation for pro-social behaviour. This obligation to pro-social behaviour is associated with both sacraments. That can be demonstrated briefly by means of primitive Christian texts.

In the case of the initiation rite of baptism the unanimous testimony of all texts is that through it human beings are changed in such a way as to 'walk in new life' (Rom. 6.4). Therefore ethical admonitions often take up the imagery of the theology of baptism: the contrast between the old man and the new man (Col. 3.9f.; Eph. 4.22–24), the bestowing of the spirit in baptism (I Cor. 6.11) or the 'bath of rebirth' (Titus 3.5). The external symbolism is focussed on a renewal: the water serves for cleansing, for separation from uncleanness. The baptismal candidates are clothed in a new garment: they put on Christ (Gal. 3.27). There is visible documentation for the whole community that they have made a break with their previous life.

In the case of the integration rite, the eucharist, what is done outwardly is in tension with the violent interpretations. For in the eucharist everyday food is divided equally. The external celebration of the eucharist itself demonstrates that life need not live at the expense of other life, but that all have their share. Therefore the eucharist, too, serves as an argument for furthering the solidarity of the community, probably most vividly in I Cor. 11.17ff. Some more prosperous members of the community have evidently displayed their status to shame the poor and either begun the common meal early or claimed better food for themselves. Paul sees this violation of equality as an offence against the meaning of the eucharist. The participants again become guilty of the death of Christ. We can 'translate' the situation by saying that they are again practising that life at the expense of other life which has become visible in the dying of one for all – and which is to be overcome by this dying.

The drifting apart of outward celebration (with an obvious everyday meaning) and religious meaning (which is orientated on the death of Christ) can go so far as to result in the two being separated. In the Gospel of John we have basically two eucharistic texts. First there is the eucharistic section in the discourse on the bread within the public first part of the Gospel of John, and then, as an introduction to the farewell discourses, which are not public, there is the narrative of the last supper with the foot-washing. The eucharistic text in John 6.51ff. emphasizes with unadorned clarity the barbarian overtones of the religious interpretation of the eucharist: 'Unless you eat (the term used here can also mean 'chew') the flesh of the Son of Man and drink his blood, you do not have eternal life in you' (6.53). But by the consumption of flesh and blood, Christ is in the believers and they are in him (6.56). However, this crude archaic and magical notion is detached from the outward celebration of the eucharist and associated with the miraculous distribution of the bread. In it Christ himself is eaten as the 'bread of life' – and in the context that clearly means that the revelation which is made possible through him is received. For 'bread' and 'food' are old images for wisdom. Therefore within this context the crudely magical eucharistic words can only have a spiritual significance. For 'it is the spirit which gives life, the flesh is of no avail; the words that I have spoken to you (i.e. the eucharistic words) are spirit and life' (John 6.63).

On the other side, in John 13 there is the description of a simple last supper without a profound religious interpretation of the elements. It stands precisely at the point where in accordance with the structure of the other Gospels we would expect the last supper. But the interpretation of this last meal is associated with an unassuming new ritual, the foot-washing. This shows that the real sense of the shared meal is mutual service and mutual love. This interpretation, which is given only in the circle of the disciples, is the real interpretation of the last supper for the Gospel of John, whether it puts it above the traditional interpretation (which is given in John 6.51ff.) and regards both as compatible, or wants to replace the old interpretation with this new one.

Thus the Gospel of John accords with our observation that the outward celebration and the inner religious meaning in the eucharist are in a dynamic tension with each other. The Gospel of John itself articulates this tension within one and the same Gospel. Elsewhere we often find a one-sided emphasis on the religious significance with an interpretation in terms of a human sacrifice appropriated by eating which is remote from everyday life (as e.g. in Paul), or a one-sided description of an everyday meal which is very close to everyday life, but in which there is no reference to the death of Jesus (Did. 9/10). The Gospel of John combines the two and sets them side by side, but clearly gives preference to the real aim of the sacraments: the creation and consolidation of a loving community of disciples of Jesus.

One important result is that it is only through reference to the death of Jesus that the symbolic actions created by Jesus and John become the mysterious primitive Christian sacraments of baptism and eucharist. Indeed the original symbolic actions were also in latent opposition to the traditional ritual sign language, which had its centre in the temple cult with its sacrifices. In competition with it, baptism offered forgiveness of sins, and the eucharist offered a shared meal based on a sacrifice. But such rival prophetic symbolic actions could not, and did not, seek to replace the traditional rites – nor were they understood in those terms either. The first Christians continued to take part in the temple cult. They in no way rejected sacrifices. But without any deliberate programme, as a result of three factors the traditional language of ritual was replaced and the sacrificial cult came to an end.

The first factor is the new *theological* interpretation of the original prophetic symbolic actions which has been worked out above. By being associated with Jesus' sacrificial death, the sacraments potentially became open to attracting the whole semantics of sacrifice and all its functions and becoming an equivalent to the sacrificial cult.

The second factor is to be seen in a *social* process. At a very early stage the first Christians accepted Gentiles as members with equal rights. In the 40s, at the Apostolic Council, they arrived at an agreement to grant them equal rights in the community. They required that these Gentile Christians should break radically with all pagan rites, but could not obtain access to the temple and its sacrifices for them, even if they dreamed of such access. Objectively the acceptance of Gentiles put the Christian communities under pressure (though they were probably not aware of it) to create a ritual sign language of their own, which covered all the semantics and all the functions of the traditional sign language and which could also replace, though not completely outdo, the temple and its sacrifices.

The third factor is a *political* event. In the Jewish War, in 70 CE the Jerusalem temple was destroyed. Jesus had foretold this in his prophecy about the temple. The Christians could understand this destruction of the temple as confirmation of their message. With the temple, the only place for legitimate sacrifice had disappeared. Therefore (after 70 CE) Jesus' message could be summed up in the Gospel of the Ebionites in his saying: 'I have come to do away with sacrifices; and if you do not cease from sacrificing, the wrath of God will not cease from you' (frag.6).

But the decisive factor was the conviction that Jesus had died a sacrificial death for all men and women once and for all, and that his death was made present and effective in the two sacraments. Only by being related to the death of Jesus does the tension between a reduction of violence in practice and an increase of violence in the imagination, which is characteristic of the primitive Christian rites, enter into them. But the interpretation of Jesus' death as a sacrificial death is only one of many interpretations in primitive Christianity. However, this very interpretation is extremely important. For there is much to suggest that only by being interpreted as a sacrificial death could the death of Jesus bring about an end to the centuries-old practice of sacrifice. Therefore we must once more investigate, even more intensively, the significance of this sacrificial death in the framework of primitive sign language. Above all we must ask why (according to the Letter to the Hebrews) it could bring about the end of sacrifice.

8

The Sacrificial Interpretation of the Death of Jesus and the End of Sacrifice

Different though the ancient religions and cults were, they had one axiom in common: the worship of a deity takes place through sacrifice. The first Christians offended against this axiom. They ceased to sacrifice. This was a revolution in the history of religion. But like many revolutions, this too is the result of a continuous development in which tendencies in the Judaism of the time (with analogies in the pagan world) were continued. So in the first part of this chapter I shall give a historical account of this *replacement of sacrifice*.

According to the primitive Christian self-understanding, this replacement of sacrifice was not fortuitous, but a consequence of the unique death of Jesus. His sacrificial death replaced all other sacrifices. Therefore in the second part I shall investigate how the first Christians interpreted this death – and what role its *interpretation as a sacrificial death* had in the framework of the manifold interpretations of his death.

In order to understand how this one sacrifice could replace the many sacrifices, we need to know what functions sacrifices performed in life. So a third part will be concerned with defining these functions, although this is almost impossible, given the many different *theories of sacrifice* in the study of religion.

Only then, in a fourth part, can we ask how far the new primitive Christian sign language offered *functional equivalents for the ritual sacrifices.* Here it will be important for us not to compare individual elements of this new sign language with the traditional sacrificial cult. Only the whole of primitive Christian religion could develop that power and dynamic which brought about the end of the practice of sacrifice.

1. The replacement of sacrifice in the primitive Christian period

When the primitive Christian groups detached themselves from the sacrificial cult, they were continuing an already existing development. There were voices critical of sacrifice in all the great religions.[1] The prophets had already castigated the contradiction between the pious practice of sacrifice and social injustice. In so doing they did not want to abolish sacrifice, but declared that a sacrificial cult without justice was invalid. So their critique of sacrifice was conditioned by their situation. Some psalms go even further. They express the thought that in principle God does not want any sacrifices, that God calls for the surrender of the whole person, which nothing can replace. So motifs from a critique of sacrifice, whether conditioned by the situation or fundamental, were already there in the Jewish tradition. After the forced interruption of the Jerusalem cult in the time of the Maccabees, they again came into play. After this desecration of the temple cult, more and more Jewish groups dissociated themselves from sacrificial worship.

The first group, which in fact ceased to participate in sacrificial worship, was that of the *Essenes*. They regarded the Jerusalem temple as desecrated. Josephus reports that they only sent dedicated gifts to it. That was not as yet a renunciation of sacrificial worship in principle. Hope for the resumption of a pure cult remained alive.[2]

The second group, which restricted sacrificial worship, was that of the *Samaritans*. After the destruction of their temple on Gerizim at the end of the second century BCE, here every year only the Passover lamb was slaughtered. So it is not fortuitous that the Johannine Christ speaks of worship in the 'spirit and in truth' in connection with Gerizim (John 4.24). Here too there was no renunciation of sacrificial worship in principle.[3]

The *movements of John the Baptist and Jesus* were an expression of a prophetic criticism of the temple. This is contained implicitly in the preaching of John the Baptist. The existing temple is impotent to offer effective forgiveness of sins. Only baptism offers this. This criticism of the temple becomes explicit in the preaching of Jesus – whether it was that he wanted to put a better sacrificial cult in its place or that in the eucharist he offered an alternative to it (conditioned by the situation). That is not yet a critique of sacrifice in principle. After Easter the first Christians took part in the Jerusalem temple cult (Acts 2.46; 21.26), but in baptism and eucharist they already had alternative rites.

The *Gentile Christians* took a further step towards cult without sacrifice. As they had separated from their old cults, they could no longer sacrifice in the framework these had provided. But at the same time, since they were uncircumcised, they had no access to the Jewish sacrificial cult in the temple. At that time the sacrificial interpretation of the death of Jesus became the substitute for all other sacrifices. Nevertheless this renunciation of sacrifice, too, was not yet a matter of principle. The first Gentile Christians probably hoped that one day the temple would be open to them and that then they too could take part in Jewish sacrificial worship.[4] In any case, the Jewish Christians continued to take part in sacrificial worship. A new situation began only with the destruction of the temple in AD 70.

As a result of this, Jews and Christians became the two largest groups in antiquity which no longer had any sacrifice. Granted, the Jews hoped for a rebuilding of the temple, but in fact they made themselves independent of the sacrificial cult. The study and practice of the Torah – above all the practice of works of love – became a complete substitute for sacrifice. Worship became worship through the word of God, following a long development which had previously taken place in the synagogues. But this renunciation of sacrificial worship, too, was not yet a mater of principle. The sacrificial laws continued to apply; they were studied and expounded, though they could no longer be practised.

Christianity first developed a renunciation of sacrificial worship in principle after the destruction of the temple. Only now, in the letter to the Hebrews, did the unique sacrifice of Jesus become the definitive replacement for all other ritual sacrifices.[5] In it Gentile Christian groups claimed, independently of the cult of the mother religion, to offer everything that other cults offered in antiquity. Certainly they had no priests on earth, but instead they had a high priest in heaven. They had no temples, but instead they had a cosmic temple which spanned heaven and earth. They had no sacrifices, but instead they had a high priest who sacrificed himself once for all for them and had thus revealed the barrenness of all other sacrifices. They had no divine images, but instead they worshipped the one who was the image of God – a reflection of his glory. In short, they offered everything that according to ancient understanding made up a religion (or better, a cult) – but in another, better and more complete way. After 70 the Jewish Christians, too, joined in this criticism of sacrifice in principle, in so doing going further than the other Jews. They knew that Jesus had prophesied the end of the temple. And after it was in fact destroyed, this prophecy was reinterpreted to mean that he had wanted to prepare the end of sacrificial worship. As we saw, in a Jewish-Christian Gospel Jesus summed up his mission like this: 'I have come to do away with sacrifices; and if you do not cease from sacrificing, the wrath of God will not cease from you' (Gospel of the Ebionites, frag.6). Moreover in the same Gospel we find references to vegetarianism, which is probably connected with the criticism of the bloody sacrifices.

Here these Jewish Christian groups met up with a fourth group, that of the *Neopythagoreans*.[6] These rejected bloody sacrifice because they supposed animals to have human souls, on the basis of their doctrine of the transmigration of souls. Because every animal sacrifice could potentially be a human sacrifice, it was rejected. By contrast, among the Christians the one human sacrifice replaced all animal sacrifices. Unfortunately we know very little about the Neopythagoreans' critique of sacrifice. It did not have a great effect on the pagan cults.

What is decisive is that around the beginning of the Christian era a violent break came about in the history of religion with the end of sacrifice. However, it did not happen all at once. Even in primitive Christianity it took place in small steps. The first Christians are only one among many other Jewish groups which distanced themselves from sacrifices. So the renunciation of sacrifice is in no way the great progress of Christianity compared with Judaism, but the result of a development within Judaism. It did not correspond to a deliberate programme. Rather, here too contingent factors like the destruction of the temple were of great significance. Only when that is clear can we say that only in Christianity was there a renunciation of sacrifice in principle which was largely put into practice. This characteristic distinguishes Christianity from all other Jewish groups which suspended the practice of sacrifice because of their situation. Renunciation of sacrifice which is consistently practised distinguishes Christianity from the philosophical critique of sacrifice in principle. Thus in what follows we can rightly limit ourselves to primitive Christianity.

According to the primitive Christian self-understanding, this critique of sacrifice in principle is bound up with the sacrificial death of Jesus. But the interpretation of the death of Jesus as a sacrificial death is not the only interpretation. It stands alongside others. So we can ask: did it really bring about the end of sacrifice, or is it only the subsequent expression of a distancing from sacrifices which already existed? Is it really the final overcoming of this sacrificial thought? Or is it rather a revival of sacrificial thought – by reverting to a form of sacrifice long outgrown, namely human sacrifice? So in a second section we shall concern ourselves with the sacrificial interpretation of the death of Jesus.

2. The sacrificial interpretation of the death of Jesus

It is improbable that the historical Jesus deliberately sought his death as a sacrificial death. The disciples experienced his execution as a catastrophe; they were not prepared for it. Only subsequently did they give it a meaning – and here too the multiplicity of interpretations still betrays the traumatic challenge of a terrible death. It had to be coped with in a whole series of new attempts and images. Nevertheless there was already a basis for the later sacrificial interpretation of his death in the life of the historical Jesus.

(a) Self-stigmatization in the life and teaching of Jesus

In his life Jesus deliberately adopted the role of despised outsiders. He was an itinerant preacher – without income, without a home, without family. He sat at the same table as people who were morally despised. He deliberately scorned some traditions, as is shown by the sabbath conflicts and his indifference to questions of purity. And this inevitably attracted both criticism and aggression. Sociologists see such a deliberate adoption of roles in which one has no chance of finding recognition as an act of self-stigmatization.[7]

In parallel to this he put forward teachings which deliberately call for self-stigmatization as a form of behaviour. The invitation to divert aggression by offering the right cheek when struck on the left is such teaching: it aims at deliberately exposing oneself to the aggression of others (Matt. 5.39). The requirement for his followers to break with their families and to omit to perform acts of basic family piety like burying one's father is similarly an invitation to self-stigmatization (Matt. 8.21).

We should also reflect that Jesus and his disciples grew up in a society with an already developed culture of self-stigmatization. The symbolic actions of the prophets were in part demonstrative self-stigmatizations. When Isaiah wandered around naked, and when Hosea married a prostitute and an adulteress, they were assuming demonstratively despised roles to present their messages. The same is true of John the Baptist. His ascetic life – his asceticism about the place where he lived, his food and clothing – is similarly an element of self-stigmatization, as is the public self-accusation which he requires before baptism: the confession of sins.

Today we recognize deliberate self-stigmatization as an important strategy in cultural change. The prevailing values are shaken by being diverted through a demonstrative adoption of roles which are seen in a negative light. Someone who deliberately practises a form of behaviour that is rejected indicates to his environment that the values underlying the rejection and contempt are false. The one who has the gift of finding adherents here can bring about a change of values – even in the face of a majority consensus about these values. We call this capacity for finding adherents even in the face of the opposition of the environment charisma. Charismatics can make self-stigmatization the pivot of changes. Even their martyrdom can serve as further justification of them. It puts the opponents of the charismatic massively in the wrong.

Jesus was a charismatic whose charisma was also grounded in the strategy of self-stigmatizing conduct. That he deliberately risked death fits into the overall picture of his life. He had the fate of John the Baptist before his eyes. He had to reckon with a violent end. However, it is highly improbable that Jesus himself already expressed this readiness for self-stigmatization in the image of a 'sacrificial death'. It is probable that he hoped to the end that God would bring about the kingdom which he proclaimed and that the cup of death would pass from him (cf. Mark 14.36).

(b) The interpretations of the death of Jesus in primitive Christianity

After Easter, the death of Jesus was interpreted in a wealth of different images.[8] Basically, two types of interpretations can be distinguished, which I shall distinguish with the terminology of the Reformers: Jesus' death was regarded as *exemplum* and as *sacramentum*. Here the term *exemplum* needs to be extended. What is meant is that Jesus is a model of divine and human behaviour. The death of Jesus shows the way in which God acts in principle – and in which the human being should bear his action and his suffering. As *exemplum*, the death of Jesus takes on its significance by analogy with divine and human conduct. By contrast, the term *sacramentum* covers all interpretations in which the death of Jesus overcomes disaster, whether by removing the disruption of an order or restoring a relationship; here the restoration of an order can be described as 'expiation' and the restoration of a relationship as 'reconciliation'.

In what follows, in addition to the distinction between *exemplum* and *sacramentum*, the integration of the resurrection into these different interpretations needs to be noted. This is particularly important for the interpretation of sacrifice. For the resurrection of the sacrificed living being is not part of traditional animal sacrifice. The resurrection a priori contains a surplus over and above the metaphor of sacrifice.

(i) The death of Jesus as an exemplum of divine and human behaviour

A *first* way of coping with the death of Jesus is to recognize it as a '*necessary event*' – as necessary and as little capable of being influenced by human beings as any event willed by God (cf. Mark 8.31; 14.21). Prophecies and pointers in the biblical writings made it possible to recognize this divine necessity of the death of Jesus (cf. Mark 14.49; Luke 24.44ff.). Belief in the resurrection could easily be integrated into this interpretation by understanding the resurrection of Jesus, too, as a necessary event – prophesied in the scriptures (I Cor. 15.3). The death of Jesus thus became a passage to glory: 'Was it not necessary that the Christ should suffer these things and enter into his glory?' (Luke 24.26). The death of Jesus could only take on significance for salvation as such a 'passage' – and then if Christ was understood as a 'pioneer' (cf. Heb. 6.20), who has paved the way to heaven for those who follow him (Heb. 10.20).

A *second* possibility of interpreting the death of Jesus consisted in putting him in the chain of *martyr prophets*.[9] Prophets had already come up against resistance in delivering their message and had paid for it with their lives. The parable of the husbandmen expresses this notion of the violent death of the prophets in the form of an allegory (Mark 12.1ff.; cf. I Thess. 2.15). Jesus was one of the many prophets who were to lose their lives in Jerusalem (QLuke 13.34; 11.49–51). The resurrection of Jesus could be integrated into this notion by being understood as a contrast event to the death of the martyr. In the parable of the husbandmen it is attached secondarily to the parable by the scriptural quotation about the rejected stone which God makes the cornerstone (Ps. 118.22 = Mark 12.10). A similar contrast scheme stamps the summaries in Acts (2.22ff.; 4.10f.; 10.39ff.; 13.27ff.). A variant on the contrast between rejection by human beings and election by God is the contrast between the self-humiliation of Jesus and exaltation by God contained in the Philippians hymn (2.6–11). Here it is also important that the death can gain saving significance only through the integration of the resurrection: that God chooses the lowly and the rejected becomes an image of hope for all those who are humiliated and rejected (cf. I Cor. 1.18ff.), towards whom God acts in an analogous way.

A *third* interpretation of the death of Jesus is to be found where he is spoken of with the motifs of the *suffering of the righteous man*.[10] Jesus' suffering is then depicted with the help of quotations from the psalms of lamentation or the suffering servant of God. He becomes the model for the suffering of Christians. Implicitly the passion narrative contains such an interpretation; its explicit form can be found above all in I Peter (2.21–25). Christians may feel bound up with Christ in their suffering. In this interpretation too, Jesus becomes significant for salvation only through the incorporation of the resurrection: then suffering and death with Christ are surpassed by the hope of a new life. The death of Jesus itself has no saving character in this context. It is the overcoming of death which first creates salvation: the σὺν Χριστῷ ('with Christ') notion of a conformity between Christ and Christians is clearly distinct from ὑπέρ notions, involving an 'on behalf of'. Christians do not die his death for others. Their dying with Christ in no way brings about salvation.

(ii) The death of Christ as a sacramentum for expiation and reconciliation

In the interpretations of the death of Jesus as *sacramentum* there is no analogy between the action of God, Christ and human beings; rather, there is particular stress on the distance between God and human beings. The ordinance of 'righteousness' which binds God and human beings has been deeply disturbed by human unrighteousness and its restoration calls for 'expiation'. The personal relationship between God and human beings has even become 'enmity', so that God and human beings have to be 'reconciled'.

Here the interpretation of death as *expiation* stands in first place.[11] When Paul writes in Rom. 3.25 that Christ 'was put forward by God as an expiation by his blood', he is referring to the vicarious suffering of God's wrath at all sinners which God has previously sworn (Rom. 3.18–20). God's sentence of annihilation has been passed on the crucified Jesus. We cannot keep this notion, which is so offensive to modern men and women, at arm's length from what the New Testament says about expiation. Only because of it can Paul say that through Jesus' death God has condemned 'sin in his flesh' (Rom. 8.3), or that Jesus became a 'curse' (Gal. 3.13) and 'sin' (II Cor. 5.21) for us. Here we find a notion which does not necessarily include the resurrection. For Paul does not continue his remarks by saying that Christ became an 'expiation', a 'curse' or 'sin' so that he could overcome this disaster through the resurrection. Rather, the statement about his death is followed by a positive statement for believers. For them his expiatory death is righteousness (Rom. 3.26; II Cor. 5.21) and blessing (Gal. 3.14). Nevertheless the resurrection can be included, most vividly in the picture of heavenly worship in Hebrews. Jesus sacrifices himself as an expiatory sacrifice in order to be able to go through the event to the holy of holies. His way into heaven is the real act which brings salvation. But we also find an extension of the notion of expiation to the resurrection in Paul, as we shall see.

A second related notion is that of *ransom*. Whereas the interpretation in terms of expiation is about liberation from a danger which threatens from God himself, the notion of ransom suggests, rather, liberation from an alien power. The vivid basic situation is ransom from enemies.[12] Here it remains obscure whether God's anger at sin has become an independent hostile force or whether the thought is in fact of demonic powers independent of God (Gal. 3.3; 4.5; I Cor. 6.19f.; 7.22; Mark 10.45, etc.). Nor does this notion of ransom, either, necessarily exclude the resurrection, but can be extended by it. Then the resurrection becomes the victory over the hostile powers, as for example in the notion that the risen Christ has destroyed the accusation that they published, disarmed his enemies and triumphed over them (Col. 2.14). Or that he has 'redeemed' Christians by his blood and made them kings and priests – and reigns for eternity (Rev. 1.4–20). However, this notion of *Jesus victor* can also occur independently of the notion of ransom (cf. I Peter 3.18–22; John 12.27–33).

In a third variant the 'dying for sins' or 'for us' can also appear as *loving surrender*. Whereas the dominant element in the notion of expiation (in the narrower sense) is the threat from God's anger, and in the 'ransom notion' the threat from other powers, now the death of Jesus appears as an expression of the love of God. Here most of all the resurrection can appear as a constitutive element of the event of redemption. Love aims at reconciliation between parties at enmity with each other, [13] but reconciliation presupposes its existence. Where Paul speaks of a loving surrender of the life of Jesus he always speaks of Jesus' resurrection (cf. esp. Rom. 6.5ff.; 8.31ff.; II Cor. 5.14ff.). But in Paul this integration of the resurrection into the saving event goes even further, as I shall now show.

(c) The incorporation of the resurrection into the interpretation of the death of Jesus

We saw that in the interpretation of the death of Jesus as *exemplum* this death first became a saving death by the incorporation of the resurrection. But in the interpretation of Jesus' death as *sacramentum* it takes on independent significance for salvation. In my view it is characteristic of Paul that he also introduces the constitutive significance of the resurrection for the saving event from the *exemplum* interpretations into his interpretation of it as *sacramentum* and so continues a line of development within Judaism.

Thus in I Cor. 15.3ff. quotes a traditional formula which says: 'Christ died for our sins in accordance with the scriptures, and was buried; he was raised on the third day in accordance with the Scriptures and appeared to Peter, then to the twelve.' Here initially only the death appears as the basis for the overcoming of sins. But in his argument with those in Corinth who deny the resurrection Paul insists: if Christ had not risen, you would still be in your sins (15.17). His death alone does not bring about a forgiveness of sins.

So in II Corinthians he can extend the formulae about 'dying for us' to the resurrection. For Christ has 'died for all, that those who live might live no longer for themselves but for him who for them died and has been raised' (II Cor. 5.15). Here the 'for them' relates grammatically not only to the dying but also to the being raised. Christ and the Christians experience both together. Paul says: if one has died for all, 'all have died'. In that case salvation can consist only in all, like Christ, attaining to new life. Now it is no coincidence that precisely in this context Paul speaks of the death of Jesus as an expression of the love of God (II Cor. 5.14) and of 'reconciliation' (II Cor. 5.18f.). It is a reconciliation which is focussed on the life of both partners in the saving event.

In Romans we then find three beginnings of a conceptual differentiation between the saving significance of the cross and the resurrection. At all events the cross has power to expiate (previous) sins. But something new is added with the resurrection:

1. If the death of Jesus represents forgiveness of sins for the *past*, the resurrection brings about the overcoming of sins for the *present and the future*. This is the sense in which we are to understand the (traditional?) formula in Rom. 4.25, which speaks of Christ as the one 'who was put to death for our trespasses and raised for our justification'.[14]

2. If the death of Christ brought reconciliation for *this life*, the resurrection (or the life) of Christ brings deliverance for *eternal life*, i.e. in the eschatological future. Romans 5.10 is to be understood in this sense: 'For if while we were still enemies we were reconciled to God by the death of his Son, much more, now that we are reconciled, shall we be saved by his life.' In this context too we find the notion of the death of Jesus as loving surrender (Rom. 5.8) and of 'reconciliation' as the aim of the saving event (Rom. 5.10f.).

3. If the death of Christ is the overcoming of sins by the love of God, the resurrection leads to the intercession of the exalted Christ at the right hand of God. So no one can accuse Christians before God's judgment. Thus we read in Rom. 8.34: 'Who is to condemn? It is Christ Jesus who died, yes, who was raised from the dead, who is at the right hand of God, who indeed intercedes for us.'

Thus in Paul the extension of the saving significance of Jesus' death to the resurrection is unmistakable. Where he not only takes up traditional formulae but constructs his own formulations, he makes it unmistakably clear that God brings about salvation not through killing but through death *and* resurrection, i.e. through the overcoming of death.

The further question now is whether here the traditional logic of sacrifice is abandoned[15] or whether this extension had not already for a long time been potentially contained within it. In this connection we shall look at expiation in the Old Testament, inside and outside the cult.[16]

In the Old Testament sacrificial *cult* there was perhaps a parallel to resurrection, a symbolic preservation of life beyond death. In the expiatory sacrifice it is not the killing of the animal which is the act of expiation but the blood rites, in which the blood of the slaughtered animal is smeared on the horns of the altar and poured at the foot of the altar. This blood-rite restores life to the deity in symbolic form: the blood is the seat of life. So expiation is not brought about by the death itself, but by the contact between the 'living substance' of the sacrificial animal and the deity after the death of the sacrificial animal. Is this an indication of an awareness that in the end it is not the destruction of life that brings salvation, but its preservation and rescue? However, by way of qualification it has to be said that the preservation of life relates to life generally, and not to the life of the individual sacrificial animal. That remains dead. No rites of restoring life – in other sacrificial cults as well – can disguise this fact.

That is confirmed by a look at the few cases of *expiatory actions outside a cultic context*. According to Deuteronomy 21.1–9 the inhabitants of a place in which an unsolved murder had been committed can make expiation by killing a cow. Its neck is broken over a stream with running water. The representatives of the place wash their hands. The water symbolically washes away the blood and thus the blood-guilt. So the blood is not preserved, nor is it given back to the deity. Rather, it is removed. The same logic appears at a second point. After the apostasy of Israel to the 'golden calf' Moses pleads for forgiveness of sins for the people and offers his life as an expiation: 'But now – if you will forgive their sin – and if not, blot me, I pray you, out of the book which you have written' (Ex. 32.30–32). The book of life is meant here. Moses does not bring expiation by remaining in this book but by being removed from it. It is the surrender of life, not the saving of life, that brings expiation. It is significant that this offer of the surrender of a human life in expiation is not accepted by God. The notion of expiation by surrendering life occurs only on the periphery of the Old Testament. It is fundamentally alien to it.

The fact that this notion occurs in Judaism in the post-Old Testament period – and becomes a central element in the interpretation of the death of Jesus in primitive Christianity – goes back to Hellenistic influences.[17] There, in the Greek world, there is often evidence of the notion of one person dying for another. Alcestis, who dies for her husband, is a well-known example. In the pagan world the possibility that this death for another includes the return from death of the person sacrificing himself or herself is a priori excluded. On the contrary, his or her death is final.[18]

Moreover the notion of vicarious dying entered the biblical world from its pagan environment. It is characteristic that in the few passages in which it occurs, it is always bound up with the hope of a new life. That also applies to the earliest passage, the Servant Song in Deutero-Isaiah. The servant of

God who sacrifices himself is promised life (in some sense): 'When he makes himself an offering for sin, he shall see his offspring and live long . . .' (Isa. 53.10).

In II Maccabees, the hope that the death of the martyrs will assuage God's anger at the people is bound up with that death. Granted, this is not yet the notion of a death as expiation for others. For the martyrs explicitly confess that they are dying for their own sins (II Macc. 7.32). There is no transfer of cultic sacrificial terminology to their death. Nevertheless, a saving effect for others is attributed to their death (in the form of an intercessory prayer). But already in these first beginnings of an interpretation of the death of martyrs as expiation, death is seen in the light of the resurrection hope. Alongside the book of Daniel, II Maccabees is one of the earliest witnesses to the resurrection hope (cf. II Macc. 7.9, 14, etc.). In contrast to the pagan world, here too the death is only accepted as a saving death for others when it is seen in the light of the promise of life.

That is even more the case in IV Maccabees. There the martyr Eleazar gives his death the significance of an expiatory sacrifice: 'Be gracious to your people. Let the punishment that we take upon ourselves be enough. Make my blood a sacrifice of purification for them, and take my life as a substitute for their life' (IV Macc. 6.28f.; cf. 17.20–22). Before the second summarizing interpretation of the death of the martyrs as an expiatory death, it is then explicitly emphasized that the martyrs 'now stand by God's throne and live in eternal bliss' (IV Macc. 17.18). Only after that is their death interpreted as a substitute action for the sins of the people. Granted, the hope of bodily resurrection is replaced by the hope of eternal life (15.3) and 'immortality' (14.5; 16.13). But there is no mistaking the fact that the interpretation of the death of the martyrs as an expiation only begins in Judaism, together with the hope of a restoration of their lives. At the end of IV Maccabees the author makes God himself say, 'I will kill, and I will make alive . . .' (IV Macc. 18.19).

Summary We can draw a provisional conclusion: according to the self-understanding of primitive Christianity, sacrificial practice was ended by the one and only sacrificial death of Jesus. But this sacrificial death is extended by the resurrection which overcomes death. That is something new by comparison with both the Old Testament sacrificial cult and the pagan notion of the expiatory death of human beings, but it corresponds to a tendency in Judaism. Judaism could imagine that a death could bring salvation only if there was the prospect of a restoration to life. God does not create salvation by killing but by overcoming death, and that also applies to expiatory death. Our further question now is: how far could this modified sacrificial interpretation of the death and resurrection of Jesus replace the traditional sacrifices? How is this replacement of sacrifices to be explained? Explanations in terms of intention are not enough. For the first Christians did not a priori have the intention of putting an end to sacrifice. They certainly criticized the cult and the temple; but there must have been something more than such an intention for them to be able to radicalize their criticism of the cult so that it became a repudiation of sacrifice in principle, and then carry it through. A functional view can provide a better explanation.

3. The functions of traditional sacrifice

The basic notion of a functional view is that new ritual forms must have fulfilled the functions of the sacrificial cult better. The sacrificial cult could only have died out when something that people had done for centuries, namely sacrifice to the gods – along with all the anxieties and wishes, obligations and obsessions which were at work in the sacrificial cult – were better satisfied than before by new religious forms of expression. In short, there was a quest for new forms of religious expression which were functionally equivalent to the traditional sacrifices. In order to define the functions of traditional sacrifice, we need a general theory of sacrifice. Unfortunately, however, there isn't one. There is only a confusing abundance of different theories. The whole undertaking is almost impossible. So I shall begin with some methodological provisos. They are meant to make it clear that I am aware of possible dangers in the explanation that I shall attempt to sketch out in what follows.

(a) Methodological reflections

General theories of sacrifice seek to be applicable to a multitude of ritual actions which are summarized under the term sacrifice. The first question to be put to them is: is there such a thing as 'sacrifice' as a universal phenomenon? Isn't the summary of all 'sacrifices' under a general term a highly artificial construct?[19] In addition, general theories of sacrifice set out to explain why people sacrifice, i.e. basically why they once began to sacrifice. Some of these theories of sacrifice reach back to a primal scene in the mists of prehistory: they may suggest a parricide in the primal horde (Sigmund Freud) or the situation in a horde of hunters (Walter Burkert). But one simple reason will never tell us why people once began to sacrifice. We have no sources for this grey prehistory. We can only make intelligent guesses.

However, there is a better way. Granted, we have no sources from primeval times to indicate why people first began to sacrifice. But we do have sources from the time in which they ceased to sacrifice. In terms of sources this period is privileged. But why shouldn't this also apply to the issue itself? Why shouldn't the end of the sacrificial cult offer just as privileged an opportunity of knowledge as the beginning? Of course this end initially allows us only to draw conclusions about the reason why people ended the sacrifices in which they engaged at that time. If we interpret sacrificial practice in terms of its end, we certainly run the risk of overvaluing these motives and projecting them back on to the preceding period. Let us discuss two instances:

1. One characteristic of post-exilic sacrificial practice is the new understanding of the whole of sacrificial practice in terms of *the notion of expiation*. Ultimately the whole cult serves to expiate transgressions. Now how far may we generalize this motive from the post-exilic period? Did the notion of expiation which emerged at that time simply bring to the surface what was already latent in every sacrifice? Wasn't any ritual slaughtering an encroachment on life? And doesn't its expression in ritual always amount to an act of expiation? I do not in fact exclude the possibility that the whole earlier practice of sacrifice can be illuminated from its penultimate stage. In that case the *hamartiocentric* interpretation of sacrifice which emerges only at the end of the development of the Israelite sacrificial cult would contain an element of truth for the interpretation of all sacrifices.

2. The same is now true of the end of sacrifice in primitive Christianity. If the first Christians replaced all sacrifices by a human sacrifice of a particular kind – namely that of a victim of human aggression or an *aggression sacrifice* – we can perhaps conclude from this for all previous sacrifices that if this one human sacrifice could take the place of all animal sacrifices, then these animal sacrifices had always already taken the place of human sacrifice. But that is to put strong emphasis on an aggressive element in sacrifices which is not evident to direct observation. One would be equally justified in emphasizing the festal atmosphere of joy. For sacrifices were communal feasts. Or one could emphasize their aesthetic character. Sacrifices were *Gesamtkunstwerke*, complete works of art. General theories of sacrifice which interpret sacrifice above all as a symbolizing and working through of aggression are therefore open to the suspicion of being a disguised *christocentric* interpretation of all sacrifice – in terms of the one and final sacrifice. From an unconscious christocentric perspective, here perhaps aggressive elements are already read into the Old Testament cult which are not (manifestly) present in it – for example when the relationship of those who sacrifice to the slaughtered animals is interpreted as one of representation and not just as the transference of guilt. But does that tell

against the element of truth in this interpretation of sacrifice which is also gained from the end of sacrifice? Of course here, too, there is the danger of over-valuing this element.

It may have become clear that to concentrate sacrifice on a sacrifice of expiation and a sacrifice of aggression corresponds to a particular historical development of sacrifice in the biblical sphere. Transfers to other sacrifices are possible only in so far as there, too, there is clearly a demonstrable (or at least a latent) place for coping with inter-personal aggression and expiating inter-personal breaches. We must also take other motives into account. The interpretation of sacrifice in terms of its end thus carries with it methodological dangers of projection on to the past. But it is also an opportunity to open up, in the light of the end, some traits which hitherto had been latent

After these methodological provisos we can attempt to define the functions of sacrifice according to the different theories, and then ask what could have taken its place.

(b) The functions of sacrifice

The different theories of sacrifice can be divided into three major groups: theories of gift see it as the act of making a gift to the deity; theories of communion see it as an act which binds together the community involved in the sacrifice (which in some instances also includes the gods and the sacrificial animal); and theories of aggression see it as an act of destroying the material sacrificed.

According to the *gift theories*, sacrifices change the relationship between God and human beings. Just as human beings attempt to win over the heads of their clans by gifts, so according to this earliest sacrificial theory they also attempt to win over the gods for themselves (Edward Burnett Taylor, 1832–1917).[20] The gift theory can be combined with a dynamistic theory of sacrifice: the power of the gods can be activated in favour of those offering sacrifice through sacrificial gifts (Gerhardus van der Leeuw, 1890–1950).[21] To be able to activate divine power for themselves, those offering sacrifice must cross the boundary between profane and sacred. There must be mediation between the two spheres. But the threshold between the profane and the sacred is particularly high. Here mediation takes place through the annihilation of the sacrificial gift (thus the mediator theory of H. Hubert, 1872–1927 and Marcel Mauss, 1872–1950).[22] One quite general feature stands out from all these theories: sacrifices are gifts to gods from which people hope for something positive. One may add the conjecture that sacrifices always take the place of the person sacrificing.

With them the person (vicariously) offers a piece of himself. Every gift is a piece of self-surrender.

By contrast, the *communion theories* emphasize the establishment of a deep bond through feeding on the animal that has been sacrificed. The gods receive their gifts only as a fiction. They are left just a few parts of the sacrificial animal – not even the best, so that rationalists in antiquity could speak of cheating the gods of sacrifices. Most of the sacrifice was consumed in a joyful communal meal. The classic communion theory (that of William Robertson Smith, 1845–1898)[23] assumed that here people felt a kinship with the deity and the animal. The gods were the ancestors of the tribes, and the sacrificial animal was the totem animal of the clan – similarly an ancestor from which one was descended, so that in the form of the animal one ultimately appropriated the power of the deity. We need not share these complicated assumptions to accept that sacrifices create community among people. They regulate the distribution of food. They represent in a real and at the same time symbolic way how scarce commodities are to be shared. If in sacrifice the self is surrendered to a higher power as a gift, in the communion of the sacrifice the others involved (sometimes also gods and animals) become part of the self – and the latent conflict in sharing is done away with. In the festal fellowship of the sacrifice all are 'one'.

By contrast, the *aggression theories* see sacrifices above all as rituals for the assimilation and overcoming of aggression. Freud's classic theory belongs here.[24] According to them, sacrifices are obsessive rituals in which people pay off a dark primal debt through parricide. The sacrificial animal stands vicariously for the father of the primal horde. In the ritual consumption of this animal, on the one hand the primal guilt is obsessively acted out (and therefore must constantly be repeated) and is atoned for. René Girard[25] offers a more general variant of this theory: not only the father but any desirable object leads to conflict, because desire is imitated – and two people cannot possess the same desired object at once. They must necessarily get involved in conflict. Sacrifices free a society for this structural conflict by directing aggression towards a scapegoat. Here in the end all sacrifices are interpreted according to the model of the scapegoat ritual, although this is quite certainly not a typical sacrifice. Walter Burkert developed a much more sophisticated theory of aggression.[26] The hunting groups of the Stone Age faced a great social challenge. They had to stimulate their aggression in order to direct it towards the prey, and at the same time strictly limit this aggression in order to direct it away from people who were to cooperate in the hunt and in distributing the booty. We need not subscribe to the individual elements of these theories either. But one thing about them is plausible: something is always destroyed in sacrificing. Parts or the whole are eliminated and removed from shared consumption. This introduces an element of aggression – in those early times even more than in our experience. For at that time animals were closer partners with human beings than they are today. And here too in the elimination of the sacrificial animal, those offering sacrifice distance themselves from a part of themselves. If the sacrificial animal is removed, it takes with it that which human beings want to remove from their midst and their lives.

The different historical manifestations of sacrifice have the function of gift, communion and aggression in varying ways.[27] The gift character emerges in offerings of first fruits, the communion character in communal sacrifices with feasts, and the function of coping with aggression in the scapegoat ritual. In many types of sacrifice, elements of all three functions are combined. Here the sacrifices choose from three possibilities of increasing their own chances when chances in life are short. Either one activates the power of a stronger one to one's own advantage, in which case the sacrifice is a gift to this stronger one. Or one foists the damage that one must otherwise suffer oneself on a weaker one, in which case the sacrifice is the aggressive sacrifice of a defenceless victim. Or one shares the opportunities in life between rivals by social rules. In that case the sacrifice becomes a communion sacrifice.

Here the self of those who sacrifice gains power either by 'surrender' to a stronger one to which it submits itself (as in the gift sacrifice), or by separating from what burdens it in foisting the burden vicariously on a weaker living being (as in the aggression sacrifice), or by identifying itself with equally strong fellow human beings, or producing the fiction of such equality in which all receive their due (as in the communion sacrifice). In that case sacrifices would be symbolic representations of the fight for opportunities in life. They document the human knowledge, fed by much observation, that life lives at the expense of other life. The weaker seeks the help of the stronger; the stronger suppresses the weaker; those of approximately equal strength strive to regulate the sharing of commodities. Sacrifices represent these ways of coping with life in symbolic form and at the same time attempt to influence this struggle in life positively. Now if so decisive a change as the end of traditional sacrifices takes place in the sign language of primitive Christianity, that would indicate that something fundamental has changed in attitudes to the struggle in life. But what? Did the first Christians perhaps simply hope to have even greater means of power in this primeval battle in life as a result of new rites? In other words: what functions in life did the new rites exercise?

4. Primitive Christian sign language as a functional equivalent of the traditional sacrifices

If the traditional sacrifices are no longer necessary in primitive Christianity, other elements of religion must have taken over their function. Now primitive Christianity developed a new sign system. Among various approaches towards a new ritual sign language, two sacraments established themselves: baptism and eucharist. Both arose out of symbolic sign actions which only later were connected with the basic primitive Christian narrative of the death and resurrection of Jesus. And both associated themselves with different sacrificial metaphors which describe the behaviour of Christians – their ethic. So all in all we have elements from three forms of religious expression which took the place of the old sacrifices:

1. Baptism and eucharist as new *rites*;
2. A new basic narrative (a *myth*) of the death and resurrection of Jesus and
3. An *ethic* which can be described by the metaphor of sacrifice: the sacrifice of praise, mutual help, the sacrifice of the martyr.

I now want to claim that no single element in this new religious sign language itself had the power to replace the traditional sacrifices. The elements needed to be combined. The combination of these different elements together took over the three traditional functions of sacrifice.

(*a*) *Gift sacrifice*. Baptism is a symbolic surrender of the whole life to God. Grounded in it is the surrender by Christians not only of individual gifts but of their whole lives to God as a 'living sacrifice' (Rom. 12.2). With baptism they activate a superior power for themselves, the power of the Holy Spirit, which dynamistically provides protection against hostile powers and makes a new life possible. With baptism they also cross a boundary between death and life: the boundary from sinful life to life in the presence of God. And here too this 'mediation' took place in the symbolic destruction of sacrifice: baptism is a symbolic death – an annihilation which through participation in the power of the resurrection leads over a threshold into a new life which is wholly consecrated to God (Rom. 6.1ff.). So the functional equivalent to the function of gift in sacrifice in primitive Christianity is baptism, but in conjunction with the basic narrative of death and resurrection and with an ethical sacrificial metaphor of the surrender of life.

(*b*) *Communion sacrifice*. The eucharist unmistakably fulfils a second function of traditional sacrifice. It forms a communion. The notion of equality is central here. Paul sees the whole significance of the eucharist endangered when social differences emerge in the course of it. Where equal distribution of the gifts of life is no longer performed in reality but represented symbolically, this amounts to a transgression against Christ himself (I Cor. 11.17ff.). In this community function, the fact that all participants eat the same food and drink from the same cup plays an important role. The gifts for the supper and the prayers said at it are 'thanksgiving' and 'praise'; at a very early stage the supper was therefore called eucharist. Sometimes in primitive Christian writings we are uncertain whether references to the 'sacrifices' of the community mean only this liturgical praise and prayer or the sacrament itself. The functional equivalent to the communion function of sacrifice in primitive Christianity is thus again a combination of a ritual action (the eucharist) with the basic narrative of the death of Jesus and a liturgical metaphor of sacrifice. The eucharist is the great 'thanksgiving' of the community to God.

(*c*) The *aggression sacrifice*. The crucifixion of Christ clearly has the character of a violent execution. It is understood as a 'dying for us' which can be described with cultic metaphors. According to Paul it is a *hilasterion*, an event of expiation, however Paul imagined that. Does the crucified Christ replace the place of expiation in the Old Testament, the *kapporet*, mercy seat, on the ark of the covenant? Is the cross of Christ a place of expiation in a quite formal sense? Or is a martyr death meant? That too would be interpreted as *hilasterion* in a cultic conceptuality. Now it is striking that this sacrificial function has a parallel only in the narrative of Christians – the one and only execution of Jesus is regarded as an expiatory sacrifice – but no parallel in the ritual and ethical sign language of primitive Christianity. There is no ritual gesture which removes guilt again. There is no parallel to the constantly renewed removal of guilt brought about by the expiatory sacrifice. It remains tied to the unique event of cross and resurrection. In primitive Christianity, the exclusive and only functional equivalent for the aggression sacrifice which expiates vicariously is the death of Jesus.

That brings us to a decisive point in our reflections. The overall system of the ritual sign language of primitive Christianity contains an irregularity which is striking only if we compare it as a whole with traditional sacrifice. The Old Testament sacrifice for sin stands out from the other sacrifices by virtue of two peculiarities:

First, the sacrificial meat is not consumed by the community which offers the sacrifice but exclusively by the priests. In the sacrifices for sin on the Day of Atonement they too are excluded from consuming it.

Secondly, the parts of the sacrificial animal which are offered to God in the community sacrifice, i.e. which are burnt on the altar, are burned outside the camp. In addition, on the Day of Atonement the priest is to wash his clothes and bathe his body afterwards (Lev. 16.28).

The implicit logic of these precepts is evident: the victim which brings expiation is excluded from the community. It is to remove from the community that which burdens it. In other words, the communion sacrifice and the expiatory aggression sacrifice are mutually exclusive.

This rule of exclusion is broken in the ritual sign language of primitive Christianity. The death of Jesus is the expiatory sacrifice. But this sacrifice is very closely bound up with the communion sacrifice of the eucharist and the existential surrender sacrifice of baptism.

In their different versions, the words of institution at the **eucharist** leave no doubt that it is a celebration of the death of Jesus which overcomes sins (Matt. 26.28). The words 'This is my body' and 'This is my blood' are bound up in different ways with a soteriological interpretation – as body 'for us' or as the 'blood which was shed for us for the forgiveness of sins', as Matthew's version says. But the eating of an expiatory sacrifice was strictly forbidden. Yet that is what happens symbolically in the eucharist. Bread and wine are interpreted as Jesus' body and blood and consumed by the community. An expiatory aggression sacrifice becomes the basis of a communion sacrifice, in marked contradiction to the rules of exclusion in the Old Testament sacrificial cult.

We can also note a comparable irregularity in the case of **baptism**. This promises the expiatory effect of the death of Jesus to each individual. It takes place 'in the name of Jesus' and 'for the forgiveness of sins'. In the great expiatory sacrifice of the Day of Atonement, however, a rite of baptism has a role only where the priest is ridding himself of all uncleanness which has come about through contact with the expiatory sacrifice. In other words, there the washing serves to distance him from the expiatory sacrifice. In Christian baptism, however, it has precisely the opposite function: it is to create a close connection with the death of Jesus. It is baptism into his death, being buried with him – growing up with him (Rom. 6.1ff.). It does not symbolize distance from the sacrifice, but identification with it.

How are we to explain these two offences against the logic of ancient sacrifice? I know of only one explanation: the resurrection does not belong to the logic of ancient sacrifice. A sacrificial animal does not experience a resurrection. But because it was the conviction of primitive Christianity that Christ is risen, his death, interpreted as an expiatory sacrifice, can be integrated into the sign system of primitive Christianity in accordance with different rules from those governing expiatory sacrifice in the Old Testament. The nature of ancient sacrifice was superseded because the one human sacrifice which according to the primitive conviction brought the overcoming of sins was superseded by the resurrection. Here too we have the key to an answer to the question how the first Christians could regress in their religious imagination to such a barbaric sacrifice as human sacrifice. This one sacrifice did not remain dead. And that is also the explanation of the end of the practice of sacrifice. The many victims were not replaced by the one sacrificial death, but by the overcoming of this sacrificial death in the resurrection.

Here I recall a result that we derived from the general theories of sacrifice. Sacrifices are symbolic depictions of the struggle for opportunities in life. The three sacrificial functions of gift, communion, and coping with aggression express the fact that the weaker seeks the help of the stronger life, the stronger foists burdens on weaker life, and seeks life of equal strength with which to share the commodities of life. Through the rites and convictions of primitive Christianity – i.e. the sacraments and faith – men and women allied themselves with a power of life which was stronger than death. This power relieved them of the heaviest burden, sin and death. And they wanted to give everyone his or her share in life. If the one sacrifice of Christ could replace the many sacrifices which kept being repeated, it could express the message that the enhancement of life does not take place only by the surrender of other life and at the expense of other life. Gain in life can also lie in the surrender of one's own life as a 'living sacrifice', which is symbolized in baptism. And such surrender does not lead to a disadvantage, but to a fair distribution of the commodities of life for all, as is depicted symbolically in the eucharist.

We have now discussed the relationship between myth and history, ethic and grace, the performance of ritual and the significance of ritual. Time and again we kept coming upon great tensions. Myth and history are in tension with one another, but in the basic mytho-historical narrative of primitive Christianity they become a unity. The radicalization of demand and grace are in tension, but can be made a unity on the basis of the two fundamental vales of love and humility. The reduction of violence in the performance of ritual and the increase in violence in the fantasy of ritual are in tension, but only together do they both make the primitive Christian sacraments effective rites which transform the violent nature of human beings into a motivation for pro-social behaviour. Thus in the three basic forms of the religious sign language we keep discovering a unity behind the manifest tensions. In the chapters which follow I shall show how this unitary religious sign language came into being.

First I shall demonstrate how as a new sign language it detached itself step by step from Judaism until this process comes to a climax in the Gospel of John. I shall also show how despite a great internal plurality and deep crises this new sign language proves itself and finds a consensus in canonical Christianity – with demarcations from variants of Christianity which are related but are repudiated as 'heretical'. In other words, in the next chapters I shall attempt to sketch out a short history of the primitive Christian religion (as the origin of an independent sign system).

Part Four: Primitive Christian Religion as an Autonomous Sign World

9

The Way from Primitive Christian Religion to an Autonomous Sign World

From Paul to the Synoptic Gospels

So far we have regarded primitive Christian religion as a semiotic cathedral, constructed from 'signs' of different kinds: first from a historico-mythical basic narrative of Jesus, secondly from an ethic which crosses boundaries, and thirdly from new rites. So we know the 'building materials' for our semiotic cathedral. What we must now investigate more thoroughly is the 'building history'. How did it come about that these new sign elements were not incorporated into the impressive Jewish religion? Why were people not content with a little side altar in its great temple? Why did they erect a building of their own? How did the new religious sign language come to be independent of its mother religion?

Here too I must begin with a paradoxical observation: historically it is not very meaningful to make non-Jewish influences responsible for this gaining of independence, as though pagan convictions which had secretly slipped in had alienated the first Christians from their Jewish mother religion. On the contrary, a genuinely Jewish heritage makes itself evident in this gaining of independence, namely the tendency for religion to develop an autonomous sign world and an independent sphere of communication. It is paradoxical that this tendency towards autonomy in a Jewish group did not just lead to the autonomy of the religion from profane spheres of life, to a demarcation from pagan religions, but to a separation from its own mother religion: to autonomy even from it.

We should be clear that in most cultures religion is only a partial aspect of culture generally. But in Judaism we find for the first time the bold attempt to construct a whole society and culture in the light of a religious faith. When after the destruction of the first temple and the exile there was a threat that Jewish society would disappear from history, it was rebuilt in the light of religion. Only YHWH's promise and his commandment had survived the catastrophe; indeed, through this catastrophe YHWH had become the one and only God. In the experience of Israel he had been the only one of the many gods of the nations to survive this crisis. If post-exilic society was constructed in the light of faith in him, religion was no longer a function of the people, society or culture; on the contrary, people, society and culture served solely to worship this one God and to show loyalty towards him. The breakthrough of monotheism led to an organization of the whole of religion and the whole of life from this one centre – and thus to a striving for autonomy from all other factors and functions of life.

However, for the moment this faith in the one and only God was tied to a single unique people – even if the hope was alive in it that one day all people would break through to the knowledge of the true God. In primitive Christianity this faith detached itself from its tie to this one people. It now created a 'new people', the church, made up of Jews and Gentiles. Thus a new society came into being solely on the basis of religious convictions. If already in Judaism religion had become an autonomous power which sought to permeate and to shape the whole life of a people, now it became an autonomous power which first created for itself a new 'people' – from all peoples and cultures – and precisely in so doing also became independent of the people from which it originated and its mother religion.

That did not happen in a single step. What later gained its independence as primitive Christianity was originally an attempt to open up Judaism to all non-Jews. A first step consisted in renouncing ritual signs which were regarded as marks of Jewish identity. That came up against understandable resistance from many Jews: most of them could not understand the new group of 'Christians' as a legitimate variant of Judaism. The renunciation of circumcision and food laws led to a schism in the first generation after Jesus: to the breaking off of fellowship, though still in the awareness that the two groups belonged closely together.

A second step was taken in the second generation: up to 70 CE, despite all the ritual differences, the temple was a common cultic bond, even if part of the Christians, the Gentile Christians, had been excluded from it. With the destruction of the temple this shared place of worship was lost. As Judaism reorganized itself, by way of compensation it reactivated all the more the traditional characteristics of Jewish religion: obedience to the Torah, with all the ritual, ethical and religious demands which went with it, that could be practised even without a temple. At the same time, with the Gospels Christians created their own basic narrative and departed from the narrative community of Judaism.

A third step was taken when primitive Christianity not only made itself *de facto* independent of Judaism but also became aware of its inner autonomy. If in the new religion everything was related to the one revealer, so all the elements of this new religion were reorganized in the light of him, and he had to be given an absolute status, as he is in the Gospel of John.

Only now (in the Gospel of John) was a fundamental contradiction between Christians and Jews noted: in the eyes of the Jews, Christians were offending against strict monotheism. A schism which could have been transitory became a heresy which amounted to apostasy.

So we can say that the origin of primitive Christianity is the history of a failed attempt to universalize Judaism. The creative force of primitive Christianity showed itself in the transformation of this failure into motives for founding an independent religion. However, 'birth scars' remained. There remained an often exaggerated demarcation from Judaism, an anti-Judaism in some writings of primitive Christianity, which time and again left it unclear that even in its best parts primitive Christianity is none other than universalized Judaism.

1. The beginning of the development towards the autonomy of primitive Christian religion: the Apostolic Council and Paul

Jesus and his followers were deeply rooted in Judaism. Nothing was further from their intentions than to supersede or to abandon Judaism. Rather, their movement was one of many which brought about revitalization in Judaism after the religious crisis of the time of the Maccabees. But at a very early stage in the Jesus movement the tendency towards an opening up of Judaism became evident – in all three forms of religious expression.

This begins in the *mythical* sign language. At a very early stage Jesus was believed in as Messiah, in whom the promises that all human beings should come to recognize God were to be fulfilled. That was imagined as the victory and world rule of Israel over its enemies. The followers of Jesus transformed such political and military dreams into the expectation of a religious and ethical world rule. The Messiah[1] would rule over the peoples through his promises and commandments. But his claim on all peoples (including all non-Jews) remained.

The *ritual* sign language of Judaism was also relativized in the Jesus movement. Jesus himself expressed the expectation that people from all nations (together with the Diaspora Jews?) would stream into the kingdom of God, to eat with the patriarchs of Israel – without the divisive food regulations playing a role. Perhaps he already dreamed of an opening up of the temple, like Stephen or the Gospel of Mark later. At all events he laid the foundation stone for relativizing the divisive commandments about cleanness as a matter of principle (Mark 7.15). After Easter, this had practical consequences in primitive Christianity.[2]

At all events the *ethical* commandments of the Torah took on an inner universality. Jesus had accentuated the Torah precisely where universal tendencies were evident in it. Here primitive Christianity had only to continue the tendencies present in Judaism itself.

The step from the open Judaism of the early Jesus movement to a special group on the periphery of Judaism was caused, as so often in the case of separations in the church and religion, by ritual questions, since rites are external signs of belonging and not belonging. In primitive Christianity these questions were discussed at the Apostolic Council and in the conflict in Antioch which followed – already soon with consequences also for the ethic and myth of primitive Christianity.

What was the *ritual* problem? At a very early stage the 'Hellenists' who had been driven out of Jerusalem also began to win over Gentiles to the new faith in Antioch and Syria without requiring circumcision of them as a condition of acceptance. In the newly founded communities, circumcised Jews and uncircumcised Gentiles lived side by side with equal rights. Circumcision was probably dispensed with as a matter of conviction. It was regarded as a sign of separation between Jews and Gentiles. If this separation was superseded in the messianic end-time, its ritual demarcation also had to be superfluous. There was resistance to this among some Jewish Christians. However, delegates from the Antiochene community, Paul and Barnabas, succeeded in gaining recognition for the uncircumcised Gentile Christians at the Apostolic Council. These were to be regarded as members of the community with equal rights – at least, that is how Paul understood the agreement.[3] This caused a problem, the extent of which no one at that time had recognized: the Gentile Christians had to stay away from all pagan rites, since only then was fellowship with the Jewish Christians conceivable. But the small Christian groups could not offer these Gentile Christians any substitute for the religious sign language that they had forsaken, since these Gentile Christians were not admitted to temple worship because they were uncircumcised. Yet for antiquity, temple and sacrifice were the centre of religious practice. Certainly there was a hope that in the near future the temple would also become accessible to Gentiles. But there was also resistance to such an opening up. In short, with the agreement at the Apostolic Council the first Christian group put themselves under internal pressure to develop a religious sign language of their own which would meet all religious needs and which could be shared by all members, Jews and non-Jews. Now baptism finally had to become the decisive rite of acceptance which replaced circumcision. The eucharist finally had to become the central rite of integration which replaced the sacrificial meals of the tradition. They had to develop a religious sign language, i.e. a religion, of their own.

The ritual problems soon had consequences for the elaboration of the primitive Christian *ethic*. The compromise achieved at the Apostolic Council was later put in question by a more radical Jewish-Christian current which wanted to reintroduce circumcision and food laws for all Christians into the Pauline mission communities. Paul developed his theology in controversy with them. Because his Jewish-Christian opponents referred to the Torah, he had to put the Torah more fundamentally in question than he had done previously. The Torah was made a problem not only as a source of ritual norms but also as a basis for ethical norms: no one can fulfil its commandments. It is an external demand on people, written on stone, whereas only the will of God written in the human heart can fulfil this (II Cor. 3.1ff.). The Torah cannot bring about this internalization of the divine will; only the Spirit can. Thus when the limited ritual norms of the Torah were made a problem, the Torah also became a problem as a basis for ethical norms.

However, this problem could only arise because for Paul another authority as a final source of revelation had appeared alongside the Torah, namely Christ. Only through him was the ambivalence of the Torah discovered, so that it became possible to distinguish in it between the letter that kills and the spirit that makes alive (II Cor. 3.4ff.). This also activated the third form of expression of the new faith in a way which introduced a detachment from Judaism: the christological *myth*.

In our context it needs to be noted that, beginning with differences in the ritual sphere, already in the first generation differences in ethics were defined and grounded in christology (i.e. in the historico-mythical basic narrative of primitive Christianity). Nevertheless, in this first generation there was only a schism, a separation in the community, without any final mutual rejection and repudiation. That calls for a brief explanation.

First of all we should recall the two basic axioms of Judaism, monotheism and covenantal nomism. In the first generation *monotheism* was still not a point of dispute, and rightly so. Paul indeed speaks of the exaltation of Jesus to divine status. But this exaltation is exclusively God's action in the crucified Jesus. It is not based on an action of the man Jesus, in whom, as we know, Paul was so little interested that he almost demonstratively denies his significance for his theology (II Cor. 5.16). Only when it was suggested that the earthly Jesus had made himself God was monotheism seriously threatened. From the first generation, apart from the letters of Paul, all that we have is the Logia source (and then only as a source for Matthew and Luke). Monotheism is not put in question in it either. Rather, in the temptation story Jesus professes monotheistic faith, against all temptations, in an exemplary way.

Nor was the second basic axiom of Judaism, *covenantal nomism*, which bound the one and only God to Israel in a privileged way, put in question in the first generation. Even if Paul makes terse remarks about the Jews, these cannot alter the fact that in Romans he counts on a salvation of all Israel (Rom. 11.25ff.). This notion is still possible, even if for Paul it is the revelation of a mystery in the face of many tribulations and complaints. In my view Paul is not alone. The Logia source also knows a comparable hope. Certainly at present Jerusalem rejects the messengers of wisdom. It kills the prophets and those sent to it, and the deity will withdraw from the temple: 'Behold, your house is forsaken. And I tell you, you will not see me until you say, "Blessed is he who comes in the name of the Lord"' (Luke 13.35). Even if this interpretation of the expectation of the parousia in Paul[4] and the Logia source[5] is disputed, we can say that in the first generation the schism between Jews and Christians is still regarded as a transitory phenomenon, which will be overcome at the latest at the parousia of the Lord.

As for the form of expression of the religion, at this early period we should remember that primitive Christianity fundamentally still did not have its own worked-out *basic narrative*. Granted, belief in Jesus as the Earthly One and the Exalted One governed the new faith. But Paul can still develop it by expounding the holy scriptures (i.e. what was later called the Old Testament) which were held in common with all Jews. It was far from his mind to collect the traditions about Jesus into a separate narrative. For him Christ is the (external) centre of scripture (the Old Testament). This is sufficient basis for his faith.[6] The Logia source is still on the way to a complete narrative of Jesus' life. It collects the sayings of Jesus as in a prophetic book,[7] and could be imagined to be an extension of the biblical (Old Testament) canon, just as at that time many apocryphal writings were added to the canon.

Nor was the separation in the *ritual sphere* yet unbridgeable. Only Gentile Christians were exempt from circumcision. For Jewish Christians it was a matter of course. The only consensus was that it was not a condition of salvation. Only Paul concluded from this that for Gentile Christians to adopt circumcision would mean that they forfeited salvation. He first presented this standpoint to the Galatians. The situation is even clearer with the Logia source. It contains no traditions critical of the Torah. There are no sabbath conflicts. There are no critical sayings about questions of cleanness like Mark 7.15. There is no saying against the temple. Jesus appears as a prophet loyal to the Torah – in line with John the Baptist. Even if he goes beyond John the Baptist, according to the Logia source (even with his preaching of judgment) he belongs as surely to Judaism as John does.

The differences in *ethic* were the least. Paul himself attached importance to the statement that in Christ the Torah in the ethical sense is fulfilled

(Rom. 13.8–10; Gal. 5.14). He contests as malicious gossip the view that he teaches sophistically that one should do evil so that goodness, the grace of God, becomes that much more powerful (cf. Rom. 3.8). Paul certainly did not teach that. Rather, we should believe him when he sees the whole Torah fulfilled in the commandment to love. His ethic, too, is in a way Torah ethic – albeit the ethic of a Torah placed in the human heart by the Spirit, so that those have been renewed spontaneously do from within what the Torah requires from the outside. Things are even clearer in the Logia source. It explicitly teaches the indissolubility of the Torah (QLuke 16.17).

Our conclusion must be that in the first generation there is really only a schism, i.e. a separation in fellowship. Christians had their own assemblies. They had their own organization as far as this had already been developed. But they still hoped to come together again. It was the second generation that also brought about a final separation in faith.

2. The way to the autonomy of primitive Christian religion and the Synoptic Gospels

In my view the writing of the Gospels is in itself a decisive step towards the final separation of Christian and Jewish faith. With the *form* of the Gospel, primitive Christianity gives itself its own basic narrative, and parts company with the narrative community of Judaism. For the Gospels were written *a priori* with a canonical claim.[8]

Whereas the letters of Paul have no formal models in the canonical writings of the Bible (the Old Testament), and their genre cannot be understood as a development of the biblical writings, the Gospels continue Old Testament historiography. That is evident to all in the Gospel of Matthew. It begins with a genealogical survey of the history of Israel from Abraham to David, from David to the exile and from the exile to Matthew's day. Jesus is related typologically to Moses in the birth narratives. Fulfilment quotations permeate the whole work. Luke too interprets the life of Jesus as the fulfilment of the Old Testament, on the one hand through hopes and expectations of pious men and women of the Old Testament in the infancy narratives, and on the other through the continuation of the history of the people of God in the Acts of the Apostles – by analogy with the history of the people of God in the Old Testament. And yet in form the Gospels are a novelty. They concentrate on a single person. They are a *bios*.[9] Such depictions of an individual life were widespread in pagan literature. By contrast, they are alien to Jewish literature. In Judaism we find them only by way of an exception in Philo's Life of Moses – and here with the remark that it has been written for Gentiles (*VitMos* 1, 1). The genre of Gospel will also have come into being when the Jesus traditions were brought together for Gentile Christians. The earliest Gospel is (also) addressed to Gentile Christians. It is a *bios*. But in it the fulfilment of salvation history is more important than the formal expectations of a *bios*.[10] For it does not begin with the birth but with an Old Testament quotation (viz. a mixed quotation from Exodus, Malachi and Isaiah: 1.2f.). Thus it signals from the start that this life is the fulfilment of a long history. So we find in the Gospels both the claim to be continuing the canonical scriptures and the claim to be surpassing them by concentrating on a single figure. The canonical claim is bound up with the awareness of depicting something new by comparison with the canon hitherto.

With the Gospels, at the same time the content of the Jesus traditions, the view of Christ, changes in a way which can collide with a strict monotheism. Whereas previously on the one hand there was belief, as in Paul, in the Exalted One who owed his whole divine status solely to God, and on the other hand there were individual traditions about the earthly Jesus, as in the Logia source, which could be understood as the words of a Jewish prophet, in the form of the Gospel the two were brought together. Jesus is depicted in such a way that his divine status becomes visible in his words and actions. These words and actions become the basis for him to be worshipped as God. Now that is to cross a boundary: at one point, Philo remarks in his criticism of the self-deification of Gaius Caligula, 'it would be easier for God to turn into a man than for a man to turn into God' (*LegGai* 118). The Pauline notion of a Son of God who has come down from heaven and assumes human form would thus still be conceivable for a Jew; the notion that by his actions and words a man could become God would be far less so.

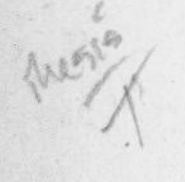

The form and content of the Gospels attest and bring about a growing separation from Judaism. Here the three Synoptic Gospels each show characteristic accents. In Mark in particular the *ritual* demarcation from Judaism becomes clear, since Mark has to deal with the loss of the temple as the ritual centre of Judaism and Christianity. In Matthew an *ethical* demarcation becomes visible through the proclamation of a 'better righteousness'. He grapples with a Judaism which is reorganizing itself, and which after the loss of the temple is reflecting on the righteousness required in the Torah. Finally, in Luke we find a *narrative* demarcation from Judaism. He develops the Old Testament salvation history in a way which is meant to provide a historical explanation of the separation of Jews and Christians and to legitimate it. Each of the first three evangelists to some degree chooses one of the three basic forms of religious expression in order to articulate his distinction between the Jewish and Christian religions.

(a) The Gospel of Mark: the ritual demarcation from Judaism

The Gospel of Mark depicts the earthly Jesus as the mysterious epiphany of a heavenly being. The glory of the Risen One shines through the person of the Earthly One and bestows an unearthly aura on it. Mark shapes this new picture of Jesus with the help of three epiphany scenes: at the beginning, in the middle, and at the end of his Gospel, which give this Gospel an unmistakable structure.[11] In each of them heaven opens, and Jesus can be experienced as a being who himself belongs to the heavenly world.

At the beginning we have the vision at the baptism, in which a voice from the opened heavens addresses Jesus as 'Son of God' (1.11). In the middle there follows the transfiguration scene, in which the same heavenly voice presents Jesus to the three closest disciples as 'Son of God' (9.7). The story of the discovery of the empty tomb, at which the angel passes on the message of resurrection (16.6), forms the end. The message at the baptism is addressed only to Jesus. At the transfiguration the disciples are addressed. If Moses and Elijah appear together with Jesus, but from now on the disciples are to 'listen to' Jesus, as the heavenly voice says, Jesus is taking the place of the Torah and the Prophets (represented by Moses and Elijah). The heavenly figures, Moses and Elijah, remain in their world. But at the empty tomb a messenger from the world beyond appears in the midst of this world and communicates a message which is to be handed on to others. The incursion of heaven into earthly reality becomes increasingly clear – and the demand for the message to be spread is constantly extended. The mystery is unveiled more and more. Only the privileged reader learns the mystery of Jesus from the beginning, experiencing his adoption as Son of God and his presentation to the disciples (9.2ff.), and hearing the message of his acceptance into the heavenly world (16.2ff.). But above all it becomes clear that Jesus owes his status solely to the heavenly world. Jesus has not given himself divine status; it has been assigned to him by a heavenly voice.

The Gospel of Mark makes clear within the text that this dignity of Jesus bestowed by God transcends all human expectations and notions. All three epiphany scenes are prepared for by human confessions. Individuals suspect and recognize Jesus' dignity, but what they suspect and recognize is inadequate by comparison with what the heavenly message reveals. John the Baptist announces a Stronger One (1.7f.); the heavenly voice at the baptism surpasses his prophecy: Jesus is not just the Stronger One but the Son of God. Similarly, Peter before the Transfiguration recognizes the dignity of Jesus as Messiah (8.29). But his confession, too, is surpassed by the title Son of God proclaimed by the heavenly voice on the mountain

(9.7). Finally, the centurion under the cross is the first person to confess Jesus as Son of God. But this confession is still provisional. For it says only that Jesus *was* a Son of God (15.39). The angelic proclamation at the tomb also corrects this confession. The Risen One is alive. He *is* the Son of God. He is not among the dead (16.6).

Not only the sovereignty of Jesus but also his lowliness transcends all human understanding. The moment the disciples (through Peter) recognize the sovereignty of Jesus, Jesus begins to teach them about the need for him to suffer (8.31). And when they see his status on the Mount of Transfiguration, he also commands them to say nothing of this until he is risen from the dead (9.9). Why is this sovereignty of Jesus connected with the cross and resurrection? Probably the evangelist Mark still sensed that the sovereignty of Jesus is compatible with Jewish monotheism only if it is rooted in the action of God in the Crucified One – and not in the miraculous actions and words of Jesus. If Jesus is 'revered' as the 'holy one of God' (Mark 1.24) or 'son of God' (Mark 3.11) on the basis of his actions, these are demonic voices which Jesus contradicts.[12] Jesus owes his status solely to divine actions. God alone can proclaim his true dignity as son of God (Mark 1.11; 9.7). And only through divine revelation is the insight into the status of Jesus bound up in actual life with the call to discipleship in conflicts with the world around. Only those readers who put themselves under the cross alongside the centurion and (going beyond his confession) confess Jesus as the living Son of God have penetrated to the complete truth.

In my view there is no doubt that Mark transfers back into Jesus' life the divine dignity of Jesus which is in substance grounded in the Easter appearances. That is the justified core of the interpretation of the Markan messianic secret by William Wrede[13] – except that the evangelist does not project the post-Easter sovereignty of Jesus as Son of God back on to an unmessianic life but on to the life of a Jewish charismatic who had always been surrounded by a numinous aura and to whom people (both in the Gospel of Mark and in historical reality) had attached messianic expectations.

To say it once again: that was a decisive step in the detachment from Judaism. Paul still worshipped in Jesus a divine being who had attained his sovereignty exclusively through the resurrection of the dead. It was not Jesus' action but solely God's action which had surrounded him with divine splendour. In transferring this Easter sovereignty of Jesus back into his life, the Gospel of Mark was already to surround the earthly Jesus with divine splendour during his lifetime. And although the Gospel of Mark wants to guarantee that this divine splendour comes only from God, it associates it very closely with the actions of Jesus: someone who multiplies loaves and walks on water can (by the standards of antiquity) only be a god. Only for that reason can Mark criticize the disciples for an incomprehensible failure when they do not understand the sovereignty of Jesus on the basis of the miracle of the loaves, but are so to speak hardened (8.21ff.). The successive divinization of the earthly Jesus begins with the creation of the Gospel form by Mark – and it was this divinization of an earthly man which first came into tension with the first basic axiom of Jewish faith, monotheism.

This detachment from Judaism has also left traces elsewhere in the Gospel of Mark. It becomes particularly clear in the way in which the ritual sign language is made independent of the Jewish sign system.[14]

The historical occasion for this demarcation was the destruction of the temple.[15] With it, the ritual sign language of Judaism lost its centre. Certainly the destruction of the temple was one of the factors prompting the composition of the oldest Gospel. For previously, for example in Paul, Jesus had been depicted above all as the fulfilment of Old Testament prophecies. However, with the destruction of the temple, in retrospect he appeared as a prophet who had forecast this catastrophe. Would not this confirmation lead to reflection on his message generally, and necessarily call attention to his past history – and not just to the one who would come in a future parousia? Certainly the Christians mourned the destruction of the temple, but they also experienced it as a confirmation of the message of Jesus. Now there must have been particular interest not only in the temple prophecy and the cleansing of the temple but also in all conflicts over ritual questions – and all conflicts with the Jewish authorities. Thus in Mark we in fact find several sets of controversy sayings; we hear of sabbath conflicts (2.23ff.; 3.1ff.), conflicts over questions of cleanness (7.1ff.), and a devaluation of the practice of sacrifice in the face of the twofold commandment to love (12.28ff.). At the end of Jesus' earthly life there is the rending of the temple curtain (15.38). From now on the Holy of Holies is accessible – also for Gentiles, who are represented by the centurion under the cross. It goes against any narrative logic for him to have seen the rending of the curtain within the temple. That makes the symbolic content of this scene all the greater.

However, the Gospel of Mark not only describes the end of the Jewish sacrificial cult, but at the same time provides a basis for the new rites of the first Christians, baptism and eucharist. After the loss of the temple it was even more necessary than before to lay a foundation for their own ritual sign system which was independent of the temple. In the Gospel of Mark, Jesus' public activity begins with his baptism. His last action is the institution of the eucharist. The Gospel of Mark is composed like an ellipse around these two narratives, which are the foundation for the sacraments. The aetiological character of the narrative in the account of the eucharist is evident. Even if, unlike the account in Paul, Mark's account does not contain the command to repeat the actions, in my view there is no doubt about the liturgical function of the text. The same will be true of the baptism of Jesus. Previously, a baptism by a Stronger One has been announced. It is said of him that he will baptize 'you' (plural) with holy spirit. Here all Christians are being addressed. Then this Stronger One appears, but he does not baptize himself, as one might expect from this announcement; he is himself baptized – in my view to show in an exemplary way how later all Christians will be baptized through him with holy spirit; how through baptism all become beloved children of God and are protected from the power of Satan. The baptism of Jesus becomes the model for Christian baptism.

The Gospel of Mark can be recognized as the basic religious narrative of a new religious community in yet one more respect. It is already evident in the earthly life of Jesus how (later) a community will gather round him made up of Jews *and* Gentiles. The preaching of Jesus has an effect from Galilee as far as the neighbouring Gentile regions, so that people stream to him from there (3.7ff.). Then Jesus himself takes steps to reach these regions. The evangelist Mark shows the difficulties that have to be overcome here. For Jesus twice crosses the sea. Not only is his voyage threatened each time by stormy winds, but the first time he reaches the Decapolis he is expelled after a successful exorcism (5.1ff.). The second time the head-wind drives him to another point on the opposite shore, so that he only arrives in Gentile territory after a long walk by foot; here he encounters the first Gentile woman, a Syro-Phoenician. Before this, not only external but also internal resistance has to be overcome. For before his encounter with the pagan Gentile there is the controversy about what is clean and what is unclean, in which Jesus raises fundamental questions about this distinction. In so doing he abrogates what separates Jews and Gentiles in everyday life – among other things the food laws, as the evangelist explicitly emphasizes (Mark 7.15ff.). Nor is it a coincidence that the Markan Jesus declares the temple the place of prayer for the Gentiles (11.17), and in the end is recognized as and acknowledged Son of God by a Gentile centurion. All these references to Gentiles cannot be fortuitous.

Thus with Mark (shortly after 50 CE) a new basic religious narrative comes into being for Christians, which can take its place alongside the Bible that they share with the Jews. It tells of a man in whom a divine being appears in a hidden way. The light of the Easter faith permeates the actions of the earthly Jesus. The Gospel of Mark itself depicts the divine dignity of

Jesus in such a way as to safeguard it against the misunderstanding of a self-apotheosis. Jesus owes his dignity wholly to the heavenly voice and the power of God which overcomes death. Nevertheless from now on a divine splendour also lies on his life. He attains a sovereignty which could threaten strict monotheism. And at all events on the basis of his sovereignty he has the authority to relativize and criticize the ritual system of Judaism. He becomes the founder of a new ritual system by which Christians distinguish themselves from Jews.

(b) The Gospel of Matthew: the ethical demarcation from Judaism (and paganism)[16]

The Gospel of Matthew continues the process of the 'divinization' of the earthly Jesus which in the Gospel of Mark is still surrounded with a great mystery. He multiplies the epiphany scenes at the beginning and end of his Gospel. At the beginning he has God intervening in events through dreams and angelic messages. At the end he relates the Easter appearances over and above the (fragmentary?) Gospel of Mark. But above all in the Gospel of Matthew, from the beginning Jesus is a divine being by virtue of his conception through the Spirit and his virgin birth. The heavenly voice at the baptism publicly proclaims his dignity: '*This* is my beloved son . . .' (3.17) instead of '*You* are my beloved son . . .' in Mark (1.11). So when Jesus walks on the water, the disciples can recognize what they were unwilling to understand in Mark: the divine dignity of Jesus. They kneel before him in the boat and confess, 'Truly you are the Son of God' (14.33). Now in fact Jesus shows himself to be Son of God through his own actions, and on the basis of these actions is recognized as such.

Matthew expresses the divine sonship of Jesus with the help of the pagan mythologumenon of the virgin birth. For Judaism the notion of a sexual union of gods and human beings is an abomination. Genesis 6.1ff. shows that only disaster can come if sons of God beget children by human beings. The apocalyptic writings elaborated this negative myth. In them evil breaks into this world with the sexual union of divine and human beings (thus in the Apocalypse of Weeks in Ethiopian Enoch 93.1–10; 91.11–17). But in the Gospel of Matthew a group close to Judaism makes use of precisely this un-Jewish notion to express the divine nature of the earthly Jesus – a notion which is similarly problematical for Jews.

Nevertheless, here we have the expression of a concern which is justified precisely on the biblical premises of the Gospel of Matthew. Virgin birth and conception through the spirit are to maintain the notion that the earthly Jesus, too, does not owe his dignity to himself but solely to God's action, which at the beginning of his life raises him above all other human beings – this does not happen only on the basis of his resurrection and exaltation after his death. Matthew finds additional support in discovering a prophecy of the virgin birth in Isa. 7.14 (LXX). So it accords with God's will. In this way even this rather pagan notion is integrated into his deeply Jewish world of ideas. By it he is saying precisely what he says at the end of his Gospel, when he makes the Risen Christ say: 'All power on heaven and earth is given to me' (28.28). It has been given to him; he does not have it from himself, but from God.[17]

But above all, Matthew copes with the problem in the ethical way which is his characteristic. He indeed depicts the earthly Jesus as a sovereign king who is humble – and renounces the demonstration and establishment of his status. This renunciation of status by Jesus becomes clear on his very first public appearance. Really he did not need to have himself baptized. John the Baptist at first refuses to baptize him, since Jesus should be baptizing John. Nevertheless, it has to happen for all righteousness to be fulfilled (Matt. 3.13ff.). Accordingly, Jesus is demonstratively 'humble' both in his teaching and also in his action. He is the master of wisdom, whose teaching is easy and who 'is meek and lowly of heart' (11.29). He acts as the lowly king when he enters Jerusalem riding on an ass (21.4 = Zech. 9.9). In the passion he dispenses with the protection of legions of angels who could have rescued him (26.53).

From these and other features we keep noticing how Matthaean Christianity, more than Markan Christianity, seeks to be the fulfilment and continuation of the Jewish sign world. The Matthaean Jesus sets out programmatically to 'fulfil' the Law and the Prophets (5.17). If Matthaean Christianity demarcates itself from Judaism, it does so by a better interpretation of the sign world that they share: above all the biblical writings that they have in common, with their promises and demands. The decisive motive is formulated programmatically in the Sermon on the Mount: 'Unless your righteousness exceeds that of the scribes and Pharisees, you will never enter the kingdom of heaven' (5.20). Christians are to present a better interpretation of the commands of the Torah than the Jews. And even where they agree in their interpretation, they are to act better than scribes and Pharisees. According to 23.1ff. they are to put the teaching of the scribes into practice, 'but do not do what they do; for they preach, but do not practise' (23.3). This ethic of the better righteousness stands out not only from the Jewish but also from the pagan environment. That is emphasized in the command to love one's enemies. What would be special about being friendly only to one's brothers? 'Do not the Gentiles also do likewise?' (5.47f.). Similarly, one is to differ from them in praying (6.7) and in dealing with everyday cares (6.31). The better righteousness is to be realized in both directions, towards both Jews and Gentiles. Here the Gospel of Matthew advocates an explicitly 'aristocratic' morality. The aim of this ethic is not the good, but the better.

What does this better righteousness consist of? The Sermon on the Mount gives the answer.[18] In it the term 'righteousness' appears five times, presumably all in passages in the Matthaean redaction (5.6, 10, 20; 6.1, 33). In addition it is associated twice more with John the Baptist (3.15; 21.32) – a sign of how little the Matthaean community claims this righteousness exclusively for itself. It strives for the same righteousness as others, but seeks to surpass others by the better righteousness.

In its three main sections, the Sermon on the Mount develops what this better righteousness is. The *antitheses* (5.21–48) demonstrate a great freedom towards tradition – regardless of whether the powerful 'But I say to you' is directed against Moses himself (and therefore the Torah) or only those who expound it (of whom Matthew was probably thinking at the redactional level). At the same time they teach a great freedom towards inner emotions – aggressiveness and sexuality – and in dealing with aggression experienced passively.

The *rules about piety* (6.1–18) are an admonition about a special way of giving alms, praying and fasting, in complete freedom from social control. If one fasts and prays in a hidden place and gives alms secretly, then the social environment has no opportunity to influence behaviour by sanctions, positive or negative.

The *social paraenesis* (6.19–7.11) calls for a sovereign freedom towards material ties. Seeking the kingdom of God and its righteousness consists in not worrying about eating, drinking and clothes. There is only an either-or where God and mammon are concerned.

This practice of the better righteousness is combined with a striving for 'perfection'. Matthew twice associates this predicate with specific behaviour, first in loving one's enemy. Those who love their neighbours are promised, 'You will be *perfect*, as your Father in heaven is perfect' (5.48). The same is true of the radical renunciation of possessions in discipleship. The rich young man who wants to follow Jesus is told, 'If you would be *perfect*, go, sell what you possess and give to the poor, and you will have treasure in heaven' (19.21).

Thus Matthew advocates an aristocratic ethic. He is not satisfied with the search for the good; his concern is with the 'better', indeed the 'perfect'. The disciples who are concerned with this are the 'salt of the earth' and the 'light of the world' (5.13, 14f.). And in fact their 'better' ethic is directed towards the whole world. Jesus' teaching is to be proclaimed to all nations.

Jesus rises from being the Jewish son of David to being the Lord of the world who rules the world through his commandments, through 'all that I have told you' (Matt. 28.20). This ethical teaching of Jesus is superior to the ethic of Jews and Gentiles. At the same time it is the fulfilment of the ethical notions of all humankind and not just a better exegesis of the Jewish Torah. Twice Jesus makes Jesus sum up what the Law and the Prophets say. Once he does this with the Golden Rule (7.12), i.e. a fundamental ethical maxim which is widespread among all peoples. The other time he quotes the twofold commandment to love (22.35ff.). It corresponds to the ancient canon of the two virtues – piety towards God and righteousness towards one's fellow human beings – which was widespread and well-known among Gentiles and Jews.

Jesus further fulfils human hopes. He claims to fulfil not only the Law but also the 'Prophets', i.e. the Old Testament promises. Therefore fulfilment quotations run right through the Gospel of Matthew – and indicate that Jesus is the expected redeemer, not only on the basis of his descent but also on the basis of his gentle and unmilitant appearance. Here too Matthew thinks it important that Gentile expectations as well as Jewish expectations are fulfilled in him.[19] So he relates how three Magi come from the East. They are motivated by an astrological oracle which prophesies to them a new ruler in Judaea. In this way Matthew takes up prophecies of a new world ruler from the East which were alive at that time – and also played a role during the Jewish War. The Gospel in particular, which most clearly has a Jewish stamp, gives a considerable amount of room to pagan expectations (including the astrology which was often vehemently rejected in Judaism).

In my view the ethical character of Matthaean theology is also the key to the question whether there is a 'rejection' of Israel in Matthew or only a removal of its privileges by putting it on the same level as all peoples. In that case Jews would have the same chances of salvation as all other peoples. Beyond doubt Matthew regards the execution of Jesus as a 'murder'. For him the destruction of Jerusalem is a just punishment for this (cf. Matt. 22.7). But with the punishment, the way to conversion would be opened up. In my opinion the great picture of judgment in Matt. 25.31ff. supports such a view, if we interpret this text in a universalistic way, i.e. see it as a judgment on all human beings (and not just on all pagans), in which there is only one criterion, whether or not one has helped sufferers. I know that this interpretation is disputed by distinguished experts on Matthew.

We can give a rough date to this conception of a universal ethic stemming from Jewish roots. The Jewish War is over (cf. Matt. 22.7). The expectations current in the East among Jews and Gentiles of a Jewish or Eastern ruler of the world have come to nothing. In this situation the Gospel of Matthew puts forward the thesis that with Jesus the ruler of the world has already come. It shows how he, the king's son from the tribe of David, has risen to rule the world. And it goes on to show that Jesus exercises this rule over the world, not by military power but by his ethical teaching and the obedience of his followers. His teaching is a universalized Judaism, in his eyes a better Judaism which is superior to other versions. Here he is competing in his time with the reorganization of Judaism which began in the school at Jabneh after the catastrophe of 70 CE. There too people reflected on how the loss of the temple was not the end of the true worship of God. The great teacher Johanan ben Zakkai comforted his Jewish contemporaries with Hos. 6.6. There God himself had said that he preferred mercy to sacrifice. So works of love could replace the sacrificial cult in the temple. It cannot be a coincidence that the Gospel of Matthew twice quotes this favourite saying of Johanan ben Zakkai – each time in a redactional addition to Mark, in Matt. 9.13 and 12.7. The Gospel of Mark is competing with the contemporary rabbinic movement to realize the 'better righteousness' on the basis of the Torah that they share.

(c) The Gospel of Luke: the narrative-historical demarcation from Judaism

For all three Synoptic Gospels, the concentration on the figure of Jesus contained in the Gospel form and the tendency to surround the earthly Jesus with a divine aura goes beyond the limits of a strict Jewish monotheism. That becomes clear in the Gospels in different forms of religious expression: in Mark we find a ritual demarcation and in Matthew an ethical demarcation from Judaism. In Luke this definition of the relationship takes place in the medium of the salvation-historical narrative: he formulates the basic historico-mythical narrative of primitive Christianity which explains the separation of Jews and Christians. He chooses a very simple way of doing this. He adds to his Gospel a second work about the followers of Jesus. In it he describes how, contrary to the will of Christians, the ways of Jews and Christians parted.

Of all the three Synoptic evangelists, Luke has the least difficulties in telling of Jesus' divine nature and activities. Like Matthew, he narrates his conception through the Spirit and the virgin birth. But in his Gospel this is no problem either for Mary's husband (in contrast to Matthew, where Joseph finds this a scandal) or for the narrator, Luke: he does not need any Old Testament quotations to demonstrate its religious legitimacy.

For Luke lives in a world in which the deification of human beings is taken for granted. The problem for him is not that it happens, but whether it happens rightly. When Herod Agrippa I without contradiction accepts the acclamation that the voice of a God and not of a man speaks through him, he is rightly punished for this hybris (Acts 12.20–23). Similarly, the two missionaries Paul and Barnabas are praised for rejecting the divine honours offered to them (Acts 14.8ff.).[20] But with Jesus the matter seems to be clear. He is a man, 'attested by God with mighty works and wonders and signs' (Acts 2.22ff.). But finally he is confirmed by God's raising him from the dead and exalting him, although he is rejected by human beings.

Nevertheless, in Luke too, the divinity of Jesus is toned down. In Mark this was done by the veil of mystery which put an aura of divinity over the earthly Jesus. In Matthew the sovereignty of the eschatological king has been ethically relativized by his humility. In Luke we find a humanization of Jesus in another form: the Lukan Jesus becomes human through his devotion to the poor, sinners and outsiders. He sums up his mission in the words 'The Son of Man has come to seek and to save that which is lost' (Luke 19.10). That is rightly already true of the composition in the central chapter of Luke with the three parables about what has been lost, the inner heart of the Gospel. Here we find a soteriological relativization of the divinity of Jesus: in a salvation-historical narrative he is depicted as the representative of true humanity.

The special feature of this salvation-historical narrative is its continuation in a second work. The history of the Son of God and that of the Christians are thus put side by side and on the same level. The result is a New Testament work which already by virtue of its form can claim to stand alongside the historical works of the Old Testament. For there – in the holy Scriptures of the Jews – no writing was concerned only with a single life. The Old Testament is literature and historiography with the whole people as its subject. Now with Luke we have a real continuation of this history: the history of a new people of God made up of Jews and Gentiles.

In Hans Conzelmann's classical scheme, [21] the characteristic features of this salvation-historical historiography have been seen in two motifs:

1. First, in a division into periods of salvation history in which a precise distinction is made between the time of Israel, the time of Jesus and the time of the church; here the transitions from one period to another lie between John the Baptist and Jesus and between the activity of Jesus and his passion respectively.

2. This salvation-historical sketch is an answer to the experience of the failure of the parousia to materialize. Previously Jesus' coming in history

was interpreted as the beginning of the end-time. But Luke interprets his history for the first time as the 'middle of time'.

Conzelmann has correct insights in both of these notions, but both need to be reformulated:

1. In place of a tripartite salvation history, one can also see in Luke-Acts a variant of the general primitive Christian picture of history which distinguishes between a time of promise and a time of fulfilment. The time of promise embraces the Old Testament and the history of Israel. But the time of fulfilment is intrinsically tripartite. It begins with a prelude in the infancy narratives, in which the following time of Jesus is depicted as the fulfilment of the expectations of pious Jews. At the centre stands the time of Jesus, the history of his activity and his suffering. It is illegitimate to separate the passion narrative from it. But after Easter (with the beginning of Acts) the time of the church begins. So instead of a tripartite salvation history we should speak of a tripartite history of fulfilment. More than others, Luke brings out how the promises are not realized all at once but successively.

2. This new view of a time of fulfilment which is itself divided into periods goes back to a more conscious perception of the way time keeps going on. No task of a (potential) imminent expectation needs to be bound up with this. Precisely because so many phases of the time of fulfilment have already passed, now the end can break in at any time. Now, where the mission has founded communities all over the world, the end can come.[22] But it is true that the notion of a fulfilment which is realized successively makes it possible to go on living as time goes on and to understand this positively as a task.

In Luke's religious 'historiography' the separation of Jews and Christians is also depicted as the result of a successive development. It comprises four phases, if we distinguish a time before and a time after the transition to the Gentile mission within the time of the church.[23]

The first step is announced in the *infancy narratives* by Simeon's prophecy: Israel is not only to be restored but to be extended. With the Messiah, salvation is to reach the Gentiles, not at the expense of Israel but in order to increase its glory (Luke 2.31). However, Simeon expands this prophecy with the announcement of a split in Israel: the Messiah will be a sign which is contradicted. Some in Israel will be caused to fall by him, but many will rise again (Luke 2.34).

The second step begins with *Jesus' preaching*: Jesus gathers Israel. As in Matthew, his activity is limited to Israel. His contacts with Gentiles are suppressed. He enters into contact with the centurion of Capernaum only through an intermediary (Luke 7.1ff.). The encounter with the Syro-Phoenician woman is left out, as part of the great Lukan omission. But in Israel itself there is a division, as Simeon had foretold: the division between the people and its rulers (cf. Luke 7.29f.; 13.17). Thus for example the parable of the tenants of the vineyard in Luke is addressed only to the people, though it clearly means the leaders of Israel. Here Jesus comes to an agreement with the people over his criticism of these leaders (20.9–19). These leaders bring Jesus to the cross. But when confronted with the crucified Jesus, the people is converted with signs of repentance (23.13ff.).

The third step takes place in the *mission to Jews* in the post-Easter period. In it the assembly of Israel is renewed by the working of the Holy Spirit. The execution of Jesus by the leaders of Israel and the Romans has not altered the offer of salvation to Israel in any way. The leaders of the people acted in ignorance (Acts 3.17). This renewed assembly of the people is successful. That is shown by the mass conversions of the three thousand and the five thousand (cf. Acts 2.41; 4.4). The fallen dwelling of David – the people of Israel – is rebuilt, so that other people can also be accepted into the people of God (Acts 15.16ff. = Amos 9.11f.). It is the time of Peter's mission.

The fourth and last step takes place only with the *mission to the Gentiles*. Only now do large parts of Israel exclude themselves from salvation. Luke wants to put the blame for this on the Jews, not on the Christians. It is the time of Paul's mission. Time and again he has Paul beginning his mission in the synagogues, in a stereotyped way. Only after Paul has been rejected there does he turn to the Gentiles (this is formulated as a programme in Acts 13.46). For Luke the mission to the Gentiles is a consequence of the refusal of the Jews to accept the message. Historically it was probably the other way round. By dispensing with circumcision and the food laws, the Gentile mission put the identity of Judaism in question and therefore came up against the opposition of Jews, so that the Gentile Christian communities became even more remote from Judaism.

The decisive thing is that in Luke the separation of Jews and Christians is not fixed from the start but develops only at a relatively late stage. So Luke does not have to project the beginnings of this separation on to the history of Jesus to the degree that the other evangelists do. Even the crucifixion is not the decisive turning point for him. Luke knows that the separation of Jews and Christians is an event in a development after Easter. He wants to demonstrate how it took place against the will of the Christians. For him it seems to have almost a final character in the present. Here he differs from Paul. In Paul the last words on Israel in Rom. 11.25f.

are of its eschatological salvation. However, Luke's last word to Israel is a statement about its hardening at the end of Acts. Or is it not the last word? Did Paul perhaps have more influence on this author working in the sphere of Pauline influence than at first appears?

At least Luke still knows something of a hope of the Christians for Israel and with Israel (was it alive only in the past?). It is emphasized at the beginning and end of each of his works. At the beginning of the Gospel, Zechariah's *Benedictus* announces the redemption of Israel (Luke 1.68ff.). At the end, the disciples on the Emmaus road doubt it. They had hoped that Jesus 'would be the one who would redeem Israel' (Luke 24.21). The same thing is repeated in Acts: at the beginning the disciples raise the question whether Jesus will at this time 'restore the kingdom to Israel' (Acts 1.6). At the end Paul asserts that he is a prisoner solely 'because of the hope of Israel' (28.20; cf. 23.6; 26.6f.). So Luke knows that both Jews and Christians share the same messianic hopes. However, these tacitly change in character if one progresses from the nationalistic messianic tones in the *Benedictus* to the later statements. Nevertheless the promises remain, though perhaps in another form. But Acts 3.20f. still emphasizes that heaven has received the messiah intended for Israel until the time of the ἀποκατάστασις πάντων, the restoration of all things, which God has proclaimed from of old through the mouth of his holy prophets. And according to Acts 15.15–17, Amos 9.11f., the promise of the restoration of the dwelling of David, is to be fulfilled.[24]

Thus Luke at least recalls the common hope. But does he also share it? Doesn't he himself share the conviction of irreversible hardening? Doesn't he end his two-volume work with that? However, we should remember that Luke does not combine any statement of judgment with the well-known saying about hardening in Isa. 6.9f. (LXX). God himself has hardened Israel, but there is no threat that he will therefore condemn it. On the contrary, one could cite small indications of a remnant of hope.

- In describing the reaction of the Jews to the message, Acts 28.24 emphasizes: 'Some were convinced by what he (Paul) said, while others disbelieved.' So the Jews of Rome are split.
- The quotation about hardening from Isa 6.9f. is introduced with the 'formula', 'The Holy Spirit was right in saying to your *fathers* through Isaiah the prophet . . .' (6.25). That does not mean that he has spoken to *you*. Initially the hardening affects only the fathers. Everything could still be open for the sons and their descendants.
- The quotation about hardening itself breaks off with a future 'And I will heal them' (καὶ ἰάσομαι αὐτούς), which replaces a previous chain of

subjunctives. Does this mean that God will redeem Israel, so that the last part of the quotation is to be understood as a main clause attached by 'and' (Acts 28.27)?

- The narrator emphasizes that Paul received *all* who came to him in his dwelling – not just all the Gentiles. Given the overall context, those who came to him must also be imagined as including (some) Jews.

There is some degree of probability that Luke keeps open the question whether the hardening of Israel is only provisional or final. For if the repudiation of the message has taken place only within the last period of salvation history (and by no means at one of its turning points), then with a certain narrative logic it would also have had to have been possible to do away with it within history. And if it has been imposed by God, it is also within God's power to overcome it.

To sum up: the writing of the Gospels is an important step towards the Christian sign system becoming independent from the Jewish mother religion. With it, the followers of Jesus created a historico-mythical basic narrative of their own which attributed a divine status to an individual human being, so that precisely for that reason this narrative could not find a place in the treasury of religious narrative in Judaism. Therefore in all three Synoptic Gospels we find a clear demarcation from Judaism. Here it must be emphasized in conclusion that in all three Gospels this demarcation always takes place against the background of an awareness of how much Jews and Christians abidingly have in common. The Gospel of Mark emphasizes the demarcation in ritual sign language. However, at the beginning it also tells the story of the leper who is explicitly sent by Jesus to the priest in Jerusalem (Mark 1.40), and in one of the last controversy and didactic sayings describes a reasonable scribe who agrees with Jesus in putting ethic above rite (Mark 12.28ff.). The Gospel of Matthew emphasizes a demarcation in the ethical sign language. It wants a 'better righteousness' which surpasses the righteousness of the Jewish authorities. But here too this takes place in the awareness of how much Jews and Christians have in common. In Luke the demarcation from Judaism is made plausible with the help of a salvation-historical narrative. It appears as a development which neither God nor the Christians wanted to be like this – but which now has to be accepted as the incomprehensible hardening of most Jews. But Luke knows a great deal about the common history and hope which points in quite another direction. It is the Gospel of John which first goes beyond the demarcation from Judaism that can be detected here.

10

The Gospel of John: The Internal Autonomy of the Primitive Christian Sign World is Brought to Consciousness

The divinization of the earthly Jesus reaches its climax in the Gospel of John.[1] This forms a synthesis of two developments which run towards each other. On the one hand we find in Paul belief in the Exalted One with divine status – and observe how individual recollections of the Earthly One are fragmentarily combined with this picture of Jesus, without the formation of a consecutive narrative. On the other hand, the tradition of the Earthly One formed in the Synoptic tradition and in the first Gospels is increasingly permeated by the sovereignty of the Exalted One without belief in the pre-existence of Jesus developing in the Synoptic Gospels. In the Gospel of John both strands of development are fused. Everywhere the glory of the Exalted One shines through the activity of the Earthly One. Jesus appears as a god walking on the earth.[2]

Let's remind ourselves of this with a few statements about the Revealer in the Gospel of John. Only in the Gospel of John is Jesus called 'God' before and after his earthly activity, at the beginning in the Prologue (1.1, 18) and at the end, when the unbelieving Thomas addresses him with 'my Lord and my God' (20.28). We saw that in principle this is no problem for Jewish monotheism. Philo knows the 'Logos', a 'second God' alongside God – the side of God which is turned towards the world; emanating from God, this shines like light in his creation. He was also familiar with the notion that this Logos was time and again embodied in human figures and angels and was at work on earth. But Philo could not have understood how the Logos could be exclusively incarnated in a single human being about whose humanity and earthly descent there was no doubt. That is precisely what the Johannine Christ asserts of himself. Even as the Earthly One, he says that he is one with God (10.30; 17.11, 21).

However, this Johannine Christ does not just exist in unity with God. He makes his unity with God the subject of his preaching. This is a decisive step beyond the Synoptic Gospels, regardless of when this step was taken.

With the Synoptic Gospels, primitive Christianity had created its own sign world with its own centre. With the Gospel of John it became aware of this. Now it grounded itself wholly in the light of the revelation in Christ. He alone is the light, the truth and the life. Everything else that is called light, truth and life comes from him. Everything in the new religion of Christianity must be grounded in this centre and legitimated by it. Christ is not only in fact the centre of this new sign language, but refers to himself as this centre. Rudolf Bultmann aptly said of the Gospel of John that in it the Revealer reveals that he is the Revealer.[3] The Gospel is stamped by references of the Revealer to himself – and they stand alongside statements which refer to the world around, from which the Gospel of John clearly demarcates itself in dualistic statements. The grounding of the new Christian religion by its own basic narrative and the demarcation from its mother religion which in fact took place in the Synoptic Gospels is reflected on in John as in a meta-Gospel. If we want to sum up this process, we can say that in the Gospel of John the new religious sign language appears as a sign system which organizes itself. It organizes itself from its own centre, christology.

1. The programme of the Johannine hermeneutic-in-stages in the prologue[4]

The Gospel of John deliberately wants to lead readers to a higher stage of understanding – beyond that faith which we find both in the Synoptics and in the Pauline literature. The prologue of the Gospel contains in itself the programme for such a 'hermeneutic-in-stages'[5] and thus gives instructions about reading the Gospel as a whole. As in all the Gospels, decisive things are said right at the beginning.

- In the Gospel of Mark the 'beginning of the gospel' is the preaching of John the Baptist, in which *Old Testament prophecy* is fulfilled: 'Behold, I send my messenger before your face, who will prepare your way; the voice of one crying in the wilderness: Prepare the way of the Lord, make his paths straight.' This is a mixed quotation. Exodus 32.30 is also used alongside the prophetic passages Mal.3.1 and Isa. 40.3. The whole of scripture is read as prophecy.
- At the beginning of the Gospel of Matthew there is the genealogy of Jesus. It divides *Old Testament history* into periods, each of fourteen generations – from Abraham to David, from David to the exile, from the exile to Jesus. Jesus is the new 'son of David'. His position in salvation history, divided up into periods, shows that with him just as decisive a

turning point must take place as with David and the exile. He brings history so far to its fulfilment. Fulfilment statements run right through the Gospel of Matthew.

- At the beginning of the Gospel of Luke we meet in the infancy narratives prophetic figures of Judaism and angels. It is less scripture than *living revelation,* which shows that now the fulfilment of what all pious Jews had always expected is taking place. That is the content of the message of the angels to Zechariah (1.13ff.), to Mary (1.30ff.), to the shepherds (2.14). That is testified to by the prophecies of Zechariah (his *Benedictus*, 1.67ff.), Simeon (the *Nunc Dimittis*, 2.29ff.) and Anna, which are spoken in the Spirit.

Compare the Gospel of John with that! According to all the Synoptics, the story of Jesus is the fulfilment of prophecy – fulfilment either of prophetic writings or of current prophecy brought about by the Spirit. But the Johannine prologue begins immediately with God. The origin of all things is present in the Revealer. He comes directly from the heart (the κόλπος) of the Father. He alone brings authentic knowledge of God – final and exclusive. For no one else has seen God (1.18). Beyond doubt the Gospel of John also relates the revelation of Christ to the existing sign system of Judaism. Here too Jesus is announced by John the Baptist, and here too his revelation is related to Moses. But it takes place in a new way. Everything that takes place before and outside Christ not only refers to him but is also determined and brought about through him. The whole of reality is a hidden 'word', which means him and is 'expressed' in him. For this word has created everything. It existed before everything else. Moses and John the Baptist have their light and their truth from him.

A second characteristic of the prologue alongside this beginning in the absolute is that the knowledge of this absolute reality comes about in stages which correspond to the two strophes of the prologue. Both strophes begin with a statement about the Logos, the first with 'In the beginning was the Word, and the Word was with God' (1.1), the second with 'And the Word was made flesh and we saw his glory' (1.14). The first strophe is mainly formulated in the third person plural and the second mainly in the first person plural. John the Baptist appears in both strophes. In both cases, the statements which refer to him were probably inserted by the evangelist. For the prosaic-sounding parts about him stand out from the hymnic prose which surrounds them. Why does John the Baptist have to appear twice? Why is it not enough for him to disseminate his message once? In my view this duplication is deliberate. John the Baptist has to appear twice because the faith which he is to create by his testimony develops in two stages. What are these stages? The following schematic survey of the prologue will bring them out.

1–5	The creation of the world through the Logos, which as a divine being (θεός) was with God (ὁ θεός) from the beginning.
	v.5: The complete failure of the darkness to comprehend the light of the Logos
6–8	The witness of John the Baptist to the light; through this witness all are to come to faith.
9–11	The rejection of the light and
12–13	the acceptance of the light by those who 'believe' in his name.
14–18	The revelation of God by the Logos in the flesh and the vision of his glory.
15	John the Baptist's witness to his pre-existence: Jesus existed before John the Baptist. He too received from him 'grace through grace'.
16–17	Moses and the law are superseded by the revelation of 'grace and truth'.
18	The authentic revelation of God by the one who is 'the only God'.

It is easy to recognize the following 'stages':

- The first strophe speaks of 'belief', the second of 'seeing'. Even if elsewhere in John both terms are synonyms,[6] here they indicate a progress in knowledge.
- The first witness of John the Baptist is a witness to the light; the second a witness to its pre-existence. It goes beyond what ordinary Christian faith (as for example in the Synoptic Gospels) saw in Jesus.
- In the first strophe the light lightens everyone and is accepted by a group of children of God. In the second strophe the glory of God is accessible only to a 'we-circle'.

It is also clear that the whole prologue depicts a way from complete misunderstanding to understanding. In 1.5 we read in the present – as a statement which continues to apply in the present day: 'The darkness has not comprehended (or grasped) it (the light).' So misunderstanding prevails at the beginning. But at the end the possibility of a complete understanding is opened up: 'The only one who has a divine nature has proclaimed him (God).' Since no one else has seen God, only he has made the inaccessible light accessible.

Our conclusion must be that the Johannine prologue describes a process from the failure to understand God in this world to a complete understanding. This takes place in two stages. The first stage corresponds to the witness of John the Baptist which is given before the appearance of Jesus. Jesus is recognized as the light of the world. The second stage corresponds to the witness of John the Baptist after the incarnation. Now John the Baptist sees the whole glory of God shining in the incarnate Logos and recognizes in Jesus the embodiment of grace and truth. Only now does John the Baptist bear witness that Jesus already existed before him. The first encounter with Jesus as *the* 'light', mediated through John the Baptist, becomes an immediate encounter with Jesus which goes beyond this. Now the believer stands alongside John the Baptist, and includes himself in the confession with the first person plural, 'And of his fullness have we all received, grace upon grace' (1.16). He becomes independent of John the Baptist. He relates everything that is to be important in his faith only to Jesus himself, not to John the Baptist or Moses.

What is the goal of this hermeneutic-by-stages? At first glance one could say that it is the high christology of the Gospel of John, specifically belief in the Pre-existent One. With this belief the Gospel of John clearly goes beyond the belief of the Synoptics. But such a concrete content of belief is not the decisive factor. What is decisive is the way in which the new Christian sign system grounds itself in its christological centre and legitimates itself from it. The inner autonomy of the Christian faith, the way in which it is defined by its own content, is the goal of the Johannine hermeneutic-in-stages.

Point

2. The implementation of the Johannine hermeneutic-in-stages

This Johannine hermeneutic-in-stages also shapes the external structure of the Gospel of John. The revelation takes place in two stages, which correspond to the two parts of the Gospel. The public activity of the Revealer (John 1–12) is surpassed by a revelation in the circle of disciples (John 13–17; 20–21). But even within these two parts we keep finding a progress of knowledge and understanding. Within the public part the reader of the Gospel of John keeps taking the step from an initial faith orientated on the visible and the manifest towards belief in the revelation of the invisible. Thus time and again the miracles of Jesus are reinterpreted symbolically and the words of Jesus take on a deeper sense – often after an initial misunderstanding. The same is true of the non-public revelation in the circle of disciples in the second part of the Gospel of John: a first farewell discourse is followed by a second, which discusses the themes of the first discourse again at a higher level.[7] This re-reading of previous texts has its climax in the high-priestly prayer (John 17), in which the whole of Jesus' career is interpreted in retrospect.

Our question now is: how far does this hermeneutic-in-stages, through which the existing Jewish and Christian traditions are reinterpreted at greater depth, form a new religious sign system, a new constellation of myth, ethic and rite? In fact all three forms of religious expression are reshaped in the Gospel of John. But the characteristic of the Gospel is that in the public part, only the transformation of the mythical and ritual sign system by Jesus is depicted. Quite unlike the Synoptic Jesus, the Johannine Christ does not put forward any ethical message in public. This happens only in the farewell section and even here it is reduced to the commandment to love. The whole ritual and mythical sign system is once again reorganized in its light. So the commandment to love is the key to the Gospel of John.

(a) The transformation of the mythical sign system in the Gospel of John

In the first part of the Gospel of John Jesus keeps encountering people's expectations of salvation which he fulfils and transcends at the same time. This becomes tangible to us in two forms: on the one hand as expectations of redeemer figures who are associated with particular honorific titles, and on the other as scriptural statements which are expected to be fulfilled in the time of salvation.

The controversy with the traditional *honorific names* already begins in the first chapter of the Gospel of John. John the Baptist directs the first disciples to Jesus. They come to him and gain further disciples because they see the traditional expectation of a redeemer fulfilled in him. They 'have found the Messiah' (1.41), or they describe this messianic figure as the one 'of whom Moses in the law and the prophets have written' (1.45). Nathanael confesses Jesus with the words, 'Rabbi, you are Son of God, you are the king of Israel' (1.49). Whereas in the Synoptic Gospels the disciples only slowly and with great difficulty penetrate to the knowledge of the dignity of Jesus, in the Gospel of John they have this knowledge from the start. They already know when they are called that he is 'Messiah', Son of God' and 'king of Israel'. But in so doing they represent only a first stage of knowledge. What is striven for in the Synoptic Gospels as the goal of knowledge is presupposed in John as its starting point. Jesus promises yet more (in his answer to Nathanael's confession): '"You shall see greater things than these." And he said to him, "Truly, truly, I say to you, you will see heaven opened, and the angels of God ascending and descending upon the Son of Man"' (1.50f.). Here all expectations are surpassed by a 'seeing', just as in the prologue the 'belief' of the children of God is surpassed by seeing the glory of the Incarnate One. The 'greater things' that the disciples will see – i.e. the content of the second stage of the Johannine hermeneutic-in-stages – is the direct unity of Jesus with the heavenly world, which is depicted by the angels ascending and descending, and is connected with the mysterious 'title' Son of Man (which in the Gospel of John is an unknown and incomprehensible title, as John 12.34 shows).

So Jesus is not yet completely known: his dignity is expressed with the traditional honorific christological titles 'Christ' and 'Son of God' and the traditional expectations of a redeemer connected with them are seen as being fulfilled. What is decisive in the Gospel of John is how the Redeemer defines himself. He does this in the *'I am' sayings*,[8] in which the christology bound up with titles is surpassed by a metaphorical christology, in other words a christology in images: I am the bread of life, the light of the world, the door, the good shepherd, the resurrection and the life, etc. The sequence of these images corresponds to a deliberate composition. The first 'I am' saying about the bread of life is an invitation to '*come*' to Jesus (6.35); the second speaks of the 'light of the world' and goes beyond the first 'I am' saying by being a call to '*follow*' Jesus (8.12) after one has come to him. Those who follow Jesus abandon their familiar life. They cross a threshold which leads to a new world. The third saying emphasizes the character of the follower's existence as a threshold: those who 'follow' Jesus (10.5) and '*enter in*' through the door enter a new sphere (10.7). In this sphere they are protected by the good shepherd, of whom the fourth 'I am' saying speaks (10.11). What they find in this new sphere of life is expressed in the last 'I am' section in the public part: Jesus is the resurrection and the life. Whoever '*believes*' in him has life not only as hope of a future, eternal life, but as a present reality. In all these images the Revealer defines himself in a way which transcends all traditional roles of Redeemer and Revealer.

In the tradition, these redeemer roles are defined by '*scripture*'.[9] Whereas elsewhere in the New Testament the Old Testament is the basis for paraenesis and promise, in the Gospel of John it exclusively becomes the reservoir of christological promise. Nevertheless it is strongly relativized. There are three indications of this:

- First, in John 5.31ff. Jesus speaks of a witness which is greater than that of John the Baptist. In so doing he mentions three factors which legitimate it: the witness of his works, the witness of his Father and – in last place – the witness of scripture. The witness of scripture in itself is not sufficient unless the Father himself bears witness to Jesus. Scripture alone does not lead to Jesus. Therefore the Johannine Jesus can say to the Jews: 'You search the Scriptures, because you think that in them you have eternal life; and it is they that bear witness to me' (5.39). One understands scripture only if one already has the Word of God 'in oneself' (5.38).

- Secondly, the Gospel of John is the only Gospel to state openly the contradiction between scriptural promises and the story of Jesus. For the Gospel of John, Jesus comes from Nazareth. He is Joseph's son (1.45). That contradicts the messianic prophecies of scripture which explicitly state: 'Has not the scripture said that the Christ is descended from David, and comes from Bethlehem, the village where David was?' (7.42).
- Thirdly, alongside the general conviction in primitive Christianity that scripture is fulfilled in Christ, the notion occurs in the Gospel of John that the words of Jesus are also fulfilled. So the word 'fulfil' (πληροῦσθαι) is used to refer not only to scripture but also to Jesus' own prophecies. Thus Jesus is crucified by the Romans, 'to fulfil the word which Jesus had spoken to show by what death he was to die' (18.32; cf. 18.9).

There is no mistaking the fact that in the Gospel of John Jesus stands above scripture. It cannot give him any ultimate legitimation; rather, he legitimates it. Jesus transcends what scripture says of him and what is alive as a traditional expectation of a redeemer. He legitimates himself through his revelation of himself. All previous stages of christological expectations and insights are surpassed in this Johannine hermeneutic-in-stages. That is true both of pre-Christian expectations of a Redeemer and of the first christological insights among Christians. Scripture and its previous Christian interpretation are surpassed. The honorific titles for a messianic figure which can be attested in Judaism are surpassed, as are the confessions of the first disciples, which are orientated on these honorific titles.

(b) The transformation of the ritual sign language in the Gospel of John

After the calling of the disciples, in the Gospel of John two signs are performed by Jesus which belong closely together: he changes water into wine and cleanses the temple in Jerusalem. Both actions have a mysterious symbolic meaning. Both point to a transformation of the ritual sign language of Judaism.

The miracle with the wine takes place in six stone water jars which are intended 'for the Jewish rites of purification' (2.6). These *rites of purification* are superseded with the appearance of Jesus. They once served to make people fit for the cult. Only those who had submitted to them could take part in the temple cult. The transformation of water into wine indicates a change in the traditional rites.

The next sign is performed in Jerusalem. Seized with 'zeal' for God's house, Jesus drives from the *temple* those who sell animals and change money. In the Synoptic Gospels this conflict stands at the end of Jesus' activity; in the Gospel of John the Johannine Jesus begins his public activity with it. It has a symbolic significance. Jesus interprets the prophecy about the temple, 'Destroy this body and in three days I will raise it up' (2.19), in terms of the temple of his body, his death and his resurrection after three days. Thus Jesus himself takes the place of the temple. This knowledge is generalized in the conversation with the Samaritan woman by the well: God does not want to be worshipped either in Jerusalem or on Gerizim, but in spirit and in truth, and the spirit of truth is bound up with Jesus, as the farewell discourses confirm.

In the Gospel of John the new Christian rites take the place of the ritual sign system of Judaism. The new ritual sign system of primitive Christianity is introduced at an early stage. *Baptism* is talked about in the conversation with Nicodemus. On the one hand it is said to be necessary for salvation: 'Unless one is born of water and the Spirit one cannot enter the kingdom of God' (3.5). On the other hand it is strongly spiritualized. Without rebirth from above it has no significance.

The *eucharist* also already occurs in the public activity of Jesus. The primitive Christian sacrament can be clearly seen through the miraculous feeding with the bread. And again a concrete interpretation stands alongside a spiritual one. On the one hand the miracle with the bread indicates that salvation is gained only by eating the flesh and drinking the blood of Jesus – the echoes of the eucharist are unmistakable; it is regarded as necessary for salvation. On the other hand the miracle with the bread is only a symbol for the spiritual food of revelation. It is expressly said that the flesh is of no avail (not even the flesh of the Revealer who has come from heaven); only the Spirit brings life. Only the words of Jesus are spirit and life. They are the true heavenly food (6.63).[10]

Thus baptism and eucharist replace the Jewish rites. But they too can be misunderstood. The fact that both sacraments are already introduced in the public part of the activity of Jesus indicates that they are to be surpassed by a revelation which goes further (in the farewell part of the Gospel).

Before we go into the content of this revelation which takes the recipients further, let us attempt to bring together the observations made on the first part of the Gospel of John. Here in the first part of the Gospel Jesus is continually confronted with people's expectations of salvation as formulated within the Jewish religion in scripture and in the ritual sign system of Judaism. In both forms he is confronted with the desire for gain in life. On the one hand he fulfils these expectations, and on the other he transcends them, coming into conflict with temple and scripture, the ritual and narrative sign system of Judaism. Yet he is the only one who gives what they promise: true life. The longing for this true life is alive in the Jewish religion, as in every other religion. Granted, within the framework of a life of Jesus the Gospel of John cannot speak directly of other religions, but these are present. Here are three features:

- The miracle of the wine is unmistakably depicted in imitation of corresponding miracles from the cult of Dionysus (John 2.1ff.).
- The healing of the paralysed man in Bethesda presents the saving activity of Jesus as the fulfilment of the longing for health and life which was alive in the ancient healing cults. Jesus surpasses Asclepios (5.1ff.).
- Through the encounter with the Samaritan women can be seen the encounter with all other religions, when the Samaritans greet Jesus as 'redeemer of the world' (4.42).

The longing for true life is present in all religions. But only in Jesus is it fulfilled. Readers of the Gospel of John know from the start that he is the embodiment of life. Already in the prologue they read: 'In him was life and the life was the light of men' (1.4). And each of the 'I am' sayings speaks of the provision of gain in life:

> I am the bread of *life*;
> he who comes to me shall not hunger,
> and he who believes in me shall never thirst (6.35).
>
> I am the *living* bread
> which has come from heaven.
> Whoever eats of this bread will *live* for ever.
> And the bread which I shall give for the *life* of the world is my flesh (6.51).
>
> I am the light of the world.
> He who follows me will not walk in darkness,
> but will have the light of *life* (8.12).

I am the door of the sheep . . .
I came that they may have *life*, and have it abundantly (10.7–10).

I am the good shepherd.
The good shepherd lays down his *life* (ψυχή) for the sheep (10.11; cf. 10.14).

I am the resurrection and the *life*.
He who believes in me will *live*, though he die.
And he who *lives* and believes in me will never die (11.25).

Where the Revealer reveals that he is the Revealer (in the 'I am' sayings), at the same time he says, 'I provide the decisive gain in life – here in the present and for all eternity.' And this is his task in the world. At the conclusion of Jesus' public activity there is a retrospect in which he gives an account of his task: he cries out (publicly) to the world:

For I have not spoken on my own authority;
the Father who sent me has himself given me commandment
what to say and what to speak.
And I know that his commandment is eternal life (12.49f.).

In the reckoning which he gives in the high-priestly prayer, Jesus repeats this significance of his mission when looking back on his activity. There he says to the Father that the Father has given him authority 'that he may give eternal life to all those whom you have given to him'. This eternal life consists in religious knowledge: 'And this is eternal life, that they know you, the only true God, and Jesus Christ, whom you have sent' (17.3). Let us recall our definition of religion: *religion is a cultural sign language which promises gain in life by corresponding to an ultimate reality*. John 17.3 is a model of this definition. Here it is clearly said that the aim of Jesus' mission is to bring about a relationship between human beings and the one and only true God. This relationship has only one aim: gain in life. Where this contact becomes 'knowledge', this life is already realized. The Gospel of John in fact wants to promise what all religions promise. In the Gospel this is predominantly described through the controversy with the Jewish religion. Jesus appears as Revealer in place of the Jewish sign system, in place of temple and scripture. He surpasses any previous revelation. He also surpasses the experience of salvation in other religions. However, this revelation of Jesus in public is once more surpassed by non-public revelation in the farewell discourses. But how can the revelation of life so far be surpassed? In the Gospel of John the answer is: through the commandment to love. That brings the third form of expression in religion into play, ethics. There is no ethical preaching in the public activity of Jesus.

(c) The transformation of the ethical sign language in the Gospel of John

In the public part of his activity, Jesus is confronted with the world's expectation of life and salvation. In the farewell part he deals with the sorrow and anxiety of his disciples. He prepares them for a life in the world without him. Just as he has one task which determines all his public activity, namely the revelation of life, so here he has one task: the revelation of the commandment to love – or more precisely, the revelation of love.[11] For what is bound up with the key word 'love' goes beyond an ethical commandment. There is little mention of love in the public part – and nothing about a human obligation to love; only now does love become the theme. The Johannine Christ speaks explicitly of a 'new commandment' which he has to communicate. And it could be that here he is referring back to the 'first commandment' with which he summed up his message at the end of his public activity: the commandment to reveal life and make it accessible (12.49f.). The new commandment goes beyond that.

But this 'new commandment', too, is revealed in two stages. It occurs for the first time in the dialogical farewell discourse (13.34f.), the second time in the monological farewell discourse (15.12–17). There is even a clear indication in the text that the most important thing in the Gospel of John is now being said. Previously Jesus has already often proclaimed that he has to proclaim the decisive message from God, that he says what he has heard from the Father. But we never hear what he has heard there, in the heavenly world. Only once in the Gospel is it expressly emphasized that Jesus has now said *everything* that he has heard from the Father, namely in the second formulation of the commandment to love:

> This is my commandment, that you love one another as I have loved you.
> Greater love has no man than this, that a man lay down his life for his friends.
> You are my friends if you do what I command you.
> No longer do I call you servants,
> for the servant does not know what his master is doing;
> but I have called you friends,
> for *all* that I have heard from the Father I have made known to you (15.12–15).

Not only is it explicitly said here that everything – really everything – that Jesus has to communicate on the basis of his familiarity with the Father has been said; in addition it is made clear that here all previous revelation has been surpassed. For hitherto the disciples were servants in their relationship to God and Jesus; now they have become his friends. The distinguishing characteristic is a religious knowledge.

This new knowledge of God is also evident in the two 'I am' sayings in the farewell discourses. These once again go beyond the self-disclosure of the Revealer in the 'I am' sayings in the first part. Only in them is God brought into play as Father. Jesus is 'the way, the truth and the life', because he opens the way to the *Father* (14.7). He is the true vine, because the Father is the gardener (15.1). If access to the Father is stressed in the first of these two 'I am' sayings, in the second the emphasis is on the consequence. In the former it is a matter of *coming* to God through Jesus, and in the latter of *abiding* in God in Jesus. This new relationship with God is to bring forth fruit, and here the Father as husbandman sees that this fruit flourishes (15.1f.). Thus in the farewell discourses, the relationship with God formally takes on a new quality.

But the previous revelation is also surpassed in content. Jesus appears as the Revealer not only of life but of love. This idea of love once again restructures the whole sign system of the Gospel of John. All three forms of religious expression – ethic, rite and myth – are transformed in the light of it.

Ethic: Even if it has been asserted time and again that the commandment to love in the Gospel of John is not an ethical commandment but rather a metaphysical statement about God's reality, the ethical content of this love cannot be denied. We have to take seriously the fact that the specific word 'commandment' is used, and that concrete modes of behaviour are indicated as love. Thus in the view of the Gospel of John, the foot-washing is an act of love – and one may generalize. All that the foot-washing symbolizes is an act of love: on the one hand hospitality which makes possible a unity of Christians whose homes are dispersed, and on the other hand the renunciation of status which produces equality among the Christians. Furthermore, in the Gospel of John love consists in the readiness to suffer martyrdom for others. Jesus himself realizes this love in exemplary fashion (John 15.13). Finally, I John makes love concrete as the material support of other Christians (3.17).

The special character of the Johannine ethic lies in the fact that all other commandments are insignificant alongside this one commandment to love. Granted, time and again commandments of Jesus in the plural are mentioned. But in fact he proclaims only one commandment. And with this one commandment he has said everything. This one commandment shows some changes by comparison with the Synoptic commandment to love.

Love of God has disappeared from the twofold commandment to love God and one's neighbour. However, this concentration on the interpersonal commandment to love also appears in Paul (cf. Rom. 13.8–10). Instead of love of God, God's love for humankind is emphasized (John 3.16).

The Synoptic tradition shows that the commandment to love is an 'old' commandment, which already appears in holy scripture. It quotes Deut. 6.4 and Lev. 19.18. By contrast, the Gospel of John emphasizes that this is a new commandment. In place of the Old Testament it introduces the model of the love of Jesus for his own to form the basis of this love.

The Synoptic tradition mentions neighbours as those to whom love is to be shown. By contrast the Gospel of John speaks of a mutual love. It is limited to fellow Christians. In I John it is called love of the brethren. By being combined with the requirement to renounce status (in the foot-washing), it preserves more strongly the element of equality which is present in mutuality.

Rites: In the farewell part the Christian rites are also reinterpreted in the light of this ethic concentrated on the commandment to love, in the foot-washing scene. Where in the Synoptic Gospels there is the account of the institution of the eucharist, in the Gospel of John we indeed read of a last supper of Jesus. However, the repetition called for is not of the sacramental eating but of the foot-washing. It is also possible to omit an account of the eucharist because the eucharist had already been mentioned earlier, in John 6.51ff. Now only a deeper interpretation of the meal is given. There are two possibilities here. Either the Johannine Christians celebrated their own rite of foot-washing in their assemblies as a church within the church, in which case a new rite would have appeared alongside the eucharist here; or the shared eucharist would be being reinterpreted in terms of its essential content. This consists in its communal character, as symbolically represented in the foot-washing. In the foot-washing the 'Lord' takes the role of the servant: the role of the slave, the woman and the pupil. At that time foot-washing was expected of these three roles. So the eucharist is to bring about a situation in which all Christians perform services for one another and none set themselves above anyone else. If we remember that Paul too sees the distinctive nature of the eucharist endangered by this social content, as I Cor. 11.17ff. shows, we will not think that such an interpretation of the eucharist in primitive Christianity was totally impossible. At the same time the second sacrament of primitive Christianity is being reinterpreted. For the foot-washing is a rite of cleansing. With it Jesus assures his own once again: 'Whoever has bathed does not need to wash, except for the feet; and you are clean . . .' (13.10). As Jesus says later in the farewell discourse, they are 'clean by the word which I have spoken to you' (15.3). They remain clean if they remain in fellowship with Jesus – like the grapes on the vine. So the binding together of all Christians is the deeper significance of both sacraments. The ritual sign language of Christians is ultimately aimed at mutual love.

Myth: the same goes for the historico-mythical basic narrative of Christianity. Already in the first summary of the Johannine 'kerygma' in the conversation with Nicodemus the whole Christ event is interpreted as an expression of the love of God:

> For God so loved the world
> that he gave his only begotten Son
> that all who believe in him should not perish, but have everlasting life (3.16).

This notion stands in complete isolation in the first part of the Gospel of John. It is developed only in the farewell discourses. First of all, at the beginning of the farewell part, there is mention only of the love of Jesus for his own: 'Having loved his own who were in the world, he (Jesus) loved them to the end' (13.1).

In the first farewell discourse this love is extended: on the one hand the disciples are to love one another in keeping with this love (thus 13.34). On the other hand, they are loved by the Father if they love Jesus and keep his word (14.23). Both will take up their abode in those who are thus bound up with God and Jesus through love. God's unity with Christians comes about through the love of Jesus. So the love of Jesus is extended to God and to the mutual love of Christians.

In the second farewell discourse a further theme is how Christians can remain in this unity with God and Jesus once they have entered into it. Here too there is a reference to the love of God.

> As the Father has loved me, so I love you;
> *abide* in my love.
> If you keep my commandments, you will *abide* in my love,
> just as I have kept my Father's commandments and *abide* in his love (15.9–10).

This abiding in the love of God cannot be taken for granted, because the world is full of hatred towards the Christians.

Finally, in the high-priestly prayer the unity of Christians with one another is extended to the future generations after the first disciples and grounded explicitly in the unity of Jesus with God:

> The glory which you have given me I have given to them,
> that they may be *one* even as we are *one*, I in them and you in me,
> that they become perfectly *one*, so that the world may know
> that you have sent me and have loved them even as you have loved me
> (17.22f.).

It is not fortuitous that the high-priestly prayer ends with the petition 'that the love with which you have loved me may be in them, and I in them' (17.26).

The basic Christian narrative of the Son of God who came into the world and is returning to the Father is redefined in the farewell discourses in terms of the motif of love. The sending of the Son into the world motivated by the love of God becomes a unity of God, Jesus and the Christians. Thus in the farewell discourses a specifically Johannine Christ-mysticism deepens even further the christology of sending,[12] which already dominated the public part of the Gospel of John.

3. The self-organization of the primitive Christian sign system in the Gospel of John

The Johannine Revealer reveals that he is the Revealer. But this revelation is not tautological. In addition, for the whole world it reveals life, and for the Christian community beyond that it reveals love. All the elements of the traditional sign system are reorganized in the light of this basic notion, so that a new sign system comes into being. Systems demonstrate their independence by being able to demarcate themselves from their environment as independent formations and to preserve themselves. The self-organization of the new sign system takes place in two directions: in the direction of the past it detaches itself from its mother religion, Judaism, and reorganizes its sign elements in a new way in terms of its christological centre. But at the same time it organizes itself in relation to its future. It incorporates into its sign world elements which ensure its survival. We find a reorganization of the tradition and a pre-organization of the future side by side.

(a) The reorganization of the traditional sign elements and forms of expression

We have already investigated the reorganization of the traditional mythical, ritual and ethical sign language. It remains to show how the primitive Christian sign language in the Gospel of John gains independence from its mother religion through this reorganization, an independence which in the texts takes the form of an abrupt demarcation from Judaism. I shall demonstrate this from the three forms of religious expression: myth, rite and ethic.

In the Gospel of John the Christian *myth* culminates in statements about unity: Jesus is the one sent by God and forms a unity with him. These statements about unity have different functions in the public part of the Gospel of John and the non-public farewell part.

In the public part they provoke the rejection of the Johannine Jews. When after a healing on the sabbath Jesus claims that he is continuing the works of his Father, they want to kill him because in doing this he has made himself equal to God (5.18). It is offensive for a human being to *make* himself God. This is repeated after the discourse about the good shepherd. When Jesus says, 'I and the Father are one' (10.30), they attempt to stone him. It is unmistakable that in the Gospel of John (and in the real life of the Johannine community) the high christology has become a point of dispute between Jews and Christians – nothing can yet be detected of this in Paul, although he too talks about pre-existence and exaltation, though not about the manifest deification of the earthly Jesus.

Such statements about unity recur in the farewell part. Just as they provoke enmity from outsiders, so they bring unity among insiders. This tendency towards integration is evident from the fact that now the disciples are taken into the unity of Jesus with God. Jesus promises them the knowledge which is only possible after Easter, 'that I am in my Father and you are in me and I in you' (14.20). Jesus prays for the preservation of this unity: 'As you, Father, are in me and I in you, that they may also be in us' (17.21). From this unity a power of conviction is to shine out into the world. It is to ensure 'that the world believes that you have sent me' (17.21).

So the sayings about unity at the same time form a feature which distinguishes the Johannine Christians from the world around, a basis on which they find one another.

The same can be said of the Christian *rite*. Here too we find the juxtaposition of a function which sets Christians apart from outsiders with an integrative function. And here too both functions can be divided between the public part of the Gospel of John and its farewell part.

In the public part, baptism is talked of in the conversation with Nicodemus. But the promise and requirement of rebirth which is bound up with it meets with complete incomprehension, although Nicodemus is portrayed as a secret sympathizer with Jesus. This function of the sacraments in making a demarcation becomes even clearer in the eucharistic section in John 6. Jesus' talk about eating and drinking the flesh and blood of the Son of man is felt to be scandalous: 'This is a hard saying, who can listen to it?' (6.60) is the reaction of many disciples to it. And even after Jesus has added a 'spiritual' interpretation to his hard saying, the offence remains. For the evangelist relates: 'After this many of his disciples drew back and no longer went about with him' (6.66). One's relationship to the sacrament becomes the test for belonging to Jesus – and therefore to the community.

In the farewell part, where Jesus is alone with his disciples, the integrative aspects of the sacraments emerge. Jesus' last meal is depicted as a love meal. And the real significance of the sacraments is seen in this mutual love. Granted, we cannot be certain whether the discourse on the vine is meant to be a deliberate allusion to the eucharist. In actual fact it has certainly aroused such associations. If the disciples remain as closely tied to Jesus as the grapes are to the vine, they will abide in his love. As for the cleanness which is brought about by the ritual washing of baptism, all disciples are equally clean. There is no gradation among them. Peter, who wants a greater cleanness for himself than the other disciples, is repudiated. The disciples need only foot-washing, no more.

Comparable remarks can also be made on the primitive Christian *ethic*. Here too the functions of demarcation and integration can be interpreted as the two sides of the same content.

The commandment to love is emphatically introduced as a 'new commandment'. But according to the self-understanding of the Gospel of John it leads not only beyond all that is 'old' (and for the Gospel that also includes the mother religion of early primitive Christianity); it is also opposed to the 'hatred' of the world. This hatred includes persecutions by the synagogue (16.2), but quite certainly not just by it. For it cannot be fortuitous that the only martyrdom that we can demonstrate is the martyrdom of Peter. In the Gospel of John it is located in a distant land – to which Peter will be taken against his will. Probably behind this lies the historical fact that Peter was executed in Rome.

The integrative function of the commandment to love does not need to be documented separately. For in the Gospel of John it is explicitly conceived of in terms of this integration as a commandment to love one another.

All in all, we will have to say that the abrupt demarcation outwards and the high integration inwards are functionally connected in the Gospel of John. The Gospel of John cannot be read one-sidedly as the Gospel of love, neatly excising its dark side, the Johannine anti-Judaism. Rather, an unprejudiced understanding of the Gospel of John will bring both sides together. So here are a few thoughts on the Johannine anti-Judaism,[13] which put it on the one hand historically in its historical world, and on the other text-immanently in its symbolic world.

When the Johannine Jews seek Jesus' life, according to the Gospel of John they do not do so of their own will. They would not do this as free children of Abraham (8.33). Rather, they stand under an alien will. They follow the will of Satan. But who stands behind Satan? In the Gospel of John he is also called the 'ruler of the world' (12.31; 14.30; 16.11) – and in fact at some points the Romans, the rulers of the world, clearly stand behind Satan. Here are two supporting arguments.

After Satan has entered into Judas to bring Jesus to the cross (13.27), in John 14.30 this Judas is announced as 'ruler of the world' and in John 18.3 can 'take a cohort' to arrest Jesus. Every reader in the Roman empire at that time knew that a cohort can be commanded only by someone who has a Roman mandate. This Judas in whom the ruler of the world is hidden commands Roman soldiers. Judas and the Roman rulers of the world belong together.[14]

The second observation arises from the condemnation of Jesus. There is no mistaking the fact that the Jewish authorities work for Jesus' death for the sake of the real rulers of the world. They blackmail Pilate into executing Jesus with the argument that Jesus has made himself king. 'If you release him, you are no longer Caesar's friend' (19.12). Because the Jewish accusers of Jesus claim that they have only one king, namely Caesar, they reject Jesus (19.15). Loyalty to Caesar is the decisive argument against Jesus which swings the vote in favour of killing him.[15]

The Gospel of John attempts to explain the death of Jesus by means of this construction. It is not 'the Jews', of whom the Gospel time and again speaks far too sweepingly, who are the cause of this death, but the Jews in so far as they have been made dependents of the ruler of this world. The Satan is a symbolic concentration of this power of the Romans which makes people dependent. So in the Gospel of John a blind 'prejudice' is not just being turned outwards. Rather, by the means of mythical language the opposition between Jews and Christians is understood as an expression of a politically-conditioned alienation of Judaism from itself.

(b) The pre-organization of the future sign language in the Gospel of John

The task still remains of showing how the self-reproduction of this new sign language in the Gospel of John is provided for. This comes about by Jesus being given three representatives in the Gospel of John: the Beloved Disciple, the Paraclete and Peter.[16] These three successors are all appointed in the second part of the Gospel of John, but in different sections of this second part.

In the farewell discourses Jesus promises the *Paraclete* as his successor. When he has returned to the Father, he will send 'another Paraclete' (14.16), his representative, the 'first Paraclete'. This other Paraclete will continue Jesus' role in the world. He will continue the trial of the world and lead the disciples into all truth. He has a task both towards the community and towards the outside world.

In the passion part the *Beloved Disciple* is appointed Jesus' representative. He is the only disciple who perseveres with Jesus to the end. Jesus appoints him his representative from the cross, when he says to Mary, 'Woman, behold your son!', and to the Beloved Disciple, 'Behold your mother!' (19.26f.). From now on this Beloved Disciple takes Jesus' place.

Finally, in the Easter part *Peter* is appointed to Jesus' role as the good shepherd. Despite failure and betrayal he is entrusted with the task of feeding the sheep (21.15–17). He assumes the role of the good shepherd who gives his life for the sheep. His martyrdom is predicted.

Now it is very important to define the functions of these representatives of Jesus in preserving the Johannine sign world.

In the Gospel of John, the *Beloved Disciple* has the task of serving as the witness to Jesus who has understood the Lord better than the other disciples. He reclines on his breast (13.23) – as Jesus reclined on his Father's breast (1.18). And just as Jesus is the true interpreter of the Father (1.18), so too the Beloved Disciple is his interpreter. His most important function for the future is to write down the Gospel of John. By attributing itself to the disciple who is superior to all the others in understanding, the Gospel of John ensures itself the highest rank among all comparable attempts to write down Jesus' words and actions in a book. There is no mistaking the fact that the Gospel of John knows such attempts. It relativizes them by saying that no book could contain the whole Jesus tradition. Therefore alongside all the Gospels which already exist there is still room for the Gospel of John; there is need for an authentic interpretation of the figure of Jesus. Now one could say that the Paraclete also assumes this task. But the Beloved Disciple has something special by comparison with him: he composes a book, whereas the Paraclete speaks. With his book he gives the Johannine sign world a stability, so that it will also be present in the future.

Like the Beloved Disciple, the *Paraclete* continues the activity of Jesus. But he does not repeat literally what Jesus has said. He does not fix it on papyrus. The Paraclete brings new, living revelation – even over and above what Jesus has said in the past. However, this new revelation is in continuity with the tradition. For first of all it is his task to recall all the sayings of Jesus and to teach them. But his task goes beyond that. Jesus himself indicated this in the farewell discourses:

> I have yet many things to say to you, but you cannot bear them now. When the Spirit of truth comes, he will guide you into all the truth; for he will not speak on his own authority, but whatever he hears he will speak, and he will declare to you the things that are to come (16.12f.).

Here the thought is of inspired discourse. The Paraclete reproduces what he himself has heard. He will reveal what is to come. Here primitive Christian prophecy is presupposed. As living discourse it supplements the revelation fixed in writing. Over and above the stability of the tradition it provides for its flexibility, i.e. for its being interpreted time and again and adapted to future situations.

Peter is the last of the three successors. Compared with the two others, he is clearly put at a lower level. The Beloved Disciple embodies the authentic understanding of Jesus. Peter accompanies his Lord with many misunderstandings. But he too has an irreplaceable function, which is directly addressed in his miraculous fishing trip in John 21 and his appointment as the good shepherd. Peter is to preserve and hold together the narrative community of the Johannine sign world. He is the shepherd who holds the Christian church together. Without this *social basis* even the sublime Johannine sign world – a new interpretation of the general primitive Christian sign world – cannot exist.

That brings us to the end of our reflections on the Gospel of John. According to the view presented here, this Gospel is a climax in the history of the origin of the primitive Christian religion.[17] Here this new religion not only actually organizes itself around its christological centre but becomes aware of this. This reflexivity is shown in the self-reference of the central statements of the Revealer, the emphatic demarcation from the environment as an alien outside world and the awareness of the need for the new sign world to ensure that it is preserved in terms of its own centre – symbolically depicted in the appointment of three representatives of Jesus who continue his work after his death. They see to the stability, the flexibility and the preservation of the *Sitz im Leben* of the Johannine sign world.

Part Five: The Crises and Consolidation of Primitive Christianity

11

The Crises of Primitive Christianity

The history of primitive Christian religion is the history of the origin of an autonomous religious sign system. It began with a departure from the ritual sign language of Judaism (by giving up circumcision and the food laws). It was completed by the formation of a distinctive narrative sign language for Christianity (as a unity of myth and history in the basic narrative of the Gospels). It safeguarded its social foundation by the development of an ethic which permeated the whole of everyday life: the obligation on the part of groups to live in a new way which had not been inherited from 'ancestors', but for which one had to make a conscious decision.

Such an autonomous sign system was something new. The pagan cults did not claim to be unique among all cults, but knew that they were embedded in a network of different cults. The Jewish religion claimed uniqueness, but remained tied to a people. Neither pagan cults nor the Jewish religion obligated their members to adopt a new way of life to which one had to convert by a deliberate decision. Rather, they came forward in the consciousness of offering a way of life legitimated by age-old traditions. By contrast, primitive Christianity developed an autonomous sign system which was international, exclusive and new.

In contrast to Judaism, but in accord with many pagan cults, it detached itself from the tie to a particular people. It denationalized that people's traditions. This detachment from the mother religion was expressed most clearly in *ritual* questions, by dispensing with the ritual signs of Jewish identity.[1]

In accord with the Jewish religion but in contrast to pagan cults, it claimed exclusive uniqueness. This exclusive uniqueness was expressed most clearly in its historico-mythical basic *narrative*: Jesus was the name above all names. All other numina are subordinate to him.[2]

In contrast to all previous religions, by a religious tie it created a new form of social life to which one converted by departing from the ancestral traditions. This turn towards a new form of life through personal decision (even against father, family and tradition) was expressed most clearly in its radical *ethic*.[3]

The crises[4] of primitive Christianity are crises of this autonomy – on three sides. On one side the detachment from a particular people could be put in question. Attempts to maintain the tie with Judaism by adopting the ritual marks of Jewish identity led to the *Judaistic crisis* in the first century. This was about independence from the mother religion. Here Paul became the founder and defender of the autonomy of the new religion. This crisis took its starting point in the elaboration of the rite and from there spread to the whole sign-system.

On another side, the uniqueness and exclusiveness by comparison with all other religious and philosophical sign systems could be put in question – and with it also the demarcation from the pagan world. Gnosticism was an attempt also to interpret the primitive Christian sign system as a variant of a universal sign system. The *Gnostic crisis* of the second century was over the independence of primitive Christian religion, which irreversibly remained tied to the one and only God of Judaism and his incarnation in Jesus. The issue here was the unity of myth and history in primitive Christianity.

Finally, in the course of time the counter-cultural consciousness of Christianity had to be toned down. Christianity itself became tradition and took on the general cultural values and patterns of behaviour of the world. However, the counter-cultural ethic of its radical beginnings kept flaring up in *prophetic crises*: in reform movements which strove for a pure and holy church. Since primitive Christianity had both tendencies, a counter-cultural protest and a general sense of cultural responsibility, within it from the beginning a structurally conditioned permanent crisis developed in the sphere of ethics. In primitive Christianity it appears in the prophecy of the Apocalypse of John and in the 'new prophecy' of the Montanist movement.

Attempts have been made to identify various crises. Thus above all pupils of Bultmann saw Paul's controversy with the Judaizers as a controversy with Gnostics (thus W. Schmithals).[5] However, both chronologically and in substance, these are different crises. Similarly, attempts have been made to interpret prophetic protest movements as movements opposing Gnostic tendencies towards assimilation to the world around.[6] But radical protest can flare up wherever life is given a liveable form.

Still, the truth is – and that is my first thesis – that the issue in all crises is the autonomy of the religious sign system, whether outwardly as a demarcation from the mother religion of Judaism or systems of pagan convictions, or inwardly as a struggle to accord with one's own radical beginnings. Here each time the crisis takes its starting point from a form of expression of the religion: in the Judaistic crisis from its rite, in the Gnostic crisis from its myth, and in the prophetic crises from its ethic. All three forms of expression first assume their final form and autonomy in these crises.

In addition there is a second thesis: the threat to inner autonomy is posed not only by religious factors but also by conditions in the political framework of the time. In the first century, political interventions by the Roman state in the communities split by the mission to the Gentiles led to the Judaistic crisis; the attempt to reintegrate Christianity into Judaism served to avoid conflict with the state and the world around. In the second century the general legal situation of the Christians, which promised them toleration if they remained socially inconspicuous, favoured the rise of Gnosticism – as a radical privatization of religion in which Christians could remain inconspicuous in public. Paul's Judaistic opponents in the first century and the Christian Gnostics of the second century therefore have one thing in common: they wanted to reduce the conflicts with the state and society. Here they differed from the prophetic movements. For these last, conflict with the world around was unavoidable. They deliberately flaunted the incompatibility of the community with the world.

1. The Judaistic crisis in the first century

Pauline theology is part of the Judaistic crisis. It provided a theological basis for the detachment from Judaism – in the doctrine of justification and its criticism of the Mosaic law. In Paul, the revelation of God in Christ becomes opposed to the revelation of God in the Torah. The result is that in Paul a religion of grace often takes the place of a religion of the law. Now Judaism itself is a religion of grace. God's positive concern for human beings precedes his demands in covenantal nomism. The opposition seems artificial. Therefore in present-day research into Paul there is a tendency to understand the tension between the revelation of the Torah and the revelation of Christ in Paul as a construct, which can be understood only in the light of immanent problems within Christianity. This is expressed in two variants. First, it is said that by virtue of an intrinsic logic the new religion has to disparage the mother religion (and therefore the Torah) and postulate in Jewish religion a need which did not exist, so that it can then celebrate itself as the fulfilment of this need.[7] Judaism had no problem with the Torah, nor did Paul, as long as he was a convinced Jew. When Paul was attached first to the Torah and then to Christ, he behaved like an immature young man who had two girl friends one after the other. The first was no problem until the second appeared. Only when the two were rivals did the first become a problem. Only now was she disparaged. In addition to this intrinsic logic (which is basically very unpleasant), there is said, secondly, to have been an external stimulus: the disparagement of the mother religion was conditioned by a conflict within Christianity.[8] Only when Judaizers in Galatia wanted to make ritual commandments of the Torah binding on the Gentile Christian communities did Paul disparage the whole law. The disparagement of the Torah is said to have its grounds in later trench warfare between parties and groups in primitive Christianity, and not in Paul's Damascus experience. In one respect, both explanations culminate in the same point: they explain a central theological doctrine of primitive Christianity, not in terms of the history of the Jewish religion, but as an expression of a detachment from this history. And in my view this is historically unsatisfactory. Must we not understand Paul and his doctrine of justification in terms of the religious and social problems of the Judaism of the time? And should that not also be possible on the premise that Judaism is a religion of grace? Therefore in what follows I shall attempt to understand the Judaistic crisis and the doctrine of justification as a sensible answer to religious and social problems of Judaism – and thus at the same time also give Pauline Christianity a place in the history of Judaism.

(a) The basic axioms of Judaism: monotheism and covenantal nomism and the aporias of Judaism

In what follows, the thesis that Judaism is a religion of grace will be accepted fully. But it will be added that even a religion of grace has its contradictions. Christianity, too, is a religion of grace, yet it is nevertheless full of contradictions and aporias. Judaism is characterized by two basic axioms:

Monotheistic faith in the one and only God, who is the God of all human beings, whether they recognize him or not. The Jewish religion is characterized by a strong theocentricity.

Covenantal nomism: God has no partner in heaven, but only the one people on earth, to whom he gave his commandments (as the representatives of all human beings). Consequently at the same time the Jewish religion has a marked anthropocentricity.

Two basic tensions of Judaism are indicated in these two basic axioms. 1. The tension between theocentricity and anthropocentricity: God is the almighty who determines all things, but only human beings are his covenant partners. 2. The tension between universalism and particularism: God is the God of all human beings, but he has chosen only one people as a covenant partner – as the representative of all human beings.

These two aporias of Judaism led Judaism to split up into different religious currents. On its periphery there are even some marginal voices which indicate that the law could also be felt to be a problem in Judaism; the Pauline critique of the law is a possibility within Judaism, even if it also may have brought about the separation of an originally Jewish group from Judaism.

The first basic tension manifests itself in the splitting up of Judaism into different religious parties.[9] According to Josephus the Essenes advocated a theocentric doctrine of election: God alone brings about salvation. By contrast, the Sadducees had an equally one-sided ethical soteriology: it depends upon human action whether or not men and women attain salvation (immanently in this life). By contrast again, the Pharisees advocate the golden mean: a synergism of divine and human action. However (at the latest after Judas of Galilee), they split into two currents. One consists of activists who are moved by the ideal of *zelos* and say that only if human beings work actively for the law and impose the observance of it on all Jews will God help. Alongside them there is a moderate majority current according to which divine action has priority over all human collaboration. Paul belongs within Pharisaism. Within it he is an advocate of an ideal of *zelos*. His statements about Judaism are statements about his Judaism. He describes this realistically and does not caricature it in any way. But he illegitimately generalizes his variant of Judaism. For him it is the only Judaism.

The first aporia of the Jewish religion arises out of the basic tension between theocentricity and anthropocentricity. If God predestines men and women for salvation, then (potentially) any 'synergism' can appear as hybris. If human beings want to bring about what only God can bring about, they are on the wrong way.[10] They succumb to an illusion. A consistent notion of election can devalue the ethic of the Torah. Conversely, a radicalized ethic of the Torah (as put forward in the ideal of *zelos*) leads to an ethical soteriology and threatens the radically theocentric, sovereign election of God.[11]

Where is the difference from the traditional picture of Judaism? The picture sketched out above does not contrast Jewish righteousness by works with a Christian religion of grace, but says that the tension between a religion of grace and righteousness by works is to be found within Judaism itself. This aporia led to the origin of Christianity out of Judaism. And I would add that this aporia was not 'resolved' in Christianity either, but lives on in it.

The contrast between theocentric election and ethical synergism can be combined with the second basic tension: those who commit themselves actively to the Torah and also want to impose it on deviant groups in Judaism in so doing emphasize the frontiers between Jews and Gentiles. The synergetic ethic can intensify particularism, especially if it is seized by the ideal of the zealot. In this way it comes into tension with the universalism of the Jewish religion. Israel worships the one and only God vicariously for all peoples. And it hopes for the universal recognition of God among all peoples.

Where is the difference from the traditional picture of Judaism here? The picture I have just sketched out does not contrast the particularistic Jewish religion with a Christian universalism, but says that this tension is an element in the life of the Jewish religion itself. It is an aporia of Judaism, which produces a universalistic group its midst. Here, too, it needs to be added that this aporia also is not 'resolved' in Christianity but continues to be active in it.

Intrinsically these aporias remained latent in Judaism. They are actualized only in marginal voices. But now and then these marginal voices on the periphery of Judaism make the law a problem from very different perspectives. Four texts may be mentioned in connection with this:

1. *Zimri's rebellion as retold by Josephus* (*Antt.* 4, 6, 10–12 = 4, 141–155): When the young Israelites fell in love with the daughters of foreign peoples and were thus ready to abandon their traditional way of life, Zambrias, himself married to a Midianite woman, came forward as their spokesman. He attacks Moses directly:

> Do you, Moses, keep these laws for which you have been so zealous (ἐσπούδακας) and which you have established through the power of custom. Were these people not as they are, by now you would often have been sorry and learned that you cannot deceive the Hebrews with impunity. I at least will not follow your tyrannical precepts (προστάσσεις). Hitherto you have striven for nothing but to enslave us (δουλείαν μὲν ἡμᾶς) under the pretext of divine legislation (better, the laws and God), and to ensure sovereignty for yourself through all kinds of scheming. You have robbed us of what is the due of a free and freedom-loving people, who recognize no law over them. Truly, the man who seeks to put what we would do of our own free will under the compulsion of laws and inflict punishment accordingly oppresses us more than the Egyptians. No, it is rather you who deserve punishment for rejecting what all others approve of and for stubbornly insisting on your own view, contrary to the view of all others. I do not regard what I have done as unjust, and I am not afraid to confess this publicly. As you say, I have married a foreign wife – accept this concession from me as a free man who does not need to hide anything. I also sacrifice to the gods what you regard as an abomination, for I think that it is permissible, since so many ways lead to the truth, not to put all one's hope tyrannically (ἐν

> τυραννίδι ζῆν) on one alone. There is no one who could boast that he has more discernment in respect of what concerns me alone than I myself' (*Antt*.4, 145–9).

Here we find the Pauline notion of the tyranny of the law – though only in the mouth of a wicked man. Slavery under the law is not replaced by God's grace but by a hybrid human claim to autonomy.

2. *The distortion of Moses' pure worship of God by his successors in Strabo of Amaseia* (*Geography* 16, 2, 35–38). Granted, Strabo is a pagan author, but the ideas expressed by him could be an echo of Jewish opinions: perhaps the echo of the moderate Hellenistic reform movement.[12] He writes that Moses himself introduced a pure worship of God – repelled by the Egyptian worship of gods in animal form and the Greek worship of gods in human form. He taught an aniconic worship of the universal God who embraces the whole of creation. He lived in peace with the surrounding peoples. He promised his people a worship of God which would not 'burden' (ὀχλήσει) them with dues, divine possession or other unreasonable things. Initially his followers kept to this form of divine worship, but then new priests came to power who were both superstitious (δεισιδαιμονίων) and tyrannical (τυραννικῶν ἀνθρώπων). Their superstition showed itself in taboos over food and circumcision, and their tyrannical nature in wars against their neighbours.

3. *Doubt about the perfect fulfilment of the law in the oration of Ezra* (IV Ezra 8.20–36). After the catastrophe of the destruction of Jerusalem, Ezra prays God not to look upon the sins of the people but upon those who serve God in truth (8.26). This brings about a split in the people: sinners and righteous come to be distinguished. But then this distinction is abandoned, since Ezra prays:

> For we and our fathers have passed our lives in ways that bring death, but you, because of us sinners, are called merciful. For if you have desired to have pity on us, who have no works of righteousness, then you will be called merciful. For the righteous, who have many works laid up with you, shall receive their reward in consequence of their own deeds. But what is man, that you are angry with him; or what is a mortal race, that you are so bitter against it? For in truth there is no one among those who have been born who has not acted wickedly, and among those who have existed there is no one who has not transgressed. For in this, O Lord, your righteousness and goodness will be declared, when you are merciful to those who have no store of good works (8.31–36).

Later the angel rejects this view:

> But you have often compared yourself to the unrighteous. Never do so! But even in this respect you will be praiseworthy before the Most High, because you humble yourself, as is becoming for you, and have not deemed yourself to be among the righteous. So you will be honoured even more (8.47–49).

Here too obedience to the Law is made a problem. Granted, this problem is dismissed by the angel. But the fact that it has to be rejected indicates that it is potentially present.[13]

4. *The radical allegorists in Philo* (*de migratione Abrahami* 89f.):

> There are some who, regarding laws in their literal sense as merely symbols of matters belonging to the intellect, are overpunctilious about the latter (the intellect), while treating the former with easy-going neglect. Such men I must blame for being too frivolous. For they ought to have given careful attention to both aspects, investigating more fully and precisely what is not seen (the meaning), and observing beyond reproach what is manifest (the wording). As it is, they live as if they were alone by themselves in a wilderness, or as though they had become disembodied souls, and knew neither city nor village nor household nor any company of human beings at all; overlooking all that the mass of men approve, they explore naked reality for itself alone. These men are taught by the sacred word to have thought for good repute, and to abandon nothing that is part of the customs fixed by divinely empowered men greater than those of our time.

In all these texts the law is made a problem. There is a 'rebellion' against the law – naturally only in the figure of someone who is in any case condemned by general opinion. But this figure, Zimri, is given life by Josephus over and above the Old Testament original: he transparently demonstrates the pull towards assimilation in Hellenistic culture and makes use of those themes in sophism which are critical of the law. Over against him Phinehas is regarded as the zealot who puts down his 'revolt'. But Moses appears as a third possibility of Judaism, which unsuccessfully calls for loyalty to the Torah through a moderate appeal. Was Paul himself a zealot for the law who with the oppression of the Christians was also putting down an 'inner' revolt against the law? Was he both Phinehas the zealot and Zimri the rebel at the same time?

But the aggression against the law embodied in Zimri is only one possibility. On the other hand we also find a high degree of identification with the law, which leads to introjected aggression against the self that is opposed to the law: to a great awareness of sin. No one can really observe the law. We find this possibility realized in the oration of Ezra.

We also find two hermeneutical attempts at a solution. On the one hand there is the distinction between Moses' original intention and the secondary additions by superstitious successors (thus in Strabo); and on the other there is the distinction between the literal meaning and the real symbolic meaning – from which is derived the freedom to neglect the external rites (thus the radical allegorists).[14]

(b) The doctrine of justification in the life of Paul

My thesis is now that Paul's doctrine of justification is an answer to these aporias of Judaism: his answer consists in a radicalization of grace and the universality of God.

Paul responds to the tension between theocentricity and anthropocentricity by radicalizing the doctrine of grace: he puts forward a theocentric doctrine of election – but this is election by God 'to be equal to the image of his son' (Rom. 8.29). Christians are not elected as part of the old creation, but as new creatures – as transformed beings, who participate in the being of Christ and will be transformed into the same form as he has. Transformed by the spirit, they do spontaneously what is required by the ethic of the Torah, at the centre of which stands the commandment to love. For Paul, to this degree Christian faith is fulfilment of the law and liberation for the law.

Paul responds to the tension between particularism and universalism by radicalizing universalism. He advocates a Jewish universalism which seeks to overcome the separatist function of the Torah by dispensing with the ritual marks of Jewish identity: circumcision, the food laws and the commandments about cleanness. In order to relativize these commandments of the Torah, he arrives at a fundamental criticism of the Torah which also relates to its ethical function. To this degree, for him Christian faith is also a matter of superseding the law and being freed from the law.

Now with this criticism of the law (along with an abiding bond with the law), does Paul drop out of the framework of Judaism? I think that the four texts from Judaism quoted above show that there was a latent problem over the law in Judaism. It was displaced and suppressed – just as Phinehas suppresses Zimri's criticism of the law, the interpreting angel dismisses Ezra's doubt about the law, or the Jewish philosopher of religion rejects the dissolution of the law by the radical allegorists. But anything that has to be repudiated is latently present. In Paul this latent criticism of the law became manifest. It broke into consciousness because he had been led astray by the law and had discovered an alternative, Christ. So we shall follow his development in broad brush strokes:

1. *The pre-Christian Paul* was a Jewish fundamentalist, characterized by demonstrative pride in the law and a zeal for the law. Paul was aware that his Judaism was not typical of Judaism generally. He emphasizes that he surpassed all his contemporaries in zeal in Judaism (Ἰουδαισμός, Gal. 1.14). His fundamentalism consisted in his transformation of his over-identification with Jewish norms into aggression against a minority which deviated from the norm – the followers of Jesus. Here Paul must already have envisaged a Judaism in which openness to the Gentiles was developing – probably not in the form of deliberately carrying on a mission to the Gentiles but in the form of an expectation that in the near future the temple would become open to all Gentiles and a hope that in a miraculous act God would bring Gentiles to Jerusalem from all points of the compass. Only if we presuppose such a burgeoning openness to the Gentiles can we explain why at his conversion Paul felt called directly to become a missionary to the Gentiles.

In addition we may reckon that the pre-Christian Paul was engaged in an unconscious conflict with the law.[15] Consciously, indeed, he was a proud Jew – 'as to the law a Pharisee, as to zeal a persecutor of the church, as to righteousness under the law blameless' (Phil. 3.5f.). But that does not exclude the possibility that at the same time unconsciously he had doubts about this law. In Romans 7.7ff. he describes a serious conflict with the law in the first person. In using 'I' he is not referring to himself; this is a typical 'I' which includes everyone. God's demand involves all in a conflict. Paul certainly does not describe this in the first person in order to exclude himself from it. What is true of all human beings is also logically true for him. Furthermore, what someone says about human beings generally is usually governed psychologically by his or her own experiences.[16] In my view, in Romans 7.7ff. Paul is indicating that originally he was unaware of this conflict. Only because of that can he speak of being deceived by the commandment; only because of that can he say that he did not understand what he was doing – and then goes on to analyse it increasingly clearly. When Paul says that human beings are by nature (as *sarx*) enemies of God, he is also referring to his own past, in which he acted as an enemy of God.

Now if we take these two characteristics of the pre-Christian Paul together, it follows that the persecution of a minority deviating from the norm by Paul, who is proud of the law, is connected with an unconscious conflict with himself which he projects on to the Christians: he sees among the Christians a freedom towards the law and an openness towards the Gentiles which he is suppressing in himself. In them he is fighting against part of himself, and the fight against the Christians at the same time helps him to suppress this 'shadow' in himself.

2. *Paul's conversion and call* is therefore the adoption of a completely new social position; he changes from being a persecutor of Christians to being the missionary of precisely this group. In the inter-personal sphere he accepts people whom he had not accepted previously – presumably because they had been more open towards strangers than he had hitherto thought possible.

Paul's conversion is at the same time an inner transformation: now he can accept all that he had previously repressed and had not wanted to perceive in himself – his indignation against the law and his hidden conflict with it. He can understand himself as a sinner. He once opposed God's will. Nevertheless he becomes an instrument of precisely this will. Personally, too, he is a justified sinner.[17]

It is therefore one-sided to emphasize either the social or the individual aspect at the expense of the other in the conversion of Paul and the certainty of justification which is grounded in it. Justification means both the acceptance of others (those who were previously rejected and the Gentiles) and acceptance of oneself.

In my view, it is similarly improbable that Paul's doctrine of justification should be understood only as an expression of later controversies,[18] as though the law had first become a problem for Paul when his opponents appealed to it to establish circumcision in his communities. Someone who is motivated by the law to persecute others and then joins those who are being persecuted must have had major problems with the law from the beginning, at his conversion. From the beginning he must have understood his new task in Christianity as grace. Nevertheless, there is a correct insight in this thesis of a later development. For Paul still had to work out his insight conceptually.[19] Here we must look briefly at Paul's further development.

3. *Paul as a Christian missionary*. We can distinguish two phases in his early period: the Nabataean mission, which he carried on from Damascus, and the mission in Cilicia and Syria, which he carried on (at least for the most part) from Antioch with Barnabas.

Questions about the validity of the law will not have played a decisive role in the *Nabataean mission*. For the Nabataeans were circumcised; they were regarded as akin to the Jews, as Arabs and sons of Ishmael – i.e. they shared Abraham as an ancestor. They worshipped a God without images. There was no substantive need to discuss the topic of the law publicly here.[20]

On the *mission to Syria* from Antioch the principle handed down on several occasions by Paul himself (as an existing formula?) probably applied, that neither circumcision nor uncircumcision mattered (Gal. 5.5; 6.15; I Cor. 7.19). Both are unimportant. But if it does not matter whether one is circumcised or not, one can think that there could be situations in which one could have oneself circumcised. Unimportant things are not forbidden.[21]

The question of the law must also have become significant for Paul's missionary activity only at the moment when Jewish Christians attempted to compel Gentile Christians to be circumcised, as in Galatia – perhaps with the argument that it was necessary for salvation. At this moment Paul must also have been confronted with his own past. For this had been governed by the fact that he had put the deviant minority of followers of Jesus under pressure. Only now did Paul activate his own conversion and introduce it as an argument into the public discussion – as a warning against accepting circumcision. He did this in two letters written against Judaistic counter-missionaries, Galatians and Philippians. A (current) crisis in the communities and a (long past) personal crisis now came together. The one interpreted the other. What is insufficiently seen is that this Judaistic crisis was also conditioned by political factors: by a changed political framework for the Pauline mission which had come about after the Apostolic Council. This needs to be described in rather more detail.

(c) The historical and political causes of the crisis in the first century

The recognition of the Gentile mission at the Apostolic Council gave great impetus to the Gentile mission. The disturbances in the community in Rome shortly after the Apostolic Council (46/48), because the message of Christ was being actively presented there, could be a remote effect of the Apostolic Council. Christianity would already have been present in Rome. However, a Jewish community could only provoke unrest if it accepted uncircumcised Gentiles as members on an equal footing. This unrest led to the Edict of Claudius in AD 49 and the expulsion of those who had played a prominent part in the unrest. The expulsion affected Jews. The Christians were not yet distinguished from them. Those who had been expelled very soon disseminated the news of the state intervention in the Jewish communities of the Mediterranean area – including Aquila and Priscilla in Corinth. They met the apostle Paul there and developed a friendly relationship with him. Quite certainly they thought as Paul did on the question of the Gentile mission.

Now we can infer two very different reactions to these political difficulties in the Jewish communities and in Jewish Christianity.[22]

After the Edict of Claudius the Jewish communities attempted even more strongly to prevent the new movement from gaining a footing in the places where they lived; if they could not prevent it doing so, they attached importance to not being identified with the Christians, so that repressive measures against the Christians did not affect them as well. They wanted to make it clear that these troublemakers were nothing to do with them.

The first reaction could have happened in Thessaloniki. According to I Thessalonians, Gentiles are the persecutors of the community. But as Paul is drawn into vigorous polemic also against Jews in connection with these persecutions (2.14–26), and Acts reports tensions with the synagogue, Jews could have attempted to prevent the dissemination of Christianity with the help of pagan authorities. The Christians in Thessaloniki were predominantly Gentiles, so the Jews there could not influence them by inter-synagogue actions. Hence the approach through pagan authorities. Probably this move was already a first reaction to the news of the expulsion of some Jews from Rome. For in Thessaloniki the central charge against Paul and his fellow-workers was that they were acting contrary to the commands of the emperor – i.e. opposing Claudius's religious policy, which was aimed at maintaining the *status quo*. Furthermore, they were accused of proclaiming Jesus as 'king', which indicates that in Thessaloniki there was the same confusion between the risen Christ and a person still living on earth as is also to be presupposed in Rome (cf. Suetonius). At all events, the Jews did not want to risk being expelled from Thessaloniki, like (some of) the Roman Jews.

By contrast, in Corinth the Jewish community appeared before the governor Gallio with a direct accusation, in order to distance itself from the Christians. The reason for this could be that here Christianity comprised some important Jews – alongside Aquila and Priscilla above all the synagogue leader Crispus. However, Gallio declared the objections presented to him to be a purely internal Jewish matter. In so doing he continued to identify Christianity as a Jewish group.

Jewish Christians reacted to the situation in a quite different way. If the synagogues got into difficulties as soon as Christians separated from them, and accepted uncircumcised Gentiles into their communities, then the tensions with Judaism had to be reduced. Christians (including Gentile Christians) who were recognizably Jews and understood themselves as Jews could be accepted by the synagogue. Only one thing was necessary: the Gentile Christians had to be persuaded to fulfil the minimal criteria of Judaism – i.e. to adopt circumcision and the food laws. This was not a direct offence against the Apostolic Council. For there it had only been agreed that circumcision was not to be an *obligation* on the Gentiles. However, that did not imply an obligation not to have oneself circumcised. What was there against doing this knowingly and voluntarily? We find this campaign for the voluntary adoption of the marks of Jewish identity for the first time in the communities of Galatia, and later in Philippi. Here the Galatian counter-mission had the following characteristics:

A positive link with Paul. His opponents said that Paul had laid the foundation for the truth. They wanted to build on it. Without such a positive link it is inconceivable that they would have made their way into the Pauline communities. So Paul's opponents did not attack him, but commandeered him. In contrast to I and II Corinthians, in my view there are no indications of personal attacks against which Paul has to defend himself. It is Paul who emphasizes the absolute gulf between the standpoints, not his adversaries. Paul escalates the conflict, not his opponents.

The claim to be perfecting Christianity. Paul asks the Galatians in 3.3: 'Are you so foolish? Having begun with the Spirit, are you now ending with the flesh?' He could have had in mind as a model the relationship of godfearers to proselytes. To some degree Paul recruited among godfearers who had not had themselves circumcised. Now circumcision was added as the perfection of this move towards the one and only God.

The concentration on the decisive marks of Jewish identity: circumcision, the food laws, the calendar. The counter-missionaries assure their audience that one need not observe the whole Jewish law. Therefore Paul urges the Galatians in 5.3: 'I testify again to every man who receives circumcision that he is bound to keep the whole law.' For the pragmatic purpose of safeguarding one's belonging to Judaism, in fact some of the decisive marks of identity are sufficient. The concern to safeguard one's membership of Israel also emerges from Paul's accusation: 'They woo you, but for no good purpose; they want to shut you out (ἐκκλεῖσαι), that you may woo them' (4.17). Thus the opponents were suggesting that the Galatians did not really 'belong' (i.e. to Israel and to Abraham's children), but should make a further effort to belong completely.

The avoidance of conflict as a motive. Paul twice insinuates a connection between the requirement of circumcision and the avoidance of conflict. 'It is those who want to make a good showing in the flesh that would compel you to be circumcised, and only in order that they may not be persecuted for the cross of Christ' (6.12). And he introduces himself personally as an example in this connection: 'But if I, dear brothers, still preach circumcision, why am I still persecuted? In that case the stumbling block of the cross has been removed' (5.11).

The passing on of political pressure. In 4.21ff. Paul makes it clear that the present Jerusalem (= Judaism) is unfree: 'It lives with its children in slavery' (4.25). Just as Ishmael, who was born unfree, persecuted the free Isaac, so it is now: the Jews, who are politically unfree, persecute the Christians, who are free. One can infer from this statement that Jews who no longer have political freedom become persecutors because of their lack of freedom. We conjectured the same situation for the Gospel of John.

Comparable Jewish Christian missionaries must have appeared in Philippi. They too propagated circumcision, even if we hear nothing directly about a demand for circumcision, but only of a demonstrative pride in circumcision. They too attached much importance to the food laws, which is why Paul tells them that their God is their belly (3.19). They too probably made the claim that they were the ones who perfected Christianity, with the result that Paul explains what perfection means for him (3.12ff.). And with all that they promised that Christians would then belong to the *politeuma* of Israel – recognized in the world around in the same way as the Jewish *politeumata* (the Jewish communities in the Hellenistic cities). But Paul counters this by saying that the *politeuma* of the Christians is in heaven (3.20).[23]

It is illuminating that in both the letters in which he is explicitly arguing with Judaizers, Paul emphatically refers back to his biography: his conversion and call is a model for turning away from Judaism in its traditional form. The question is: is he exploiting his past here as a rhetorical means of winning arguments in the present against his opponents, or is he experiencing his former situation in the light of his conversion?

(d) The Judaistic crisis and the response of Pauline theology

The relationship between Paul's personal crisis and the Judaistic crisis in early primitive Christianity is often defined as a projection of this general crisis to some degree on to the personal crisis in his memory. When he depicts his conversion in Phil. 3 as the breakthrough of the certainty of justification, he is projecting back on his beginnings the doctrine of justification which arose only much later. Because he wants the Philippians to turn from Judaism in the present, he depicts his conversion as a radical departure from all Jewish traditions. In my view the opposite thesis is more probable: all through his life Paul is stamped by his Damascus experience. And he projects it on to situations in which he is confronted indirectly with his own Judaistic past by Judaistic opponents. He cannot perceive these opponents objectively. For him they are a piece of his own past which he repudiates vehemently. Even in Galatia his opponents did not seek the fight. Paul introduces it into the situation.

These opponents compel him after a long period once again to grapple with his own Judaistic past. And in the course of this grappling he arrives at an increasingly clear conceptual grasp of his ambivalence towards the law. Here in my view he derives the conceptuality with which he criticizes the law from the general critique of the law familiar in antiquity. Fragments and individual themes had circulated as far as Hellenistic Judaism, even if they had been attributed only to malicious critics of the Mosaic Torah, about whose rejection there was general agreement. That is the case with Josephus, when he makes Zimri attempt a rebellion against Moses. Or they were applied only to the pagan laws as distinct from the Torah of Moses. This is the case in Philo, when he depicts Joseph as the lawgiver of Egypt (*de Jos.* 28ff.). In short, in Galatians Paul applies to the law of Moses categories and concepts which elsewhere among Jews were applied only to the pagan laws.

The first argument against the law is that it is merely an addition to the promise, which was added a long time chronologically after the promise to Abraham. Paul says that the law was added (προσετέθη) because of sins (Gal. 3.19). That recalls Philo's description of the legislation of Joseph. Joseph means 'addition' (from the Hebrew *yasap*), or in Greek πρόσθεσις. This name is interpreted as meaning that Joseph makes further additions to the universal law of nature which is identical with the Torah of Moses: special laws for the pagan Egyptians (*Joseph* 28ff.). Paul by contrast regards the Mosaic Torah itself as an addition.

The second argument against the law is that it goes back to a multiplicity of legislators, that it was mediated through one, but that the one mediator is always a mediator of many. Explicit mention is made of the angels. Now the idea that the angels communicated the Torah on Sinai is not alien to Jews (cf. Stephen's speech in Acts 7.53). However, in Jewish understanding the 'many angels' can also be the angels appointed over the different peoples.

The third argument is that the law has a repressive function. It was added because of sins (Gal. 3.19) – i.e. primarily in order to suppress them. It is a 'pedagogue' (παιδαγωγός), under whom the one who is protected by it has not yet come of age and is no different from a 'slave' (δοῦλος, 4.1). This notion that the law is a tyrannical instrument is expressed by Josephus in connection with the rebel Zimri. Moses rules over the Israelites with its help in order to oppress them.

If the law is regarded in the way in which otherwise only pagan laws are regarded, it becomes understandable that the place of the lawgiving is sought by Paul in Arabia and is identified with Hagar[24] – and therefore not with Sarah, the matriarch of the Israelites, but with a concubine of Abraham's, from whom non-Jews also descended. In fact the Jews assume the role of Gentiles.

Only now can we also understand why Paul can criticize the adoption of the law by the Galatians as a relapse into their paganism. For this argument is in reality contrary to the facts. In their pre-Christian period the Gentile Galatians did not observe the law. But if the Jewish law can be depicted as a pagan law, then the pagan gods and the Jewish law can be lumped together as 'elements of the world' (στοιχεῖα τοῦ κόσμου). The argument about a relapse is also so attractive because the counter-missionaries had celebrated the adoption of the law as progress and perfection. Against this, Paul argues that the Galatians are achieving the opposite of what has been promised them: the perfection of the beginnings which he brought about. What in their eyes is 'progress' is in reality a step backwards.

Paul goes into this promise to some degree. The law is not fulfilled through circumcision and other ritual sign actions, but only through love. That is his thesis in Gal. 5.14. The law which previously had been devalued so strongly is revalued tremendously in his central ethical commandment. In Galatians both still stand side by side in juxtaposition: first the tremendous devaluation of the law which is scandalous in a Jew, and at the end its revaluation. Paul does not mediate between the two value judgments. He does not say that the devaluation relates to the law as the embodiment of ritual demands and its revaluation to the law as the embodiment of ethical commands. He does not have this terminology at his disposal – and as a Jew does not even think of splitting the law in this sense.

Only after writing Galatians[25] did he find in II Cor. 3 a conceptuality which expresses this tremendous ambivalence towards the law. The law has two sides: it is on the one hand the letter that kills, and on the other the spirit that makes alive (II Cor. 3.6). Here he is not thinking of specific substantive demands. The ritual demands are not identical with the letter that kills, nor are the ethical demands identical with the spirit that gives life. Rather, Paul is clearly alluding to the ethical commandments of the Decalogue when he sees the letters in the tablets engraved in stone, and the spirit where their content is inscribed on the heart.

Paul uses this terminology again in Romans. Because he now has a conceptuality which allows sharp opposing statements about the law, we now find side by side on the one hand Paul's most negative statements about the law, namely that it came in order to increase sin (5.20), and on the other the most positive: that the commandment is holy, righteous and good (7.12). Only in the hands of sin does it become a law that kills.

Now what is the abiding historical contribution of the Pauline critique of the law and the doctrine of justification? With it Paul laid the theological foundation of the independence of Christianity from Judaism. We can also say that with it he made possible the acceptance of Gentiles into the Christian community without prior circumcision, which was in fact the occasion for the separation from Judaism. This independence is expressed with abrupt antitheses which point far beyond this concrete occasion.

The first antithesis is works of the law versus faith. The works of the law do not justify, but only faith. First of all what Paul means is merely that when one is accepted into the community the Jewish ritual marks of identification no longer play a role. The sole condition for acceptance into the Christian community is faith in Jesus. In my view it is indisputable that in addition Paul generalizes this notion. For him there are also no ethical presuppositions for acceptance into Christianity. The works of the law embrace both ethical and ritual actions. But the antithesis 'works of the law versus faith' first of all relativizes, and above all relativizes the ritual sign system of Judaism. Ritual questions were the starting point of the Judaistic crisis .

The second antithesis is law versus Christ. The law played a particular but limited role in salvation history. The revelation in Christ has now taken the place of the revelation in the Torah. With this new revelation the narrative-mythical sign system of Judaism is taken further. It finds a new centre in Christ. So here we can see the emergence of independence in the mythical sign world.

The third antithesis is letter versus spirit. This antithesis similarly comprises several aspects, but also ethical opposites. The letters written on stone denote the ethical Decalogue. As demands coming from outside, the ethical commandments, too, are the 'letter' which kills. But the spirit is the power of the new, ethically determined life, of which the first fruit is 'love'. Thus in these antithesis an ethical demarcation from Judaism is also indicated.

Paul grounds and defends the autonomy of the new religion in all forms of expression of its sign language by this demarcation from Judaism. This is all the more notable, since the changed political conditions must have made a renunciation of this autonomy seem the simpler way. Had Christianity remained a part of Judaism, it could have avoided many conflicts with Jews and Gentiles at that time.

However, Paul's significance is not seen adequately if one regards it as being that of demarcating the new religion from Judaism. His greatness consists in the fact that he maintains the continuity with Judaism. For him the Christian faith is the fulfilment of Judaism, not just as a fulfilment of the Old Testament promises. Rather, with his theology Paul offers responses to the basic aporias of Judaism. Romans works on these questions. Paul does not resolve the aporias, but he does reformulate them in such a way that a universally accessible faith comes into being. I shall demonstrate this briefly from Romans.

The conflict between universalism and particularism appears in the summary of the doctrine of justification in Rom. 3.28–30: 'For we hold that a man is justified by faith apart from works of law. Or is God the God of Jews only? Is he not the God of Gentiles also? Yes, of Gentiles also, since God is one; and he will justify the circumcised on the ground of their faith and the uncircumcised through their faith.' Because the universalism of God leads to there being no difference between circumcision and uncircumcision, one could understand justification as a replacement of requirements for ritual segregation. But in Romans that would be too little. The first chapters contain a 'moral' attack on all human sin, regardless of whether it is the sin of Jews or of Gentiles. Because all are sinners, the differences between Jews and Gentiles disappear. Gentiles take the role of Jews: they too perceive in their hearts the requirement of the law and bear witness to it through their consciences (Rom. 2.14f.). They too can be regarded as 'circumcised' in a transferred sense if they fulfil God's demands (Rom. 2.26). The advantage that Jews have over them, the promises, illuminates above all human infidelity in contrast to God's fidelity (Rom. 3.1ff.). In short, in the first chapters of Romans the unity of human beings is brought about through their infinite distance from the God who makes ethical demands. There are no righteous. Therefore all human beings are equal (Rom. 1.18–3.20).

In the next chapters (Rom. 3.21–5.21), the universality of the grace of God for all believers is set over against this in a positive way. That is demonstrated by means of the two Old Testament figures of Abraham and Adam. Abraham , the forefather of the Jews, becomes the forefather of all believers, regardless of their national origin (Rom. 4.1ff.). Christ as the new Adam is set over against the tribal ancestor of all human beings, Adam. The point of this is that all are thus shaped by this new Adam – just as they were all shaped by the old Adam: 'Then as one man's sin led to condemnation for all men, so one man's act of righteousness leads to acquittal and life for all men' (Rom. 5.18). But this universality is *de facto* limited: namely to the believers (Rom. 3.21ff.) or to those who have received grace through Jesus Christ (Rom. 5.15, 27, 21).

So the aporia of the clash between God's will for universal salvation and the particularity of the 'people' of God is not resolved. It is also repeated for Christians. This particularity no longer consists in belonging to a particular people, but in faith in Christ. In chapters 9 and 10 Paul is tormented by the sting of this new limitation of the universality of God: not all Israelites believe, although the promises apply to them. So will the offer of salvation in Christ lead to the doom of those to whom it first applied? Paul adopts several approaches in seeking an answer. He finds it only when he fights his way through to the conviction that all Israel will be saved (Rom. 11.25) – although most of Israel in his day rejects the faith. The basis for this salvation is God's mercy. This transcends the repudiation of the gospel. Thus the idea of grace is radicalized. But that leads to the second aporia.

We saw the second aporia of Judaism as lying in the tension between the theocentric grace of God and human action. Romans is stamped by this tension too. Through grace, God creates salvation for all without any human contribution. Here the 'works' of the law are excluded. The type of the recipient of salvation is Abraham, not through the binding of Isaac, which elsewhere in Judaism and Christianity is the demonstration of his exemplary obedience (cf. James 2.20–24; Heb. 11.17–19), but through his faith in the power of God which overcomes death. Abraham's faith is trust in a power before which human beings are utterly passive. His faith is faith in the one who calls into being that which is not (Rom. 4.17). And in the part about Israel, too, this God appears as a God who acts in a sovereign way, who can dispose freely of his creatures like a potter. Before there can be any question of a human act, God decides on doom and salvation.

Even if human beings seem to sink to nothingness before the sovereignty of God, in Romans they are raised to a dignity which transcends human limits. They are destined to share the likeness of the image of the son of God (Rom. 8.29). They are to 'rule' with Christ in life (Rom. 5.17). They are to be 'glorified' with him as an independent heritage (Rom. 8.17). They are transformed into beings who again achieve their freedom and dignity: the freedom of the glory of the children of God (Rom. 8.21)? How is that possible?

Romans does not just extent the limits of salvation to a universal dimension quantitatively. Salvation is not just offered to all human beings. It also changes them qualitatively. Paul depicts this in the central part of his letter, in chapters 6 to 8. Whereas elsewhere in Romans he has described God and his action with metaphors from political life – as king, judge and cultic lord – here he goes over to metaphors from private life: redeemed human beings are compared one after the other with a slave who changes his master (Rom. 6.12ff.), with a woman who enters a second marriage (7.1ff.), and with a human being who becomes a son instead of being adopted (8.12ff.). All three roles in a house, those of slave, wife and son, are conjured up to make it possible to describe the change in the human being.[26]

Paul begins with the greatest dependence, with slavery, and here he plays on its ugliest aspect, the way in which slaves are sexually available, when he writes: 'For just as you once yielded your members to impurity and to greater and greater iniquity, so now yield your members to righteousness for sanctification' (Rom. 6.19). Once they were delivered over to sin, as slaves are delivered over to the sexual lusts of their master. But now they are 'set free from sin, becoming slaves of righteousness' (Rom. 6.18). With the image of the slave who changes master, he seeks to depict freedom from sin.

The next image conjures up the fate of a woman whose husband has died and is now free for a new marriage. She is 'free from the law of the husband' (7.3). There is a jump in the picture: the general premise says that the death of a person brings freedom from the law. The example then speaks of the death of a husband as a result of which his wife who survives him becomes free. The application then speaks again of the death of Christians – although they are presented in the image of the surviving wife. This jump is understandable, for resurrection is thought of along with death. Christians are already living now as if they have been raised from the dead (cf. Rom. 6.11, 13; 7.4). They belong to the one who has the power to free beyond death those who have died with him. The image of the remarriage of the wife is meant to depict freedom from the law.

This series of images finds its culmination in the image of adoption, which deliberately surpasses all the images used so far. With adoption to become sons (and daughters) of God, Christians have not received a 'spirit of slavery' so that they have to fear, but the 'spirit of sonship'. The sons have the same form as the son of God (Rom. 8.29). In retrospect we can understand why Paul relativizes the image of the slave with the remark that he is speaking in human terms (Rom. 6.19). For slavery is associated with a lack of freedom and with fear. Only as sons have Christians received 'the freedom of the glory of the children of God' (Rom. 8.21). This freedom is freedom from slavery to transitoriness (Rom. 2.21).

Thus in three images Paul expresses what he understands by human 'freedom'. In Rom. 7.7ff. he contrasts it with the lack of freedom of those who are not redeemed. In antiquity freedom is the capacity to do what one wants.[27] In Rom. 7.15, 19 Paul denies that the unredeemed have this freedom: 'For I do not do what I want; I do the very thing that I hate.' But it is certain that human beings can attain this freedom again through a transformation with Christ and through the spirit of this freedom.

In the next two parts of Romans, in fact humans reappear as God's partners. In the Israel part (Rom. 9–11) we find a collaboration of human beings in the proclamation of salvation. The feet of those who, according to Rom. 3.15 (= Isa. 59.7), hasten to shed blood are now activated to preach the gospel: 'How beautiful are the feet of those who preach good news' (Rom. 10.15; Isa. 52.7). In the paraenetic section of Romans this human collaboration is extended to all ethical action. Human beings put on the armour of God in order to wage a battle against darkness in the dawn of the new world (Rom. 13.11–14). So in Romans we find a kerygmatic and an ethical synergism: human beings are called to be partners of God in his proclamation and in the implementation of his will in the world. When they are called they are completely passive. But the goal of their call is for them to become active.

If we ask how Paul overcomes the two basic aporias of Judaism, we can say that he does so through his faith in Christ: through faith in Christ salvation becomes universally accessible to all men and women. This faith is in principle through 'works of the law' – without adopting specifically Jewish rites, and also without moral presuppositions. Similarly, the transformation of human beings by Christ is not brought about so much through faith (in Romans 6–8 the word 'faith' appears only in 6.8) as through being conformed to Christ. The aporias of Judaism appear in a different form: if God is radically gracious, why then should human beings labour for the good (cf. the questions in Rom. 3.5–8 and 6.1)? If God wants to save all believers universally, what happens to the unbelievers? Paul attempts to put these aporias in a new balance. How does he do that?

In the aporia of the conflict between theocentric grace and anthropocentric human activity he emphasizes the two forms of relations to Christ: faith in his saving action and being transformed by his fate. The saving act of Christ is understood exclusively in the first case: Christ does and suffers vicariously for human beings what these do not need to do and suffer. In the second case it is understood inclusively: the fate of Christ is repeated in every Christian. Every Christian will die with him and enter a new life. The saving event understood in exclusive terms makes possible a radical and universal understanding of grace. It applies to all human beings, and they have only to accept it in faith. The saving event understood inclusively prevents a libertinism which relies on grace without motivating itself to good actions. It is impossible for those who have been transformed with Christ to want to sin. They are free from sin.

Paul only works on the second aporia between universalism and particularism; he does not resolve it. Here too he argues with his faith in Christ. Christ is the new Adam. Just as all human beings are formed through Adam, so with intrinsic consistency all must also be reshaped by the new Adam. The Adam-Christ typology is potentially universalistic. But the juxtaposition of the two appearances of 'man' is insufficient to allow all really to participate in salvation. In Rom. 5.12ff. the 'new Adam' is the earthly Jesus who through his act of obedience made good the disobedience of the first Adam. According to I Cor. 15.47ff. the new Adam is the one who will return at the parousia. Paul activates his expectation in Rom. 11 in order to advocate a universal doctrine of redemption at least in respect of Israel: all Israel will be saved, regardless of whether Jews believed or did not believe. All will meet the returning Christ at his parousia – and Christ will forgive them their unbelief.

In conclusion, it must be emphasized that although Paul provides the foundation for the independence of Christianity from Judaism, he maintains a continuity in all forms of religious expression. He does not break completely with the ritual sign system of Judaism. He still shares its abhorrence of all pagan ritual. He can accept the eating of meat offered to idols, but not if it becomes the expression of a participation in pagan cults. Nor does he break with the history of Israel. He simply sees it in the light of a new centre. And he quite certainly does not break with the Jewish ethic. Rather, he wants to fulfil it in an exemplary way – driven by the almost enthusiastic longing for God's commandments to be given by the spirit in human hearts. In his self-understanding Paul remains a Jew. And it accords with his deepest convictions that despite the separation of Christians and Jews, he continues to hope that at the end – the parousia of Christ – they will be united in a miraculous way.

2. The Gnostic crisis in the second century

As a result of the Judaistic crisis in the first century it was decided that Christianity is not a part of Judaism. That made all the more urgent the question whether it could not be part of Hellenistic religion generally – part of a new movement which was permeating a variety of religions and cults. Gnosticism can be interpreted as such an inter-religious movement, which embraced Christianity along with other religions.

(a) What is Gnosticism? An attempt at a definition[28]

Gnosis, from which 'Gnosticism' derives, means 'knowledge' (in German the same word, *Gnosis*, is used for both). The special character of the Gnostic movement is that it promised salvation through knowledge. This knowledge has a special content: the identify of the essence of the inner person with the transcendent deity. Here it is decisive that there is on the one hand the innermost self, a self unknown to the Gnostic before his enlightenment, which is first discovered in the process of Gnosis. And on the other side there is the transcendent God, who is not identical with the gods known previously – not even with the monotheistic God of the philosophers or the Jews. Thus God and the self both stand dualistically over against the world and the body. All religious traditions are reinterpreted in the light of this basic knowledge – as symbols of human self-discovery. So a brief definition of 'Gnosis' could run: *Gnosis means the gaining of salvation through knowledge. The subject of the knowledge is the identity in essence of the transcendent self in the human being with the transcendent deity beyond the world.* It is characterized by the combination of a radical revaluation of the self with an equally radical devaluation of the world (here the body is part of the world).

Now the Gnostic myth explains in narrative form how this dualism of world and God, self and body, Gnostics and other human beings came about.

The *cosmic* dualism of the world and God is explained by a myth about the creation of the world which explains the origin of the world as an accident, a mistake or a rape. It is attributed to a subordinate demiurge whom ignorant human beings worship as creator of the world.

The *anthropological* dualism of self and body is explained by a narrative about the creation of human beings in which, contrary to the will of subordinate powers which created the world, a divine spark found its way into human beings, who however have forgotten their origin. Only through 'gnosis' do they become conscious of it again.

The *social* dualism of Gnostics and other human beings follows from the drama of redemption. Gnosis is communicated by a heavenly cry or through a redeemer. By their 'gnosis' the redeemed know themselves to be different from all other human beings – including those whose system of religious convictions they once shared. At best these are at a prior stage – they are 'pistics' (from Greek *pistis,* faith).

(b) The historical context of Gnosticism as a universal movement

The condition for the rise of Gnosticism was a dissatisfaction with the traditional religions. In the Hellenistic period people had been content with a synthesis of the different religions by identifying different deities with one another – to the point of a synthetic monotheism which ultimately sees the same God behind all gods. In the long run, this way of dealing with religious pluralism was not enough. In Gnosticism the religious situation of pluralism was overcome, not by making all religions of equal value but by radically devaluing them as an imperfect preliminary stage towards a higher religion. So Gnosticism could nest in quite different religious sign systems, and promised to surpass them all.

Of course this promise was particularly attractive to people who had just experienced a devaluation of their ancestral faith. However, this devaluation is the reason not for the rise of Gnosticism but for receptiveness towards it.[29]

After AD 70, Jews had experienced their tie to YHWH as a restriction. Because of it they were subjected to a special tax. In these circumstances the devaluation of the creator God to a jealous and ignorant demiurge could seem plausible to some Jews.

Pagans who had been influenced by the trend towards monotheistic faith as it could be traced at that time throughout philosophy and religion could remedy their dissatisfaction with all existing religions through a quest for a new 'meta-religion'.

Christians must have felt a strong temptation to present the new revelation which they offered as a mediation of this meta-religion: among them Jesus became the revealer of the true Gnosis.

Now we have no accurate insight into the beginnings of Gnosticism. The church fathers regarded Simon Magus as the first Gnostic. The brief account in Acts from the end of the first century knows nothing of this. Therefore the church fathers were probably wrong in making Simon Magus the first Gnostic.[30] But on one point we may trust them more than is customary at present. They were right that the Gnostic myth which became associated with Simon Magus at a secondary stage is one of the earliest Gnostic systems. The historical Simon will have been a Samaritan charismatic who – as Luke also shows – regarded himself as a manifestation of the deity.[31] The people in Samaria say that he is the 'great power', which is a Samaritan predicate for God. Around 180 Irenaeus gives the following report about him, the essential features of which are confirmed by a very much briefer report by Justin from the middle of the second century (cf. Justin, *Apology* I, 26, 2–3; Irenaeus, *Adversus haereses* III, 23, 2–4):

> He carried around with him a certain woman named Helen whom he (Simon) had ransomed from prostitution in Tyre, a Phoenician city, and said that this woman was his first thought, the mother of all, by whom in the beginning he conceived in his mind to create angels and archangels . . . But his Ennoia was detained by those powers and angels which had gone forth from her and suffered all kinds of shame from them, so that . . . through the centuries she passed in succession from one female body to another, as from vessel to vessel. She was, for example, in that Helen

> on whose account the Trojan war was begun . . . Passing from body to body, and suffering insults in every one of them, she at last found herself in a brothel – and she was the lost sheep.

This myth, too, has a historical nucleus.[32] The historical Simon Magus probably went around with a female companion – as did the primitive Christian charismatics. It is not significant that Luke does not mention this companion. He is also silent about the female companions and wives of the primitive Christian missionaries. Nowhere is Peter provided with a wife, though according to Paul's credible earlier testimony in I Cor. 9 she accompanied him. Contrary to the Lukan tendency, we may assume that Peter had a woman companion, and so we may also concede that the historical Simon had a Helen. It is also probable that he performed a *hieros gamos*, a sacred marriage, with her as a prophetic symbolic action – corresponding to Hosea, who also married a woman who was an adulteress and a prostitute in order to proclaim his message of the love of God to his unfaithful people.[33] That in John 4, in the conversation with a Samaritan woman, the woman's relationship to the Revealer and to her many men is used in a symbolic relationship also fits this picture. It is quite credible that Simon's Helen came from Tyre. For there was already a large group of people from Phoenicia in Samaria.[34] In contrast to the Jews and Judaeans, the Samaritans saw themselves as a variant of the biblical faith which was more open to the world. They said a great deal about themselves when in the Hellenistic reform attempt of 168/7 BC they called their God 'Zeus Xenios', the hospitable Zeus.[35] Simon symbolized this hospitable tie to an alien people by his tie to Helen. It is quite conceivable that he purchased his Helen from a brothel, since in Acts 8 too the tendency to gain the religious power of salvation through money is imputed to him. There he wants to purchase from the apostles the capacity to hand on the Holy Spirit.

In the course of between fifty and one hundred years, one of the earliest Gnostic myths came to cling to this historical Simon. The Gnostic Simon no longer depicts divine redemption through a *hieros gamos*; rather, he regards himself as the incarnation of the supreme God. Helen is not a symbol for his redemptive action, but the embodiment of the first thought of this deity, which has become lost in the world. Former symbolic actions – i.e. images of salvation – are remythologized in this Gnostic system.

This Gnostic myth expresses a deep dissatisfaction both with the indigenous religion (monotheistic Samaritan religion) and with pagan myth.

Dissatisfaction with the indigenous religion becomes evident in the reinterpretation of creation as the botched work of subordinate powers. In this way the creator God of the Old Testament is degraded. He is experienced as a repressive power who mistreats the thoughts of God in this world. It is in keeping with this that the law of this creator God is also devalued among the Simonians.

But the same dissatisfaction is also expressed towards paganism. The *Iliad* is its basic myth. The story told there was sparked off by the abduction of Helen, and according to the Gnostic-Simonian myth this becomes a history of constant rapes with a humiliating end: it leads to a brothel in Tyre. It is a representative of the true God from Samaria who first brings about the saving change.

The two mythical traditions are fused into a unity. There is a kind of syncretism, but this is not the classic kind of syncretism in which existing cults and deities are fused. Rather, the existing mythical traditions are reinterpreted in terms of a hitherto unknown transcendent God – often clearly against their meaning. Accordingly, Gnosticism is the attempt to restructure the different particular religious systems in the light of a unitary thought and to discover the same basic figure of the creation of the world and redemption in all of them. But why did this Gnosticism, which came into being independently of Christianity, become the great temptation within Christianity in the second century? Why did the Gnostic crisis come about? Why did Gnosticism develop more strongly in Christianity than in other religions? The answer to this question is connected with the social and political situation of primitive Christianity in the second century.

(c) Christian Gnosticism

At the beginning of the second century the legal situation of Christianity was clarified by Pliny's letter and Trajan's rescript. As governor of Bithynia, Pliny the Younger had had to deal with denunciations of Christians. He had had them executed, not because of the charges against them but because in legal proceedings they had refused to sacrifice to the gods. However, he is not quite sure how he should act in future, especially as he has anonymous lists of Christians. He probably shrank from mass executions. Hence the enquiry to the emperor – with the information that the Christians were morally above reproach: they committed themselves only to general ethical commandments. What marked them out was an excessive superstition – the worship of an executed Christ as though he were a god (Pliny, *Epistles* X, 96).

It emerges from the emperor's answer (*Epistles* X, 97) that:

1. The state will not take the initiative in proceedings against Christians.
2. Christians may not be prosecuted on the basis of anonymous denunciations.

3. If they dispute that they are Christians before the court and call on the gods, they will be acquitted.

The tendency is clear: on the one hand being a Christian is as such a criminal offence – regardless of whether there are specific crimes. It is officially maintained that the sole crime of Christians consists in their being different from others. On the other hand, proceedings against Christians will be avoided as far as possible. Christians could live unmolested if they were socially inconspicuous. Only if they attracted undue attention in public or caused offence to their neighbours could there be criminal proceedings. In this situation, objectively there was pressure towards forms of Christianity which made it possible for Christians to be socially inconspicuous, and which provided guarantees and legitimation. In other words, there was now a call for forms which privatized Christianity. Gnosticism was such a privatization of religion.[36] It experienced a tremendous boom in second-century Christianity. However, here we must add the qualification that those forms of Gnosticism were stimulated which furthered such privatization.

The following observations on confession, martyrdom and the food laws may be cited as evidence of such a privatization of religion in important currents of Christian Gnosticism:

The need for public *confession*:[37] some Gnostics taught that one need not make a confession before the state archons (the earthly rulers and authorities), but only before the heavenly archons. In other words, in a decisive situation one might deny one's Christian identity. According to Tertullian (*Scorpiace* X, 1), the Valentinians taught this.

Martyrdom:[38] many Gnostics denied the crucifixion of Jesus with the help of a deception theory. The Romans had not executed Jesus, but had erroneously executed Simon of Cyrene in his place. Jesus himself had stood by the cross and felt superior to the foolish people who could not harm him. Here no doubt we find a portrait of the Gnostic: he stands unmolested and unrecognized alongside the martyrs.

On the *food laws:* many Gnostics taught that one could eat meat offered to idols without coming to any harm. So they could take part in all pagan banquets: they did not stand out – at least here – by deviant behaviour.

In the Christianity of the time the political and legal situation sketched out above led to another effort to defend the Christian faith as being beyond reproach. Apologetic flourished in the second century almost contemporaneously with Gnosticism. It is an attempt to reconcile Christianity with general public opinion. The truth which is present in nucleus everywhere in the best people first comes fully into view in Christianity. Gnosticism is an alternative to apologetic. It too claims to find a universal truth in Christianity. It too understands this universal truth as a truth which is already present. The truth is communicated by an intuitive insight into revelation which can be found enciphered in all religious systems. The basic problem is the same in both Gnosticism and apologetics: Christianity and universal truth are to be brought together. And that was no academic problem in a time when there was a concern to achieve toleration of Christianity by society.

So the controversy with Gnosticism was again about the inner autonomy of Christianity or a new religious sign system. In the Judaistic crisis of the first century the question had been whether it could not form a small substructure within the great Jewish sign system without parting company with Judaism. It would have shared the ritual, mythical and ethical sign world of Judaism – but in addition would also have introduced some special features: belief in the Messiah who had already come (in its myth), two sacraments (as additional rites), and a concentration on the commandment to love (as ethic). At that time it had been decided that these new sign elements were to be the nucleus of an independent sign world – independent of Judaism, yet related to it. So the issue in the Gnostic crisis was whether this new sign world which had been constructed in the meantime should itself be merely a small sub-system of a more universal sign world – a sign language which was present in all traditional religions as images and symbols of a process of self-discovery, and which combined a radical revaluation of the self with an equally radical devaluation of the world. Why did this fascinating attempt not succeed?

We must even ask: why could a 'Gnostic crisis' come about at all? A current which did not like conflict with the non-Christian world might also have sought to avoid conflict with its Christian environment. In fact the Gnostics usually saw themselves as good members of the community and by no means as heretics. They lived inconspicuously as an 'inner circle' in the community and regarded the ordinary members as potential Gnostics who had not yet attained to full knowledge.[39] Important Gnostic teachers like Valentinus in Rome[40] and Basilides in Alexandria[41] were active as Christian teachers without coming under attack. No one wanted to excommunicate them as heretics. So how was there nevertheless a conflict – which can be seen in the anti-heretical writings of Christians like Justin, Irenaeus, Tertullian and Hippolytus, the central task of whom is to fight against the very different 'Gnostic' groups? Must we take the activity of Marcion into account as a catalyst?[42] Marcion was not a Gnostic in the strict sense, but his teaching is reminiscent of Gnosticism: his proclamation of an alien God of love alongside the Old Testament creator God of justice recalled the juxtaposition of the true God and the subordinate demiurge who was responsible for creation. There were analogies to his docetic christology in the docetism of many Gnostic systems: the Redeemer could not really come into contact with this evil world. But there were also great differences: Marcion did not advocate a privatizing of religion, but called for public witness to the faith to the point of martyrdom. Similarly, he did not know any deprivatizing of faith inwards – no retreat into small inner circles. Rather, after he separated from the Roman community he organized his followers into separate communities. Did the Marcionite shock perhaps cast suspicion on anything that looked like 'Gnosticism'? Was that the reason why in the subsequent people it was more the representatives of mainstream Christianity who went on the attack against the Gnostics – rather than the Gnostics themselves? Be this as it may, the controversy brought out incompatibilities between a general Christian consensus and Gnostic systems. These contradicted some basic axioms of the new sign world – basic axioms which were expressed above all in the character of the fundamental 'myth' in primitive Christianity. Gnosticism contradicted the fundamental unity of myth and history.

This unity corresponds to the first basic axiom of Christianity (and Judaism), namely monotheism. Monotheistic faith says that God has no social partner in heaven, but only human beings as his partners. Precisely that was put in question if alongside the supreme God one also accepted a subordinate demiurge, and over and above that chains of emanations and aeons. At the least, Gnostic monotheism was no longer belief in the creator of heaven and earth – but at best belief in the creator of heaven.

The second basic axiom, belief in a redeemer, was similarly put in question. For all Gnostic systems put in question the real entry of the redeemer into this world. In itself this world is misfortune and a mistake. Therefore the redeemer cannot really associate himself with it. He only has a phantom body, or only transitorily associates himself with an earthly body. So one can say that both the unity of the creator God and the unity of the redeemer was threatened in Gnosticism – on the basis of a devaluation of the world and the body which contradicted the biblical sign system of primitive Christianity.

The two problems can be summed up like this. In Gnosticism primitive Christianity developed into a radical religion of redemption which denied the Old Testament belief in creation and the New Testament belief in incarnation – the unconditional entry of the redeemer into creation and corporeality. The resolution of the Gnostic crisis was achieved by a theology which brought belief in creation and belief in redemption into equilibrium and which held fast to both Old and New Testaments. This theology appears for the first time as a reaction to the Gnostic crisis in Irenaeus: it is the first to give a basis to the two-part canon of Old and New Testament and develops a salvation-historical theology according to which redemption is the restoration of creation: Christ restores the image of God in human beings which had been lost as a *similitudo* but had been preserved as an *imago*.

Of course in addition to the points discussed, Gnostic thought offended against the basic Christian convictions in yet other ways. These related not only to the primitive Christian myth of history but also to the ethic and rites of primitive Christianity. But they were far less important.

In the sphere of ethics the division of communities into pistics and Gnostics with two different truths contradicted the Christian commandment to love. If the one prays to the creator God and the other regards this as an error because the supposed creator God is merely a subordinate, foolish and ignorant demiurge, the unity of the community is put in question.

In the sphere of the rite we find interesting special developments among the Gnostics. For example, the Valentinian Gospel of Philip knows five sacraments: baptism, anointing, eucharist, redemption and the mystery of the bridal chamber (cf. EvPhil 68). Regardless of how one interprets them in detail, the three additional sacraments are rites which symbolically depict the salvation of the individual: his anointing, his redemption and the union of the soul with the heavenly bridegroom. Here the ritual sign language loses its social significance for the whole community.

It is amazing that the Gnostic movement did not establish itself, although it was favoured by the political and legal situation of primitive Christianity in the second century. Gnosticism was a 'form of adaptation' to the precarious situation of Christians. In the second century, Gnostic forms of primitive Christianity avoided conflicts in the same way as did the development of Judaistic forms of Christianity in the first century. Christianity could have more easily come to terms with its environment both as a part and an extension of Judaism and as a variant of a universal symbolic language. Each time the political situation favoured the form of Christian faith and community life which in the end did not become established within the church. In other words, the inner autonomy of the new religious sign system asserted itself against structural political circumstances which really pointed in a different direction. So in conclusion we must ask: from where did primitive Christianity derive the power to offer such resistance? What drove it to kept distinguishing itself from the surrounding world? To answer this question we must consider the ethical radicalism of primitive Christianity and the prophetic crises which were caused by it.

3. The prophetic crises in the first and second centuries

Ethical radicalism as a radical fulfilment of the law was nothing strange in Judaism. Since the religious persecution of the time of the Maccabees, movements had kept forming which advocated an intensified fulfilment of the Torah as a defence against the Hellenistic pull towards assimilation. In the time of Hellenistic rule they included the Essenes and the Pharisees in the time of Roman rule Judas of Galilee and John the Baptist. Judas of Galilee advocated an ethical radicalism when he inferred from the first commandment that the acknowledgment of the one and only God excluded the acknowledgment of the emperor by paying tax. He proclaimed the radical theocratic alternative: God or the emperor. In him the Jewish ethic is radicalized as a result of opposition to alien rule. He gave it an aggressive turn outwards. We find a comparable radicalization of the Jewish requirements of cleanness in John the Baptist. All existing rites of cleanness are inadequate preparation for a holy people of God. John the Baptist gives his ethical radicalism a turn 'inwards': it is expressed as a call to repentance addressed to his own people. Both possibilities keep reappearing in the history of primitive Christianity: here the turn outwards (to preserve the community in situations of political oppression) and the turn inwards (to create a pure community) could be combined in different ways.

(a) The Jesus movement and the Logia source

Jesus and his followers advocated an ethical radicalism. Indeed Jesus rejected the alternative put forward by Judas of Galilee. But he too was influenced by Judas' radical theocratic spirit. His message of the kingdom of God which will break in soon is an expression of radical theocracy: in the end God alone will rule. Granted, we find no explicit alternative, 'God or the emperor', in Jesus. In any case direct political statements are rare with him. Rather, in the political sphere Jesus chose an indirect form of communication: communication by symbolic political actions – for example when he appointed twelve countrymen and fishermen as the future government of Israel; when he entered Jerusalem with peaceful pilgrims from the country in a counter-demonstration to the entry of the Roman prefect and his cohorts; or when he answered a question about the legitimacy of taxes by means of the symbolic medium of a coin and the image on it. If we decipher the 'figurative language' of these symbolic political actions, we soon recognize that *implicitly* behind Jesus' message of the rule of God which will break in soon stands the radical theocratic alternative 'God or the emperor'. If God really accedes to power, no other power has a place alongside him. The co-existence between the kingdom of the emperor and the kingdom of God can only be provisional.

At the same time the radical theocratic spirit appears *explicitly* as an alternative between God and mammon, i.e. in the economic sphere: 'No one can serve two masters: for either he will hate the one and love the other, or he will be devoted to the one and despise the other. You cannot serve God and mammon' (Matt. 6.24). The polemic against the rich is almost intolerably sharp. If it is easier for a camel to go through the eye of a needle than for a rich man to enter the kingdom of heaven, no rich person has a chance (Mark 10.25). The woes against the rich speak a clear language (Luke 6.24ff.). And beyond question the invitation to the rich young man to sell all his possessions and follow Jesus breathes the spirit of Jesus (Mark 10.21ff.).

This ethical radicalism of the early Jesus movement had a *Sitz im Leben* among the itinerant charismatics of primitive Christianity.[43] It could be advocated credibly because it was practised by the homeless itinerant charismatics: they required people to follow Jesus, to leave house and home, to break with family and parents, and to live without employment and possessions. They recommended demonstrative defencelessness in case of attack. These first disciples of Jesus were free from the ties and obligations of family and job. They lived an ascetic life – dependent on the unpredictable giving and the hospitality of many people in the villages of Galilee. In short, initially this movement was a counter-cultural movement of drop-outs, but from the beginning contrary impulses were also alive in it: namely the will to embody a universal and exemplary ethic accessible to all. So we can say that two souls lived within primitive Christianity. The one pressed for an exodus from this society – but the other wanted to realize the ethic represented by the best people in this world. The one pressed for a revolution in values, the other for conformity to values.[44]

The ethical radicalization in the Jesus movement is conditioned both by (latent) resistance to political power (as in the case of Judas of Galilee) and also by (manifest) moral aggression against its own people – by the call to repentance (as in the case of John the Baptist). We will observe that ethical radicalism keeps flaring up in the further history of primitive Christianity where either a political crisis challenges the counter-cultural power of resistance in primitive Christianity – or signs of staleness within the church give rise to the call for repentance.

Possibly this ethical radicalism was already revived and shaped by a political challenge in the first generation after Jesus' death – if the origin of the Logia source can be connected with a political crisis. The Logia source is a collection of sayings of Jesus which is stamped by the spirit of primitive

Christian itinerant radicalism.[45] As a rule this Logia source contains sayings of Jesus, but at three points it breaks through this form-critical framework and also includes narratives: the narratives of the temptation of Jesus, the centurion of Capernaum, and an exorcism which introduces the saying about Beelzebul. These three narrative elements could belong together. Many scholars conjecture that they were included only at the redactional level.

The temptation story culminates in the temptation on the mountain, which in my view gives literary and mythical form to the Caligula crisis (though there is no consensus about this among exegetes). In AD 39/40 the emperor Gaius Caligula attempted to set up a statue of himself in the Jerusalem temple. This experience is worked over in mythical form in the Logia source in the figure of the devil, who rules over the world and requires worship of himself. The Caligula crisis could have been the challenge for the Jesus movement to reflect on its radical ethic and to gather its traditions in a written work. In that case, the major narrative of the temptation story which introduces this work indicates the historical context of this prophetic collection of sayings. As a counterbalance to the counter-cultural impulses, the narrative about the centurion of Capernaum could show how a representative of the world power acknowledges Jesus and his words. Again in a counter-move, the saying about Beelzebul emphasizes the opposition between the kingdom of Satan and the kingdom of God. The exorcism is related in order to give a vivid picture of the victory of Jesus over this world and its powers.

Whereas symbolic political forms of the clash with the political power can be found with Jesus, the controversy now shifts into the language of myth. The Satan of the temptation story transparently represents Roman imperial power. Though that may still be disputed in the case of the Logia source, there is consensus over it in the case of the Revelation of John.

(b) The Revelation of John

In the prophecy of the Revelation of John, primitive Christian radicalism revives once again in the face of a new political challenge.[46] In it the emperor and the emperor cult are attacked as a satanic power: not directly, but enciphered in mythical language. However, this language can be clearly deciphered. Formerly the Apocalypse of John was interpreted as the response to a persecution of Christians under the emperor Domitian, who was the first emperor to have himself addressed with the titles *dominus et deus* (Lord and God). Over against him is set the Lamb whom the assembly before the heavenly throne acclaims as 'Lord and God' (Rev.

4.11). Today scholars do not think in terms of a persecution of Christians initiated by the emperor himself but of local limited pressure against Christians which in some obscure way is connected with the emperor cult practised by the local aristocracy in Asia Minor.[47]

The difficulties are hard to define because there is a clear tension between the letters of the prophet to the seven churches in Asia Minor and the following apocalyptic visions about the destiny of the whole world. Only limited conflicts with the emperor cult can be inferred from the letters. These are mentioned directly only in one letter, that to the community in Pergamon. There a Christian by the name of Antipas has suffered a martyr death. But that, too, lies some time in the past, since there is talk in retrospect of 'the days' in which the community had to show its steadfastness. If we assume that such a sharp opponent of the emperor cult as the seer had been punished 'only' with banishment to the island of Patmos – and not with death – an acute bloody persecution becomes improbable. What emerges far more in the letters is a crisis within the communities: there is an attack on a teaching of Balaam and the prophet Jezebel, who is promoted by so-called Nicolaitans. This teaching reduces the distance from the pagan world. It says that one can eat meat offered to idols (Rev. 2.14, 20). It is accused of leading people astray into fornication – which probably means engaging in pagan idolatry.

By contrast, the visions in the Revelation of John make quite a different impression. They propagate an irreconcilable opposition between the Roman empire and the kingdom of Christ, between the beast from the abyss who had been fatally wounded and made whole, and the Lamb which has been killed and raised to life again; between the earthly city on the seven hills and the heavenly city Jerusalem; between the whore Babylon and the pure bride. How are we to explain this discrepancy? There are three possibilities:

1. In the cryptic mythical and symbolic language of the visions, the seer is speaking much more openly about the brutal experiences of persecution than in the direct language of the letters. Most primitive Christian writings were composed after the Neronian persecution. But usually they are silent about this persecution, and often mention it only in hints. One thinks simply of the few very guarded references in I Clement, which comes from Rome. We would never be able to infer from it the cruelty of this persecution of the Christians in Rome. A criminalized minority does not necessarily have an interest in emphasizing its criminalization.

2. In the letters the seer is describing present reality, but in the visions he is giving expression to his fears and intimations of the future. The present

pressures were limited. There can be no question of a bloody persecution. So the visions are not reflections of experiences of persecution but of fears of persecution. The less one sees these as real experiences, the more one must admire the visionary power of the seer. With great perspicacity he had intimations of the incompatibility of the Roman empire with Christianity – and already at the end of the first century foresaw a conflict which became reality only more than a century later, in the great persecutions of Christians. He would really have been a prophet – with a remarkable gift of precognition.

3. But over and above this a third notion suggests that the seer is using relatively minor difficulties with an emperor cult enforced by the local aristocracy in one of the provinces of Asia Minor in order deliberately to drive a wedge between the community and the world. It was not the emperor cult that was the great problem, but the lack of demarcation between many Christians in the churches and the pagan world, its affairs and its society. Most Christians did not regard the emperor cult as a basic problem. Only the prophetic seer takes it as an occasion to declare war on this world, so as to be able to resist more effectively tendencies in the community to assimilate to this world – with striking success. Some time later Pliny says that it is generally known that in no circumstances will Christians sacrifice to the emperor.

Probably a combination of all three perspectives is closest to the truth. We do not know all the difficulties that Christians had at that time. The seer keeps quiet about some of them. In a visionary way he has developed pressures experienced in the present into a dark picture of the future. But above all he has made the emperor cult enforced in Asia Minor at that time the occasion for a fundamental declaration of war on this world. The Roman empire did not declare war on the Christians; a Christian prophet declared war on the Roman empire.

Here he was following an intrinsic necessity. As long as the Christians were still part of Judaism, in principle they were free of any contact with the emperor cult. Only after they had been perceived by those around them as an independent group alongside the Jews could they be perplexed by their confrontation with the emperor cult. In this situation attitudes necessarily arose which taught indifference towards the pagan cults – comparable to the so-called 'strong' in Corinth. They would have made it possible to perform the emperor cult outwardly, but to distance oneself from it inwardly. The apocalyptist fights against this attitude – with striking success. Around two decades later in Bithynia, Pliny met former Christians who turned their back on Christianity about the time that the Apocalypse of John is assumed to have been written. They said that they had done so out of obedience to the emperor's prohibitions. One might add that they also did so because at the same time an ethical radicalism had driven them out of the community.

In one respect this ethical radicalism stands in continuity with the original itinerant radicalism. The prophet of the Apocalypse of John was probably himself an itinerant prophet who once lived in Palestine and then emigrated to Asia Minor.[48] There he claims an authority which extends beyond the region. None of the seven churches to whom he writes can be recognized as his home community; he is equally influential in all of them. Probably he travelled from community to community. But in his Apocalypse he addresses the whole community from exile – and in so doing completely ignores the offices in the church which already existed at that time: the presbyters, the episkopoi and the deacons. His ideal community is egalitarian and charismatic internally, but externally he insists on a clear separation from this world. As formulated in 18.4 his message runs: 'Come out from her, my people, lest you take part in her sins!'[49] Once again we hear the prophetic summons to an exodus from this world.

(c) The Shepherd of Hermas

Whereas the Logia source and the Apocalypse of John are reacting to a political challenge, the prophecy of the Shepherd of Hermas is governed by the situation within the church. In the first half of the second century a prophet formulated the message of just one chance for a second repentance – even for those Christians who had already lost themselves in the world through their sins. His concern is to build a pure and holy church – but above all a church in solidarity. His second concern is the readiness of the rich to support the poor in the community. In the parable of the elm and the vine he shows that the rich and the poor are dependent on each other. The poor man receives material support from the rich man. Therefore the poor man prays for the rich man to God that God will bless the rich man with material goods. For the poor man is rich before God, whereas the rich man has a deficit before God. If his prayer is successful, he thus also sees indirectly to his own well-being – within the community. Both concerns could be combined, in a way which does not immediately become visible. The rich are the members of the community who are in danger of losing themselves to the world. They are in danger before God. They need the spiritual intercession of the poor. The call to a second repentance applies above all to them. By opening up to them a way to reintegration into the community through the possibility of a second repentance, the author ensures that important givers are preserved for the community (thus P. Lampe).[50]

Although the message of Hermas seems to be more moderate than that of the Apocalypse of John, the same prophetic solemnity lives on it: this insists on one holy and pure church which stands apart from the world. In his first parable he expresses this in the image of the foreign city. The Christians dwell in a foreign city. They do not have to go by the laws of this city but by those of their home city. Therefore: 'Because you live in a foreign land, make no preparations except for enough to live on, and be ready, if the lord of this city wills to expel you as an opponent to his law, to leave his city and go to your city and joyfully follow your law, suffering no harm' (Sim. I 6). Here too the basic tenor is an exodus from this society.

(d) The new prophecy of Montanism[51]

The spirit of ethical radicalism comes to life once again in the final phase of primitive Christianity. The 'new prophecy' which forms itself around the three main figures of Montanus, Maximilla and Priscilla embraced large parts of the church. These prophets, men and women, speak inspired words in the name of the 'Paraclete'. And again the theme is that of all prophetic holiness movements: the purity of the church. One of the sayings of the Paraclete runs:

> The church can forgive sins, but I will not do so, lest yet others sin (Tertullian, *De pudicitia* XXI, 7).

Again this prophetic message indicates a twofold oppositional character, opposition both to the community and to the outside world. The new prophecy is a summons to martyrdom in relation to the world. The saying that has been preserved is addressed to women, who had equal rights in this movement, and indeed may have dominated it: 'Do not wish to die in bed, nor in childbirth nor in a fever which puts you to sleep, but in martyrdom, so that he who has suffered for you may be glorified' (Tertullian, *De fuga* IX, 4).

At the same time, however, the new prophecy comes to be in tension with the church. Its representatives know that they are being persecuted by the church. The criticism of the opposition is directed inwards. Maximilla laments: 'I am persecuted like a wolf from (the flock) of sheep; I am not a wolf; I am word and spirit and power' (Eusebius, *HE* V, 16, 17).

It is characteristic that this movement soon got the reputation of being heretical. But there is no doubt that it was orthodox, in that it was a Christianity orientated on the 'canon' of the New Testament. What was provocative was not the content of its message but the prophetic form which appealed to direct inspiration – although it was one of the genuine expressions of primitive Christianity. This movement was even to win over the great Christian author Tertullian; it spoke to the ethical rigorism of this unquestionably orthodox theologian.

As is shown by the enumeration of the four prophetic 'crises' in primitive Christianity, there was not just a single crisis caused by the radicalism. Structurally, rather, this radicalism was integral to the new religion. It was given with its radical beginnings. The radical spirit of the first itinerant charismatics kept flaring up. Here it is not just an anachronism, but rather continues to have an important function in the shaping and preservation of the new religion. The temptation to adapt to the surrounding world and to deny its own identity was chronic, and simply assumed different forms. In the first century it became acute in the form of the Judaistic crisis, and in the second century in the form of the Gnostic crisis. But it was always present in the everyday life of all Christians – even when inconspicuous forms of a 'bourgeois' Christianity were developed and remained within the framework of 'orthodoxy'. Primitive Christianity derived its power to resist these manifold forms of temptation to assimilation from its solemn stand against culture: the awareness of being different from the world and the claim also to depict this difference from the world in a visible life-style. For abstract radicalism alone bestows only a problematical social identity. But ethical radicalism which leads to visible patterns of behaviour that are socially binding and also gives power to deviate from 'behavioural norms' could time and again keep safeguarding the identity of primitive Christianity. Here this power of resistance often established itself against the structural tendencies which were given by the social and political overall framework of the Roman empire.

In this survey of the three crises of primitive Christianity I have not yet mentioned a great crisis which in fact has a special position: the crisis brought about by Marcion.[52] Marcion combines elements from all three crises:

1. He radicalizes the outcome of the *Judaistic* crisis, namely the demarcation from the Jewish religion, in an extreme form. He dissolves the unity of the creator God and the redeemer God. For him the Old Testament is the revelation of another God. A hitherto alien God of love and mercy has revealed himself in Jesus. The new and singular element in Christianity is here abruptly emphasized. Here the notion of love comes into the centre, in accord with the basic convictions of primitive Christianity.

2. The *Gnostic* features in his thought are unmistakable. He dissolves not only the unity of the creator and redeemer God but also the unity of the divine and human essence in the redeemer. Marcion advocated a dualistic christology. His Jesus was not born, but descended directly from heaven. But in contrast to the other Gnostic systems, Marcion dispensed with any speculation on emanations and processes within the deity. Nothing was further from his mind than to dissolve Christianity into a timeless system of symbols; rather, he presented Gnostic motifs with a prophetic solemnity: as an expression of the uniqueness of the new revelation, which differed from all previous revelations.

3. These *prophetic* features of his appearance, the strict belief in revelation which he advocated and which he combined with an ethical radicalism – he taught asceticism and a readiness for martyrdom – gave great impetus to his emergence. Here someone was presenting a deviant form of Christianity which issued neither in an integration of Christianity into Judaism nor in its dissolution into a symbolic language which could be varied at will.

Precisely because of this combination of unusual features, Marcion was probably the greatest challenge to the church that was coming into being. Challenged by him, it developed the canon – and there arose a canonical Christianity which on the one hand preserved the plurality of primitive Christianity and on the other side also limited it. That leads to our next theme: plurality and unity in primitive Christianity and the question whether and from when a distinction which I have used without further justification is in fact justified, namely that between orthodoxy and heresy. It may be surprising that this question is an important topic in a decidedly undogmatic analysis of primitive Christianity. But religions are normative systems. We do not understand them unless we recognize what intrinsic norms are at work in their internal conflicts.

12

Plurality and Unity in Primitive Christianity and the Origin of the Canon

The great crises of primitive Christianity were not resolved in a uniform way. In the controversy over the basic question 'What is Christianity?' we encounter many attempts at an answer aimed at demarcating Christianity from its Jewish mother religion and from the universal symbolic language of Gnosticism, or renewing it in the spirit of ethical radicalism. This variety often seems so great that some hesitate to speak of primitive Christianity in the singular, saying that we can recognize only a multiplicity of primitive Christian groups.[1]

Already in the nineteenth century there was an attempt to recognize a hidden dialectical unity in this great variety: the historical picture of primitive Christianity created in Tübingen.[2] This distinguished two parties which were so to speak thesis and antithesis: Petrinism and Paulinism. These two parties were said to be represented in the literature by the original Gospel of Matthew on the one hand and the authentic letters of Paul on the other. All further writings could be assigned to them, depending on the 'tendency' that they represented. Thus I Peter and James represent an attempt at mediation on the part of the Petrine party, Luke-Acts and the Deutero-Paulines an attempt at mediation from the Pauline side, in order to bring the two parties together. Catholicism formed a synthesis – represented by the Gospel of John. With it, primitive Christianity finds its culmination and its conclusion.

The Tübingen picture of history also recognizes the two great crises of primitive Christianity. The internal conflicts between the religious parties in the first century were sparked off by the question how far Christianity should and might depart from Judaism in order to become a universal religion for all peoples. F. C. Baur saw here a conflict between particularism and universalism. This conflict is identical with what I have called the Judaistic crisis.

In the second century this conflict was replaced by another: the controversy with Gnosticism. According to F. C. Baur this is brought to an end in the Gospel of John by the acceptance of Gnostic ideas into the system of Christian convictions.

The controversy with Gnosticism is no longer about independence from Judaism but is a controversy with the Hellenistic philosophy of religion.

The Tübingen picture of history is outdated in this form, but not the basic notion of a development which takes place in conflicts and finds its goal in a synthesis. The following corrections need to be made to the Tübingen picture of history:

1. In primitive Christianity there were not just two parties but a multiplicity of currents, between which there were tensions and conflicts: Jewish Christianity, Synoptic Christianity, Pauline Christianity and Johannine Christianity. In the first part of this chapter I shall survey these currents and their undercurrents, and the connections between them. Here I shall work out the plurality of primitive Christianity and gather indications of its unity in and behind all the multiplicity. Only this unity explains the formation of the canon, which succeeded in establishing itself in primitive Christianity in the course of the second century without any organized central authorities. Its origin is the decisive event in the history of primitive Christianity in the second century.

2. The synthesis at the end of this development is not represented by the Gospel of John but by the canon. The conscious affirmation of multiplicity in primitive Christianity is the characteristic of the formation of the canon. The canon includes writings of almost all the representative currents. The Johannine corpus is not this synthesis. It represents only one current in it, though it may have played a special role in the formation of the canon. So in the second part I shall discuss the formation of the canon as a collection of heterogeneous writings – to some extent the 'external canon', with which primitive Christianity comes to an end and the early church begins.

3. With the formation of the canon, 'heretical' currents were excluded.[3] Not all currents and tendencies in primitive Christianity were represented in the canon by writings. There are no Gnostic writings. Jewish-Christian writings are under-represented. In, with and through the formation of the canon a consensus must have been arrived at about what is 'Christian' in the normative sense. Only writings which accorded with this consensus became established. In the third part I shall attempt to work out this consensus. Here we are looking for a series of implicit axioms and basic motifs which were shared by most Christians. We can call this consensus an 'internal canon' within the external canon.

Thus the formation of the canon has decisive significance for a theory and history of primitive Christianity. So the first question is: what is a canon? And what was the significance of the formation of the canon for primitive Christianity?

A theoretical definition of the canon is:[4] *a canon consists of the normative texts which are appropriate for constantly reconstructing the sign system of a religion and by means of exegesis for making it possible for a community to live within that system.* The significance of the canon for the community lies in the fact that a canon enables internal consensus between different groups, marks them off from the outside world and makes possible a continuity which spans the generations. Canonized writings are a cultural memory which is protected by the aura of the holy, a memory which stubbornly resists the temptation to forget and suppress. Through the formation of the canon the primitive Christian religion defines itself as a normative sign system.

Now what is the significance of this formation of the canon for the history of primitive Christianity if we understand it theoretically as the history of the origin of a new religious sign system?

1. This formation of the canon is the *end of primitive Christianity*. The history of primitive Christianity is the history of the origin of a religious sign system. Its origin is completed and concluded the moment that this sign system is no longer developed by the composition of new writings but is regarded as closed. From now on the further development of the religion is carried on by interpretation of a sign system which is regarded as closed – by exegesis. To exaggerate: primitive Christianity dies with the exegetes. The productive phase of the formation of a new symbolic language comes to an end. The formation of the canon separates primitive Christianity from the early church.

2. Further, the the formation of the canon defines primitive Christianity over against Judaism and at the same time documents both its final *separation from its mother religion* and its permanent bond with it. New holy scriptures are set alongside the holy scriptures of Judaism. As 'Old Testament' the holy scriptures of Judaism are subordinated to the 'New Testament'. In this way emphasis is put on the newness of Christianity. However, the new scriptures gain their normative character only as the continuation of an already existing collection of canonical writings of Judaism; moreover, primitive Christianity owes the idea of the canon to its mother religion.[5] It is dependent on the 'invention' of the canon, i.e. the idea which became established in the post-exilic period of making a collection of writings the normative basis of a religious sign system – first of all alongside and in combination with the temple cult (and thus embedded in its ritual sign language), but after the destruction of the temple in AD 70 also independently of the temple. However, the bond with the mother religion is not just expressed at a formal level. In content, too, with the formation of the canon an important decision is taken: over against Marcion, primitive

Christianity maintains the unity of the Old Testament creator God with the God of the New Testament.

3. Finally, the formation of the canon completes *the self-definition of primitive Christianity over against paganism*. With the Old Testament it takes over the self-demarcation of the 'people of God' from all other peoples. The form of the canon already implies such a self-demarcation: the canon is the document of the bond with a quite special history, the history of the election of Israel and the revelation of the one and only God. Hence the claim remains to bear witness to this one God in a unique way, in competition with all other religions. We saw that because of this, primitive Christianity developed a competitive syncretism, a tendency to proclaim its own superiority to rival religious sign systems (to other gods and promises of salvation) by heightening statements about the exalted character and the lowliness of Jesus. This competitive syncretism is completed with the formation of the canon. Through the normative collection of different writings, maximal statements about Jesus in both directions are put side by side – and thus become the key signature for *all* traditions. Late New Testament writings explicitly name Jesus 'God' (John 1.1, 18; 20.28; Heb. 1.8; Titus 2.13; II Peter 1.1). Now his divinity shines out in the canonical context above all other writings. The same is true of the lowliness of Jesus. The earthly appearance of Jesus in the Synoptics to the point of the Gethsemane scene gives vivid content to abstract statements about his incarnation in the letters.

At first sight it may seem surprising that a theoretical depiction of primitive Christianity raises the question of the canon and its limits, and of orthodoxy and heresy. Its concern is not to state what Christianity should be in a normative sense. Rather, it seeks to understand the value judgments which were made in the historical processes and decisions of that time. Religion is always a normative force. There is therefore a struggle in any religion over what can claim normative validity in it. How 'norms' and criteria developed for what at that time was regarded as orthodox and what heretical is the subject of an analysis which need in no way be obligated to the norms under investigation. Anyone who loses sight of religion as a normative power of definition thus loses sight of an element in the essence of religion generally.

1. Plurality in Christianity up to the formation of the canon

The attempt which follows, to put the plurality of primitive Christianity in historical order and to understand it, proceeds methodologically by combining two groups of 'data' that we have about the history of primitive Christianity.

- For the time up to AD 70 we have the historical monograph of the Acts of the Apostles[6] and the authentic letters of Paul. Both together provide valuable information about some conflicts in which clearly different groups emerge, though we do not possess writings from all these groups.
- For the time between 70 and around 110 we have no consecutive historical account; instead we have a wealth of primitive Christian writings from this period which we can hardly put in a historical context that can be described in a narrative. Four groups stand out among them: Jewish Christian, Synoptic, (Deutero-)Pauline and Johannine writings.
- For the period up to around 180 controversies with representatives of a radical religion of redemption, Gnosticism, and with prophetic renewal groups can be recognized directly through (vague) reports and also indirectly through writings that have been preserved; between these an early catholic church Christianity develops.

Now we can attempt to attribute to the groups which become visible in the first period the writings which can be recognized in the second period. This gives us four basic currents in primitive Christianity. It is then natural to regard the early catholic church Christianity as a continuation of these currents, which must be demarcated on two sides: against radical prophetic currents and against Gnosticism. In these controversies 'orthodoxy' and 'heresy' can be differentiated.

(a) Conflicts and groupings in the first generation

The first conflict that becomes visible is that between *Hebrews* and *Hellenists*.[7] The Hebrews include the Twelve, and the Hellenists the Seven. The number twelve shows that here not only the primitive community in Jerusalem, but all Israel, is represented. The Twelve are itinerant missionaries who know themselves to be sent to all twelve tribes. By contrast, the number seven corresponds to the representatives of a place. Here we find a first beginning of structures of authority in a local community. Both groups are shaped differently in cultural terms (by different languages). There is no mistaking the fact that the Hellenists came into a major conflict with the central institution of Judaism, the temple. Their leader, Stephen, was stoned for his criticism of the temple. Probably he proclaimed that the temple would soon be opened to Gentiles. His followers were banished. Some of them, above all Philip, carried on a mission in Samaria and in the Graeco-Palestinian coastal cities. Another part of them reached Antioch, where they founded the first community that also included Gentile

Christians. Thus already at a relatively early period we can distinguish three groups and tendencies (see the diagram on p.258).

The controversies between Antioch and Jerusalem over circumcision as a condition of accepting Gentile Christians enable us to make this picture more precise. At the *Apostolic Council*[8] in Jerusalem two parties faced each other: on the one side the three pillars in Jerusalem, James, Peter and John (the last never makes an independent appearance) – and on the other side Paul and Barnabas (who are both delegates of the Antioch community, with equal standing). A group of 'false brothers' is not integrated into the consensus.

The subsequent *conflict in Antioch*[9] shows a new coalition. Peter and Barnabas on the one hand stand apart from James (and the false brothers) because in Antioch they eat with Gentile Christians. On the other hand they part company with Paul, who declares eating together to be a *status confessionis*: according to Paul it is not only permissible for Christians but absolutely compulsory, and may not be put in question in any way. Thus a third mediating current becomes visible between strict Jewish Christianity (the false brothers and James) and Paulinism: a coalition of moderate Jewish Christian 'Hebrews' like Peter and moderate Jewish Christian 'Hellenists' like Barnabas. Thus not just three but four groups and basic currents emerge in earliest primitive Christianity, the fourth coming into being through a convergence of two groups.

(b) Four basic currents in the second generation

It is natural to connect these four groupings with the four complexes of writings which have come down to us from the next two generations. And having made some differentiations, it is tempting to undertake yet further differentiations within this complex of writings.

I begin with the clearest example: *Pauline Christianity*. It is evident that there is a historical connection between the historical Paul and the Deutero-Paulines. Here we have indisputable evidence that emphatic positions from the first generation continue to exercise an influence for a long time. Similarly, different wings can be detected within such currents: Colossians and Ephesians (which are not only dependent on each other in literary terms but are also related theologically) bear witness to a 'left-wing' Paulinism[10] that advocates a present eschatology and a characteristic 'body of Christ' ecclesiology which distinguishes between the head and the body, but maintains a high opinion of each member. The Pastoral Epistles and II Thessalonians differ. Here we find a repudiation both of an imminent expectation of the end (II Thessalonians) and of present eschatology (II

Tim.2.18). The 'body of Christ' ecclesiology is absent from them. Instead we have the key image of the 'house'. The community (in the Pastoral Epistles) is the house of God. Only the bishop has a charisma in it. Here we can speak of a 'right-wing' Paulinism.

The connection with James of *Jewish Christianity* and the 'false brothers' (who can clearly be distinguished from him by their more recalcitrant attitude) is also relatively plausible. After the departure of Peter, James was the decisive figure in Jerusalem. Not only do we know this from Acts, but we can also infer it from Josephus.[11] From this Jewish Christianity come the Jewish Christian Gospels, which only have been preserved in fragments:the Gospel of the Hebrews, the Gospel of the Ebionites and the Gospel of the Nazareans. Here too we can detect two wings. Like the Pseudo-Clementines (which are very much later), the Gospel of the Hebrews knows the Gnostic notion of a change in the form of the redeemer. Parts of Jewish Christianity were in fact embraced by Gnostic currents. The best evidence of this is the Gospel of Thomas, which presents a theology close to Gnosticism and at the same time gives James a unique status (12). Over against this wing of Jewish Christianity which is close to Gnosticism is another which stands close to the Synoptic Gospels. The Gospel of the Nazareans is a revision of the Gospel of Matthew. In some traditions the letter of James stands close to the Sermon on the Mount. The social ethic in both of them is impressive: seldom has a sense of obligation to solidarity with the poor been expressed so clearly as in these primitive Christian writings.[12]

It is harder to give a context to this *Synoptic Christianity*. Beyond question it combines Gentile and Jewish Christianity. Both the Logia source and the Matthaean special material clearly have a Jewish Christian colouring. By contrast, the Gospel of Mark and Luke-Acts are clearly influenced by a Gentile Christianity. So here too we find two wings. But the relative opposite element is not absent from any of the Synoptic Gospels. Jewish Christianity and Gentile Christianity are always combined, though we do not find the radical Pauline theology, the goal of which was the unity of Jewish and Gentile Christians. Peter and Barnabas would be good representatives of this combination in the first generation: Peter as the missionary to Israel, Barnabas as the missionary to the Gentiles. This attribution is supported by the tradition of the early church, which associates the Gospel of Mark with Peter – and attributes it to John Mark, a kinsman and companion of Barnabas. Such attributions need not be correct, but they show that if the Gospel of Mark was already always attributed to a 'Mark', we should look for it in circles in which John Mark stood in high repute. And these must have been circles in which both Peter and Barnabas were esteemed.[13]

Johannine Christianity remains, as the great historical enigma of primitive Christianity. There is something to be said for associating it with that branch of the Hellenists which carried on a mission in Samaria.[14] The connection with the Gospel of John comes about on the one hand through the place Samaria and on the other through Philip. Samaria has a positive significance in the Gospel of John. Whereas the whole 'world' seems to reject the message, here by way of exception it is given a positive welcome. The story of the Samaritan woman indirectly relates the founding of Samaritan Christianity. That Christ himself is called a 'Samaritan' (8.48) fits this picture. Philip plays a special role in the Gospel of John. The 'Greeks' turn to him in order to make contact with Jesus. According to Acts 8 he is the great missionary to the Samaritans.[15] The later reports about him lead to Asia Minor, where the Gospel of John is also located (later). In my view a strand in the prehistory of the Gospel of John leads to Samaria, though that does not illuminate all the prehistory of the Gospel. We can also distinguish different wings within Johannine Christianity. I John shows that there was a schism in the Johannine community: the dissidents could have presented a christology close to Gnosticism – a faith for the advanced (cf. II John 9). Unfortunately, in the literature we have only the writings of the other side.

Thus in all the basic currents of primitive Christianity we can discover at least two different wings. And this very situation also relativizes a differentiation into four basic currents. For it is easy to see that the wings of different basic currents stand close to one another. The Jewish Christianity of the Gospel of the Nazareans and the letter of James stands close to the Jewish Christianity of the Logia source and the Gospel of Matthew. The Gentile Christian wing within Synoptic Christianity, represented by Mark and Luke, indisputably stands close to Pauline Christianity: for Luke Paul is one of the great figures of Christianity. With its present eschatology, the 'left-wing' Paulinism of Colossians and Ephesians has a certain affinity with Johannine Christianity, etc. Thus numerous cross-connections arise between the four basic currents. Certainly they do not as yet represent a 'unity' of primitive Christianity, but they do indicate that communication could prevail between the different currents. However, the production of such a unity was still a special task. It was achieved in the early catholic church Christianity of the second century.

(c) Early catholic church Christianity and its controversy with heresies

In the second century these four basic currents flow together in *early catholic church Christianity*. In my view the most significant evidence of this is the *canon*.[16] Writings from all four basic currents are united in the New Testament canon. However, writings are absent both from the more radical wing of Jewish Christianity (the Gospel of the Hebrews and the Gospel of Thomas) and from the more radical wing of Johannine Christianity, to which in any case we cannot assign any of the writings that have come down to us. In addition all Gnostic writings are absent. By collecting, and also by refusing to accept, many writings, the formation of the canon is the great achievement of this church Christianity which brought about a consensus. However, not only did this early catholic church Christianity gather together the New Testament writings; it also produced writings of its own: a*pologetic,* in which it attempted to interpret itself to others (Aristides, Justin, Theophilus of Antioch and others) offered accounts addressed to the outside world; for its own communities there were those writings which are collected under the term '*Apostolic Fathers*'; and for the controversy with heretics there were the first heresiological writings.

This early catholic church Christianity was put in question from two sides. On the one side it was challenged by Gnosticism, the radical religion of redemption which had dissolved the Christian sign system into a universal symbolic language. On the other side it was challenged by prophetic renewal movements of different intensity: the Apocalypse of John from the end of the first century and the Shepherd of Hermas from the second century are already prophetic writings which seek to renew the church. Above all in the 'new prophecy' of Montanism there dawns the longing for an inner renewal of Christianity from its original prophetic spirit. But the most dangerous challenge was probably made by Marcion. He presented a theology close to Gnosticism, with the prophetic claim to mediate a unique new revelation and a radical ethic. In his figure the two movements which provoked early catholic church Christianity are combined: on the one hand the Gnostic heresies and on the other the prophetic renewal movements.

However, the early church also showed a power of integration in the face of these provocative and disturbing currents on the left and right wings. Tertullian was able to integrate Montanism into his theology. Although his orthodoxy was beyond question, in a late phase of his life he became a Montanist. Again, Clement of Alexandria was able to integrate Gnosticism into his early catholic theology. By contrast, Irenaeus emerged as a theoretician of the canon. His salvation-historical theology, which brought faith

Plurality in primitive Christianity

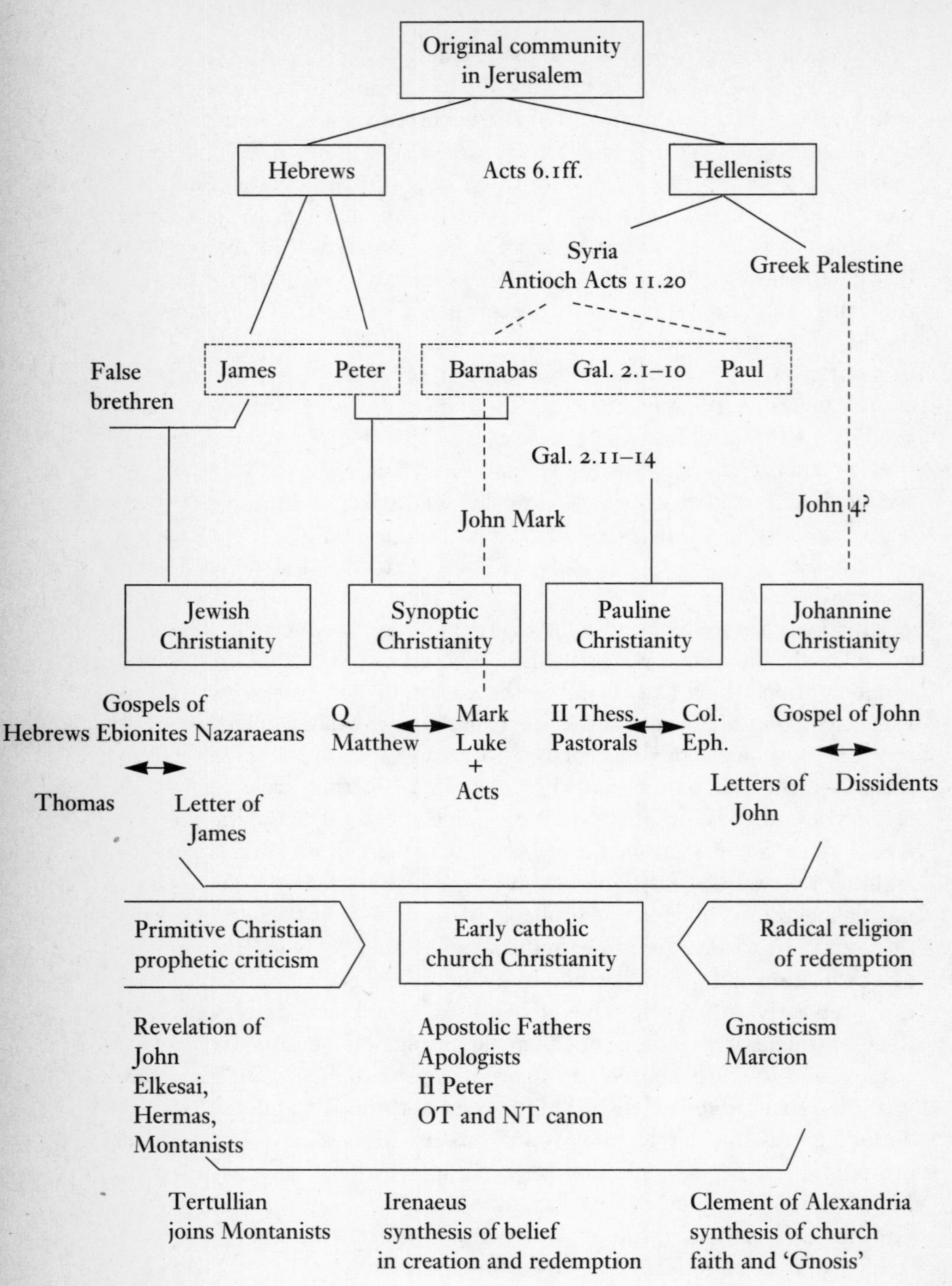

in creation and faith in redemption into equilibrium, can be understood as a mature answer to the questions of Marcion. All in all, the canon is the great answer to the identity crisis of the church at the end of Christianity.

All schemes simplify reality. So does the diagram on the opposite page. It does not claim to depict historical reality point by point, but is merely intended as an aid in assessing its complexity in terms of agreements and deviations. In the first primitive Christian generation (up to AD 70) it includes only conflicts which emerge from the sources. There will certainly have been far more. For the next period between c.70 and 110 it includes only groups of writings and currents which can be recognized as unities. There will have been more than these four basic currents in primitive Christianity. It attempts to indicate the complex history of the second century only in very broad outline. In reality everything is far more complicated. Some comments on the diagram may make this clear.

1. The diagram suggests that primitive Christian history had a unitary origin. Here it is governed by Luke's picture of history, in which the original Christian community in Jerusalem stands at the beginning of all developments. However, there are good reasons for supposing that primitive Christianity had a pluralistic beginning: Jesus' followers in Galilee and his disciples will also have handed on their memories of Jesus independently of the original community in Jerusalem. The itinerant primitive Christian charismatics, a record of whom is found in Q and who influenced the Didache, cannot be regarded as an 'offshoot' of Jerusalem, even if the Twelve – the core of Jesus' disciples – had links with Jerusalem.

2. The Judaistic crisis, i.e. the counter-mission against Paul after the Apostolic Council and the conflict in Antioch, is not included in the diagram. We do not know precisely which groups stood behind this counter-mission. In Galatia and Philippi the mission has Judaistic traits. Here it could have been made up of groups close to the 'false brethren' of the Apostolic Council (Gal. 2.4). But there could also have been more moderate Judaizers who argued for voluntary acceptance of circumcision – and precisely for that reason gave rise theologically to a psychological 'group pressure'.

3. Perhaps the four basic currents of primitive Christianity need to be supplemented with the Gospel of Thomas. In the diagram this Gospel is put on the Jewish-Christian wing, close to Gnosticism. In the Gospel of Thomas we find a further development of Jewish Wisdom theology: without devaluing the God who created the world it regards the world as alien; without devaluing the pistics it advocates a higher knowledge. It is possibly a continuation of the radicalism of the primitive Christian itinerants in an independent form.

4. The basic currents of Christianity which emerge in writings after 70 are put side by side in the diagram. Indeed the groups will have existed roughly contemporaneously. But this contemporaneity does not apply to the writings that they produced. The majority opinion is that the Gospel of John is later than the Synoptics and presupposes the existence of one or two Synoptic Gospels, even if these did not serve as a direct 'source'. The Jewish Christian Gospels (at least the Gospel of the Nazaraeans) are a reworking of Matthew – and thus are clearly later in time. The final version of the Gospel of Thomas may similarly be later than the Synoptic Gospels.

5. The different wings in the four basic currents touch one another. The best example is the Gospel of Luke with Acts. This two-volume work unmistakably came into being in the sphere of Pauline influence. Some points of contact are not immediately clear in the diagram: the dissidents in the letters of John show a proximity not only to later Gnostic ideas but also to Jewish Christianity. These dissidents standing on the right edge of the diagram thus have points of contact with the Jewish Christianity close to Gnosticism which is to be found on the extreme left edge – as if they were particularly remote from the Johannine dissidents.

6. The history of the influence of Paul is even more complex. Alongside the left-wing and right-wing Paulinism of Colossians and Ephesians on the one hand and the Pastorals on the other, we may conjecture a further more radical ascetic current which has been preserved for us in the Acts of Thecla. There Paul appears as a preacher of continence. He persuades young women to refrain from marriage – and on decisive points is opposed to the Paul of the Pastorals.

7. Primitive Christian prophetic criticism is indicated in the diagram as if it were to be put chronologically after the four basic currents of primitive Christianity. But it is the expression of a structural crisis which dogged Christianity from the beginning. Usually it displays a marked Jewish-Christian stamp. That applies particularly to the prophets behind the Logia source, the prophets of the Revelation of John, and the prophets Hermas in Rome and Elkesai in Transjordan, both of whom preached a second repentance.

8. The label 'radical religion of redemption' hides an intrinsic multiplicity of currents which call for a separate description. The first Gnostic 'systems' in Cerinthus, the Simonians and Carpocrates are to be distinguished from the later Gnostic systems. Valentinus and Basilides form a 'class' of their own. Only when we have recognized how far they are from the later Gnostic systems can we also put Marcion with the Gnostics in a broader sense. Certainly with his preaching of two deities he is diametrically opposed to the monism of the great 'Gnostics' Valentinus and

Basilides, but precisely for that reason he is as much and as little a typical Gnostic as these two are. The 'distance' of Gnosticism from Judaism suggested in the diagram could also give a false impression: many Gnostic writings show a nearness to Jewish Christianity. One need think only of the prominence of James, the brother of the Lord, in these writings.

9. The separation of the four basic currents from the Apostolic Fathers is chronologically misleading: the late New Testament writings (the Pastorals and II Peter) belong to the same phase as the Apostolic Fathers. The Didache could still belong in the first century; at least it represents very old traditions. Otherwise, the Letter to the Hebrews and Barnabas, the Gospel of John and the letters of Ignatius, the Pastorals and Polycarp stand very close to one another in terms of content. The boundaries between the canonized writings and the so-called 'Apostolic Fathers' are fluid.

2. The formation of the canon as a confession of plurality

The canon preserves (and limits) the plurality of primitive Christianity which had come about. We can read a fourfold decision for plurality from the formation of the canon: 1. The Old Testament is preserved alongside the New Testament. 2. Gospels and letters are put side by side. 3. Four Gospels are canonized instead of one. 4. The Catholic letters appear alongside the letters of Paul. Even if we can only guess at the motives behind this development towards the preservation of plurality, since we have no direct sources on the formation of the canon, we can venture some statements.

(a) The decision to divide the canon as a whole into Old and New Testaments

It would be a misunderstanding of the decision to form a two-part canon from the Old and New Testaments if one were to assume a deliberate decision to adopt the Old Testament. Rather, our 'Old Testament' was a priori the holy scripture of the Jews – and therefore also the Bible of Jesus, the first disciples and the primitive Christian communities. It is better to say that there was a deliberate decision to put other writings alongside this given Old Testament – not as an extension of the one canonical collection of writings but as a new collection alongside the old, as 'New Testament' alongside the 'Old Testament'. How natural it would have been to accept the Gospels as a continuation of the historical books of the Old Testament – and to assess the epistolary literature as the testimonies of new prophecy![17] Be this as it may, primitive Christianity had occasion to examine its bond with the Old Testament, which had come to be taken for granted, when Marcion developed a canon which did not contain the Old Testament.

Marcion[18] came to Rome around 140. He was a rich shipowner from the Black Sea who initially emerged as a benefactor of the Roman community; however, as early as around 144 he parted company with it. The reason for this was his theology, which also had a background in contemporary history. In 132–135 the Jews had been defeated in a war waged with great cruelty, after two rebellions had already been put down in bloody fashion: in 66–74 in Palestine, and in 115–117 throughout the Near East. After 135, Jews were no longer allowed to enter Jerusalem. After 135, Marcion appeared in Rome with his 'Antitheses' between Old and New Testament. This, the clearest distancing from its Jewish mother religion, took place in early Christianity at the moment when all the world was distancing itself from a beaten and defeated people.[19] Marcion interpreted the Old and the New Testaments as the revelation of two different deities. In his book 'Antitheses' he pointedly summed up the oppositions between Old Testament and New Testament which he had discovered.[20]

The God of the Old Testament is a God of righteousness and retribution.	The God of the New Testament is a God of love and mercy.
The God of the Old Testament is a lower God, the creator of this imperfect world and the God of Israel.	By contrast, Jesus is an emissary of the supreme God, who has not previously revealed himself in this world.
The God of the Old Testament teaches an eye for an eye and a tooth for a tooth.	By contrast, Jesus emphasizes a refusal to offer retribution and a love of enemies.
Elijah has children eaten by a bear in the name of the God of the Old Testament.	By contrast, Jesus exclaims in the name of his God, Let the children come to me.
In the Old Testament Joshua stops the sun in its course.	By contrast, in the New Testament Paul admonishes: Let not the sun go down upon your wrath.
The God of the Old Testament allows polygamy and divorce.	The God of the New Testament commands monogamy and prohibits divorce.
The God of the Old Testament makes the sabbath and the law compulsory.	By contrast, Jesus brings freedom from the sabbath and from the law.

There is still a dispute as to whether and how far the primitive Christian formation of the canon was a deliberate response to Marcion.[21] But we do have a very unassuming sign that in holding on to the Old Testament, a deliberate difference from Marcion was maintained. In all the Christian manuscripts of the Greek Old and New Testaments the *nomina sacra* and especially the *nomina divina* are abbreviated.[22] The usual abbreviation for God, ΘΕΟΣ, is ΘΣ, for ΚΥΡΙΟΣ, ΚΣ, and for ΠΝΕΥΜΑ, ΠΝ. This happens throughout both the Old *and* the New Testaments – and is a peculiarity of Christian scribes which is not attested anywhere else. To some degree it becomes the 'hallmark' of Christian calligraphy (alongside the form of the codex, a book) to use such abbreviations. The Christian scribes may have been prompted to do it by the tetragrammaton יהוה, which they found in Greek transcription in the Septuagint manuscripts from which they copied. But it is essentially their own creation. By it they emphasize that the God of the Old Testament is the same as the God of the New Testament. The same holy reality reveals itself in both places.

(b) The decision to divide the New Testament into a gospel part and an apostle part

The New Testament part of the canon was itself divided into two. Marcion's canon, too, comprised a gospel and an apostle part. As gospel he used the Gospel of Luke, and as the apostle part the ten letters of Paul, i.e. our canonical letters of Paul without Hebrews and the Pastoral letters. But as both had been falsified and worked over by Judaistic 'false brothers', in the original version adopted by Marcion they were reconstructed by means of literary criticism. The Gospel of Luke was heavily abbreviated (e.g. the whole of the infancy narratives was deleted). The letters of Paul were purged of Judaistic interpolations.

Marcion was not the first to develop the idea of such a two-part canon. Rather, it already appears implicitly in the Johannine corpus. Here we have a collection of writings which belongs together in theology and linguistic style (modern analysts were the first to be able to note the subtle differences between the Gospel and the Letters of John). Here for the first time the two most important genres of the New Testament canon – gospel and letter – were combined in a single collection of writings which emerged with an authoritative claim: the Gospel of John seeks to be the authentic and true testimony to Jesus. I John is not far behind it in its claim.

As the Johannine corpus has its *Sitz im Leben* above all in Asia Minor – here the history of its influence is best attested[23] – and as Marcion comes from Asia Minor and is also said to have been active in the cities of Asia

Minor and the Aegean, it would not be inconceivable that he was stimulated to the idea of his two-part canon by the Johannine corpus. However, we have no evidence of this.

Marcion's canon and the Johannine corpus were at any rate comparable in one respect: they contained only writings in which there was just one theology – or for which one could postulate the same theology. In the Johannine corpus that is given by the uniformity of style and world of ideas. In the case of Marcion's canon we must presume that Marcion already knew the attribution of the Gospel of Luke to Paul's companion 'Luke' and therefore among other reasons decided for this Gospel. However, that is not certain. For him, the Gospel of Luke is *the* Gospel.

At all events, the formation of the canon is stamped by the fact that it brings together (both in the Gospels and in the letters) writings of a different theological stamps. We shall investigate this decision for plurality in each instance.

(c) The decision for the fourfold Gospel

When Marcion based his canon on only one Gospel, that was no more a revolutionary innovation than having a two-part New Testament canon. For in many communities and areas well in to the second century a tendency towards the 'one-Gospel principle' was dominant. A community had only one Gospel and believed that this was sufficient basis for its own faith. For over a long period the basis of this faith was 'the gospel' as an oral message of salvation, not as a particular writing. The evidence of the one-Gospel principle is particularly thick in the region of Syria.

- The Didache often refers to 'the Gospel' as a written text and probably means the Gospel of Matthew,[24] as it cites the Our Father in a form which stands close to the Gospel of Matthew. Since the Gospel is always mentioned in the singular, the Didache probably knew only one Gospel – presumably still without the attribution of this Gospel to a particular author, i.e. as an anonymous writing.
- The Syrian Tatian certainly made the acquaintance of the four-Gospel canon in Rome. But when he made it into a single Gospel, the Diatessaron, which became the normal form in Syria, he was hardly introducing an innovation, since there people were used to hearing the message of the one Gospel from *one* Gospel writing.
- The Jewish-Christian Gospels are a third piece of evidence for the one-Gospel principle. Certainly three Gospels can be demonstrated here: the Gospel of the Hebrews, the Gospel of the Nazareans and the Gospel of

the Ebionites. However, these Gospels were not assigned to particular authors but to different Christian groups. Attribution to groups in this way makes sense only if each individual Gospel enjoyed exclusive canonical recognition in a particular group. Here, too, the indications point towards Syria. We know that the Gospel of the Nazareans was read by Jewish Christians in Beroea.[25]

- A fourth piece of evidence is possibly the Gospel of Peter, which is written in the first person. According to Eusebius (*HE* VI 12, 36), it was read in a community in Rhossos in Syria at the end of the second century – the report leaves open whether it was read alongside other Gospels. That is improbable, since the Gospel is not called, say, 'The Gospel according to Peter', but 'The Gospel of Peter'.
- However, the one-Gospel principle may have spread beyond the region of Syria. Irenaeus regards it as a characteristic of the heretics that each of them had only one Gospel. According to him the Gospel of Matthew is the Gospel of the Ebionites, Luke the Gospel of the Marcionites, and Mark is favoured by those 'who separate Jesus from Christ and (make) Christ impassible, but Jesus suffer'. Finally, he says that the Gospel of John is preferred by the Valentinians (Irenaeus, *Adversus haereses* III 11, 7–8). Thus these heretics are probably just continuing a much more widespread tradition. Only after the rise of the four-Gospel canon could the continued adherence to just one Gospel become a sign of heresy.

The four-Gospel canon must have existed around the middle of the second century. Around AD 180 Irenaeus defends the 'quadriform Gospel' (the εὐαγγέλιον τετράμορθον) as a theological necessity with many analogies from cosmology and salvation history. Thus just as in the creation there are four regions of the world and four winds, and just as salvation history is divided up by four covenants (with Adam, Noah, Moses and Jesus), so too there are four Gospels. These correspond to the four heavenly figures described in Rev. 4.7: John (not Mark!) is the lion, Luke the bull, Matthew the human figure, and Mark the eagle (Irenaeus, *Adversus haereses* III 11, 7–8).

However, there are already references to the four-Gospel canon before Irenaeus. Thus in the middle of the second century Justin writes of the 'reminiscences whose authors I claim to be the apostles of Jesus and their successors' (*Dialogue* 103, 8). He also calls these 'reminiscences' (ἀπομνημονεύματα) 'Gospels' (*Apology* 66). Among them he distinguishes writings of the apostles and their disciples (both in the plural), thus presupposing at least two Gospels by apostles and two by disciples of apostles.[26] Since he demonstrably quotes the Gospels of Mark and Luke which were composed by disciples, and Matthew from the Gospels composed by apostles – and probably also John (namely John 3.3–5 in I *Apology* 61.4) – , he quite certainly knows our four canonical Gospels. That would demonstrate the canon of four Gospels in Rome in the middle of the second century. For Asia Minor Papias would be the earliest evidence, if we could infer that he knew further canonical Gospels alongside Matthew and Mark. Unfortunately we cannot.[27]

The reasons why Papias may know further canonical Gospels, and especially John (which are no more than inferences), are as follows:

1. Papias mentions the disciples in the sequence Andrew, Peter, Philip, Thomas, James, John, Matthew, etc. (Eusebius, *HE* III 39, 4 = frag.5): in the case of the first three Gospels that is precisely the order in which these disciples are mentioned at the beginning of the Gospel of John (1.40ff.). Is that possible without knowledge of John? However, this is not very convincing. In John 1 there is also an anonymous disciple in addition to Andrew. And Nathanael is not mentioned anywhere in Papias.
2. Papias criticizes the Gospel of Mark for its order of individual pericopes (Eusebius, *HE* III 39, 15 = frag.5). If, on the other hand, he gives the sequence of disciples in accordance with the 'order' in John, is he then using the Gospel of John as a secret criterion for his judgments on other Gospels? Or is it enough to see the priority he accords to the oral tradition as the basis of his critical judgment – and the defence of his own work, in which various Jesus traditions are given with no chronological order.
3. The attribution of the Gospels to Matthew and Mark is certainly attested for Papias. If we are convinced that this attribution to individual authors took place only at the formation of the four-Gospel canon, when a distinction had to be made in the one Gospel 'according to four authors', that would suggest that he knew the four-Gospel canon. However, this argument depends on a hypothesis over which there is no consensus.
4. Papias demonstrably knows I John (Eusebius, *HE* III 39, 17). Must he not then also have known the main writing of the Johannine corpus? Is that not historically probable for other reasons? The Gospel of John had a broad reception above all in Asia Minor.
5. A later prologue to the Gospels (the *Argumentum secundum Iohannem* = frag.20) appeals to the fifth book of Papias for the claim that the evangelist John dictated his Gospel to Papias.
6. In an Armenian source Papias becomes the author of the story of the woman taken in adultery (John 7.53–8.11) – probably on the basis of an erroneous inference from Eusebius (*HE* III 39, 17), who claims to have read this or a similar story in Papias and in the Gospel of the Hebrews.[28] So this note is worth no more than the tradition in Eusebius – and is silent about any knowledge of the Gospel of John on the part of Papias.

Unfortunately none of these arguments is strong enough to make it possible to draw a firm conclusion. For they do not invalidate the counter-argument that despite his great interest in demonstrating the canonical writings to be as early as possible, Eusebius says nothing of any knowledge of the Gospels of Luke and John on the part of Papias.

Now since the Gospels are cited down to the middle of the second century without the names of their authors, there is something to be said for the conjecture that the four-Gospel canon came into being shortly before the middle of the second century, deliberately breaking with the tendency towards the principle of one Gospel. Marcion perhaps indirectly encouraged the acceptance of the four-Gospel canon, since after him, his early catholic opponents could brand the restriction to one Gospel as a characteristic of heretical groups. In short, the four-Gospel canon is the 'revolutionary innovation' in the second century, and not Marcion's one-Gospel canon.

This is also suggested by the fact that in the four-Gospel canon, two of the four canonical Gospels were 'torn' from their original context. The Gospel of Luke was conceived as a two-part work composed of the Gospel and the Acts of the Apostles; the four-Gospel canon separated the Gospel of Luke from its sequel, and it continued to be separated from it in the later history of the canon. As a rule the Acts of the Apostles is handed down with the Catholic letters. 'Acts of the apostles' were found in Acts, and the corresponding 'letters of the apostles' in the Catholic letters. Similarly, the Gospel of John had to be detached from the Johannine corpus. Thus the formation of the four-Gospel canon broke with tendencies towards collections of writings (Luke + Acts and the Gospel of John + the letters of John) which were already clearly recognizable.

Finally, the formation of the canon also contradicted the intrinsic claim of some canonical Gospels. The Gospel of Matthew sets out to sum up the teaching of Jesus in final form. 'Everything' that Jesus commanded his disciples (Matt. 28.20) is to be found in it, and in a form in which Jesus will be present among his disciples until the end of the world, i.e. a final form. Perhaps Matthew deliberately differs from other forms of the Jesus tradition at two points. Twice in connection with preaching the gospel all over the world he speaks of '*this* gospel of the kingdom of God' (Matt. 24.14; 26.13). He wants to see only his 'gospel'[29] preached throughout the world. So the Gospel of Matthew is by no means intended to be read as a supplement alongside the Gospel of Mark. It seeks to replace this earliest Gospel – and includes practically all of it.

The same goes for the Gospel of Luke. In the prologue it makes the programmatic claim to surpass all its predecessors. Before it, many had already 'attempted' to give an account of Jesus, but only Luke promises the necessary reliability in his report. The Gospel of Luke, too, includes almost all the Gospel of Mark and the Logia source. Its readers are to know everything necessary to be informed about the Christian faith and to be confident in their own faith.

We find the first beginnings of an affirmation of different Gospels only in the Gospel of John. In its two conclusions the Gospel emphasizes that it offers only a selection from a much greater Jesus tradition – certainly a selection which is sufficient for attaining eternal life through faith (John 20.30f.), and which is the true testimony of the Beloved Disciple (John 21.24f.). But alongside this testimony there is still room for further Gospels: 'If one wanted to write down everything (about Jesus), I suppose that the world itself could not contain the books that would have to be written' (John 21.25). Here no exclusive collection of Gospel writings is yet envisaged. There is emphasis on the abundant wealth of possible Gospel writings. Nor is the equivalence of different Gospels in view. Before this, the 'truth' of the testimony to Jesus which is specifically contained in the Gospel of John is emphasized. But here the way opens up towards the acceptance of many Gospels. Just as the Johannine corpus was pioneering in its combination of the Gospel form and letters, so too it showed the way in the acceptance of several Gospels.

(d) The decision for the letters of Paul and the Catholic letters

The letters of Paul stand at the beginning of the history of primitive Christian literature. They must already have had an influence in many communities before the Gospels. That is the only explanation of the fact that at a very early stage, pseudepigraphical letters were written which similarly claimed influence in the communities under the name of Paul. There is no better evidence of the early 'canonical' respect for the letters of Paul than the fact that – beginning with Colossians – a wealth of pseudonymous Pauline letters was produced: first of all the Deutero-Pauline writings Colossians, Ephesians and II Thessalonians, which, together with the authentic letters, Philippians, I Thessalonians and Philemon, were added as a first appendix to an original collection of letters of Paul consisting of Romans, I Corinthians, II Corinthians and Galatians.[30] Then came the Pastoral Epistles, which clearly form a second division within the Pauline corpus and were absent from Marcion's canon. As a result of this Pauline corpus, which developed quickly and dynamically, Paul gained an importance in primitive Christian literature which did not correspond everywhere to his real position in the Christianity of the time. At least the Catholic letters, which were only collected later, served as a counterbalance to the dominant Pauline influence.

It is no chance that these Catholic letters were attributed above all to the three 'pillars' of primitive Christianity, who according to Gal. 2.9 were the partners of Paul and Barnabas in the negotiations at the Apostolic Council: Peter, James and John. The Lord's brother Jude is the only one to whom we find no parallel, unless he was seen as the Jude who is mentioned in the Apostolic Decree along with Silas as the person who communicates it (Acts 15.27), and who is identified as Judas Barsabbas only by the narrative which frames it (Acts 15.22).

The Johannine letters also play an important role as a counterbalance to the Pauline corpus. These three letters form the centre of the five Catholic letters. For the groups which formed the canon, their author was at the same time the author of the Apocalypse, and the seven letters to churches in Asia Minor were regarded as his letters. The Muratorian Canon even thinks that Paul took these letters to the seven communities as his model, since he similarly wrote to seven communities (cf. Muratorian Canon, lines 47f., 57ff.). Thus the letters of John, which numbered ten in all, formed the strongest counterbalance to the canonical letters of Paul, which were thirteen in all. Together with the four further Catholic letters (I and II Peter, James, Jude), the non-Pauline letters even exceeded the Pauline letters in number.

That the collection of Catholic letters was deliberately created as a counterbalance to the Pauline corpus emerges from II Peter. II Peter clearly presupposes all parts of the New Testament canon. It is directly related to a further Catholic letter, I Peter (II Peter 3.1). It knows the canon of four Gospels. It is certainly familiar with the Gospel of Matthew, since it refers in II Peter 1.16–18 to the Transfiguration story in its Matthaean version, though it probably also knows the Lukan version, since it introduces the key word 'glory' (δόξα) from the Lukan version (Luke 9.32). In addition it alludes to the Gospel of Mark when it asserts that it wants to ensure that the community can 'recall all these things' after his death (1.15; cf. 1.13), as if Peter wanted to leave behind a written account of his 'reminiscences'. This could only refer to the Gospel of Mark. From the Gospel of John it knows Jesus' prophecy of Peter's martyr death (John 21.18f.; II Peter 1.14). However, for us it is decisive that it knows the Pauline corpus. It speaks summarily of 'all' the letters of 'dear brother Paul', but clearly distances itself from them: they are difficult to understand. There are ignorant and frivolous people who twist them (II Peter 3.16). The immanent expectation in them is an offence to the author of II Peter. Therefore he declares apodictically that Paul called for eschatological patience in all his letters, which is objectively false, but indicates how the author wants the imminent eschatology of the letters of Paul to be understood.

Since II Peter already presupposes large parts of the whole of the New Testament canon, it may have been written near to the formation of the canon. Perhaps it was written as a pseudonymous letter only in connection with the formation of the canon, as a kind of 'editorial' by the compilers of the canon, who hid behind the name of the first apostle. They took over the polemic of the letter of Jude against heretics and in so doing betrayed something of the anti-heretical thrust of the formation of the canon, in which among other things they could have been referring to Gnosticism. At the same time they contested the imminent expectation of prophetic movements in primitive Christianity which kept flaring up in the Apocalypse of John, the Shepherd of Hermas and the new prophecy, and led to ever new disappointments and mockery. If we read II Peter on these premises, it unmistakably betrays that the Catholic letters are meant to be a counterbalance to the letters of Paul. But despite the distance from the letters of Paul, it does not attempt to remove the letters of 'dear brother Paul' from the canon.

The canon is the great achievement of early catholic primitive Christianity, which I would prefer to call 'canonical primitive Christianity'. It established itself on two fronts. It opposed the many Gnostic currents which led to a fundamental crisis in the understanding of the basic 'narrative' myth by dissolving its indissoluble unity with history; similarly, it opposed prophetic movements which with their radical ethic revived the spirit of earliest primitive Christianity. With the formation of the canon, early catholic church Christianity did not seek dissolution either in its 'myth' or in its ethic. Rather, the canon is one of the forms of ritual expression, in that it comprises the books which are to be read in worship. In fact we have indications that the very earliest Gospel manuscripts were prepared for liturgical use. Here the texts are divided into short pericopes. Contradictions between them remain hidden. And they were even productive, since life itself is contradictory and requires that time and again other sides of a religious sign system should be actualized, even if they point in different directions.

It is decisive that the canon did not suppress the inner plurality of primitive Christianity, but preserved it. That is the only reason why it was accepted so quickly and without conflicts in a pluralistic primitive Christianity. Its basic features are already present in Irenaeus around AD 180. His canon includes the four Gospels, the letters of Paul, Acts and the Catholic letters, of which he cites only I Peter and I and II John (though we cannot conclude from this that he does not know the others). However, unlike our canon he knows two apocalypses, the Shepherd of Hermas as well as the Apocalypse of John. Only writings on the periphery continue to be disputed: Hebrews because of the impossibility of a second repentance, the Apocalypse of John because of its 'materialistic' eschatology, and the shorter Catholic letters.

Nor was there much dispute about excluding the great flood of Gnostic writings. There must have been an amazing consensus here, which made it possible to exclude them, and which gave early catholic primitive Christianity a feeling of cohesion and orthodoxy. Can we go on to analyse this consensus? In other words, can we also work out its content from the various New Testament writings? Can we still reconstruct why a Christian stamped by Synoptic theology could also feel at home in a Pauline community? Or why a Johannine Christian could celebrate the eucharist with others in a community which was influenced by the radical ethic of the Gospel of Matthew, and why with the formation of the canon all these basically different traditions could be appropriated by all?

3. The inner canon within the canon: the grammar of primitive Christian faith

A canon consists of the texts from which one can time and again reconstruct the sign language of a religion. Like any language, this sign language presupposes a 'grammar' – rules by which the different sign elements of language can be used and connected. Competence in the language presupposes competence in, but not (cognitive) knowledge of, such rules. For they are unconsciously learned when acquiring the language, and usually practised without conscious reflection. The new religious language of primitive Christianity was also guided by such rules, which had been 'internalized' along with the narrative and images, the rites and ethic of primitive Christianity. These rules indicate a certain hierarchy. Two 'basic axioms' form the most fundamental rule: the axioms of monotheism and belief in the redeemer. Primitive Christianity shares the first with Judaism, and the second separates it from Judaism. Combining them changes both of them: strict monotheism is modified by the divine worship of the redeemer, and belief in the redeemer is limited by monotheistic belief in creation; in my view this explains the repudiation of the Gnostic temptation by early Christianity, which was backed by a large consensus.

In addition to that there are limited 'rules' which I call 'basic motifs', to distinguish them from the fundamental axioms. These are relatively formal convictions, which recur in different themes, genres and spheres of tradition. An example can illustrate better than abstract definitions what such a basic motif is, and how it can be analysed as an invariable from different themes, genres and spheres of tradition.

The example I shall take is the basic motif of the change of position: we find it formulated explicitly in the logion about the first and the last. Whoever will be the first should be ready to adopt the position of the last (Mark 10.43, etc.).

- This motif occurs in different *themes*: in the interpretation of history, the ups and of which are interpreted as God's humbling and exalting. It occurs in ethical admonitions as an invitation to humility; in christology, when Christ humbles himself to the depth of the cross to be exalted by God (Phil. 2.6ff.). And in eschatology, where the last will be first and the first last.
- The motif also occurs in different *genres*: in hymns like the *Magnificat* and the Philippians hymn (Luke 2.46ff.; Phil. 2.6ff.), in logia of the Jesus tradition; and in narratives: the foot-washing scene in John enacts the exchange of the roles of master and slave (John 13.1ff.).
- Finally, the motif occurs in different *spheres of tradition*. Assuming that a Christian with a Synoptic stamp found his way into a Pauline community, he could join in singing the Philippians hymn there. The notion of pre-existence might be unknown to him, i.e. the idea of a figure who came from heaven in order to return there; however, he knew the story of the way of the son of God to the cross – he knew the sayings of Jesus about humbling and exaltation. And if a Johannine Christian were present, he will have reinterpreted the humiliation on the cross in terms of a hidden exaltation more boldly than all the rest. Even a friend of the letter of James could have felt that texts with this basic motif spoke to him: 'Humble yourselves before the Lord and he will exalt you' (James 4.10).

We can work out such axioms and basic motifs inductively from the texts and infer their influence in life. If they are taken for granted, they make understanding possible between all people whose thought, feeling and wills they have shaped. In respect of the whole of primitive Christianity, it is not necessary to demonstrate all the basic motifs in all the groups of texts, and not just because each group of texts always gives only extracts from the interpreted world of a group. It is even more important that the basic convictions bring together different traditions and people like family similarities. Not all members of a family have all its characteristics, but a web of different characteristics unites constantly changing sub-groups, so that each feels connected with each. Here of course it is conceivable that as a result of such family similarities (as understood by Ludwig Wittgenstein) a nuclear family also crystallizes out.

I shall go on to give an open list of such axioms and basic motifs. It will never possible to formulate them completely.

The first basic axiom of primitive Christian faith is *monotheism*, belief in the one and only God. In the religious sign system this serves as a fundamental positive connecting link: everything in reality, in life and in faith must be related to this one and only God and be determined by him. All human beings are directed towards him, whether they know it or not. This one axiom gives religious sign language a single centre from which it can organize itself and differentiate itself from the environment as an independent force. At the same time, the basic axiom of monotheism serves as a negative rule of exclusion: nothing may be equated with God. Everything is to be separated from God. Everything that is the world is not God. This rule of exclusion holds particularly in relation to the religions. All connections with other gods are excluded – and everything that creates a connection with these gods. If the first Christians gave up many of the ritual traditions of Judaism, the horror of being polluted by idolatry remained – or was at least vigorously disputed. As in any monotheistic religion, the strict exclusivity of the one God was time and again qualified: the abundance of negative experiences which people could not and would not attribute to the one God motivated faith in intermediate beings: Satan and his demons. And the abundance of positive experiences motivated belief in the angels (and later the saints). Such intermediate beings filled the vacuum between God and human beings in the religious imagination. But these subordinate numinous beings had only a subordinate meaning.

The second basic axiom of primitive Christianity is *belief in a redeemer*. It is subordinated to the first and yet is unmistakably in tension with it. It is subordinate, because through the figure of the redeemer the one and only God becomes universally accessible to all peoples. With the help of the redeemer, only now can monotheism establish itself correctly: its universal aspect is brought to bear. But belief in the redeemer is also subordinated to monotheism because it takes back the 'deviation' in monotheism caused by numinous intermediaries: Christ is the Lord over all numinous powers – both demons and angels. The redeemer conquers all enemies and rules over all angels, in order at the end to hand over the rule to God alone (I Cor. 15.11–28). This belief in the redeemer not only establishes the monotheistic dynamic; it ties it to a human form: God is firmly linked with Christ. The notion of incarnation surpasses all previous forms of the presence of God in history and in the world.

The tension between monotheism and christology remains. In the end it is resolved by means of a creative use of the basic axiom of monotheism: nothing may stand alongside God – except God himself. In a long process of reflection in the early church, the way in which Father and Son stood over each other was attributed to an indissoluble unity of being – in order to overcome any belief in two gods. Similarly, in a long process of reflection the redeemer was fully bound up with human existence – despite the temptation to limit this bond only to the higher part in human beings in order to restrict it in time or to demote its reality. Belief in the full incarnation became established.

Both basic axioms served as criteria for demarcation. In the long term all theological convictions would be rejected which threatened the unity of God, whether by putting a creator and a redeemer God side by side (as in Marcion) or by subordinating a limited demiurge to the true God (as in Gnostic systems). Similarly, all christologies would be rejected which denied the full incarnation, whether they assumed only an apparent entering of the deity into human life or taught that only a subordinate part of the deity became human.

These basic axioms become concrete in many basic motifs.

1. The *creation motif. God has created the world through his will. Everything could also not have been, and everything could have been different*. Formulated as a rule of association, that means that the being and non-being of all things is exclusively connected with the one and only God – and not with anything else: with matter alongside God, with another demiurge who completed the creation, or with emanations, but only with the will of God. This will of God manifests itself both in the creation at the beginning (John 1.1ff.; I Cor. 8.6) and in the dawn of every new day (I Clem. 24.2f.); both in an individual conversion as in the origin of a 'new creation' (Gal. 6.15, etc.), and also in the repeated everyday renewal of men and women (II Cor. 4.16); both in the prototypical overcoming of death through the resurrection of Jesus and in the future resurrection of all Christians. Throughout we find a juxtaposition of a fundamental act of creation and a continual creation which is made possible by it – in different spheres and themes: in the cosmos, in human life and in eschatology. The motif of creation shapes the image of God: God is *the* Creator. It defines christology: Christ is the mediator at creation (I Cor. 8.6; John 1.2; Col. 1.16) and the firstborn of those who are risen from the dead (Col. 1.18). It shapes the picture of human beings, in so far as they are creatures by nature – but in Christ become a 'new creation' (Gal. 6.15; II Cor. 5.17). Even if creation is not yet envisaged as *creatio ex nihilo* in the strict sense (as later with the Gnostic

Basilides and other writers of the second century), God can be formally characterized as the God 'who gives life to the dead and calls into existence the things that do not exist' (Rom. 4.17). No long explanation is needed of the fact that the motif of creation drew a clear dividing line from Gnosticism. No demiurge, no emanation, no unformed matter had any influence on creation.

2. The *wisdom motif. The world has been created by God's Wisdom and Word (John 1.1ff.). However, this is inappropriate for human wisdom, though it is nevertheless accessible in a paradoxical way through Christ, 'in whom are hid the treasures of wisdom and knowledge' (Col. 2.3).* That too can be formulated as the rule of association of interpreting the world. An order and rationality which make life possible is presupposed in all things and must be related to them, even where it goes against appearances and wisdom seems to be folly. It is a characteristic of the New Testament understanding of miracle that Wisdom has to establish itself in the face of resistance: the messengers of Wisdom are rejected and killed (Luke 11.59ff.). Precisely those who elsewhere are excluded from wisdom, the 'foolish' and the 'babes', the 'weary and heavy laden', experience the wisdom of God (Matt. 11.25–30; I Cor 1.26f.). God's peaceful wisdom from above is in tension with the aggressive wisdom from below (James 3.13–18). And only with the help of the divine pneuma can wisdom become master over human emotions, i.e. perform the classical task which was expected of a wise man in antiquity (Gal. 5.16ff.). Wisdom establishes itself everywhere in the face of resistance: cosmically in the world, historically in Christ, socially and ethically among men and women. Here the motif of wisdom shapes and permeates many themes. Trust in an order which stands behind the world continues to be maintained – but the deep disruption of this order is evident in the fact that God chooses the way of folly to establish himself in the world (I Cor. 1.18ff.). Gnosticism, too, knows the motif of wisdom. But in it wisdom often takes a false step out of folly and ignorance, which leads to the origin of the world and of disaster. By contrast, in primitive Christianity wisdom even in the form of the folly of the cross is the foundation of salvation and an expression of God's superior wisdom.

3. The *motif of miracle. Everything that happens in the world is open to miraculous events which go against all expectations. Nothing is completely determined.* Formulated as a rule of association, this means that nothing is linked in so determined a way that it cannot spontaneously be broken through by the power of miracle. This power of miracle is activated in order to overcome suffering. Two of its special features may be mentioned. 1. Miracles

are actions of a kind that are performed by God and by human beings. The formula 'Your faith has saved you' (Mark 5.34; 10.52; Luke 17.19, etc.) and the saying about the faith which moves mountains (Mark 11.22–24; I Cor. 13.2) bear witness to an active power of miracle in human beings which becomes effective through faith and prayer. The first Christians have gifts which go beyond the normal: manifold charismata like the 'charism of healing' (I Cor. 12.28). But they also reflect the limits of such miraculous power: Paul must bear his illness (II Cor. 12.9); no miracle saves Jesus from the cross (Mark 15.31f.). 2. Miracles are signs. They illuminate the meaning of events – the star of Bethlehem the birth (Matt. 2.1ff.) and an earthquake the death of the redeemer (Matt. 27.52). Cosmic signs will announce the end of the world (Matt. 24.4ff.). But the miracles performed by Jesus and other human beings are also understood as 'signs'. Already with Jesus they are signs of a new world – and especially in the Gospel of John they are symbols of all the dimensions of redemption. Because the miracles are understood symbolically, they are connected with every possible theme of New Testament faith. Miracles are part of its understanding of God and history, its picture of Christ, its understanding of the church (as charisma) and its anthropology. Through miracles the world is drawn into redemption. Despite some miracles in apostolic Acts with a Gnostic colouring, miracles and miracle stories are far from having the same importance in Gnosticism as they do in the Christianity of the church.

4. The *motif of alienation. All life lives at a distance from God. Human beings are separated from God by guilt and suffering, finitude and death, and also by dark numinous powers, and in this way are also alienated from their own origin.* Formulated as a rule of association in interpreting life, that means that in their present existence human beings must be bound up with sin, death and powers hostile to God, but with God it is the opposite. God is holy and eternal. In the New Testament, too, we meet the three basic possibilities of interpreting evil. It is either attributed to God – with the consequence that God becomes incomprehensible and the *deus absconditus*. Or it is attributed to human sin or the structure of the world – as a third element alongside God and human beings, in that this hostility of the world is interpreted anthropomorphically as Satan and his demons. We find a radicalized consciousness of sin – from John the Baptist, who sees everyone threatened by the divine wrath and calls on all to repent (Mark 3.7ff.), to Paul, for whom human nature as 'flesh' (σάρξ) represents fundamental hostility to God (Rom. 8.7). In primitive Christianity a main emphasis lies on human sin. In addition, demons and powers threaten human beings. Their conquest through exorcisms is already proclaimed by Jesus (Matt. 12.28), but even

more so in the rest of the New Testament. There the Risen Christ becomes Lord of all powers and authorities (Rom. 8.31ff.). But God too can become incomprehensible: the simile of the potter gives him the freedom to reject without reason when he wills (Rom. 9.19ff.). In the great schemes of the New Testament we find a balance between these three factors: in Romans sin (Rom. 1.18ff.; 5.12ff.), the powers (Rom. 8.31ff.) and the incomprehensible God (Rom. 9.19ff.) are all made responsible for evil – but always in the awareness that Christ has overcome sin, has conquered the powers and created access to a gracious God. The motif of alienation also draws a dividing line from Gnosticism. Gnosticism shifts the origin of evil away from human beings – in a drama before time, whose prisoner human beings are.

5. The *motif of renewal. History is permeated by an expectation of a new world which has already begun in the midst of this world. Christians are citizens of two worlds, who with their 'sarx' are imprisoned in the old world, but who already belong to the new world through the 'pneuma'*. Formulated as a rule of association, everything in this world must be connected and contrasted with its eschatological counterpart: this world with the new heaven and earth, this human being with the new human being. The view of the world and human beings as an eschatological transition occurs throughout the New Testament – with Jesus as the expectation of the kingdom of God that is dawning, which for him begins in the present and calls for the conversion of human beings (Mark 1.14f.). After Easter it appears as the conviction that with the resurrection of Jesus the new world has already begun. This awareness of a transition could be expressed as an imminent expectation (Mark 13; Apocalypse of John) and as present eschatology. Now already Christians have passed from death to life (John 5.24; I John 3.14) or have been transported to another realm of being (in the spatial sense, Col. 1.13; 3.1ff.; Eph. 2.1ff.). They walk in a 'new life' (Rom. 6.4), are a 'new creation' (Gal. 6.15; II Cor. 5.17), and are newly created human beings (Col. 3.10; Eph. 4.24). This sense of a transition can also be expressed as the scheme of a history (of fulfilment) with Jesus as the centre of this time (thus in Luke-Acts). It is characteristic that this motif of renewal determines both the view of the cosmos and that of human beings: just as the whole world has to be renewed, so too do human beings if they want to correspond to the will of God. The call for repentance has a markedly ethical accent: fruits of repentance and works are required of men and women (Matt. 3.8; Rev. 2.5, 22f.). Here renewal takes place in human action. At the same time the motif of renewal appears as the action of God. It makes possible 'new life' (Rom. 6.4) and human rebirth (John 3.5; Titus 3.5). The parallelism of cosmos and human renewal can be summed up in the heading 'participa-

tion eschatology'. It is alien to Gnosticism. There human renewal and redemption do not take place with the world, but against it.

6. The *motif of representation. There is a close connection between all life, so that one life can take the place of another. What happens to it thus also happens to others or benefits them.* Formulated as a rule of association, persons and living beings can be bound together as active analogies. If they accord with one another, they influence one another. So representation is a structure of the whole of life in the primitive Christian interpretation of the world. As their ancestor, Adam already represents all human beings. All are formed after him, but his sin also has an effect on all. By analogy to this and in contrast to it, Christ is the 'ancestor' of a new humanity (Rom. 5.12ff.). Abraham is the ancestor of Israel. He becomes the ancestor of the Gentiles. The righteousness promised to him will benefit all (Rom. 4.1ff.), and the blessing resting on him will become a blessing for all peoples (Gal. 3.6ff.) – provided that one is 'related' to Abraham by faith. A second notion appears alongside that of the ancestor: as the one who is sent, Christ is the representative of God: 'Whoever sees me sees him who has sent me' (John 12.45). Correspondingly, it is true of the disciples that 'Whoever hears you, hears me' (Luke 10.16). And of the children: whoever accepts them accepts Jesus, and whoever accepts Jesus accepts the one who has sent him (Mark 9.37). A third notion is action for others: one can pray for others (Rom. 1.8), be baptized for the dead (I Cor. 15.29), bear burdens for others (Gal. 6.2). The notion of 'dying for others' is embedded in a wealth of representative relationships. 'If one has died for all, then they have all died' (II Cor. 5.14). Like Jesus, they will also rise – and be a 'new creation' (5.17). An 'exclusive' representation appears alongside this 'inclusive' representation, in which there is a basic analogy: Christ suffers precisely what the others need not suffer: a punitive death (Rom. 8.3) and curse (Gal. 1.3f.). Similarly, the apostle Paul can say of himself that death is at work in him, so that life may be at work in the community (II Cor. 4.12). However, before this he says that he wants life also to become manifest in him (4.11). Thus the analogy is preserved: he comes through death to life. So too will the Corinthians! The same is the case with the statements about the representative character of Christ. In Paul it is not just Christ's death which brings about salvation, but death together with resurrection (cf. Rom. 4.25; 5.10; 6.1ff.; 8.34). Gnosticism also knows thought in effective analogies. However, it does not activate it in order to bind redemption to the representative action of the one Christ. Rather, redemption comes about through human 'knowledge' (*gnosis*).

7. The *motif of indwelling. God takes up his abode in the concrete world of the senses. God is present in human beings through his spirit, in Christ through incarnation, in the rites through sacramental presence, in the church as 'house' and 'body'*. Formulated as a rule of association, God can be so closely connected with concrete parts of the world that this connection can be interpreted as real presence. The Old Testament already knows the indwelling of God – above all in two forms: as the indwelling of God's Spirit or his wisdom in chosen people (Wisdom 7.27), and as the indwelling of God's name in the temple. Both forms will be continued in the New Testament – initially related to Christ; there the indwelling is heightened so that it becomes the exclusive incarnation of the Logos in the *sarx* (John 1.14; cf. Col. 2.9). Here at the same time Christ takes the place of the temple (John 2.18ff.). Something similar applies to Christians: their body is a temple of God in which his spirit is present (I Cor. 6.19) – and at the same time 'a member in the body of Christ' (I Cor. 6.15). Their community is at the same time the house and temple of God (I Cor. 3.16) and the 'body of Christ' (I Cor. 12.12ff.; Rom. 12.3ff.). Granted, initially the image of the 'body' is only a widespread ancient image for a political society, but in primitive Christianity it is remythicized because it is related to the mysterious presence of the Risen Christ in his community. The motif of indwelling also includes belief in the sacramental presence of Christ – regardless of whether this is depicted as presence in the memory, as the personal presence of the host, as a social presence of the community or as a material real presence in bread and wine (John 6.51ff.). On the basis of such statements about indwelling, sometimes reciprocal formulations appear – and thus the mystical language of 'being in Christ'. The Christians are in Christ (Rom. 8.1), and at the same time Christ is in them (8.10). According to the first farewell discourse Christ comes, and God, to dwell in the believers. They are in them – and at the same time they are in Christ (John 14.20ff.). In I John 4.16 there is even a reciprocal 'mystical' statement which is related to God: 'God is love, and whoever abides in love abides in God, and God in him.' The motif of indwelling firmly contradicts a basic Gnostic conviction about the incompatibility of God and matter, spirit and body.

8. The *motif of faith. God and salvation disclose themselves to human beings through faith as a total act of trust, with which human beings give a basis to their lives that is outside themselves.* Formulated as a rule of association, for human beings faith is connected in a privileged way with the divine reality. Where faith and human beings are firmly bound together, it is possible for human beings to extricate themselves from their alienation from God. It is striking that there are correlations between statements about faith and external

events. The New Testament speaks of a coming of faith – and a coming of Christ (Gal. 3.23; Mark 2.17); of the victory of faith and the victory of Christ (I John 5.4; John 16.33); of the omnipotence of faith and the omnipotence of God (Mark 9.23; 10.27). In it, faith becomes 'judgment' – as an inner process – and at the same time remains the external judgment of God (John 3.18; 5.29). Faith justifies – just as God justifies. All this is more than a shorthand way of speaking. Faith establishes the centre of the self in the external saving action of God and in the person of the redeemer. Accordingly, it varies depending on the manifold character of this action. Faith is rarely 'faith in God' – in the sense of faith in the one and only God and creator (James 2.19; Heb. 11.3). It is more often trusting faith in a helping divine power – as faith in miracle and prayer (Mark 2.5; Mark 11.22f.; James 1.6; 5.15). It is above all confessing faith which confesses redemption in Jesus (Mark 1.14f.; Rom. 10.9f.). This faith has power to justify and redeem. It is finally a proving faith – trust and perseverance on the long way through history (Heb. 11.4ff.). So it is bound up with belief in God, with christology, with ethics. The motif of faith is almost a reversal of the motif of indwelling. There God from his beyond becomes transcendent in earthly reality, whereas in faith human beings become transcendent in the divine reality, to find a firm ground beyond themselves: 'the assurance of things hoped for, the conviction of things not seen' (Heb. 11.1). Because faith was a basic motif in primitive Christian religion, a demarcation from Gnosticism became automatic, since there redemption came about through knowledge. Faith was only a preliminary stage on the way to it.

9. The *motif of agape. Love is the foundation of a positive relationship to God and human beings – especially in its extension to the enemy, the stranger and the sinner.* Formulated as a rule of association, through love God, Christ and human beings may be bound together, and human beings may be bound together among themselves – always in a relationship of mutuality (whereas faith goes one-sidedly from human beings to God and Christ and in this context is not applied to any interpersonal relationship). In the Synoptic tradition we have only the twofold love of God and neighbour – in a characteristic extension beyond traditional limits, which in nucleus may go back to Jesus (Matt. 5.43ff.; Luke 10.25ff.; 7.36ff.). In Paul the love of God and Christ for human beings is added, without interpersonal love being grounded by definition in this divine love. Instead, love is almost absolutized in a hymn of praise: it becomes a personified power which develops in the community (I Cor. 13). The Gospel of John fuses both traditions: just as God and Jesus have loved the disciples, so too the disciples are to love one another (John 13.34f.; 15.9ff.). Here love is limited to the members of

the community, but it also has an effect on the world around and a significance for it. Finally, in the Johannine corpus we find the definition of God as love (I John 4.16). The understanding of God, christology, ethics and ecclesiology is thus shaped by the basic motif of love. As the 'greatest commandment' it is explicitly given a central significance as the basic conviction of primitive Christianity. In the light of the Gnostic self-understanding, the notion of love does not lead to any demarcations from Gnosticism, but it does in the light of church Christianity. What Paul says to his 'Gnostics' (who were not yet Gnostics in the strict sense) – namely, 'Knowledge puffs up, but love builds up' (I Cor. 8.2) – the church Christians could repeat in connection with their Gnostics.

10. The *motif of change of position. God casts down and exalts, makes the first last and requires a readiness to relinquish status.* Formulated as a rule of association, wherever there are high and lowly in a relationship, the two poles can be exchanged. We find this basic motif in the interpretation of God's action in history: 'He puts down the mighty from their thrones and exalts the lowly', as Mary sings in the *Magnificat* (Luke 1.52). She is herself an example of this, since despite her 'lowliness' she becomes the mother of the Messiah. The motif occurs in *christology*, thus in the New Testament picture of Jesus: the one who was like God has humbled himself to the point of the cross in order to be exalted by God (Phil. 2.6ff.). It similarly occurs in *ethical admonitions*, as an invitation to humility and renunciation of status or as a warning against arrogance (I Peter 5.5). Anyone who wants to be first in the community must be prepared to be the servant of all – and in this way to distinguish himself from the rulers of this world (Mark 10.42ff.). Jesus himself is the model for this. When in the Gospel of John he washes the disciples' feet, as master he is assuming the role of the slave, as teacher the role of pupil, and as man the role of the woman (John 13.1ff.). One can even see *whole Gospels* governed by this notion of a change of position: the one whom the angels serves all by giving his life (Mark 1.13; 10.45). And finally it appears in *eschatology* – as an expectation that in the last judgment the last will be first and the first last (Mark 10.31). The notion of martyrdom can also be regarded as a variant on this change of position: martyrdom is prophesied for the sons of Zebedee – in it, as first they will become last (Mark 10.35ff.). Certainly the motif of a change of position did not create any acute distinctions from Gnosticism – but quite certainly many church Christians found the Gnostic sense of being superior to the simple pistics arrogance and an offence against the admonition to humility.

11. The *motif of judgment. Human beings will be answerable before God's*

forum of judgment but on the basis of their faith they will be justified apart from their deeds. Formulated as a rule of association, in the judgment good and evil human works will be closely connected with their positive and negative sanctions, but God's grace cuts through this connection. The sinner will be justified. This notion of judgment was originally part of eschatology. But it also moves over into anthropology: Paul depicts the 'work of the law' written in the heart and the conscience as an inner process of judgment on which the last judgment casts its shadow (Rom. 2.12ff.). The notion of judgment is further bound up with the redemption that has already taken place: in Christ, God condemned the sins in the flesh so that the Christians could fulfil God's demand in the spirit (Rom. 8.3f.); for them there is no longer any condemnation. Soteriology knows the acquittal which already has its effect now. But usually the talk is of the 'last judgment'. The notion of judgment is in tension with salvation. So in the New Testament there are three important variants on the notion of judgment. 1. In the Synoptic tradition, in the judgment a paradoxical reversal takes place: the first will be last (Matt. 20.16). In particular the sinners and the lost will have a chance. 2. In the Deutero-Paulines the judgment is relativized by a tendency towards universal reconciliation. It also fades right into the background in Ephesians. The goal is the summing up of all things in Christ (Eph. 1.10). There is no place here for the harshness of judgment. 3. The judgment is internalized. It already takes place now in the decision of faith or unbelief (John 3.17; 12.47). So Jesus himself does not judge anyone, but human beings judge themselves through their unbelief (12.47). And if this point is nowhere carried through consistently, the acquittal of the sinner in the judgment does away with the ethical rationality of action and consequence, but it can take place only in a forensic framework. Here Gnosticism goes a step further: the notion of salvation completely displaces the notion of judgment. Those who in the intuitive certainty of Gnosticism are certain of their identity with the deity have left all judgment behind.

Let us note the result: the consensus of primitive Christianity is governed by two basic axioms, monotheism and belief in the redeemer. In addition there are eleven basic motifs: the motifs of creation, wisdom and miracle; of renewal, representation and indwelling; of faith, agape and a change of position; and finally the motif of judgment. One could certainly also compile other lists. If we begin by assuming that the consensus over this 'grammar' of primitive Christian faith developed organically, then the exclusion of Gnostic texts and groups from canon and church would be the natural consequence of these religious axioms. This set of axioms inevitably had to separate a radical religion of redemption from a religion the basic axioms of which contained a balance between faith in creation and faith in redemption. It was not external means of power but the inner normativeness of primitive Christian faith which led to the exclusion of the Gnostics. Thus the grammar of primitive Christian faith forms the inner canon within the canon. The writings merely established themselves because they corresponded to this inner canon.

If we make a cross-check, however, we come to a different result. Certainly the writings collected in the canon by and large correspond to the 'grammar of primitive Christian faith', but there are writings which do not contradict it, yet nevertheless remained outside the canon. And we can ask whether here there are not some currents and important aspects of primitive Christian faith which have been under-represented.

That is true of a series of Jewish Christian writings. There is no reason to exclude the Jewish-Christian Gospels from the canon. Only some fragments of them have been handed down to us. And perhaps they were regarded as variants of the Synoptic gospels. But perhaps they did not become established only because the canon came into being in a region which had little contact with Jewish Christianity in the East.

Thus we do not have the *Gospel of the Nazareans*, which makes some important emphases with its social motifs. In it, the man with the paralysed hand is healed so that he can earn his own living. He himself asks to be healed so that he does not have to go on begging (frag.10). The pericope about the rich young man is characteristically developed further. Now there are two rich men. This does away with any suggestion that Jesus addressed his call to renounce possessions and become a disciple only to a single individual: rather, he means many rich people, if not all. The renunciation of possessions is motivated with the social distress of fellow Jews. It is the fulfilment of the Torah (namely love of neighbour), and not an additional requirement for the perfect. The fundamental character of its demand is also worked out in this way (frag.16). The parable of the talents is full of a human ethic relating to possessions. The servant who buried his talent is not punished but only censured. Only the servant who squandered his possessions in debauchery is thrown into prison. All this is morally more illuminating than the punishment of the fearful servant (frag.18).

Similarly, the *Gospel of the Ebionites* does not appear in the canon. With its absence we lack the voice of a primitive Christian vegetarianism which we already find in an early form in Romans 1.4; 2.21. Here John the Baptist eats 'wild honey, the taste of which was like manna, like cakes in oil' (frag.2). Jesus refuses to celebrate the passover because it involves eating meat (frag.7). His whole mission is summed up in the saying that he has come to abolish sacrifice (6). Sacrifices were predominantly the sacrifices of animals – and many involved eating meat. Just as the Gospel of the Nazaraeans shows a special sensitivity towards the poor, so the Gospel of the Ebionites shows a sensitivity to all fellow-creatures. The renunciation of possessions and vegetarianism are a legitimate protest against the harshness of life in which life lives at the expense of other life and human beings live at the expense of other human beings.

The *Gospel of the Hebrews* is full of a spirit which is close to Gnosticism. In it the motif of rest plays a role which unites God and human beings. Through the voice at Jesus' baptism, God identifies himself with Jesus: 'My Son, I expected in all the prophets that you would come and that I should rest in you. For you are my rest; you are my firstborn son, you who rule in eternity' (frag.2). Here God longs for a resting place. And through Jesus he promises rest and rule to all. What he finds in the Son, men and women find in Jesus: 'Whoever is amazed will attain glory, and whoever attains glory will rest' (frag.4a; cf. also the variant of this same saying in 4b). But this fulfilment of divine and human longing is closely connected with a concern for fellow human beings: 'And you shall never be joyful unless you look on your brother in love' (frag.5). The worst crime is that of the one 'who has disturbed his brother's spirit' (frag.6). One can only guess that in these Jewish Christian Gospels we have lost the voices of a very impressive Christianity which was no less valuable than the Christianity close to Judaism in the Letter of James or in Matthew.

That only becomes clear when we read one of the very few extant writings from this milieu, the *Didache* or the 'Teaching of the Apostles'. Here we find a very early form of primitive Christianity with a Jewish Christian ethic, which is presented in the doctrine of the two ways. In it, itinerant charismatic Christianity is still alive. The eucharist is celebrated as spiritual food and spiritual drink, but without the sacramental real presence of the Crucified. The church order combines charismatic and democratic features: the bishops and deacons are elected by the community.

The Jewish Christianity of the *Gospel of Thomas*, which is close to Gnosticism, deserves special mention. When it was not accepted in the canon, a valuable variant of primitive Christian faith was lost: an individual primitive Christian mysticism. The book cannot be accused of Gnosticism. It knows no second creator of the world who is distinct from the true God. And nowhere does it recognizably advocate a docetic christology. On the contrary, it embodies in a pure form the message of the infinite value of the individual human soul. The kingdom of God is the sphere from which human beings come and to which the redeemed return – and at the same time it is the inner self. Recognition of the kingdom of God is therefore recognition of the self: '. . . the kingdom is inside you, and it is outside you'

(3). The redeemer who communicates knowledge by no means radically transcends this world: Jesus has 'revealed himself to them in the flesh' (28). The redeemer is omnipresent: 'I am the light which is above them all. I am the all. From me did the all come forth and to me did the all extend. Split a piece of wood and I am there. Lift up the stone and you will find me there' (77). Despite all the disparagement of the world it remains the medium of revelation. We find traits of a cosmic piety. Stones will minister to the disciples (19). What distinguishes the Gospel of Thomas from all other primitive Christian writings is its radical individualism. No community is visible. It speaks to individuals and the solitary. And it offers them a mysticism of union with God, a return to where everything comes from. But in my view, according to the 'grammar of primitive Christian faith' constructed above it is not a 'heretical' book.

Most of the Jewish Christian writings I have mentioned may have been composed in Syria (or elsewhere in the East). They were also probably disseminated there. But in its final form the canon seems above all to have been shaped by a consensus between Christianity in Asia Minor and Christianity in Rome. Most pseudepigraphic writings point to this sphere: the Pastorals could have been written in Rome but address communities in Asia Minor. Hebrews directs the imagination of the reader to 'Italy' (Heb. 13.24). The (pseudepigraphic) prison letters Colossians, Ephesians and II Timothy suggest a Roman origin – and at the same time point to recipients in the East. Was Jewish Christianity in the second century too much off the beaten track to leave traces of itself in the final form of the canon?

With other books, as with the Gospel of Thomas, a colouring close to Gnosticism may have made reception more different. After Marcion, everything that led in the proximity of Gnostic ideas was regarded increasingly heretical – even if these points of contact did not affect the decisive points. For that reason alone the Gospel of Thomas would have had little chance – quite apart from the fact that its individualistic and mystic piety was not to the taste of an early Catholicism which was establishing itself as an institution. A fundamental possibly of human religion – mysticism – thus remained under-represented, to the detriment of the inner riches of Christianity. Here a theory of primitive Christianity can reconstruct lost riches and in the light of the norms of primitive Christian faith which historically developed into a system can recognize them as 'legitimate'. For it would have been completely in keeping with the tendency to recognize an inner plurality that can be seen in the formation of the canon also to accept a voice of individualistic mysticism in the concert of the canonical writings – and thus supplement the community mysticism of Paul and the Gospel of John from another side.

13

Conclusion: The Construction and Plausibility of the Primitive Christian Sign World

I have described primitive Christian religion as a sign system which the first Christians constructed on the basis of Jewish religion. They built a semiotic cathedral out of narrative, ritual and ethical materials, a world of signs *and* a world in which to live. For its inhabitants this world was quite simply 'true' and plausible. Before we raise the question how this plausibility came about, I shall once again give a brief summary of the 'building history' and of the appearance of this impressive semiotic cathedral.

1. The construction of primitive Christian religion: a summary

The material used in this semiotic cathedral comes largely from the Jewish mother religion. That applies first to the narrative material which underlies the *basic narrative* of Jesus in primitive Christianity. This basic narrative reformulates the messianic hopes of Judaism under the impact of the Jewish prophets and the charismatic Jesus of Nazareth. Here myth and history enter into a unity in tension. According to the conviction of primitive Christianity, something as decisive happened in the midst of history as had happened in primal times and would happen in the end-time, and therefore the history of Jesus was narrated like an event of these times, in mythical form, and at the same time as a concrete historical event. The history of Jesus was transformed into mythical statements; mythical expectations were transformed into his history. This mythicizing of history and historicizing of myth begins with Jesus' proclamation of the kingdom of God – a mythical dramatization of the basic monotheistic conviction of Judaism. Since then a unity of myth and history has stamped the narrative sign-world of primitive Christianity.

The *rites* also derive from Judaism. John's washing became baptism in Christ; the everyday Jewish meal became the Lord's supper. Both Jewish rituals were originally related to the end-time; they were the condition of entering the new world and an anticipation of it. In primitive Christianity both were related at a secondary stage to the death of Jesus and his resurrection, in which for the first Christians the new world had already begun. In their outward performance both rites reduce violence; both manage without animal sacrifice. But at the same time they intensify the violence in the ritual imagination which accompanies them, in that both rites point to the death of Jesus. The hidden violence in all relationships in life is brought into the open by recollection of the violent execution of Jesus. But at the same time this violence which is intensified (in imagination within the ritual) is transformed into real non-violence. A tension between an increase in violence and a reduction in violence stamps the ritual sign world of primitive Christianity and the world in which the Christians live.

In *ethics*, too, the content comes from Judaism. The Jewish norms are reorganized around two central values, love of neighbour and renunciation of status. In this ethic we find a tension between upper-class and lower-class values: an aristocratic self-confidence seeks to outdo all others by a better 'righteousness' – and a popular ethic of neighbourliness at the same time calls for inter-personal reconciliation. An aristocratic ethic with radicalized demands is 'transferred' downwards, and an ethic of little people with a radicalized readiness for reconciliation is transferred upwards. The two are mixed. The ethical sign world of primitive Christianity and the world in which the Christians lived is shaped by a tension between an accentuation of norms and a relaxation of norms.

The first Christians built their semiotic cathedral from the materials of this narrative, ritual and ethical sign world and the world in which they lived. With growing awareness they claimed *autonomy* for themselves: they were not just to be a subsidiary temple in a larger sanctuary, but an independent sanctuary which replaced all other sanctuaries. That came home to them step by step in the course of the writing of the Gospels. In the earliest Gospel we find primarily a ritual demarcation from Judaism: baptism and eucharist take the place of the temple. In the Gospel of Matthew the ethical demarcation comes to the fore through a 'better righteousness'. And in the Gospel of Luke there is a narrative account of the separation between Jews and Christians, which Luke interprets as parts of Judaism excluding themselves from salvation. This development reaches its climax with the Gospel of John. Only in it does the primitive Christian sign system which has newly come into being become consciously aware of its complete autonomy: all the content of the new religion is now consciously governed by its relationship to the one redeemer, who makes himself the theme of his message. He legitimates himself in statements which refer to himself. He brings an unconditional truth. Myth and history become perfectly one. The historical Jesus is the primeval creator and the eschatological judge in the present. He is one with God. In this way the first Christians articulate a consciousness that they are presenting the final truth; here they link up with the truth-claim of the Jewish mother religion formally, but depart from it in content. Formally they link up with Judaism, for only in the Jewish religion was the question of the true worship of God unavoidably raised and the one and only God set over against the idols. The first Christians regarded their new semiotic temple as the only true temple, as a fulfilment of all Jewish expectations. But through the content of their faith they made the separation from Judaism final, by worshipping in their inner sanctuary a second figure alongside God as God's revealer.

At all events the inner *dynamic* of this development derives from Judaism. The God of Israel also owed his exaltation to become the one and only God to a great historical crisis. After the catastrophe of the destruction of Jerusalem his 'defeat' on earth (which it manifestly was in the eyes of the mentality of the ancient Near East after the defeat of his people) was re-interpreted as a victory in heaven: he became the only God. All other gods were non-existent. This monotheistic dynamic repeated itself in primitive Christianity. The one who was executed on the cross by the powers of this world was enthroned in heaven after his death as ruler over all other powers and authorities. He entered into competition with all others, so that his image was elaborated through a *competitive syncretism*, i.e. not through the direct adoption of pagan content, but through the activation of the Christians' own traditions in controversy with and assimilation to the beliefs of the world around – for example in notions of the redeemer being begotten through the Spirit and of his incarnation, or in the development of the primitive Christian sacraments.

That the cathedral built of such materials had really been built on its own foundations was confirmed in *crises*. These were always about the autonomy of the new religion. In these crises we rediscover the monotheistic dynamic which was inherited from Judaism. Only it gave the new religion the power to assert its independence.

The independence of the *ritual* sign language of primitive Christianity was at stake in the *Judaistic crisis* of the first century. It laid the foundation for the replacement of circumcision by baptism. For Gentiles who had newly been won over, and who could not take part in either the Jewish or the pagan sacrificial cult, the 'sacrificial death of Jesus' came into the centre. Gradually all other sacrifices were repudiated with reference to this one and only sacrificial death. The one and only human sacrifice in mythical imagination replaced the many violent animal sacrifices in reality. With the rite, all ritual commandments were relativized. Their relativization specifically affected the visible Jewish marks of identity – circumcision, the food laws, the sabbath, the bond with the cult in the Jerusalem temple. In this way, in primitive Christianity much that separated Jews from those around them in everyday life disappeared. Primitive Christianity worked as a Judaism without frontiers. And this removal of frontiers corresponded to the monotheistic dynamic in Judaism. For one day the one and only God would be recognized by all peoples. In opening itself to Gentiles, primitive Christianity followed this dynamic. In defending this universal dynamic and opening itself up to all peoples, in the Judaistic crisis the independence of primitive Christianity established itself over against Judaism.

The independence of its basic *narrative* came under discussion in the *Gnostic crisis.* This was about the indissoluble bond between myth and a concrete history which could be dated to the first century and localized in Palestine. The unity of the creator God with the true God was as much at risk as the unity of the redeemer with the concrete human being Jesus of Nazareth. Gnostics could not accept his incarnation in a human body. In this crisis the independence and autonomy of the primitive Christian religion was defended from its dissolution into a universal symbolic language – and the bond with the mother religion and the Old Testament was established for all times. Here too the monotheistic dynamic of the Jewish legacy won through: not only in the rejection of a subordinate creator God alongside the true God of the other world, but in the strict link between God and the world. The one and only God has only the world as his counterpart and only human beings as his partners – and not countless emanations and aeons which separate him from a world that has come into being against his will.

As for *ethics*, primitive Christianity was exposed to a chronic crisis which kept being sparked off in *prophetic crises* about the radical nature of the demands with which the first Christians set themselves apart from 'normal life'. These were crises which at the same time kept challenging the radical nature of grace and reconciliation, when radical demands threatened to split the community. Only with a great readiness for reconciliation did it become possible for people who wanted to achieve a special holiness and radicalism to live with the many others who put forward more moderate norms. Without the radicalism which kept flaring up, Christianity would have forfeited its identity; without the moderate forms of assimilation it would have lost its viability. And here too we trace the radical theocratic spirit of the beginning: that consistent monotheism which shows itself in Jesus' preaching of the establishment of the kingly rule of God.

These manifold crises were an endurance test for the narrative, ritual and ethical building materials of the new semiotic cathedral, and they were a test for the unity of its inhabitants. Every crisis provoked different attempts at an answer and also provoked separations. Therefore primitive Christianity appears as a seething chaos of many groups, as a *plurality* of currents, among which Jewish Christianity, Synoptic, Pauline and Johannine Christianity shaped the further development – but in so doing excluded both radical forms of Judaism and Gnosticizing tendencies in Johannine Christianity. Each of these currents continued to build on the common edifice in a very arbitrary way. Nevertheless the same principles of construction can be established in all the areas of the cathedral that was constructed. These principles of construction are the basic axioms and basic motifs of primitive Christian religion: they form the *grammar* of the new religious sign language, which is close to the grammar of Judaism.

Primitive Christianity begins from the two *basic axioms* of Judaism, monotheism and covenantal nomism. It believes in the one and only God who has bound himself to a single people in his covenant. But with monotheism it combines belief in a redeemer, through which this tie to a single people is extended to all peoples. Here the belief in a redeemer heightened worship of Christ in a way which was rejected by most Jews as a threat to strict monotheism.

The individual *basic motifs* with which this belief in a redeemer is elaborated and connected to the sign cosmos of the primitive Christian religion are usually basic motifs of the Jewish religion. They bind primitive Christianity closely to Judaism, just as they distinguish it from Gnosticism.

The *creation motif* is Jewish, as is the fact that God created the creation through his independent wisdom or reason. The only new thing is that Christ comes to occupy this place.

The *wisdom motif* is Jewish, as is the revelation of wisdom in a history of its rejection. But it is a scandal for Jews that wisdom reveals itself in the folly of the cross.

The *motif of miracle* shapes the texts of both the Old and the New Testaments. The only new conviction is that in the miracles of Jesus the threshold to the new time has already been crossed.

The *motif of alienation* is worked out with increasing clarity in the history of the Old Testament tradition. Human beings are far from God not only as transitory creatures but also as sinners. The New Testament radicalizes this notion of sin: as 'flesh', human beings are hostile to God.

The *motif of renewal* is Jewish tradition in relation both to the world and to the individual. But the transformation of the human being into a pneumatic being in accord with the transformation of the world goes beyond Judaism.

The *motif of indwelling* is already present in the Jewish belief in the presence of God in the temple and the prophets. Its focus on belief in the incarnation in the New Testament goes beyond Judaism.

The *motif of representation* is an element of ancient mythical thought generally. But that Jesus is the representative – of human beings to God, of God to human beings – in fact goes beyond Jewish belief.

The *motif of faith* derives from the Old Testament and in Judaism increasingly becomes a comprehensive characteristic of the relationship of God, to the point that in the New Testament 'faith' becomes the designation of the relationship to God and the one whom he has sent.

In the New Testament the *motif of agape* is explicitly derived from the Old Testament. Here too the motif is heightened, in being extended to love of the enemy, the stranger and the sinner – but this tendency towards extending it is already suggested in the Old Testament.

The *motif of a change of position* comes into being under the impact on the history of Israel of the God who raises up and brings down, and in Judaism and primitive Christianity becomes a human ethical form of behaviour: interpersonal humility.

The *motif of judgment* extends the Old Testament notion of an ethical responsibility before God to all eternity and heightens the Old Testament trust in God's mercy so that it becomes belief in the justification of the godless.

What is decisive here is that in the depth structure of its convictions, primitive Christianity largely participates in convictions of Judaism. The difference from Judaism lies at this level above all in the christocentric reorganization of the images, motifs, narratives and sign elements which the two religions share. Otherwise most of the differences are more at a superficial level: the notion of incarnation certainly goes further than the notion of indwelling and is unimaginable without borrowings from pagan language. But even the incarnation can be understood as a limit formulation within the motif of indwelling shared by both Judaism and Christianity.

The theory of primitive Christian religion as a whole which has been presented here understands this religion as an objective sign system which organizes itself from a centre with the help of a few axioms – on the basis of two fundamental basic axioms and many basic motifs, which could be further multiplied and differentiated. With these axioms I am attempting to detect the principles by which the interpreted world of primitive Christianity has been constructed. To this degree the comment of a friendly colleague of mine is justified. He remarked that my theory of primitive Christianity set out to find the 'formula of the primitive Christian world'. His gentle mockery is justified, in so far as this theory indeed seeks the formulae, rules and principles of construction which underlie the primitive Christian sign world.

Time and again I have used the image of a semiotic cathedral to depict this sign world. This architectural metaphor is in one respect paradoxical as an image of primitive Christian religion. The first Christians did not have any architectural forms of expression of their own. The communities assembled in private houses. All other cults displayed themselves in public temples. The first Christians did not miss these very much. For them in any case the world was caught up in a profound transformation. In this change they experienced their own community as a 'living temple'. In it they performed a 'reasonable service' with their whole lives (Rom. 12.1f.). In this 'semiotic cathedral' eternal being was not to be symbolized by hard stone, but by living beings who were undergoing a profound change. In it there was a celebration of the 'transubstantiation' of the world and human beings.

For me this primitive Christian sign world is an amazing human construction: a semiotic cathedral which was built to worship God and to change life. Although it is a human construct, for those who inhabited it, it was manifestly the response to a revelation. Even now it brings people under its spell. So in a last section we shall investigate the plausibility of this sign world.

2. The plausibility of primitive Christian religion

When I speak of a 'constructed' world, I do not meant to devalue it by comparison with an allegedly objective world. For we know today that even worlds which we experience as 'objective', i.e. our everyday world and our scientific world, are constructs which are no less based on particular axioms than was the primitive Christian sign world. However, for us there is a difference. We have little difficulty in finding the results of science plausible. And we are aware that we have reasons for this. But what about a religious interpretation of the world? Here we often fail to understand how some imaginative statements have seemed time and again to carry a high degree of conviction. How does this come about? An answer calls for some preliminary methodological considerations, which I shall sum up in three theses:[1]

1. Religious axioms as a basis of plausibility

My first thesis is: *It is not so much the content of the statements of religion which create plausibility as the network of basic axioms and basic motifs which forms its grammar.*[2] An example may illustrate this. In my view it is very difficult to find sources of evidence in individual substantive statements of the Philippians hymn. Was there a divine being who descended from his pre-existence in order to be exalted to the name above all names? The first Christians could not verify or falsify such statements any more than we can. They are poetry of the holy. But it is meaningful to ask whether the axiom of change of position contained in this poetry corresponds to reality – and also an ultimate reality. Or to put it more cautiously: can people meaningfully interpret reality in the light of this axiom, and can they lead their lives under the guidance of this axiom? For those whose fundamental convictions included the axiom of a change of position, the Philippians hymn was plausible because it expressed these convictions. To put it more generally: those who were convinced of the truth of the Christian faith had intuitively read the fundamental 'grammatical rules' off the narratives, images and poems of the Bible, had internalized them, and trusted that these 'grammatical rules' organized their experience of the world, corresponded to their own being, made communication with other people possible – and above all were a chance of making contact with God.

2. Three sources of evidence as confirmation of religious axioms

My second thesis is: *The plausibility of a set of religious axioms is grounded in the way in which they correspond to three sources of evidence: in their 'agreement' with the world, the self and other people.* Traditional theology may serve as an analogy to these three ways. It attempts: 1. To infer God from the order of the world and to read God's action off history, in other words to practise theology as a deeper interpretation of reality. 2. To find pointers to God in the depths of one's own self – say in the longing of the heart for God or in the (transcendental) conditions of the possibility of experiences of the self. Finally, 3. It seeks the agreement of others – either by bringing about a new consensus in mission (thus by conversion to its own axioms) or by demonstrating in ecumenical and inter-religious dialogue that a consensus has always existed between the religions. The plausibility of religious axioms can be confirmed in the same three ways:

- The first question is: does the world agree? Can religious axioms make possible experiences which are constantly confirmed, i.e. which can be repeated and be communicated from one person to another? Here I follow a *correspondence theory* of plausibility (and of truth). Convictions are plausible which correspond to a reality which is intended by them and can be confirmed by experiences which stream in from outside.

- The second question is: Does the self which has these experiences agree? Religious axioms are learnt. They are acquired a posteriori. They are experienced as plausible if in addition they correspond to 'innate' axioms and categories, i.e. to even more fundamental conditions of the possibility of experience which a priori belong to the endowment of the self. They include, for example the requirement of unity and absence of contradiction. Here I follow a *coherence theory* of plausibility (and truth): whatever accords with fundamental conditions of thought is plausible.
- The third question is: Do other people agree? Here I follow a *consensus theory* of plausibility (and truth): whatever gains the agreement of others is plausible. Plausibility is dependent on social reinforcement. If we wanted to reformulate that as a criterion of truth, we would have to say that what people can accept under ideal conditions of communication is true.

Here an important qualification needs to be added: religious axioms also reflect the limits and the collapse of their own plausibility: the world refuses to correspond, the self contradicts itself, and other people reject consensus. The failure of one's own plausibility is accepted in the set of religious axioms, which makes them more resistant to objections. In the course of the development, the conviction is increasingly clearly bound up with the basic monotheistic axiom that God is incomprehensible and escapes human experience. In the course of history many individual axioms have been modified for so long that they have often come to incorporate their limits. This failure of plausibility often becomes the basis of a strict theology of revelation which says that God can be understood only through himself. We know of God only through his self-disclosure. For like can be understood only by like.

3. Religious axioms as the result of trial and error

The third thesis is: *The set of axioms of a religion correspond to the three sources of evidence, the world, the self and others, because it came into being in a historical process of trial and error. In this process these axioms have been adapted to the basic structures of the world; they have been shaped actively by the human self and survived because they furthered community. Their plausibility is based on the concentrated experiences of many generations.* Just as our organs came into being in a long period of trial and error and therefore contain relevant pre-information about the world in which we live, so religion as an organism also contains signs of such pre-information about the world. And just as the physical organism developed only such organs as corre-

sponded to its given possibilities, so too in religion the human spirit works out only what corresponds to its a priori possibilities. Finally, this axiomatic pre-information only becomes established when it is capable of guiding our lives (both our individual and our social lives). So religions are sign worlds which have undergone a long period of testing. Nevertheless they often clash with reality. Here is an example. The motifs of creation and of wisdom teach trust in a structure of reality which is meaningful, even if it is often hidden. This trust keeps discovering corresponding objective structures in the world, indeed so great a rationality that people have often experienced their own reason merely as a weak echo and reflection of this 'objective wisdom'. The motif of wisdom is continually reinforced from outside (through experience of the world) and from within (by corresponding to our rationality). It is indispensable to the way in which individuals and societies live. For it furthers the motivation to strengthen order in social life. Any community would disintegrate without such motivation. But this motif of wisdom has constantly experienced the stubborn resistance of reality to this trust: Job and Ecclesiastes are witnesses to this. This failure, too, is part of the objective pre-information about religion: it is expressed in the transformation of the motif of wisdom into wisdom which is concealed in folly and is manifested on the cross – in other words, in a failure. The set of primitive Christian axioms made a correct discovery in reality here. To this degree these axioms could be experienced as being 'true'.

I shall now go on to sketch out an attempt to apply these general considerations about plausibility and the sources of evidence to primitive Christian faith.

(a) Experience of the world as a source of evidence: the axioms of primitive Christianity make a dynamic view of the world possible

The first thesis: *By its set of axioms primitive Christianity opened up a dynamic view of the world as process. In this process a new world breaks into the old world, in which the previous foundation of all evolution, the principle of selection, is included in, and partially abrogated by, solidarity.*[2] The foundation of this dynamic view was the experience of the rise and fall of states and empires – and the hope that this stimulated of a fundamental change by the dawn of a kingdom of God. This experience, with a social foundation, was developed further into a view of the world in which intuitively appropriate structures of reality were discovered. This can be demonstrated by means of some of the axioms of primitive Christian religion.

- The *motif of renewal* allows the world to be experienced as a transition in which human beings are themselves embedded on the way between being sarkic and pneumatic beings. In the great vision of Daniel 7 the series of different kingdoms had been interpreted as a transition from a 'bestial' being to the power of 'one like a human being'. Primitive Christianity transferred this power to an actual human being who had been exalted by God. The new kingdom had a human character, in contrast to the beasts. Is there not here for the first time the dawning of an awareness that we are embedded in an evolutionary process: in a transition from biological to cultural evolution? That in the midst of history we are still in transition from beast to human being? And is there not some truth in this awareness?
- The *motif of judgment* allows reality to be understood as a process of division: all life is subject to the harsh pressure of selection, which divides out the adapted forms of conduct and life from the unadapted. This objective pressure of selection is expressed in the fantasies of the last judgment: only what accords with the criteria of the new world will enter into it – and in the decisive New Testament texts that is precisely what is elsewhere sorted out by selection: the weak and the unadapted. The godless is justified by God in the judgment. The Gospel of the acquittal of the sinner is the removal of the pressure of selection – and contains a protest against selection.
- In the primitive Christian texts the *motif of miracle* assumes a special form. Miracles serve to make life possible and to help it. They intervene where otherwise life has no chance: among the hungry, those in danger, the sick and the dying. We may sometimes be irritated by the bizarre miracles of the Gospels, but they contain in a simple and urgent form that protest against selection which stamps the whole Bible.
- The *creation motif* is also transformed by this protest. In the New Testament it emerges most clearly in the midst of history in the resurrection of Jesus from the dead. The crucified Jesus was the rejected one who was to be removed from history. He was the weak one whose impotence was publicly demonstrated. But he was the very one to whom God gave new life.
- The *motif of agape* shows what becomes different in the transition from biological to cultural evolution. In biological evolution, love towards those who are genetically akin is combined with aggression towards the others. In primitive Christianity this combination is stood on its head. Love is required towards enemies, aliens and sinners – and aggression against those who are genetically akin: a break with father and family is tersely called for.

- The *motif of change of position* can be understood in precisely the same way. In animal communities hierarchies and pecking orders have a clear significance for survival. The strongest animals are favoured, because they are important for the group in warding off external dangers and in internal co-ordination. But if the first is the one who occupies the position of the last, this basic feature of biological evolution hitherto is also robbed of its force.
- The *motif of representation* intrinsically contains both the principle of selection and the protest against it. On the one hand life always lives at the expense of other life. Defective beings die vicariously for the life of superior beings. To this degree representation is an expression of selection. In the struggle for life the costs of preserving the life of the others are loaded on to the less competent. On the other hand, in christological symbolism the representative dying for others is reversed: here life no longer lives at the expense of other life, but voluntarily accepts death in order to make possible other life – but above all, this sacrificed life does not remain in death. It overcomes death and thus breaks through the law that life lives at the expense of other life.

It is not necessary to relate all axioms to such an evolutionary view of the world. Nor is it necessary to attribute an evolutionary consciousness to the men and women of primitive Christianity. We need only assume that all human beings are involved in a transition from biological to cultural evolution – whether they know it or not. In their religious images and symbols they grope for the basic structures of reality and of their situation, long before they can put them into words. But where they encounter this situation intuitively, their sign worlds take on a power to disclose reality which goes far beyond the understanding of those who inhabit these worlds.

It was its accord with the human condition, with the situation of human beings in a world in a process of evolutionary change, that gave the religious sign world of primitive Christianity its inner plausibility.

But this experience of being in accord with a world which was in process of change was threatened from the beginning by experiences to the contrary. In primitive Christianity the expectation of a change of the whole world, which was already dawning in the present, was very much alive. And precisely this expectation was disappointed. There are amazingly few voices which register that directly (e.g. II Peter 3.3f.; I Clem. 23ff.; II Clem. 11; Justin, *Apol.* I 28, 2). There was never a great crisis over the failure of the parousia to materialize. However, indirectly adaptation to the abiding world has left its traces behind in many theological schemes – for example in Luke-Acts, which evaluates the period between Jesus and the end as the time of the church and of mission; in the Gospel of John, which in the farewell discourses reinterprets the traditional expectation of the parousia in a spiritualizing way (John 14.1ff.) and advocates a present eschatology (John 5.24ff.); or in Hebrews, in which a spatial eschatology is an overlay for temporal eschatology: everything is already present in heaven. The way to the holy of holies has already been pioneered. But at the same time, in all these schemes we have the traditional future expectation of a decisive turning point for the whole world. The basis for the mystery of the amazing 'noiselessness' in coping with the delay of the parousia is that the means for doing so were already there in primitive Christianity from the beginning.

At the beginning there is John the Baptist's expectation of an imminent end: the axe has already been laid to the root of the trees. The fact that Jesus appears after him is the first 'delay of the parousia'. This is already the presupposition for Jesus' appearance. The words on which it has left its traces are by no means always a priori inauthentic. Thus in sayings of Jesus the abiding existence of the world is interpreted as the grace of God: the way in which God continues to make the sun rise and set, drawing no distinction between the just and the unjust, is implicitly an answer to the 'disappointed' expectation that he will soon come to distinguish between the righteous and the unrighteous in the judgment (Matt. 5.45). When a saying of Jesus cites Jonah as a type of present prophecy, it chooses precisely the Old Testament prophet whose announcement of judgment did not take place: would not Jesus too have seen the real meaning of the expectation of an imminent end in the opportunity to repent – with the possibility that the great judgment would not take place (cf. Luke 11.29f.)?

The same experience is reflected in the parable of the barren fig tree, which is given a reprieve (Luke 13.6–9). In short, already with Jesus the failure of the judgment to materialize imminently is coped with by preaching about the grace of God. From the beginning in primitive Christian preaching, alongside the expectation of the great turning point, we find the cognitive, emotional and motivational means of coping creatively with the failure of this shift to come about. The world was experienced as a period of transition – and even the experiences which told against this were interpreted as a confirmation of Christians' experiences.

But that was not all. In their religious sign systems the first Christians wanted to disclose not only the 'world' but also God – i.e. something that went far beyond the world, something that is unconditioned and eternal. If we are to understand the inner plausibility of this relationship of the primitive Christian sign world to a 'transcendence' we must consider the way in which it corresponds not only with the experience of the 'objective' world but also with the transcendental conditions of this experience in the human subject.

(b) Correspondence to the self as a source of evidence: the axioms of primitive Christianity and the religious a priori

(R, Fort)

The second thesis is: *The set of axioms in primitive Christianity was plausible because it corresponded to the inner conditions of human beings: human beings a priori have a sense for the eternal and the unconditional and a sense of responsibility, but empirically they experience themselves as transitory, conditioned and determined, and live with at odds with themselves.* The history of religion produced religious symbols and images adequate for the a priori conditions of religious experience in a long historical process of trial and error. What are these a priori conditions? In my view three elements are presupposed in any claim to validity, which are not necessarily conscious (though potentially they can become conscious) and which make transcendental experience possible (if they are related to particular content). Here I am following the insights of the transcendental philosophy of religion which is more widespread on the European continent.[3]

- *The first insight*: a claim that something which is true (or false) is an intrinsic claim that it will also be true (or false) in x + n years. A 'claim to eternity' is also presupposed in any claim to validity. Even if one relativizes a claim to validity and says that it is limited to particular places and times, for this relativizing statement one requires a claim to validity of x + n years. So in all claims to validity we implicitly document a sense of the 'eternal', [4] even if we explicitly deny it – and keep denying it in the face of the overwhelming experience of transitoriness.
- *The second insight*: all claims to validity also have an unconditioned element. In so far as we measure anything by a norm, we prefer whatever corresponds to the norm to whatever contradicts it. We cannot do other than prefer what we have subjectively recognized to be the truth to the error that we have recognized. Those who nevertheless prefer the illusion of truth can do so only because they prefer other values to the cognitive criteria of true and false. What serves life is more valuable for such people than what serves truth. They too recognize an unconditioned priority of what is normatively higher. So as soon as we make any normative judgment at all, we activate an unconditioned element in our thinking – even if we explicitly deny it.
- *The third insight*: if we claim validity for a statement, we claim to be responsible for it. Were our statements completely determined by factors

which lie in the past, we could always only register the fact of such statements; we could never claim validity for them. And any discussion of claims to validity would consist in waiting to see whether our 'determination' would be different in the future from the past. The thesis that everything is determined also claims that it is not completely determined by past causal factors. It claims for itself a freedom grounded in 'responsibility'.

This sense of the eternal and the unconditioned, this sense of responsibility, becomes productive in religion. With images from the world in which we live, it constructs images which go far beyond that world. But above all we find the traces of such a transcendental poetry which goes beyond all that is empirical in the two basic axioms of primitive Christianity:

- The monotheistic basic axiom of Jewish and primitive Christian belief became increasingly plausible in many ancient societies after the sixth century BC. Not only Deutero-Isaiah, but also the Pre-Socratics developed an understanding of God which left the polytheism which was widespread everywhere far behind. We cannot explain such processes by social plausibility – as if the rise of great empires with a king at the head had also furthered the breakthrough of monotheism. Neither the Greek city states nor little Israel lived in such structures. And with their subordinate commanders and provinces, the great empires suggested more the notion of a pantheon of gods with a monarchical focus. Among the pre-Socratics the pull towards a unitary explanation of the world became united with monotheistic approaches. An a priori need of the human spirit established itself historically in their schemes: the human spirit a priori prefers explanations of the world which derive a great multiplicity from a unity. The discoveries of logic and of the one God go hand in hand. Here we find a cognitively motivated monotheism. For a long time it remained the concern of a few intellectuals. By contrast, in Israel's ethically motivated monotheism other motifs emerge. Responsibility becomes more responsible if it is responsibility to only one authority. And the commandments of the one and only God make possible that unity of ethical conduct which we admire in Judaism. Through the intuition of an unconditional human responsibility to the one God, Israel activates above all a sense of the unconditional and a sense of freedom. This image of God was developed further in the post-Old Testament period: God became the judge in the last judgment, an authority who for eternity makes human beings responsible and measures them by an unconditional standard. In this image, on the one hand the empirical experience of selection, which distinguishes between adequate and inadequate variants of life and conduct, is heightened beyond anything empirical. On the other, the religious a priori of the eternal comes into play: it is precisely for this reason that the image of the judge before whom all human beings must be responsible occurs among so many peoples. It is a piece of 'transcendental poetry', a religious poem which is based on aprioristic ideas of the human self: an unconditioned responsibility to eternity.

- This sense of the eternal and the unconditioned, this sense of responsibility, also helped to shape the second basic axiom of primitive Christianity, belief in a redeemer. The exaltation of the historical Jesus to deity is not just to be explained as a way of coping with cognitive dissonance. A transitory phenomenon, a figure who lived under limiting conditions in which determinative social and political factors can be recognized, was acknowledged on the basis of a religious a priori to be the manifestation of an eternal and unconditional which demands our responsibility, a manifestion who in a poetic way is surrounded by that mythical aura which pertains to a divine being. But his appearance was not absorbed by this mythical aura. For the memory was preserved at the same time of Jesus as a mortal, conditioned and unfree person, i.e. as a concrete piece of earthly history. Was not the great plausibility of his image for the Christians to rest on the fact that this christology corresponded to the structure of the human self: a human self which has a sense of the eternal and the unconditioned, a sense of freedom – but which is exposed to transitoriness, conditions and compulsions? In interpreting Christ as a symbol for the human self, the Gnostic groups therefore had a correct insight – except that they denied the unity of the eternal and the transitory, the unconditioned and the conditioned, freedom and compulsion in this symbol, and presented an illusory (or narcissistic) view of the self which in principle knew itself to be free from this world of the transitory, the conditioned and the determined.

Anyone who has the history of philosophy in mind will certainly have noticed that my three aprioristic elements are an analogy to Kant's three transcendental ideas: immortality, God and freedom – except that Kant made these ideas concrete with the notions of the Christian religion.[5] Immortality also comprises the eternal, but it is less than the eternal. The unconditioned also comprises God – but God is far more than the unconditioned. The responsibility involved in claims to validity always presupposes freedom as a causation of the subject, but in addition it presupposes that the subject is bound to norms. In my view, the activity of these formal a prioris of the eternal, the unconditioned and of freedom in the human spirit is the only explanation why human beings in their religious constructions time and again transcend the finite empirical world and perceive in the transitory something eternal, in the conditioned something unconditional, and in inexorable destiny the call to responsibility – and do so with great inner conviction.

Here, too, however, it should be emphasized that primitive Christianity did not just offer plausibility by corresponding with transcendental categories of human consciousness. It could also shake up such categories. We can deliberately deny what has always been presupposed in our consciousness because powerful experiences tell against it. The sense of the eternal is contradicted by the experience of transitoriness; the sense of responsibility by the experience of compulsion and dependence; and the sense of the unconditional by the experience that everything is relative. Transcendental categories of our consciousness do not establish themselves automatically in experience, but can be severely shaken, so that a whole 'world' collapses with them. In limit experiences, what seems 'automatically' to determine our consciences is 'de-automated'.[6] What is supposed to be the most obvious thing in the world is put in question. This shaking of the 'self' is depicted with impressive imagery in primitive Christian religion – perhaps most impressively in the Gnostic metaphors and myths. Here the human 'self' is a spark which has been thrown into a hostile world – subject to transitoriness and corporeality, although it has within itself a spark of the 'eternal' and the 'unconditioned', of 'freedom', even if this is often covered up. Church Christianity could have taken up notions close to Gnosticism. In the sayings in the Gospel of John, Christ is the only Gnostic who knows where he comes from and where he is going (John 8.14). All Christians could understand themselves in accordance with this model: through him a small light of eternity had been kindled in them again.

However, the two previous sources of evidence, correspondence to the experience of the world and correspondence to the transcendent subjective conditions of this experience, are still not enough to explain the plausibility of primitive Christian religion or any other religion. Religion is not just a world of ideas, but a power in life. It first gains its force in living communities. Its plausibility is bound up with the agreement of others.

(c) Correspondence to other people as a source of evidence: the power of the axioms of primitive Christianity in forming a community

The third thesis is: *The sign world of primitive Christianity was plausible to its inhabitants because its axioms contributed towards forming a community. This new religion brought people together beyond cultural and national boundaries and must have strengthened the impression that here there was a breakthrough which could become the consensus of all men and women.* In the previous chapter I introduced the axioms (i.e. the basic convictions and the basic motifs) of primitive Christianity in order to explain the astonishing consensus in primitive Christianity which made possible the formation of the canon and the exclusion of some 'heresies'. Despite theologies in the basic currents of primitive Christianity which were very different in content, these were currents bound together by formal basic convictions. As a result, a sense of belonging could come into being right across different currents, which retroactively strengthened their own convictions. Plausibility increases with the agreement of others.

In addition, the basic motifs of primitive Christianity in themselves furthered community. Granted, by definition only those interpretations and convictions survive in the history of religion which are compatible with the communities which hand them down. To this degree it is a tautology to say that a set of religious axioms furthers community. But there were clear differences between the axioms, as there were between the groups which handed them down.

It makes a difference whether these groups first form on the basis of the set of religious axioms – or whether they already belong together on the basis of other factors. We saw that primitive Christianity is one of the first social formations in which primarily religious convictions gave form to the community. It had been preceded by Judaism. Originally its religion could be based on a people. But according to its understanding of itself, this people owed its existence to its religion: election by God and the obligation to observe his commandments. Post-exilic Judaism corresponded to this self-understanding in so far as in it the renewal of the community after the exile, if not its founding, was motivated by religious impulses. The primitive Christian communities continued this development: they formed on the basis of their common confession of the ΚΥΡΙΟΣ ΙΗΣΟΥΣ. They were not based on pre-existing communities, but brought together people from different communities. They were a refounding of community, not just its renewal.

A priori their axioms must therefore have been a great force in forming communities. We can certainly say that of the motifs of agape and of the change in position. The proclamation of love as the supreme value supports social cohesion, but is not sufficient in itself. Equally important are convictions which resist the constant endangering of such ties and cooperation. Communities are divided and destroyed through rivalry over internal hierarchies. The motif of change of position works against that. It makes possible an awareness that equal status is being maintained – in the face of de facto differences in status. Communities with a high moral sense of social obligations are further often deeply split by the violation of these obligations, because all parties in the conflict accuse themselves of violating norms. The motif of judgment works against this: it prohibits final judgments on others and argues for the acceptance of the sinner and the justification of the godless.

But how did the Christians deal with the vigorous rejection which often hit them in the world in which they lived? Here they had to build on a possible consensus in the face of the manifest dissent – strengthened on the one hand by experiences in missions. Even opponents of Christianity could be converted to it. Paul was a shining example of this. The set of axioms in primitive Christianity proved to be so strong in its interpretative power that it kept embracing new people – including former opponents. But on the other hand early Christianity made sure of itself by engaging in consensual dialogue with others: the Apologists saw a grain of truth in every human consciousness, the λόγος σπερματικός.[7] In our terminology one could say that they saw their own axioms latently at work in all human beings. The best of the non-Christians were potential or anonymous Christians. A plausible example for the first Christians was the basic axiom of all Jews and Christians: belief in the one and only God. Many Greek philosophers had also come to accept a single God, without their monotheism having cultic consequences in the religion that they practised. Here Jews and Christians could see themselves as perfecting what the most acute minds in pagan antiquity had begun. But where the opposition was totally obdurate, they resorted to theories of hardening, which attributed a failure to see to supernatural powers. They imputed to their opponents an extreme alienation from themselves which made them incapable of the truth, but to a degree also exonerated them: being hardened is not something of which one is guilty, but a fate.

So in the framework of a theory of primitive Christian religion it is possible to explain how these heightened convictions were arrived at: the first Christians were deeply convinced of the superiority of their sign world to all other rival worlds of convictions. However bizarre the content of their narrative rites and ethical demands might be, on the basis of the axioms on which it was based this sign world had a high power of interpretation. It corresponded to experiences of a world which was dynamically changing, to transcendental conditions of the self and a community which was increasingly capable of communication. These were the sources of their convictions. In addition, in their basic convictions they could also express the limitations of such convictions – in statements about the *deus absconditus*, the folly of the cross and the failure of communication.

That ends my outline of a theory of primitive Christian religion, but does not complete it. This theory needs to be expanded. It puts the emphasis on the objectivity of the primitive Christian sign world. But particularly in the last part, it has become clear that primitive Christian religion is at the same time a sign world *and* a world in which people live. Only this unity of a sign world and a world in which people live gives plausibility to the set of religious axioms in primitive Christianity. Even if the world in which the first Christians lived has been constantly addressed in the different chapters, it deserved a deeper treatment. So the theory presented here needs to be deepened:

- by a *psychology of primitive Christian religion*. A psychology describes and interprets the typical features of the individual experience, behaviour and consciousness of the first Christians. Here the subjective experience which for many people today is identical with religion would come into its own. Such a psychology could also work out better the subjective evidence of primitive Christian belief and its contribution towards guiding conduct and experience in both everyday and exceptional contexts.
- It is possible to deepen the theory further by a *sociology of primitive Christian religion*, which analyses the structures of primitive Christian groups over and above the individual in connection with the society of the time. Here non-religious factors which also shaped this religion would also come into play. Such a sociology would work out the social plausibility of the new faith: its rapid dissemination and the vitality of the small sub-culture within which it spread in the ancient world.

Finally, one could move over from theory to a *philosophy of primitive Christian religion.* That has already happened in this last chapter. But the real transition takes place only where there is a discussion of the actual claim of the primitive Christian sign world to validity and truth, in other words where the question is not only 'Why was the primitive Christian faith plausible to some people in the first century?' but 'Why is it still valid today?'. The interpretation of it given in this theory of religion as an objective sign world is an important preliminary here. It opposes a reductionist explanation of religion. It can understand the internal autonomy of primitive Christian religion conceptually as the autonomy of a sign system which is organizing itself. As an autonomous construction it is more than an expression of struggles for social prestige and power, of an infantile anxiety about punishment or a longing for regressive security. In such a structure with an inner autonomy the question of the truth makes sense, without a decision being taken against religion a priori. Even with this question of the truth we are not yet doing theology in the narrower sense. Rather, the *question* of the truth can be put in general philosophical terms. But I am convinced that any answer has an element of confession – i.e. it is governed by a confession of a theological, an anti-theological or an agnostic kind.

I often ask myself about the character of a theological answer. I suppose that in it all the sources of evidence mentioned above are at work, but that they will once again be transcended in living religious experience. In it, the truth of faith is guaranteed not just by agreement with the world, with the depths of the self and a community of men and women, but by God himself. It rests on the certainty that a contact with God has come about. That is conceivable only by the self-disclosure of God. If God is experienced in a religious experience as a power which determines all things, God is self-evidently also experienced as the cause and foundation of this one religious experience. Theology is bound up with living religious experience, and because of that it will always be more or less a 'theology of revelation'.

Once again I would like to turn to the main image I have used in this discussion. Primitive Christian religion is a marvellous cathedral of signs,[8] built on the basis of religious experience, to worship God. One can visit such a cathedral as a tourist, without taking part in its worship. One can also take part in that worship. I am one of those who still preach and pray in this cathedral. But I am also fond of analysing its architecture and the forms of its language. I would like to show this cathedral to all visitors and communicate to them something of its meaning and significance. I do not mind whether or not the visitors also want to take part in worship, whether they are at home in another cathedral, or whether they avoid such places. But in my walk round the cathedral it would not be enough for me, even if I were guiding uninvolved visitors, merely to relate historical facts about the history of its building or to give aesthetic descriptions of its style. I would also want to communicate something of its religious significance to all the visitors. If I left this out, I would be leaving out the reason why I love my cathedral. Hence this attempt at a theory of primitive religion: it is a visit to and an explanation of the primitive Christian sign world which gives everyone the freedom to get to know it, yet leave it without a prayer. Of course I would be delighted if the visitors understood why one can pray in such a cathedral and why in the view of those who built it and developed it that is the primary significance of this place.

Bibliography

Adam, Traute, *Clementia Principis*, KiHiSt 11, Stuttgart: Klett 1970

Aland, Barbara, 'Marcion', *TRE* 22, 1992, 89–101

Alkier, Stefan, *Urchristentum. Zur Geschichte und Theologie einer exegetischen Disziplin*, BHTh 83, Tübingen 1993

Alvarez, David, *Die Religionspolitik des Kaisers Claudius und die paulinische Mission*, HBS 19, Freiburg and Vienna: Herder 1999

Amir, Yehoshua, 'Die Begegnung des biblischen und des philosophischen Monotheismus als Grundthema des jüdischen Hellenismus', *EvTh* 38, 1978, 2–19

Andresen, Carl and Ritter, Adolf M., 'Die Anfänge der christlichen Lehrentwicklung', in *HDThG* 1, Göttingen: Vandenhoeck & Ruprecht ²1999

—, *Handbuch der Dogmen- und Theologiegeschichte* 1, Göttingen: Vandenhoeck & Ruprecht ²1999 (= *HDThG*)

Assmann, Aleida und Jan, 'Mythos', *HRWG* IV, 1998, 179–200

Augenstein, Jörg, *Das Liebesgebot im Johannesevangelium und in den Johannesbriefen*, BWANT 134 = Folge 7, Heft 14, Stuttgart, Berlin and Cologne: Kohlhammer 1993

Barth, Gerhard, *Der Tod Jesu Christi im Verständnis des Neuen Testaments*, Neukirchen-Vluyn: Neukirchener Verlag 1992

Bauer, Walter, *Orthodoxy and Heresy in Earliest Christianity*, Philadelphia: Fortress Press 1971 and London: SCM Press 1972

Baur, Ferdinand C., *Das Christenthum und die christliche Kirche der drei ersten Jahrhunderte*, Tübingen : Fues 1853

Beckwith, Roger T., 'Formation of the Hebrew Bible', in Jan M. Mulder (ed.), *Mikra. Text, Translation and Interpretation of the Hebrew Bible in Ancient Judaism and Early Christianity*, Assen: Van Gorcum and Philadelphia: Fortress Press 1988, 39–86

—, *The Old Testament Canon of the New Testament Church and its Background in Early Judaism*, London: SPCK 1985

Berger, Klaus, *Theologiegeschichte des Urchristentums*, Tübingen and Basel: Francke Verlag ²1995

Betz, Hans D., *Der Apostel Paulus und die sokratische Tradition*, BHTh 45, Tübingen: Mohr (Siebeck) 1972

—, *Galatians. A Commentary on Paul's Letter to the Churches in Galatia*, Hermeneia, Philadelphia: Fortress Press 1979

Beyschlag, Karlmann, *Simon Magus und die christliche Gnosis*, WUNT 16, Tübingen: Mohr (Siebeck) 1975

Bianchi, Ugo (ed.), *Le Origini dello Gnosticismo. Colloquio di Messina 13–18 Aprile 1966. Testi e Discussioni*, SHR 12, Leiden: Brill 1967, [2]1970

Bickermann, Elias, *The God of the Maccabees: Studies on the Meaning and Origin of the Maccabean Revolt*, SJLA 32, Leiden: Brill 1979

Bolkestein, Hendrik, *Wohltätigkeit und Armenpflege im vorchristlichen Altertum. Ein Beitrag zum Problem 'Moral und Gesellschaft'*, Groningen: Bouma's Boekhuis 1967 (reprint of the Utrecht 1939 edition)

Bousset, Wilhelm, *Kyrios Christos. A History of the Belief in Christ from the Beginnings of Christianity to Irenaeus* (1913), Nashville: Abingdon Press 1970

Bovon, François, *Das Evangelium nach Lukas*, EKK III, 1, Zürich: Benziger Verlag and Neukirchen-Vluyn: Neukirchener Verlag 1989

Brandt, Sigrid, *Opfer als Gedächtnis. Zur Kritik und Neukonturierung theologischer Rede von Opfer*, Habilitation dissertation, Heidelberg 1997

Breytenbach, Cilliers, *Versöhnung. Eine Studie zur paulinischen Soteriologie*, WMANT 60, Neukirchen-Vluyn: Neukirchener Verlag 1989

Bühner, Jan – A., *Der Gesandte und sein Weg im 4. Evangelium. Die kultur- und religionsgeschichtlichen Grundlagen der johanneischen Sendungschristologie sowie ihre traditionsgeschichtliche Entwicklung*, WUNT II/2, Tübingen: Mohr (Siebeck) 1977

Bultmann, Rudolf, *The Gospel of John: A Commentary*, Oxford: Blackwell 1971

—, *Theology of the New Testament* (2 vols), London: SCM Press 1952, 1955

Burchard, Christoph, *Der dreizehnte Zeuge. Traditions- und kompositionsgeschichtliche Untersuchungen zu Lukas' Darstellung der Frühzeit des Paulus*, FRLANT 103, Göttingen 1970

Burkert, Walter, *Homo Necans. Interpretationen altgriechischer Opferriten und Mythen*, RVV 32, Berlin and New York: de Gruyter 1972

—, 'Opfertypen und antike Gesellschaftsstruktur', in Gunther Stephenson (ed.), *Der Religionswandel unserer Zeit im Spiegel der Religionswissenschaft*, Darmstadt: Wissenschaftliche Buchgesellschaft 1976, 168–86

—, *Wilder Ursprung. Opferritual und Mythos bei den Griechen*, Kleine Kulturwissenschaftliche Bibliothek 22, Berlin: Klaus Wagenbach 1990

Burridge, Richard A., *What are the Gospels? A Comparison with Graeco-Roman Biography*, Cambridge: Cambridge University Press 1992

Campenhausen, Hans von, *The Formation of the Christian Bible*, London: A. & C. Black 1968

Cancik, Hubert, 'Bios und Logos. Formgeschichtliche Untersuchungen zu Lukians "Demonax"', in id. (ed.), *Markus-Philologie, Historische, literargeschichtliche und stilistische Untersuchungen zum zweiten Evangelium*, WUNT 33, Tübingen 1984, 115–30

Cassirer, Ernst, *Essay on Man*, New Haven: Yale University Press 1944

—, *Philosophy of Symbolic Forms, II, Mythical Thought*, New Haven: Yale

University Press 1955

Charlesworth, James H. (ed.), *Jesus' Jewishness. Exploring the Place of Jesus within Early Judaism*, New York: Crossroad Publishing Company 1991

Chester, Andrew, 'Jewish Messianic Expectations and Mediatorial Figures and Pauline Christology', in Martin Hengel and Ulrich Heckel (eds), *Paulus und das antike Judentum*, WUNT 58, Tübingen 1991, 17–90

Conzelmann, Hans, *The Theology of St Luke*, London: Faber 1960 reissued SCM Press 1982

Coser, Lewis A., *The Function of Social Conflict,* New York: Free Press 1964

Countryman, Louis W., *The Rich Christian in the Church of the Early Empire. Contradictions and Accommodations*, New York and Toronto: Edward Mellen Press 1980

Cullmann, Oscar, *The Johannine Circle*, London: SCM Press 1976

Davies, William D., and Allison, Dale C., *The Gospel According to Saint Matthew*, ICC, Edinburgh: T. & T. Clark 1988

Deissmann, Adolf, *Light from the Ancient East*, London: Hodder & Stoughton ²1927

Dettwiler, Andreas, *Die Gegenwart des Erhöhten. Eine exegetische Studie zu den johanneischen Abschiedsreden (Joh 13, 31–16, 33) unter besonderer Berücksichtigung ihres Relecture-Charakters*, FRLANT 169, Göttingen: Vandenhoeck & Ruprecht 1995

Dinkler, Eberhard, 'Friede', *RAC* 8, 1972, 434–505

Dodd, Charles H., *The Interpretation of the Fourth Gospel*, Cambridge: Cambridge University Press 1953

Drexler, Josef, *Die Illusion des Opfers. Ein wissenschaftlicher Überblick über die wichtigsten Opfertheorien ausgehend vom deleuzianischen Polyperspektivenmodell*, Münchener Ethnologische Abhandlungen 12, Munich: Akademischer Verlag 1993

Drijvers, Hendrik J. W., 'The Origins of Gnosticism as a Religious and Historical Problem', *NedThT* 22, 1967/8, 321–51 = Kurt Rudolph (ed.), *Gnosis und Gnostizismus*, WdF 262, Darmstadt: Wissenschaftliche Buchgesellschaft 1975, 798–841

Ebersohn, Michael, *Das Nächstenliebegebot in der synoptischen Tradition*, MThSt 37, Marburg: Elwert 1993

Ebertz, Michael N., *Das Charisma des Gekreuzigten. Zur Soziologie der Jesusbewegung*, WUNT 45, Tübingen: Mohr (Siebeck) 1987

Ebner, Martin, *Jesus – ein Weisheitslehrer? Synoptische Weisheitslogien im Traditionsprozess,* HBSt 15, Freiburg, Basel and Vienna: Herder 1998

Elert, Werner, 'Redemptio ab hostibus', *ThLZ* 72, 1947, 265–70

Elsas, Christoph, 'Herrscherkult', *HRWG* III, 1993, 115–22

Etzioni, Amitai, *The Active Society: A Theory of Societal and Political Processes*, London: Macmillan 1968

Faust, Eberhard, *Pax Christi et Pax Caesaris. Religionsgeschichtliche, traditionsgeschichtliche und sozialgeschichtliche Studien zum Epheserbrief*, NTOA 24, Freiburg CH: Universitätsverlag and Göttingen: Vandenhoeck & Ruprecht 1993

Feldtkeller, Andreas, 'Der Synkretismus – Begriff im Rahmen einer Theorie von Verhältnisbestimmungen zwischen Religionen', *EvTh* 52, 1992, 224–45

—, *Identitätssuche des syrischen Urchristentums. Mission, Inkulturation und Pluralität im ältesten Heidenchristentum*, NTOA 25, Freiburg CH: Universitätsverlag and Göttingen: Vandenhoeck & Ruprecht 1993

—, *Im Reich der syrischen Göttin. Eine religiös plurale Kultur als Umwelt des frühen Christentums*, Studien zum Verstehen fremder Religionen 8, Gütersloh: Gütersloher Verlagshaus 1994

Festinger, Leon, *A Theory of Cognitive Dissonance*, Stanford, CA: Stanford University Press 1957

Fitzer, Georg, 'Der Ort der Versöhnung nach Paulus', *ThZ* 22, 1966, 161–83

Frend, William H. C., 'Montanismus', *TRE* 23, 1994, 371–9

Freud, Sigmund, 'Obsessive Actions and Religious Practices', in *Origins of Religion*, Penguin Freud Library 13, Harmondsworth: Penguin Books 1985, 43–224

—, 'Totem and Taboo', in ibid., 27–42

Gager, John G., *Kingdom and Community. The Social World of Early Christianity*, Englewood Cliffs, NJ: Prentice-Hall 1975

Gamble, Harry Y., 'Canon, New Testament', *ABD* I, 1992, 852–61

Geertz, Clifford, 'Religion as a Cultural System', in *The Interpretation of Cultures*, New York: Basic Books 1973, 87–125

Gehlen, Rolf, 'Liminalität', *HRWG* IV, 1998, 58–63

Gemünden, Petra von, and Theissen, Gerd, 'Metaphorische Logik im Römerbrief. Beobachtungen zu dessen Bildsemantik und Aufbau', in Reinhold Bernhardt and Ulrike Link-Wieczorek (eds), *Metapher und Wirklichkeit. Die Logik der Bildhaftigkeit im Reden von Gott, Mensch und Natur, FS Dietrich Ritschl*, Göttingen: Vandenhoeck & Ruprecht 1999, 108–31

—, *Die urchristliche Taufe und der Umgang mit den Affekten*, Leiden: Brill 1999, 115ff.

—, *Vegetationsmetaphorik im Neuen Testament und seiner Umwelt*, NTOA 18, Freiburg CH: Universitätsverlag and Göttingen: Vandenhoeck & Ruprecht 1993

Gerlitz, Peter, 'Opfer I', *TRE* 25, 1995, 253–8

Gese, Hartmut, 'Die Sühne', in id., *Zur biblischen Theologie. Alttestamentliche Vorträge*, BEVTh 78, Munich: Christian Kaiser Verlag 1977

Gese, Hartmut, 'Τὸ δὲ Ἁγὰρ Σινὰ ὄρος ἐστὶν ἐν τῇ Ἀραβίᾳ (Gal 4, 25)', in id., *Vom Sinai zum Zion*, BEvTh 64, Munich: Christian Kaiser Verlag 1974, 49–62

Girard, René, *The Scapegoat*, London: Athlone Press 1986

—, *Violence and the Sacred*, London: Athlone Press 1988

Gladigow, Burkhard, 'Ritual, komplexes', *HRWG* IV, 1998, 458–60

Gnuse, Robert K., *No Other Gods*, Sheffield: Sheffield Academic Press 1997

Grom, Bernhard, *Religionspsychologie*, Munich: Kösel Verlag and Göttingen: Vandenhoeck & Ruprecht 1992

Gubler, Marie-Louise, *Die frühesten Deutungen des Todes Jesus. Eine motivgeschichtliche Darstellung aufgrund der neueren exegetischen Forschung*, OBO 15, Freiburg CH: Universitätsverlag and Göttingen: Vandenhoeck & Ruprecht 1977

Harnack, Adolf von, *Markion. Das Evangelium vom fremden Gott. Eine Monographie zur Geschichte der Grundlegung der katholischen Kirche,* Leipzig: Hinrichs 1924

Harnisch, Wolfgang, *Verhängnis und Verheissung der Geschichte. Untersuchungen zum Zeit- und Geschichtsverständnis im 4. Buch Esra und in der syrischen Baruchapokalypse*, FRLANT 97, Göttingen: Vandenhoeck & Ruprecht 1969

Heine, Ronald E., 'Montanus, Montanism', *ABD* IV, 1992, 898–902

Hengel, Martin, *Acts and the History of Earliest Christianity*, London:SCM Press 1979

—, *The Atonement. A Study of the Origins of the Doctrine in the New Testament*, London: SCM Press 1981

—, 'Between Jesus and Paulus. The "Hellenists", the "Seven" and Stephen (Acts 6.1–15; 7.54–8.3)', in id., *Between Jesus and Paul,* London: SCM Press 1983, 1–29

—, 'The Gospel of Mark: Time of Origin and Situation', in id., *Studies in the Gospel of Mark*, London: SCM Press 1985, 1–30

—, 'Jakobus der Herrenbruder – der erste "Papst"?', in Ernst Grässer and Otto Merk (eds), *Glaube und Eschatologie, FS Werner Georg Kümmel*, Tübingen: Mohr (Siebeck) 1985, 71–104

—, *The Johannine Question,* London: SCM Press and Philadelphia: Trinity Press International 1989

—, *Property and Riches in the Early Church,* London: SCM Press 1974

—, *Die Schriftauslegung des 4. Evangeliums auf dem Hintergrund der urchristlichen Exegese*, JBTh 4, Neukirchen-Vluyn: Neukirchener Verlag 1989, 249–88

—, 'Der stellvertretende Sühnetod Jesu. Ein Beitrag zur Entstehung des urchristlichen Kerygmas', *IkaZ* 9, 1980, 1–25, 135–47

—, *The Zealots. An Investigation into the Jewish Freedom Movement in the Period from Herod I to AD 70*, Edinburgh: T. & T. Clark 1989

—, and Schwemer, Anna M., *Paul Between Damascus and Antioch. The Unknown Years,* London: SCM Press 1997

Hodgson, Robert, Jr, 'Holiness (NT)', *ABD* III, 249–54

Holm, Nils G., *Einführung in die Religionspsychologie*, Munich: Reinhardt Verlag 1990

Hölscher, Gustav, 'Der Ursprung der Apokalypse Mrk 13', *ThBl* 12, 1933, 193–202

Holtzmann, Heinrich J., *Die synoptischen Evangelien. Ihr Ursprung und ihr geschichtlicher Charakter*, Leipzig: Engelmann 1863

Hooker, Morna D., *The Signs of a Prophet. The Prophetic Actions of Jesus*, London: SCM Press and Harrisburg, Penn.: Trinity Press International 1997

Horn, Friedrich, W., 'Die Gütergemeinschaft der Urgemeinde', *EvTh* 58, 1998, 370–83

Hübner, Hans, 'Unclean and Clean (NT)', *ABD* VI, 741–5

Isenberg, Sheldon R., 'Millenarism in Greco-Roman Palestine', *Religion* 4, 1974, 26–46

Jensen, Anne, *Gottes selbstbewusste Töchter*, Freiburg, Basel and Vienna: Herder 1992

Karrer, Martin, *Die Johannesoffenbarung als Brief*, FRLANT 140, Göttingen: Vandenhoeck & Ruprecht 1985

—, *Jesus Christus im Neuen Testament,* GNT 11, Göttingen: Vandenhoeck & Ruprecht 1998

Käsemann, Ernst, *The Testament of Jesus*, London: SCM Press 1968

Kippenberg, Hans G., *Die vorderasiatischen Erlösungsreligionen in ihrem Zusammenhang mit der antiken Stadtherrschaft*, stw 917, Frankfurt: Suhrkamp Verlag 1991

Klauck, Hans-Josef, 'Das Sendschreiben nach Pergamon und der Kaiserkult in der Johannesoffenbarung', *Bib* 73, 1992, 153–82 = in *Alte Welt und neuer Glaube. Beiträge zur Religionsgeschichte, Forschungsgeschichte und Theologie des Neuen Testaments,* NTOA 29, Freiburg CH: Universitätsverlag and Göttingen: Vandenhoeck & Ruprecht 1994

—, *Die religiöse Umwelt des Urchristentums* I, Stuttgart, Berlin and Cologne: Kohlhammer 1995

—, *Die religiöse Umwelt des Urchristentums* II, Stuttgart, Berlin and Cologne: Kohlhammer 1996

Klein, Günter, 'Galater 2, 6–9 und die Geschichte der Jerusalemer Urgemeinde', *ZThK* 57, 1960, 275–95 = id., *Rekonstruktion und Interpretation; Gesammelte Aufsätze zum Neuen Testament*, BEvTh 50, Munich: Christian Kaiser Verlag 1969, 99–118 + 118–28

Klinghardt, Matthias, *Gesetz und Volk Gottes. Das lukanische Verständnis des Gesetzes nach Herkunft, Funktion und seinem Ort in der Geschichte des Urchristentums*, WUNT II, 32, Tübingen: Mohr (Siebeck) 1988

Kloft, Hans, *Liberalitas Principis*, Cologne and Vienna: Böhlau 1970

Kokins, Ralfs, *Das Verhältnis von ζωή und ἀγάπη im Johannesevangelium. Stufenhermeneutik in der Ersten Abschiedsrede*, Heidelberg dissertation 1999

Körtner, Ulrich H., *Papias von Hierapolis. Ein Beitrag zur Geschichte des frühen Christentums*, FRLANT 133, Göttingen: Vandenhoeck & Ruprecht 1983

Koschorke, Klaus, *Die Polemik der Gnostiker gegen das kirchliche Christentum*, NHS 12, Leiden: Brill 1978

Köster, Helmut, *Einführung in das Neue Testament im Rahmen der Religions-*

geschichte und Kulturgeschichte der hellenistischen und römischen Zeit, Berlin and New York: de Gruyter 1980

Krüger, Gustav, *Das Dogma vom neuen Testament*, Giessen 1896

Küchler, Max, *Frühjüdische Weisheitstraditionen*, OBO 26, Freiburg CH: Universitätsverlag and Göttingen: Vandenhoeck & Ruprecht 1979

Kümmel, Werner G., *Römer 7 und das Bild des Menschen im Neuen Testament*, ThB 53, Munich: Christian Kaiser Verlag 1974

Laato, Timo, *Paulus und das Judentum. Anthropologische Erwägungen*, Aabo: Aabo Akademis förlag 1991.

Lampe, Peter, 'Der Brief an Philemon', in Nikolaus Walter, Eckart Reinmuth and Peter Lampe, *Die Briefe an die Philipper, Thessalonicher und an Philemon*, NTD 8, 2, Göttingen: Vandenhoeck & Ruprecht 1998, 205–32

—, *Die stadtrömischen Christen in den ersten beiden Jahrhunderten*, WUNT II, 18, Tübingen: Mohr (Siebeck) 1987

—, *Die Wirklichkeit als Bild: Das Neue Testament als Grunddokument abendländischer Kultur im Lichte konstruktivistischer Epistemologie und Wissenssoziologie*, Neukirchen-Vluyn: Neukirchener Verlag 1999

—, 'Keine Sklavenflucht des Onesimus', ZNW 76, 1985, 135–7

—, 'Wissenssoziologische Annäherung an das Neue Testament', *NTS* 43, 1997, 347–66

Lang, Bernhard, 'Kanon', *HRWG* III, 1993, 332–5

—, 'Monotheismus', *HRWG* IV, 1998, 148–65

—, 'Ritual/Ritus', *HRWG* IV, 1998, 442–58

Latte, Kurt, 'Synkretismus', *RGG* V, [2]1931, 952

Leeuw, Gerhardus van der, 'Die do-ut-des-Formel in der Opfertheorie', *ARW* 20, 1920/1, 241–53

Lindbeck, George A., *The Nature of Doctrine. Religion and Theology in a Postliberal Age*, Philadelphia: Westminster Press 1984

Lipp, Wolfgang, 'Charisma – Social Deviation, Leadership and Cultural Change. A Sociology of Deviance Approach', *The Annual Review of the Social Sciences of Religion* 1, 1977, 59–77

—, *Stigma und Charisma. Über soziales Grenzverhalten*, Schriften zur Kultursoziologie 1, Berlin: Reimer 1985

Lips, Hermann v., *Weisheitliche Traditionen im Neuen Testament*, WMANT 64, Neukirchen-Vluyn: Neukirchener Verlag 1990

Löhr, Winrich A., *Basilides und seine Schule*, WUNT 83, Tübingen: Mohr (Siebeck) 1996

Lüdemann, Gerd, 'The Acts of the Apostles and the Beginnings of Simonian Gnosis', *NTS* 33, 1987, 279–359

—, 'Die Bekehrung des Paulus und die Wende des Petrus in tiefenpsychologischer Perspektive', in Friedrich W. Horn (ed.), *Bilanz und Perspektiven gegenwärtiger Auslegung des Neuen Testaments, FS Georg Strecker*, Berlin and New York: de Gruyter, 91–111

—, *The Resurrection of Jesus. History, Experience, Theology*, London: SCM Press 1995
—, *Untersuchungen zur simonianischen Gnosis*, GTA 1, Göttingen: Vandenhoeck & Ruprecht 1975
Luz, Ulrich, *Das Evangelium nach Matthäus*, EKK I, 1, Zurich: Benziger Verlag and Neukirchen-Vluyn: Neukirchener Verlag 1985
—, *Das Evangelium nach Matthäus*, EKK I, 1–3, Neukirchen-Vluyn 1985, 1990, 1997
—, *Die Jesusgeschichte des Matthäus*, Neukirchen-Vluyn: Neukirchener Verlag 1993

Malinowski, Bronislaw, *Myth in Primitive Psychology*, New York 1926 = Westport, Conn.: University Press 1971
Malter, Rudolf, 'Kant', *TRE* 17, 1988, 570–81
Markschies, Christoph, *Valentinus Gnosticus? Untersuchungen zur valentianischen Gnosis mit einem neuen Kommentar zu den Fragmenten Valentins*, WUNT 65, Tübingen: Mohr (Siebeck) 1992
Martyn, James L., *History and Theology in the Fourth Gospel*, Nashville: Abingdon Press [2]1979
Mathys, Hans Peter, *Liebe deinen Nächsten wie dich selbst. Untersuchungen zum alttestamentlichen Gebot der Nächstenliebe (Lev 19, 18)*, OBO 71, Freiburg CH: Universitätsverlag and Göttingen: Vandenhoeck & Ruprecht 1986
Meeks, Wayne A., *The Origins of Christian Morality. The First Two Centuries*, New Haven: Yale University Press 1993
Meisinger, Hubert, *Liebesgebot und Altruismusforschung. Ein exegetischer Beitrag zum Dialog zwischen Theologie und Naturwissenschaft*, NTOA 33, Freiburg CH: Universitätsverlag and Göttingen: Vandenhoeck & Ruprecht 1996
Metzger, Bruce, *The Canon of the New Testament*, Oxford: Oxford University Press 1987
Mieth, Dietmar, 'Normen', *HRWG* IV, 1998, 243–50
Mödritzer, Helmut, *Stigma und Charisma im Neuen Testament und seiner Umwelt. Zur Soziologie des Urchristentums*, NTOA 28, Freiburg CH: Universitätsverlag and Göttingen: Vandenhoeck & Ruprecht 1994
Müller, Ulrich B., *Zur frühchristlichen Theologiegeschichte. Judenchristentum und Paulinismus in Kleinasien an der Wende vom ersten zum zweiten Jahrhundert n.Chr.*, Gütersloh: Mohn 1976

Nygren, Anders, *Die Gültigkeit der religiösen Erfahrung*, Gütersloh: Bertelsmann 1922

Ortwein, Gudrun, *Statusverzicht im Neuen Testament und in seiner Umwelt*, Heidelberg dissertation 1997 (forthcoming in NTOA c.1999)
Otto, Eberhard, *Die biographischen Inschriften der ägyptischen Spätzeit. Ihre geistesgeschichtliche und literarische Bedeutung*, Leiden: Brill 1954

Otto, Eckart, *Theologische Ethik des Alten Testaments*, Theologische Wissenschaft 3, 2, Stuttgart, Berlin and Cologne: Kohlhammer 1994

Pagels, Elaine, *The Gnostic Gospels*, New York: Random House 1979

Parsons, Talcott, *Theory of Social Action*, London and New York: McGraw-Hill 1937

Pilhofer, Peter, *Philippi Bd I. Die erste christliche Gemeinde Europas*, WUNT 87, Tübingen: Mohr (Siebeck) 1995

Räisänen, Heikki, *Beyond New Testament Theology: A Story and a Programme*, London: SCM Press 1990

—, 'Comparative Religion, Theology, and New Testament Exegesis', *StTh* 52, 1998, 116–29

—, 'Die frühchristliche Gedankenwelt: Eine religionswissenschaftliche Alternative zur "neutestamentlichen Theologie"', in Christoph Dohmen and Thomas Söding (eds*), Eine Bibel – zwei Testamente: Positionen biblischer Theologie*, Paderborn: Schöningh 1995, 253–65

—, 'The "Hellenists"- a Bridge Between Jesus and Paul?', in id., *The Torah and Christ. Essays in German and English on the Problem of the Law in Early Christianity*, SESJ 45, Helsinki: Kirjappaino Raamattutalo 1986, 242–306

—, *Marcion, Muhammad and the Mahatma*, London: SCM Press 1997

—, *The 'Messianic Secret' in Mark's Gospel*, Edinburgh: T. & T. Clark 1990

Ritschl, Dietrich, 'Die Erfahrung der Wahrheit. Die Steuerung von Denken und Handeln durch implizite Axiome', in id., *Konzepte*, Munich: Christian Kaiser Verlag 1986, 147–66

—, 'Paul's Theological Difficulties with the Law', in id., *The Torah and Christ. Essays in German and English on the Problem of the Law in Early Christianity*, SESJ 45, Helsinki: Kirjappaino Raamattutalo 1986, 3–24

—, and Jones, Hugh O., *'Story' als Rohmaterial der Theologie*, TEH 192, Munich: Christian Kaiser Verlag 1976

Roloff, Jürgen, *Einführung in das Neue Testament*, Stuttgart: Reclam 1995

—, *Die Kirche im Neuen Testament*, GNT 10, Göttingen: Vandenhoeck & Ruprecht 1993

Rowland, Christopher, *Revelation*, Epworth Commentaries, London: Epworth Press 1993

Rudolph, Kurt, *Gnosis: The Nature and History of Gnosticism*, Edinburgh: T. & T. Clark 1983

—, 'Simon-Magus oder Gnosticus? Zum Stand der Debatte', *ThR* 42, 1978, 279–359

Ruppert, Lothar, *Jesus als der leidende Gerechte?*, SBS 59, Stuttgart: Katholisches Bibelwerk 1972

Sabbatucci, Dario, 'Kultur und Religion', *HRWG* I, 1988, 43–58

Sandelin, Karl-Gustav, *Wisdom as Nourisher: A Study of an Old Testament Theme*, *its Development within Early Judaism and its Impact on Early Christianity*, AAAbo 64, 3, Aabo Akademi 1986

Sanders, E. P., *Jesus and Judaism*, London: SCM Press 1985

—, *Judaism. Practice and Belief 63 BCE–66 CE*, London: SCM Press and Philadelphia: Trinity Press International 1992

—, *Paul and Palestinian Judaism. A Comparison of Patterns of Religion*, London: SCM Press 1977

Schaeffler, Richard, *Fähigkeit zur Erfahrung. Zur transzendentalen Hermeneutik des Sprechens von Gott*, QD 94, Freiburg, Basel and Vienna: Herder 1982

Schäfers, Bernhard, 'Krise', in id (ed.), *Grundbegriffe der Soziologie*, UTB 1416, Opladen: Leske & Budrich 1986, 167–9

Schlüter, Astrid, *Die Selbstauslegung des Wortes. Selbstreferenz und Fremdreferenzen in der Textwelt des Johannesevangeliums*, Heidelberg dissertation 1996 (forthcoming c.2000)

Schmeller, Thomas, *Brechungen. Urchristliche Wandercharismatiker im Prisma soziologisch orientierter Exegese*, SBS 136, Stuttgart: Katholisches Bibelwerk 1989

Schmithals, Walter, *Neues Testament und Gnosis*, EdF 208, Darmstadt: Wissenschaftliche Buchgesellschaft 1984

Schnelle, Udo, *The History and Theology of the New Testament Writings*, Minneapolis: Fortress Press and London: SCM Press 1998

Schottroff, Luise, 'Gewaltverzicht und Feindesliebe in der urchristlichen Jesustradition, Mt 5, 38–48/Lk 6, 27–36', in Georg Strecker (ed.), *Jesus in Historie und Theologie, FS H. Conzelmann*, Tübingen: Mohr (Siebeck) 1975, 197–221

Schrage, Wolfgang, *Ethics of the New Testament*, Philadelphia: Fortress Press and Edinburgh, T. & T. Clark 1988

Schürmann, Heinz, *Die Symbolhandlungen Jesu als eschatologische Erfüllungszeichen. Eine Rückfrage nach dem irdischen Jesus* (1970) = id., *Jesus – Gestalt und Geheimnis*, ed. Klaus von Scholtissek, Paderborn: Bonifatius Verlag 1994, 136–56

Schüssler Fiorenza, Elisabeth, *The Book of Revelation. Justice and Judgement*, Philadelphia: Fortress Press 1984

—, 'Apocalyptic and Gnosis in Revelation and in Paul', *JBL* 92, 1973, 565–81 = ibid., 114–32

—, *Revelation. Vision of a Just World*, Proclamation Commentary, Minneapolis: Fortress Press 1991

Schweitzer, Albert, *The Quest of the Historical Jesus*, London: A. & C. Black [3]1954, reissued SCM Press 1981 (the first complete translation of the second edition will be published by SCM Press in 2000)

Scott, Martin, *Sophia and Johannine Jesus*, JSNT.S 71, Sheffield: JSOT Press 1992

Seeley, David, 'Rulership and Service in Mark 10:41–45', *NT* 35, 1993, 234–50

Seiwert, Hubert, 'Opfer', *HRWG* IV, 1998, 268–84

Sellin, Gerhard, 'Mythologeme und mythische Züge in der paulinischen

Theologie', in Hans H. Schmid (ed.), *Mythos und Rationalität*, Gütersloh: Mohn 1988, 209–23
Siegert, Folker, 'Unbekannte Papiaszitate bei armenischen Schriftstellern', *NTS* 2, 1981, 605–14
Söding, Thomas, *Das Liebesgebot bei Paulus. Die Mahnung zur Agape im Rahmen der paulinischen Ethik*, NTA NF 26, Münster: Aschendorf 1991
Stanton, Graham N., 'The Fourfold Gospel', *NTS* 43, 1997, 317–46
Steck, Odil Hannes, *Israel und das gewaltsame Geschick der Propheten*, WMANT 23, Neukirchen-Vluyn: Neukirchener Verlag 1967
Stegemann, Hartmut, *Die Essener, Qumran, Johannes der Täufer und Jesus*, Herder Spektrum 4128, Freiburg, Basel and Vienna: Herder 1993
Stemberger, Günter, *Pharisäer, Sadduzäer, Essener*, SBS 144, Stuttgart: Katholisches Bibelwerk 1990
Stendahl, Krister, 'The Apostle Paul and the Introspective Conscience of the West', *HThR* 56, 1963, 199–215
—, *Paul among Jews and Gentiles and Other Essays*, Philadelphia: Fortress Press 1976
Stern, Menahem, *Greek and Latin Authors on Jews and Judaism*, I, Jerusalem: Israel Academy 1976
Stolz, Fritz, *Einführung in den biblischen Monotheismus*, Darmstadt: Wissenschaftliche Buchgesellschaft 1996
—, *Grundzüge der Religionswissenschaft*, KVR 1527, Göttingen: Vandenhoeck & Ruprecht 1988
—, 'Der mythische Umgang mit der Rationalität und der rationale Umgang mit dem Mythos', in Hans H. Schmid (ed.), *Mythos und Rationalität*, Gütersloh: Mohn 1988, 81–106
Stommel, Eduard, '"Begraben mit Christus" (Röm 6, 4) und der Taufritus', *RQ* 49, 1954, 1–20
—, 'Christliche Taufriten und antike Badesitten', *JAC* 2, 1959, 5–14
Stoops, Robert F., 'Simon. 13', *ABD* VI, 1992, 29–31
Strauss, David F., *The Life of Jesus Critically Examined* (1835), reissued Philadelphia: Fortress Press 1972 and London: SCM Press 1973
Strecker, Christian, *Transformation, Liminalität und Communitas bei Paulus. Kulturanthropologische Zugänge zur paulinischen Theologie*, Neuendettelsau dissertation 1995 (forthcoming in FRLANT c. 1999/2000)

Talmon, Shemarjahu, 'Die Samaritaner in Vergangenheit und Gegenwart', in Reinhard Pummer (ed.), *Die Samaritaner*, WdF 604, Darmstadt: Wissenschaftliche Buchgesellschaft 1992, 379–92
Theissen, Gerd, 'The Ambivalence of Power in Early Christianity, in Cynthia L. Rigby (ed.), *Power, Powerlessness, and the Divine. New Inquiries in Bible and Theology*, Atlanta: Scholars Press 1997, 21–36.
—, 'Auferstehungsbotschaft und Zeitgeschichte. Über einige politische Anspielungen im 1. Kapitel des Römerbriefs', in Sabine Bieberstein and Daniel

Kosch (eds), *Auferstehung hat einen Namen. Biblische Anstösse zum Christsein heute, FS Hermann-Josef Venetz*, Lucerne: Edition Exodus 1998, 59–68

—, 'Autoritätskonflikte in den johanneischen Gemeinden. Zum "Sitz im Leben" des Johannesevangeliums', in *Diakonia, Gedenkschrift B. Stogiannos*, Thessaloniki: Theologische Hochschule 1988, 243–58 = (revised) 'Conflits d'autorité dans les communautés johanniques. La question du Sitz im Leben de l'évangile de Jean', in id., *Histoire sociale du christianisme primitif. Jésus, Paul, Jean*, MoBi 33, Geneva: Labor et Fides 1996, 209–26

—, *Biblical Faith. An Evolutionary Approach*, London: SCM Press 1984 and Philadelphia: Fortress Press 1985

—, 'Evangelienschreibung und Gemeindeleitung. Pragmatische Motive bei der Abfassung des Markusevangeliums', in Bernd Kollmann, Wolfgang Reibold and Annette Steudel (eds), *Antikes Judentum und Frühes Christentum, FS Hartmut Stegemann*, Berlin and New York: de Gruyter 1999, 389–414

—, *Frauen im Umkreis Jesu, Sexauer Gemeindepreis für Theologie 1993*, Sexau 1993

—, '"Geben ist seliger als nehmen" (Apg 20, 35). Zur Demokratisierung antiker Wohltätermentalität im Urchristentum', in Andrea Boluminski (ed.), *Kirche, Recht und Wissenschaft, FS Albert St*ein, Neuwied: Luchterhand 1995, 195–215

—, 'Gewaltverzicht und Feindesliebe (Mt 5, 38–48/Lk 6, 27–38) und deren sozialgeschichtlicher Hintergrund', in id., *Studien zur Soziologie des Urchristentums*, WUNT 19, Tübingen: Mohr (Siebeck) [3]1989, 160–97

—, *The Gospels in Context. Social and Political History in the Synoptic Tradition*, Edinburgh: T. & T. Clark 1992

- , 'Gruppenmessianismus. Überlegungen zum Ursprung der Kirche im Jüngerkreis Jesu', *JBTh* 7, 1992, 101–23.

—, 'Hellenisten und Hebräer (Apg 6, 1–6). Gab es eine Spaltung der Urgemeinde?', in Hermann Lichtenberger (ed.), *Geschichte – Tradition - Reflexion, Bd III. Frühes Christentum, FS Martin Hengel*, Tübingen 1996, 323–43

—, 'L'hérméneutique biblique et la recherche de la vérité religieuse', *RThPh* 122, 1990, 485–503

—, 'Jesus – Prophet einer millenaristischen Bewegung? Sozialgeschichtliche Überlegungen zu einer sozialanthropologischen Deutung der Jesusbewegung', *EvTh* (forthcoming 1999)

—, *Jesus und das Judentum*, KuI 1999

—, 'Jesus und die symbolpolitischen Konflikte seiner Zeit. Sozialgeschichtliche Aspekte der Jesusforschung', *EvTh* 57, 1997, 378–400

—, 'Jesusbewegung als charismatische Wertrevolution', NTS 35, 1989, 343–60

—, 'Judentum und Christentum bei Paulus. Sozialgeschichtliche Überlegungen zu einem beginnenden Schisma', in Martin Hengel and Ulrich Heckel (eds), *Paulus. Missionar und Theologe und das antike Judentum*, WUNT 58, Tübingen 1991, 331–56

—, 'Mythos und Wertrevolution im Urchristentum', in Dieter Harth and Jan Assmann (eds), *Revolution und Mythos*, Frankfurt: Fischer Verlag 1992, 62–81

—, 'Pax Romana et Pax Christi. Le christianisme primitif et l'idée de la paix', *RThPh* 124, 1992, 61–84

—, 'Die pragmatische Bedeutung der Geheimnismotive im Markusevangelium. Ein wissenssoziologischer Versuch', in Hans G. Kippenberg and Guy G. Stroumsa, *Secrecy and Concealment. Studies in the History of Mediterranean and Near Eastern Religions*, Leiden, New York and Cologne: Brill 1995, 225–45

—, *Psychological Aspects of Pauline Theology*, Edinburgh: T. & T. Clark 1987

—, 'Die Rede vom grossen Weltgericht (Mt 25, 31–46). Universales Hilfsethos gegenüber allen Menschen?', in Arnd Götzelmann, Volker Steinmann and Jürgen Stein (eds), *Diakonie der Versöhnung. Ethische Reflexion und soziale Arbeit in ökumenischer Verantwortung, FS Theodor Strohm*, Stuttgart: Quell Verlag 1998, 60–70

—, 'Theoretische Probleme religionssoziologischer Forschung und die Analyse des Urchristentums', *NZRSTh* 16, 1974, 35–56 = in id., *Studien zur Soziologie des Urchristentums*, WUNT 19, Tübingen: Mohr (Siebeck) [3]1989, 55–78

—, 'Urchristlicher Liebeskommunismus. Zum "Sitz im Leben" des Topos in Apg 2, 44 und 4, 32', in Tornd Fornberg and David Hellholm (eds), *Texts and Contexts. Biblical Texts in Their Textual and Situational Contexts, FS Lars Hartman*, Oslo and Copenhagen: Scandinavian University Press 1995, 689–711

—, *Die urchristliche Taufe und die soziale Konstruktion des neuen Menschen*, forthcoming Leiden: Brill 1999

—, 'Vom Davidssohn zum Weltherrscher. Pagane und jüdische Endzeiterwartungen im Spiegel des Matthäusevangeliums', in Michael Becker and Wolfgang Fenske (eds), *Das Ende der Tage und die Gegenwart des Heils, FS Heinz W. Kuhn*, Leiden: Brill 1999, 145–64

—, 'The Wandering Radicals. Light Shed by the Sociology of Literature on the Early Transmission of Jesus Sayings, Social Reality and the Early Christians', in *Theology, Ethics and the World of the New Testament*, Minneapolis: Fortress Press 1992, 33–59

—, 'Weisheit als Mittel sozialer Abgrenzung und Öffnung. Beobachtungen zur sozialen Funktion frühjüdischer und urchristlicher Weisheit', in Aleida Assmann (ed.), *Weisheit. Archäologie der literarischen Kommunikation* III, Munich: Fink 1991, 193–204

—, 'Wert und Status des Menschen im Urchristentum', *Humanistische Bildung* 12, 1966, 61–93

—, and Merz, Annette, *The Historical Jesus*, London: SCM Press and Minneapolis: Fortress Press 1998

Thyen, Hartwig, 'Ich-Bin-Worte', *RAC* 17, 1994/96, 147–213

—, 'Johannesevangelium', *TRE* 17, 1988, 200 -25

Trautmann, Maria, *Zeichenhafte Handlungen Jesu. Ein Beitrag zur Frage nach dem geschichtlichen Jesus*, FzB 37, Würzburg: Echter Verlag 1980

Trevett, Christine, *Montanism. Gender, Authority and the New Prophecy*, Cambridge: Cambridge University Press 1996

Trobisch, David, *Die Endredaktion des Neuen Testaments*, NTOA 31, Freiburg CH:

Universitätsverlag and Göttingen: Vandenhoeck & Ruprecht 1996

—, *Die Entstehung der Paulusbriefsammlung*, NTOA 10, Freiburg CH: Universitätsverlag and Göttingen: Vandenhoeck & Ruprecht 1989

—, *Die Paulusbriefe und die Anfänge der christlichen Publizistik*, KT 135, Gütersloh: Christian Kaiser Verlag 1994

Tuckett, Christopher, *Q and the History of Early Christianity*, Edinburgh: T. & T. Clark 1996

Turner, Victor, *The Ritual Process. Structure and Anti-Structure*, Chicago: Aldine Press 1969

Uro, Risto (ed.), *Symbols and Strata. Essays on the Saying Gospel Q*, SESJ 65, Göttingen: Vandenhoeck & Ruprecht 1996

Versnel, Hendrik S., 'Quid Athenis et Hierosolymis? Bemerkungen über die Herkunft von Aspekten des "Effective Death"', in Jan W.van Henten (ed.), *Die Entstehung der jüdischen Martyrologie*, StPB 38, Leiden: Brill 1989, 162–96

Veyne, Paul, *Le Pain et le cirque. Sociologie historique d'un pluralisme politique*, Paris: Editions du Seuil 1976

Vielhauer, Philipp, 'Erwägungen zur Christologie des Markusevangeliums' (1964), in id., *Aufsätze zum Neuen Testament,* ThB 31, Munich: Christian Kaiser 1965, 199–214

—, and Strecker, Georg, 'Jewish-Christian Gospels', in Wilhelm Schneemelcher and R. McL. Wilson, *New Testament Apocrypha I. Gospels and Related Writings*, Cambridge: James Clarke and Louisville: Westminster John Knox Press 1991, 134–78

Walzer, Michael, *Interpretation and Social Criticism*, Cambridge, Mass.: Harvard University Press 1987

Wengst, Klaus, *Bedrängte Gemeinde und verherrlichter Christus*, BThSt 5, Neukirchen-Vluyn: Neukirchener Verlag 1981 = Munich: Christian Kaiser Verlag [2]1990

—, *Humility – Solidarity of the Humiliated*, London: SCM Press 1988

Wilson, Robert McLachlan, 'Gnosis/Gnostizismus II', *TRE* 13, 1984, 535–50

Windisch, Hans, 'Friedensbringer – Gottessöhne. Eine religionsgeschichtliche Interpretation der 7. Seligpreisung', *ZNW* 24, 1925, 240–60

Wischmeyer, Oda, 'Macht, Herrschaft und Gewalt in den frühjüdischen Schriften', in Joachim Mehlhausen (ed.), *Recht – Macht – Gerechtigkeit*, Gütersloh: Christian Kaiser Verlag 1998, 355–69

—, 'Matthäus 6, 25–34 par. Die Spruchreihe vom Sorgen', *ZNW* 85, 1994, 1–22

Wlosok, Antonie (ed.), *Römischer Kaiserkult*, WdF 372, Darmstadt: Wissenschaftliche Buchgesellschaft 1978

Wolters, Michael, 'Verborgene Weisheit und Heil der Heiden. Zur Traditionsgeschichte und Intention des "Revelationsschemas"', *ZThK* 84, 1987, 297–319

Wrede, William, *The Messianic Secret in the Gospels* (1901), Cambridge: James

Clarke 1971
—, 'Paulus', *RV* I, 5–6 = Halle. GebauerSchwenschke 1904 = Rengstorf, Karl H., *Das Paulusbild in der neueren deutschen Forschung*, WdF 24, Darmstadt: Wissenschaftliche Buchgesellschaft 1969, 1–97
—, 'The Task and Methods of New Testament Theology', in Robert Morgan (ed.), *The Nature of New Testament Theology*, SBT 25, London: SCM Press 1973, 68–116
Wright, David P., 'Holiness (OT)', *ABD* III, 237–49
—, 'Unclean and Clean (OT)', *ABD* VI, 728–41

Zeller, Dieter, *Christus unter den Göttern. Zum antiken Umfeld des Christusglaubens*, Stuttgart: Katholisches Bibelwerk 1993
—, 'Die Menschwerdung des Sohnes Gottes im Neuen Testament und die antike Religionsgeschichte', in id (ed.), *Menschwerdung Gottes – Vergöttlichung von Menschen,* NTOA 7, Freiburg CH: Universitätsverlag and Göttingen: Vandenhoeck & Ruprecht 1988, 141–76
—, 'Die Mysterienkulte und die paulinische Soteriologie (Röm 6, 1–11). Eine Fallstudie zum Synkretismus im Neuen Testament', in Hermann P. Siller (ed.), *Suchbewegungen. Synkretismus – kulturelle Identität und kirchliches Bekenntnis,* Darmstadt: Wissenschaftliche Buchgesellschaft 1991, 42–61
Zimbardo, Philip L., *Psychology and Life*, Glenview, Ill.: Scott, Foresman [12]1988
Zumstein, Jean, 'L'évangile johannique: une stratégie de croire', *RSC* 77, 1989, 217–32 = id., *Miettes exégétiques*, MoBi 25, Geneva: Labor et fides 1991, 237–52

Notes

Introduction: The Programme of a Theory of Primitive Christian Religion

1. The programme of a scientific analysis of primitive Christian religion goes back to William Wrede, *Über Aufgabe und Methode der sogenannten Neutestamentlichen Theologie* (1897), English translation 'The Task and Methods of New Testament Theology', in Robert Morgan (ed.), *The Nature of New Testament Theology,* SBT 25, London: SCM Press 1973, 68–116. This programme is being revived at the present time by Heikki Räisänen, cf. id., *Beyond New Testament Theology: A Story and a Programme,* London: SCM Press 1990; id., 'Die frühchristliche Gedankenwelt: Eine religionswissenschaftliche Alternative zur "neutestamentlichen Theologie"', in Christoph Dohmen and Thomas Söding (eds), *Eine Bibel – zwei Testamente: Positionen biblischer Theologie*, Paderborn: Schöningh 1995, 253–65; id., 'Comparative Religion, Theology, and New Testament Exegesis', *StTh* 52, 1998, 116–29. This programme has three characteristics which are governed by its opposition to a 'theology of the New Testament' tied to norms, and to this degree are variations of the same concern:

1. It distances itself from the *normative claim* of religious texts. Their 'claim' becomes the object but not the presupposition of the analysis of them. The analysis of primitive Christianity takes place 'with an open identity' (i.e. accessible to people with different religious identities) and 'remote from application' (i.e. independently of whether the results can be used in the praxis of the church).
2. It goes beyond the limits of the *canon.* All primitive Christian literature up to around Irenaeus is included in the investigation; here the precise demarcation of primitive Christianity from the early church is disputed. The canonical and non-canonical literature are in principle regarded as being of equal value.
3. It emancipates itself from the categories of '*orthodoxy*' and '*heresy*': all currents in primitive Christianity are regarded as equally justified in principle. To exaggerate the point: in cases of doubt orthodoxy is regarded as the 'heresy' which has established itself.

Three further definitions bring out more positively what such a scientific analysis of primitive Christianity is striving for. It is here that the strengths of the programme lie:

4. The recognition of the *plurality* and contradictory nature of the theological schemes in primitive Christianity. There is no necessity to work out a

uniform kergyma from the primitive Christian writings, although the question of their unity remains a justified historical and religious concern (and by no means just a theological concern): the theory of primitive Christian religion presented here investigates the unity in the plurality far more intensively than the programmatic recognition of the plurality suggests.

5. The interpretation of theological ideas in the light of their *context in real life*. Religion does not consist (only) in ideas, but is the expression of all of life. Theological notions are an expression of religious and social experience – and in each case are also governed by non-religious factors. Therefore political and social conditions are also included in the analysis.

6. Openness towards the *history of religion*: primitive Christian religion is seen in its interaction with other religions – especially as a current deriving from Judaism which is shaped by its controversy with pagan religions. These other religions are described without disparagement – and not from the standpoint of a superiority of Christianity which is stated a priori. It is another matter that the sense of superiority among Jews and Christians in the pagan world also requires to be explained.

There is still no detailed outline of such a scientific analysis of primitive Christianity. However, it should be clear that such an approach leaves great scope for different schemes. The attempt presented here stands out probably: 1. By its use of theoretical models, even if they always have only an auxiliary function. I shall mention them in advance here simply by their catchwords: religion as sign language; its guidance by implicit axioms; its independence as a self-organizing system; the assimilation of cognitive dissonances in religion; the reaction of millenarianism to the conflict of indigenous cultures with imperial cultures; the interpretations of ethics in terms of conflict theory, as an expression of a way of coping with the fight over the distribution of opportunities in life; the theory of ritual liminality with constitutive breaches of taboo. None of these theories or theoretical approaches serves to outline a general theory of religion; they depict the beginnings of a concrete religion in categories that are generally accessible. 2. More markedly than in other schemes, religion is understood as a normative power in life. The working out of, for example, a canon (i.e. a collection of writings with a claim to authority) plays a major role for this 'theory of primitive Christian religion'. Therefore great importance is attached to the question of the unity of primitive Christian religion (in the form of the question of the grammar of its sign language).

2. The definition of religion as 1. cultural sign language which 2. corresponds to an ultimate reality and 3. promises a gain in life is influenced by Clifford Geertz, 'Religion as a Cultural System', in *The Interpretation of Cultures*, New York: Basic Books 1973, 87–125: 90. According to him, religion is 'a symbol system aimed at creating strong, comprehensive and lasting moods and motivations in people by formulating notions of a universal order of being and surrounding these notions with such an aura of activity that the moods and motivations seem to correspond completely to reality'. I have simplified this definition at two points:

1. Instead of a symbol system I speak of a sign system, since 'symbols' in the stricter sense (like the 'cross') are only a particularly complex kind of sign, and while imperatives like 'You shall not kill' are linguistic 'signs', they are not 'symbolic' (in the narrower sense).
2. The formulation 'corresponding to an ultimate reality' summarizes the differentiated description of the correspondence of mood and motivations to an order of being believed to be a fact.
3. In addition there is a pragmatic motive: religion promises a gain in life, i.e. an improvement, preservation or intensification in life.

3. This view of the human being as an *animal symbolicum*, which transforms the world into a home by an interpretation bound up with signs, appears in Ernst Cassirer, *Essay on Man*, New Haven: Yale University Press 1944.

4. My definition of the three forms of expression of religion borrows from Fritz Stolz, *Grundzüge der Religionswissenschaft*, KVR 1527, Göttingen: Vandenhoeck & Ruprecht 1988, 79ff.: he distinguishes between 'possibilities of description' or 'possibilities of codification' of the religious message in the sphere of acting, seeing and speaking, i.e. performative, representational and linguistic forms of expression. The performative and representational forms of religion are here summed up as ritual forms of expression: the eucharist and the altar belong together. The linguistic forms of expression appear as myth – but they can also be developed further to become theology and reflection. Ethic is regarded as a separate form of expression – in accordance with its great importance within the Jewish-Christian tradition.

5. In my view, three dimensions of myth need to be distinguished: it is a text, a power that shapes life and a thought-structure. In so far as theories of myth each concentrate on one of these dimensions, they do not contradict one another.

1. Myth is a *text*: a narrative the action of which is in a decisive time for the world, in which numinous subjects (gods, angels and demons) transform (or will transform) a fragile state of reality into a stable state. Cf. Fritz Stolz, 'Der mythische Umgang mit der Rationalität und der rationale Umgang mit dem Mythos', in Hans H. Schmid (ed.), *Mythos und Rationalität*, Gütersloh: Mohn 1988, 81–106.
2. Myth has a *function*: it is a narrative with legitimizing or utopian force which is the basis for a form of social life or puts such a form in question (the latter is the case with some eschatological myths). Functionalism has investigated this aspect of myth. Cf. Bronislaw Malinowski, *Myth in Primitive Psychology*, New York 1926 = Westport, Conn.: University Press 1971.
3. Finally, myth is a *mentality* or a *thought structure*. Myths are narratives based on another way of ordering the world in forms of perception and interpreting it in categories. To this degree myth is not opposed to the Logos, but a first form of the Logos. Cf. Ernst Cassirer, *Philosophy of Symbolic Forms, II, Mythical Thought*, New Haven: Yale University Press 1955.

A characteristic of myth within the forms of space and time is its structuring by the opposition between the sacred and the profane: there is a holy centre to the world, a decisive holy time (or holy places and times) – always in opposition to profane space and time.

Within the thought categories with which impressions are ordered in space and time the most important are:

(a) A concept of substance in which things appear to have souls: *animation* is therefore the first category of mythical thought. The mythical world is a world of wills and intentions which are active in all things. The hostility of the world is, for example, personified and ensouled – and then presented in the form of the Satan and his demons (cf. Aleida and Jan Assmann, 'Mythos', *HWRG* IV, 1998, 179–200: 191).

(b) A concept of causality which also has analogous things influencing one another: the individual sin of the human being does not just take place in analogy to human sin but is brought about by it. *Analogical causality* is a second basic category of mythical thought.

(c) A concept of relationship, in which an *in-depth identity* of things which are clearly separated in our everyday perception is possible: for example, Adam's sin is repeated in every human being. Every human being is Adam. For thinking in terms of such an in-depth identity cf. especially Gerhard Sellin, 'Mythologeme und mythische Züge in der paulinischen Theologie', in Hans H. Schmid (ed.), *Mythos und Rationalität*, Gütersloh: Mohn 1988, 209–23.

The most important thought structures are summed up in the following table:

Forms of perception			
(a) Space	holy space	–	profane space
(b) Time	holy time	–	profane time
Categories of thought			
(a) Substance	animation: all things act in a personified way		
(b) Causality	analogous causality: things that are analogous have an effect on one another		
(c) Relationship	in-depth identity: what is separate is identical in depth		

6. Cf. Bernhard Lang, 'Ritual/Ritus', *HRWG* IV, 1998, 442–58. If we want to distinguish between rite and ritual, Lang's definition is an obvious one: 'Whereas "rite(s)" denotes the smallest elements in sacred actions, ritual is reserved for the overall event which is built up of rites' (444).

7. The 'systemic' approach to religion sketched out in the following pages has been stimulated by three insights.

1. Systems of religious convictions are governed by a few '*implicit axioms*' or regulative statements which need not be present as formal propositions but in principle are capable of becoming conscious and expressed in language. I owe this insight to Dietrich Ritschl, 'Die Erfahrung der Wahrheit; Die Steuerung von Denken und Handeln durch implizite Axiome', in id., *Konzepte*, Munich:

Christian Kaiser Verlag 1986, 147–66.

2. The religions are languages in which such implicit axioms form a grammar by which, among other things, associations and inconsistencies are determined. This notion of a grammar of faith comes from George A. Lindbeck, *The Nature of Doctrine. Religion and Theology in a Postliberal Age*, Philadelphia: Westminster Press 1984.

3. Religions are systems which refer to themselves and outside themselves, and have a capacity for self-organization: they attempt to direct themselves through implicit axioms (or through their grammar). For such a system-theoretical approach to religions and their interaction I am indebted to two Heidelberg dissertations by Andreas Feldtkeller and Astrid Schlüter. Cf. A. Feldtkeller, *Identitätssuche des syrischen Urchristentum. Mission, Inkulturation und Pluralität im ältesten Heidenchristentum,* NTOA 25, Freiburg CH: Universitätsverlag and Göttingen: Vandenhoeck & Ruprecht 1993; id., *Im Reich der syrischen Göttin. Eine religiös plurale Kultur als Umwelt des frühen Christentums*, Studien zum Verstehen fremden Religionen 8, Gütersloh: Gütersloher Verlagshaus 1994. Here a system-theoretical analysis is applied to whole religious systems. By contrast, Astrid Schlüter, *Die Selbstauslegung des Wortes. Selbstreferenz und Fremdreferenzen in der Textwelt des Johannes-evangelium*, Heidelberg dissertation 1996 (to be published around 2000), applies a system-theoretical analysis to a concrete religious text-world.

8. Wolfgang Lipp has worked out the connection between stigma and charisma in a number of publications: id., *Stigma und Charisma. Über soziales Grenzverhalten*, Schriften zur Kultursoziologie 1, Berlin: Reimer 1985; id., 'Charisma – Social Deviation, Leadership and Cultural Change. A Sociology of Deviance Approach', *The Annual Review of the Social Sciences of Religion* 1, 1977, 569–77. His ideas were initially applied only to Jesus and his followers (Michael N. Ebertz, *Das Charisma des Gekreuzigten. Zur Soziologie der Jesusbewegung*, WUNT 45, Tübingen: Mohr [Siebeck] 1987), then to the whole of primitive Christianity (Helmut Mödritzer, *Stigma und Charisma im Neuen Testament und seiner Umwelt. Zur Soziologie des Urchristentums*, NTOA 28, Freiburg CH: Universitätsverlag and Göttingen, Vandenhoeck & Ruprecht 1994).

9. Many psychologists of religion put a one-sided emphasis on emotional aspects of religion. Justice is done to the different functions of religion by Bernhard Grom, *Religionspsychologie*, Munich: Kösel Verlag and Göttingen: Vandenhoeck & Ruprecht 1992; Nils G. Holm, *Einführung in die Religionspsychologie*, UTB 1952, Munich and Basel: Reinhardt 1990.

10. I have made an attempt which also takes into account apparently opposed social functions of religion in Gerd Theissen, 'Theoretische Probleme religionssoziologischer Forschung und die Analyse des Urchristentums', *NZRSTh* 16, 1974, 35–56 = *Studien zur Soziologie des Urchristentums*, WUNT 19, Tübingen: Mohr (Siebeck) [3]1989, 55–78.

11. In principle the following approaches can be distinguished in the theory of religion.

1. Cognitivistic theories of religion see religion as a system of ideas which are related to specifically religious objects.

2. Expressive (or expressivistic) theories of religion see religion as the expression of human life, especially its emotional dimension (as for example with Schleiermacher).

3. Pragmatic-functional theories of religion see religion above all as a system of guidance for human behaviour – for example, if they interpret the power of the holy as an objectivizing of the supremacy of society over the individual (as e.g. with Emile Durkheim).

This book puts forward a cultural-linguistic (or semiotic) theory of religion: religions are sign systems with three dimensions. They organize cognitions, emotions and behaviour. For such a cultural-linguistic theory of religion see above all Lindbeck, *The Nature of Doctrine* (n.7).

12. The classical analysis of religion as an offer of roles which restructures the perception of reality in a specifically religious way has been developed by Hjalmar Sundén, *Die Religion und die Rollen* (Swedish 1959), Berlin: Töpelmann 1966; cf. id., *Gott erfahren. Das Rollenangebot der Religionen*, GTB 98, Gütersloh: Mohn 1975. This is taken further in a positive way by Bernhard Lang, 'Rolle', *HRWG* IV, 1998, 460–76, esp. 469ff. Also in Nils G. Holm and J. A. Belzen (eds), *Sundén's Role Theory – An Impetus to Contemporary Psychology of Religion*, Religionsvetenskapliga skrifter 27, Aabo: Aabo Akademi 1995.

13. The ambivalent term symbol can be used clearly only if one mentions each of the different thought traditions within which it is used.

(a) We are familiar with the opposition of symbol and allegory from the aesthetic tradition. Here the symbol is regarded as the meaningful appearance of an idea in the concrete, whereas allegory makes possible only a relationship between what can be sensed concretely and its sense which is communicated by thought. In both cases something objective is revealed in the symbol or in the allegory (Goethe). We are familiar with this opposition from the classic German theory of poetry.

(b) From the philosophical tradition we know the concept of symbol as an expression of the unconscious in dream and myth – either as a veiling of socially unacceptable impulses and wishes which cannot be communicated directly (in Freud the dream is more an 'allegory' which veils), or as a language which makes the unconscious accessible to public communication (in Jung and others the dream is more a symbol which reveals).

(c) In the neo-Kantian tradition the concept of symbol is an overall concept for different 'symbolic forms' for ordering and structuring the world: by myth, language, art and knowledge (Cassirer). Here the concept of symbol does not relate to the appearance of an objective or subjective 'transcendent' reality but is the expression of an intellectual 'transcendent' act of human beings, by which they order their world.

Independently of these three traditions, all of which have an influence on the concept of symbol used above, in linguistic imagery one should distinguish between symbol and metaphor without separating the two: a symbol is the depiction of a real object which becomes transparent to a deeper meaning. A real flame, for example, is depicted in such a way that it become transparent to a real passion. Symbols are based on the capacity to perceive the real world symbolically. Symbolic texts must therefore always be understood both literally and in a transferred sense. They have a primary meaning – and at the same time a surplus of meaning. By contrast, if one speaks of the 'flame of passion' (without meaning a real fire), one has made the reality which is perceived symbolically into a linguistic metaphor. Whereas symbols have to be taken literally (and at the same time may be understood in a transferred sense), metaphors may be understood only in a transferred sense. To understand them literally would always be to misunderstand them. So the same 'image' can appear in a text as a symbol (as a transparent reality) or as a metaphor (as a transferred notion). Thus the religious images which I have called 'symbols' above often occur in texts as metaphors. For the demarcation of the different forms of imagery cf. Petra von Gemünden, *Vegetationsmetaphorik im Neuen Testament und seiner Umwelt*, NTOA 18, Freiburg CH: Universitätsverlag and Göttingen: Vandenhoeck & Ruprecht 1993, 1–49 (with bibliography).

14. The two terms 'ethical norms' and 'commandments' belong to different cultural thought contexts: a 'commandment' is part of an objective law which is given to human beings. The term 'norm' arose only in modern times as a term for 'purposive regulations', but then became a quite general term which can denote anything 'normative' in everyday life, science and religion. Cf. Dietmar Mieth, 'Normen', *HRWG* IV, 1998, 243–5. A characteristic of the normative system of biblical language is that two distinctions are present but not carried through.

1. The distinction between legal and moral norms. Certainly in the Old Testament one can distinguish norms that are clearly defended by sanctions from norms without the sanctions of a human judge, for the notion of God as judge appears in these passages. But often the two appear immediately side by side in the Old Testament collections of law.
2. The distinction between ethical norms which make human social life possible, and ritual norms which make worship of God possible. The fulfilment of ethical norms is also understood as 'worship' – often even as the real worship. This leads to a tremendous revaluation of ethics.

15. Since the time of the exile, monotheism has been the basic confession of Israel. This is an exclusive monotheism, which excludes the existence and worship of other gods – as opposed to a philosophical monotheism, which is compatible with the practical worship of many gods in popular cults, in that it ultimately sees only one God behind the various deities. The encounter between them is the basic theme of ancient Judaism in the Hellenistic period. Cf. Yehoshua Amir, 'Die Begegnung des biblischen und des philosophischen Monotheismus als Grundthema des jüdischen Hellenismus', *EvTh* 38, 1978, 2–19. In the case of exclusive monotheism, in theory one can distinguish between a prophetic and a practical monotheism: prophetic monotheism is mediated by a prophetic figure

with a claim to revelation (by Akenaten in Egypt or Deutero-Isaiah in Israel); practical monotheism develops from the worship of one God (from temporary henotheism or lasting monolatry). This can often arise in a crisis situation in which people expect their salvation wholly from one God. In Israel the two came together: prophetic revealer figures established faith in the one and only God; a chronic situation of crisis made their message plausible. Cf. Bernhard Lang, 'Monotheismus', *HRWG* IV, 1998, 148–65. For a distinction between prophetic, practical and philosophical monotheism see ibid., 151–4.

16. The term 'covenantal nomism' expresses the fact that the election of the people by God (his covenant) presupposes its being obligated under the law. The law does not have the task of constituting the covenant of God with Israel but of preserving Israel in this covenant. So in terms of salvation, the law does not bring about a getting in but a staying in. Accordingly Judaism is just as much a religion of grace as Christianity. This basic structure of Jewish religion has been worked out by E. P. Sanders, *Paul and Palestinian Judaism. A Comparison of Patterns of Religion,* London: SCM Press 1977.

17. Instead of 'myth' one can speak neutrally of a 'basic narrative'. For particularly in the biblical religion, the mythical and the historical were closely interconnected – and within the historical 'poetry and truth' were mixed. The concept of story embraces everything: the mythical, the fictitious and the historical in the narrower sense. Such basic narratives form the foundation for the identity of both whole groups and individuals. What we call 'christology' in the New Testament is always based on a narrative (which is more or less developed). The christological honorific titles are abbreviations of narratives. For the theory of the relationship between summary abstractions and narratives in religion cf. Dietrich Ritschl and Hugh O. Jones, *'Story' als Rohmaterial der Theologie*, THE 192, Munich: Christian Kaiser Verlag 1976. Martin Karrer, *Jesus Christus im Neuen Testament*, GNT 11, Göttingen: Vandenhoeck & Ruprecht 1998, gives an account of New Testament christology which departs from a fixation on titles and evaluates these in the framework of their 'narratives'.

18. Although in the scholarly study of religion myth and rite are usually mentioned side by side – and ethic is mentioned at best as an enlargement of this – , in the following pages, after the basic narrative of primitive Christianity (in which its myth is to be sought) I shall first analyse its ethic. This approach both corresponds to the great importance of ethics in biblical religion and indicates the great significance of the rite: in the rite we find a concentrated summary of the whole religion – including its ethic. Only when this is known do we recognize the way in which it is symbolized in the rite.

19. Eckart Otto, *Theologische Ethik des Alten Testament,* Theologische Wissenschaft 3, 2, Stuttgart, Berlin and Cologne: Kohlhammer 1994, in particular has worked out how in the Old Testament all norms are theologized. Here it is striking that God often comes into play in the norms which are not provided with a sanction. In the Book of the Covenant there are no legal sanctions for: the release of Hebrew slaves (Ex. 21.1–11); respect for aliens, widows and orphans (22.20–23);

the prohibition against usury (22.24–25); the prohibition against bending the law (23.1ff.); help for the enemy (23.4f.); sabbath year and gleaning (23.10–11); the hallowing of the sabbath also for animals, slaves and aliens (23.12), i.e. particularly the social commandments in which a human spirit can be detected.

20. Sigrid Brandt, *Opfer als Gedächtnis. Zur Kritik und Neukonturierung theologischer Rede von Opfer*, Habilitation dissertation, Heidelberg 1997, gives a theological analysis of the rites of sacrifice.

21. The notion of an 'autonomy of religion' is not a general category in the study of religion. In one branch of the discipline it is now stressed, rather, that the segregation of religion within society and its separation from the state is a special European development and may not be projected on to other societies. Cf. Dario Sabbatucci, 'Kultur und Religion', *RWG* I, 1988, 43–58.

2. The Significance of the Historical Jesus for the Origin of Primitive Christian Religion

1. The liberation of the Jesus tradition from the mythical garb of church dogmatics was the concern of the liberal quest of the historical Jesus, in so far as it was governed by a historical impulse. Characteristic of this was the work of Heinrich J. Holtzmann, who thought that he could outline a valid historical picture of Jesus on the basis of the two-source theory which he brought to widespread attention. Cf. id., *Die synoptischen Evangelien. Ihr Ursprung und ihr geschichtlicher Charakter*, Leipzig: Engelmann 1863. An impulse then became established in a late phase of liberal theology, influenced by the history-of-religions school, which increasingly found reminiscences of the historical Jesus changed by pre-existing hopes for a redeemer. Wilhelm Bousset, *Kyrios Christos. A History of the Belief in Christ from the Beginnings of Christianity to Irenaeus* (1913), Nashville: Abingdon Press 1970, is characteristic of this phase. The vacillation between a historical and a mythical reconstruction of the Jesus tradition was still very much stronger in popular and semi-scholarly literature than in professional New Testament research. Albert Schweitzer, *The Quest of the Historical Jesus* (1906), reissued London: SCM Press 1981, gives a vivid account of both theological research and research in general (the English text of the much-expanded second edition of 1912, not previously translated, is to by published by SCM Press in 2000).

2. The concept of myth was explained above, Chapter 1, n. 5. It was introduced by D. F. Strauss, *The Life of Jesus Critically Examined* (1835–36), reissued Philadelphia: Fortress Press 1972 and London: SCM Press 1973. On the one hand myth explains for him how the supernatural has been woven into the history of Jesus: as a 'poetic saga without a purpose' it veiled Jesus in expectations which existed previously. On the other hand, a truth is expressed in it: the idea of the unity of God and human beings. Myth is the 'history-like' clothing for this idea, on the realization of which the whole of history is focussed.

3. For what follows see Gerd Theissen and Annette Merz, *The Historical Jesus*, London: SCM Press and Minneapolis: Fortress Press 1998, especially 9. Jesus as

Prophet: The Eschatology of Jesus, 240–80.

4. The interpretation of the Jesus movement and primitive Christianity as a millenarian movement was made for the first time by S. R. Isenberg, 'Millenarism in Greco-Roman Palestine', *Religion* 4, 1974, 26–46, and John G. Gager, *Kingdom and Community. The Social World of Early Christianity*, Englewood Cliffs, NJ 1975, independently of each other. I shall be publishing an extended critical discussion of this approach as 'Jesus – Prophet einer millenaristischen Bewegung. Sozialgeschichtliche Überlegungen zu einer sozialanthropologischen Deutung der Jesusbewegung', *EvTh* 1999.

5. For a more detailed discussion of the ethic of Jesus see Theissen and Merz, *The Historical Jesus* (n.3), 347–404.

6. Cf. John P. Meier, *A Marginal Jew. Rethinking the Historical Jesus, Vol.1: The Roots of the Problem and the Person*, New York: Doubleday 1991; *Vol.2: Mentor, Message, and Miracles*, New York: Doubleday 1994.

7. While in the period of the so-called 'new quest of the historical Jesus' (from 1953 to around 1980) Jesus was often contrasted with Judaism in order already to find Christianity (and a christology) implicit in him, now there is a growing consensus that he belongs within Judaism. This insight appears both in the 'forefather' of historical-critical research into Jesus, Hermann S. Reimarus, in the eighteenth century (1694–1768), and in the greatest New Testament scholar of the twentieth century, Rudolf Bultmann (1884–1976). E. P. Sanders, *Jesus and Judaism*, London: SCM Press 1985, helped this insight to break through. There is a survey of the discussion in the composite volume edited by James H. Charlesworth, *Jesus' Jewishness. Exploring the Place of Jesus within Early Judaism*, New York: Crossroad Publishing Company 1991. I shall discuss the problem once again in an article 'Jesus und das Judentum' in *Kirche und Israel* 1999.

8. I have substantiated the thesis of a political background to the activity of Jesus which is summed up briefly in what follows in Gerd Theissen, 'Jesus und die symbolpolitischen Konflikte seiner Zeit. Sozialgeschichtliche Aspekte der Jesusforschung', *EvTh* 57, 1997, 378–400.

9. Not all the symbolic actions of Jesus are symbolic political actions. He makes use of them to present his whole message. Cf. Heinz Schürmann, *Die Symbolhandlungen Jesus als eschatologische Erfüllungszeichen. Eine Rückfrage nach dem irdischen Jesus* (1970) = id., *Jesus – Gestalt und Geheimnis*, ed. K. Scholtissek, Paderborn: Bonifatius Verlag 1994, 136–56; Maria Trautmann, *Zeichenhafte Handlungen Jesu. Ein Beitrag zur Frage nach dem geschichtlichen Jesus*, FzB 37, Würzburg: Echter Verlag 1980.

10. We have attempted to describe the very complicated situation in Theissen and Merz, *The Historical Jesus*, 16. The Historical Jesus and the Beginnings of Christology, 512–68.

3. How Did Jesus Come to be Deified? The Transformation of the Jewish Sign System by Post-Easter Belief in Christ

1. In what follows I shall work with a classical theory of social psychology: the theory of cognitive dissonance put forward by Leon Festinger, *A Theory of Cognitive Dissonance*, Stanford CA: Stanford University Press 1957. 'Cognitive dissonance is the concept and general theory used . . . to explain the state of conflict experienced by someone after he has made a decision, performed an action or been exposed to information which stands in contradiction to previous opinions, feelings or values' (Philip L. Zimbardo, *Psychology and Life*, Glenview, Ill.: Scott, Foresman [12]1988). In such a situation one can tone down or eliminate the dissonant elements – or reinforce and add consonant elements. The experience of Jesus' failure on the cross was certainly a 'dissonant' experience for the disciples, which was in conflict with their expectations and convictions – and this dissonance was further heightened by the Easter experiences. The deification of God can therefore be understood as a way to reduce dissonance.

2. There has been a lively discussion of the origin of monotheism. The present consensus is that it did not stand at the beginning of the history of Israel but was the result of a long development involving much conflict, which only broke through and came to be established in the time of the exile with Deutero-Isaiah. For good information on the discussion see Fritz Stolz, *Einführung in den biblischen Monotheismus*, Darmstadt: Wissenschaftliche Buchgesellschaft 1996; Robert K. Gnuse, *No Other Gods*, Sheffield: Sheffield Academic Press 1997, who on pp.92–94 makes positive use of my contribution in *Biblical Faith. An Evolutionary Approach*, London: SCM Press 1985, 45–81.

3. The term 'syncretism' denotes either the exchange of elements between different religious systems or even the fusion of these systems. Cf. e.g. the definition by Kurt Latte, 'Synkretismus', *RGG* V, [2]1931, 952: 'Syncretism denotes the fusion of different religions in the age of Hellenism and the empire, especially the incursion of beliefs from the East into the Graeco-Roman world and the partial Hellenization of them.' Here we can hardly define syncretism without establishing the perspective from which such an exchange takes place: either individuals determine the relationship between religions by their view of religion or their participation in different religions; or the religious systems relate to one another in their practice of religion; or they choose particular elements from their forms of expression with a view to other religions. Andreas Feldtkeller, 'Der Synkretismus – Begriff im Rahmen einer Theorie von Verhältnisbestimmungen zwischen Religionen', *EvTh* 52, 1992, 224–45, distinguishes these four perspectives. A 'competitive syncretism' appears when a religion chooses traditions and means of expression from within itself with which it can outdo other rival religions. It need not take over anything 'alien' directly in order to do this, but only activate something of its 'own' – in such a way that its reactivation is shaped by encounter with the alien element. A simultaneous adoption of alien elements (which are nevertheless experienced as belonging to the religion) can easily be combined with this.

4. In my view the Easter experiences are not produced by cognitive dissonance, but in fact produce cognitive dissonance: they increase the dissonance which already exists. And this dissonance, heightened to an unbearable degree, produces the interpretations of the Easter appearances as the exaltation of a human being to divine dignity; this interpretation is legitimated and made plausible by the tradition (i.e. through the reinterpretation of passages like Ps. 110.1). The fact of the Easter experiences also explains the difference from other prophetic charismatics who left behind a cognitive dissonance among their followers through their failures. The sign prophets came forward with the promise of a future miracle. Each time the Romans intervened. The movements disappeared after the death of the prophet. Their authority was dependent on the promised sign and collapsed when this was not given. By contrast, it is probable that Jesus deliberately refused to give such an authenticating cosmic sign (cf. Mark 8.11–13 par.). He himself was the representative of the rule of God. He himself was 'the sign'. The appearance of his person in visions after death could therefore be experienced as a confirmation of his person.

5. The subjective vision theory has been renewed most recently by Gerd Lüdemann, *The Resurrection of Jesus. History, Experience, Theology*, London: SCM Press 1995. In what follows I have taken ideas from him but without adopting the subjective vision hypothesis, according to which the visions were exclusively products of the psychological processes in the disciples. It completely depends on our construction of reality whether we think it possible that an objective message can also be communicated to people through internal psychological processes. To take an analogy: in my view there can be no doubt about the 'objectivity', i.e. the factual correctness, of some transfer of information after the death of people (of which stories are told above all in time of war), even if we cannot fit them into our scientific constructions of reality. We cannot exclude them. For the dependence of our statements about reality on more comprehensive constructions, specifically in the case of the Easter sayings, cf. Peter Lampe, 'Wissensoziologische Annäherung an das Neue Testament', *NTS* 43, 1997, 347–66, and his forthcoming book *Die Wirklichkeit als Bild: Das Neue Testament als Grunddokument abendländischer Kultur im Lichte konstruktivistischer Epistemologie und Wissenssoziologie*, Neukirchen-Vluyn: Neukirchener Verlag 1999.

6. The Davidic origin of Jesus is attested at a very early stage by Paul (Rom. 1.3), but is disputed elsewhere (John 7.42; perhaps also Mark 12.35–37). We can hardly imagine that a family of Davidic origin would have emphasized this publicly in times when kings and princes from non-Davidic royal houses were ruling over the Jews. That could only cause difficulties. Only when one of their number, Jesus, was believed in as 'messiah' in quite a different way could one perhaps confess that one belonged to this family. However, that is by no means certain.

7. Granted, many New Testament scholars think it impossible to say anything about the psychological dynamics in the biography of Paul. I am not so completely sceptical: Paul could have been in unconscious conflict with the Law in his pre-Christian period. This conflict would be compatible with his assertion that –

as far as he was aware – he was blameless before the law (Phil. 3.6). Cf. Gerd Theissen, *Psychological Aspects of Pauline Theology,* Edinburgh: T. & T. Clark 1987, 228ff.

8. Once again it has to be emphasized that here I am not attempting any psychological derivation of the Easter appearances. The fact that one is investigating psychological aspects of an event does not necessarily mean that one is deriving it from psychological factors. If one is investigating the psychological aspects of the birth of a small child for a family one will accept that child as a reality that transcends all the psychological processes. We can be clear about the limits of a psychological explanation of the Easter appearances by experimentally reversing the beginnings of an explanation given above.

1. The Easter appearances are connected with conflicts with other Christians (as in the case of Paul) or with the family (as in the case of James?) but they can hardly be derived from that. For in the early period of primitive Christianity there will have been many Christians who accepted Christian faith after an initially negative attitude to Christianity (like Paul), or who with their conversion to Christianity redefined their relationship to the family (possibly like James). Nevertheless, none of these people had visions of Christ. In short, the presumed psychological factors continued – but they did not produce any more appearances of Christ.
2. Easter experiences certainly also formed the basis of authority. The battle over authority was a chronic problem of early primitive Christianity. If the Easter appearances had been produced by this social need for recognition, authority and legitimacy, such appearances would have had to have been far more frequent and to have gone on for longer: the presumed sociological factors continued, but they did not produce any more appearances of Christ.

We have presented an extended analysis of the Easter traditions in Gerd Theissen and Annette Merz, *The Historical Jesus*, 474–511.

9. Adolf Deissmann, *Light from the Ancient East*, London: Hodder & Stoughton [3]1927, 342: in primitive Christianity 'a polemical parallelism arises between the cult of the emperor and the cult of Christ'.

10. I have developed the thesis that a controversy with Gaius Caligula and his attempt to have himself worshipped in the temple in Jerusalem instead of the one and only God underlies the temptation on the mountain in Gerd Theissen, *The Gospels in Context. Social and Political History in the Synoptic Tradition,* Edinburgh: T. & T. Clark 1992, 206–21.

11. The conjecture that the Caligula crisis underlies a tradition taken up in Mark 13 has a long tradition. Gustav Hölscher, 'Der Ursprung der Apokalypse Mrk 13', *ThBl* 12, 1933, 193–202, was a lasting influence with his advocacy of it. I have attempted to revive this conjecture with further arguments in *The Gospels in Context* (n.10), 125–65.

12. Cf. Gerd Theissen, 'Auferstehungsbotschaft und Zeitgeschichte. Über einige politische Anspielungen im 1. Kapitel des Römerbriefs', in Sabine Bieberstein and Daniel Kosch (eds), *Auferstehung hat einen Namen. Biblische*

Anstösse zum Christsein heute, FS für Hermann-Josef Venetz, Lucerne: Edition Exodus 1998, 59–68.

13. I have developed this interpretation of the Gospel of Mark further in *The Gospels in Context* (n.10), 258–71.

14. I have given further reasons for this interpretation of the Gospel of Matthew in Gerd Theissen, 'Vom Davidssohn zum Weltherrscher. Pagane und jüdische Endzeiterwartungen im Spiegel des Matthäusevangeliums', in Michael Becker and Wolfgang Fenske (eds), *Das Ende der Tage und die Gegenwart des Heils, FS Heinz W. Kuhn,* Leiden: Brill 1999, 145–64.

15. For the opposition between the image of Christ and the emperor cult in the letter to the Ephesians see Eberhard Faust, *Pax Christi et Pax Caesaris. Religionsgeschichtliche, traditionsgeschichtliche und sozialgeschichtliche Studien zum Epheserbrief,* NTOA 24, Freiburg CH: Universitätsverlag and Göttingen: Vandenhoeck & Ruprecht 1993.

16. Andrew Chester, 'Jewish Messianic Expectations and Mediatorial Figures and Pauline Christology', in Martin Hengel and Ulrich Heckel (eds), *Paulus und das Antike Judentum*, WUNT 58, Tübingen 1991, 17–90, gives an excellent typology and analysis of the mediator figures standing between God and humankind.

17. François Bovon, *Das Evangelium nach Lukas,* EKK III, 1, Zurich: Benziger Verlag and Neukirchen-Vluyn: Neukirchener Verlag 1989, 69.

18. The following remarks on the notion of incarnation are dependent on Dieter Zeller, 'Die Menschwerdung des Sohnes Gottes im Neuen Testament und die antike Religionsgeschichte', in D. Zeller (ed.), *Menschwerdung Gottes – Vergöttlichung von Menschen*, NTOA 7, Freiburg CH: Universitätsverlag and Göttingen: Vandenhoeck & Ruprecht 1988, 141–76.

19. For the following remarks cf. above all Dieter Zeller, 'Die Mysterienkulte und die paulinische Soteriologie (Röm 6, 1–11). Eine Fallstudie zum Synkretismus im Neuen Testament', in Hermann P. Siler (ed.), *Suchbewegungen. Synkretismus – kulturelle Identität und kirchliches Bekenntnis*, Darmstadt: Wissenschaftliche Buchgesellschaft 1991, 42–6.

20. The table of different partner deities reproduced below comes from Dieter Zeller, *Christus unter den Göttern. Zum antiken Umfeld des Christusglaubens,* Stuttgart: Katholisches Bibelwerk 1993, 42. There is more information about the individual cults in Hans-Josef Klauck, *Die religiöse Umwelt des Urchristentums I. Stadt- und Hausreligion, Mysterienkulte, Volksglaube,* Stuttgart, Berlin, Cologne: Kohlhammer 1995, 77–128.

4. The Two Basic Values of the Primitive Christian Ethic: Love of Neighbour and Renunciation of Status

1. German has at its disposal two words, *Ethos* and *Ethik*. *Ethos* denotes a moral which is socially binding, characteristic of a group, a profession, a class or a whole society. That does not mean that this *Ethos* is always practised in the particular society. But it is recognized in it. It is the foundation for the demonstration of

respect and contempt. It is expressed in sentences and in maxims and in a tendency of behaviour. Here of course it must be remembered that alongside the 'official' *Ethos* there are always 'unofficial' subsidiary programmes. By contrast, *Ethik* is theological reflection on moral norms and values – either limited to the critical development of the *Ethos* dominant in a group (in the framework of a hermeneutical ethic), or expressed as a concern to (re)construct the morality from the ground upwards (in the framework of a rational ethic) or a desire to communicate the vision of ethical values (in the framework of a phenomenological ethic). For these three approaches to ethics cf. Michael Walzer, *Interpretation and Social Criticism*, Cambridge, Mass.: Harvard University Press 1987.

2. Wolfgang Schrage, *Ethics of the New Testament*, Philadelphia: Fortress Press and Edinburgh, T. & T. Clark 1988, is a good general account. In the following three chapters I sum up ideas which I want to develop in a book on primitive Christianity and the change in values, on which I have been working for a long time. The programme is contained in 'Jesusbewegung als charismatische Wertrevolution', *NTS* 35, 1989, 343–60; 'Wert und Status des Menschen im Urchristentum', *Humanistische Bildung* 12, 1966, 61–93.

3. From the many discussions of the commandment to love I would single out Michael Ebersohn, *Das Nächstenliebegebot in der synoptischen Tradition*, MThSt, Marburg: Elwert 1993, and Thomas Söding, *Das Liebesgebot bei Paulus. Die Mahnung zur Agape im Rahmen der paulinischen Ethik*, NTA NF 26, Münster: Aschendorff 1991. There is a comprehensive account of all the New Testament evidence in Hubert Meisinger, *Liebesgebot und Altruismusforschung. Ein exegetischer Beitrag zum Dialog zwischen Theologie und Naturwissenschaft*, NTOA 33, Freiburg CH: Universitätsverlag and Göttingen: Vandenhoeck & Ruprecht 1996.

4. Hans Peter Mathys, *Liebe dein Nächsten wie dich selbst. Untersuchungen zum alttestamentlichen Gebot der Nächstenliebe (Lev, 19.18)*, OBO 71, Freiburg CH: Universitätsverlag and Göttingen: Vandenhoeck & Ruprecht 1986, has shown that this tendency to 'delimit' the commandment to love is already present in the Holiness Code, the first formulation of it.

5. Cf. our account of the commandment to love as the centre of the ethic of Jesus in Gerd Theissen and Annette Merz, *The Historical Jesus*, 381–94.

6. The command to love one's enemy and the renunciation of violence were not just the postulate of a utopian society but had their *Sitz im Leben* in the Palestine of the time. Twice we hear from the first half of the first century CE that Jews were successful with non-violent protest and a demonstrative readiness to sacrifice themselves without putting up a defence. This happened in demonstrations first against Pilate's attempt in the 20s to introduce imperial emblems into Jerusalem (*BJ* 2, 169–174; *Antt.* 18, 55–59), and then against the attempt of Gaius Caligula at the end of the 30s to rededicate the temple (Philo, *Leg ad Gaium* 197–337; *BJ*, 2, 184–203; *Antt.* 18, 256–309). Such events are the expression of an existing 'mentality' and at the same time indications of objective 'opportunities' for non-violent resistance – and to this degree there is an indirect connection with Jesus' preaching here. Cf. Gerd Theissen, 'Gewaltverzicht und Feindesliebe (Mt. 5,

38–48/Lk 6, 27–38) und deren sozialgeschichtlicher Hintergrund', in *Studien zur Soziologie des Urchristentums*, WUNT 19, Tübingen: Mohr (Siebeck) [3]1989, 160–97.

7. Here moreover the Samaritan is following an indigenous tradition: it is certainly no coincidence that in the Hellenistic reform of the cult at the beginning of the second century BCE the Samaritans dedicated their temple on Gerizim to Zeus Xenios – the hospitable Zeus who openly welcomes strangers (*Antt.*12, 257–64). Nor is it a coincidence that the hospitality shown by Melchizedek to Abraham was obviously one of the foundation stories behind the Samaritan temple on Gerizim (cf. Pseudo-Eupolemos in Eusebius, *Praep.Ev.* IV 17, 4–6). The Samaritan village which rejects Jesus (Luke 9.51ff.) goes against the Samaritans' own ethos.

8. Today it is generally recognized that Onesimus was not a fugitive slave but came to Paul with a request to be reconciled with his master (cf. Peter Lampe, 'Keine Sklavenflucht des Onesimus', *ZNW* 76, 1985, 135–7; id., 'Der Brief an Philemon', in Nikolaus Walter, Eckart Reinmuth and Peter Lampe, *Die Briefe an die Philipper, Thessalonicher und an Philemon*, NTD 8.2, Göttingen: Vandenhoeck & Ruprecht 1998, 205–32). Nor is the question whether or not Paul is arguing for his release important. For even the freeman, the *libertus*, continued to be dependent on his master. To regard him and treat him as 'brother' was something quite unusual in antiquity, regardless of whether he was bound to his master as a *servus* or a *libertus*.

9. Jörg Augenstein, *Das Liebesgebot im Johannesevangelium und in den Johannesbriefen*, BWANT 134 – Folge 7, Heft 14, Stuttgart, Berlin and Cologne: Kohlhammer 1993, has shown that the commandment to love has an effect on attitudes towards outsiders even in the Johannine writings.

10. This section on the renunciation of status and humility is based on Gudrun Ortwein, *Statusverzicht im Neuen Testament und in seiner Umwelt*, Heidelberg dissertation 1997 (forthcoming in NTOA c.1999).

11. David Seeley, 'Rulership and Service in Mark 10:41–45', *NT* 35, 1993, has thoroughly investigated this humane ideal of kingship. It appears not only in pagan antiquity but also in the sphere of Jewish tradition.

12. Despite the criticism of the conduct of pagan rulers, this criticism recalls a humane ideal of kingship widespread both in early Judaism and in paganism. Cf. Oda Wischmeyer, 'Macht, Herrschaft und Gewalt in den frühjüdischen Schriften', in Joachim Mehlhausen (ed.), *Recht – Macht – Gerechtigkeit*, Gütersloh: Christian Kaiser Verlag 1998, 355–69.

13. Cf. Klaus Wengst, *Humility – The Solidarity of the Humiliated*, London: SCM Press 1988, 54ff.

14. Albert Schweitzer, *The Quest of the Historical Jesus*, London: SCM Press 1981, described the ethic of Jesus as an interim ethic – as an ethic for a state of emergency in the short time before the end of the world.

5. Dealing with Power and Possessions in Primitive Christianity. The Ethical Demands in the Light of the Two Basic Values: I

1. Amitai Etzioni, *The Active Society: A Theory of Societal and Political Processes*, London: Macmillan 1968.

2. For an example of a conflict theory of society see Lewis A. Coser, *The Function of Social Conflict,* New York: Free Press 1964. For an example of an integration theory see Talcott Parsons, *Theory of Social Action*, London and New York: McGraw-Hill 1937.

3. For what follows see Gerd Theissen, 'The Ambivalence of Power in Early Christianity', in Cynthia L. Rigby (ed.), *Power, Powerlessness, and the Divine. New Inquiries in Bible and Theology*, Atlanta: Scholars Press 1997, 21–36. It should be emphasized once again that the separation of state and church, of the political and the religious system, is a development characteristic of European history. The beginning of this development lies in ancient Judaism and primitive Christianity.

4. Cf. Christoph Elsas, 'Herrscherkult', *HRWG* III, 1993, 115–22. The ruler cult must not be understood as a naïve transgression of the frontier between human beings and the deity. 1. In Greece the beginnings of the ruler cult do not relate to the person of the ruler but to his benefactions for a city, on which its existence depended. 2. The veneration of many rulers was often first that of the dead rulers who had entered the world of the gods, thus in the Old Kingdom in Egypt, in China, and in Rome itself (cf. Elsas, 116, 119). 3. The veneration was of the ruler only in association with a representative of power distinct from him: his 'living image on earth' in the New Kingdom in Egypt, or his image in association with the goddess Roma. Cf. further Antonie Wlosok (ed.), *Römischer Kaiserkult*, WdF 372, Darmstadt: Wissenschaftliche Buchgesellschaft 1978.

5. I have developed these ideas in Gerd Theissen, 'Gruppenmessianismus. Überlegungen zum Ursprung der Kirche im Jüngerkreis Jesu', *JBTh* 7, 1992, 101–23. The observation that the share of the disciples in rule is a continuation of the traditional idea of the participation of the righteous in the judgment is no objection: the decisive point is that this is participation in the rule of the messiah, as is clearly expressed in Rev. 2.26f.; 3.21 and 20.6.

6. Cf. already Hans Windisch, 'Friedensbringer – Gottessöhne. Eine religionsgeschichtliche Interpretation der 7. Seligpreisung', *ZNW* 24, 1925, 240–60; Gerd Theissen, 'Pax Romana et Pax Christi. Le christianisme primitif et l'idée de la paix', *RThPh* 124, 1992, 61–84.

7. Thus rightly Luise Schottroff, 'Gewaltverzicht und Feindesliebe in der urchristlichen Jesustradition, Mt 5, 38–48/Lk 6, 27–36', in Georg Strecker (ed.), *Jesus in Historie und Theologie, FS H. Conzelmann*, Tübingen: Mohr (Siebeck) 1975, 197–221. For the ancient idea of the *clementia* of the ruler cf. Traute Adam, *Clementia Principis*, KiHiSt 11, Stuttgart: Klett 1970.

8. Cf. Hans Kloft, *Liberalitas Principis*, Cologne and Vienna: Böhlau 1970; Paul Veyne, *Le Pain et le cirque. Sociologie historique d'un pluralisme politique*, Paris: Editions du Seuil 1976.

9. Hendrik Bolkestein, *Wohltätigkeit und Armenpflege im vorchristlichen Altertum. Ein Beitrag zum Problem 'Moral und Gesellschaft'*, Groningen: Bouma's Boekhuis 1967 (reprint of the Utrecht 1939 edition).

10. For the rooting of love of neighbour in the morality of little people cf. Veyne, *Le Pain et le cirque* (n.8). There he does not write without a critical undertone, since he has erroneously attributed John the Baptist's preaching about different classes in Luke 3.10–14 to Jesus himself: 'This was an "irresponsible ethic" . . . because it was created by a man for people who did not have to bear any shared responsibility. All that remains for them is to convince one another that it is to the advantage of all of them to tone down and mitigate an order and laws of which they are not the author, either in fact or by consent. This popular morality does not develop any abstract principles. It is expressed in maxims and typical examples. To love one's neighbour as oneself is no longer the nationalistic solidarity of the old warlike Israel but the solidarity of the weak. So too is to turn the other cheek instead of appealing to the law of an eye for eye when a brother is in need. One is not to exercise one's rights to the utmost, for even if one is in the right, one must go some way to meeting one's opponent. What gain could a poor man have here if he presented his case to the powerful?'. 'The popular morality of mutual help and almsgiving became a sectarian morality.' 'The sectarian solidarity goes back to Jesus himself; the Gospel of John sketches a lifelike, passionate and completely unconventional picture of Jesus.' The reference to the Gospel of John in an attempt to depict the ethics of the historical Jesus as sectarian is certainly a perversion of the historical facts. But Veyne has seen a grain of truth: the morality of loving one's neighbour and giving help is a morality of small people. However, it should be added that in primitive Christianity this popular morality 'from below' is steeped in a morality of rule 'from above', in which little people labour to act in a way analogous to kings and princes.

11. Cf. Gerd Theissen, '"Geben ist seliger als nehmen" (Apg 20, 35). Zur Demokratisierung antiker Wohltätermentalität im Urchristentum', in Andrea Boluminski (ed.), *Kirche, Recht und Wissenschaft, FS Albert Stein*, Neuwied: Luchterhand 1995, 195–215.

12. Quoted from Eberhard Otto, *Die biographischen Inschriften der ägyptischen Spätzeit. Ihre geistesgeschichtliche und literarische Bedeutung*, Leiden: Brill 1954, 222. For the disputed exegesis of the pericope cf. Gerd Theissen, 'Die Rede vom grossen Weltgericht (Mt 25, 31–46). Universales Hilfsethos gegenüber allen Menschen?', in Arnd Götzelmann, Volker Steinmann and Jürgen Stein (eds), *Diakonie der Versöhnung. Ethische Reflexion und soziale Arbeit in ökumenischer Verantwortung, FS Theodor Strohm*, Stuttgart: Quell Verlag 1998. In my view, the Jewish tradition contained in Matt. 25.31ff. originally posed the question how the Gentiles would fare in the last judgment – and gave all Gentiles a chance if they had helped Israelites (the brothers of the messianic king according to Deut. 17.5). The tendency of this tradition (originally particularly tied to Israel) would then have been universalistic. Matthew himself would have reinforced it further by

bringing not only the 'Gentiles' but 'all peoples' to judgment and measuring them by what they had done to 'the least'. Behind this may stand experiences with itinerant Christian charismatics, but all sufferers are meant: Matthew does not repeat the term 'brother' from the phrase 'the least of my brothers' (25.40), which might have suggested a limitation to Christian missionaries, but repeats the term 'the least' (25.45). In them people have helped the messiah unaware. Being confronted with a deity in the stranger without knowing it is a widespread motif from antiquity (cf. just the entertaining of angels unaware in Heb. 13.2). This can hardly be relativized as a literary motif in order to emphasize the amazement of the righteous at their own actions. I am aware that distinguished exegetes of Matthew interpret 25.31ff. differently.

13. M. Hengel, *Property and Riches in the Early Church*, London: SCM Press 1974, esp. 60–73, 'The Compromise of Effective Compensation'.

14. The idea of the primitive Christian sharing of possessions is also to be mentioned here: it was probably always only a dream of the first Christians, but it is possible that it was already dreamed of (i.e. already used as a slogan) in the primitive community in Jerusalem. I have attempted to show this in Gerd Theissen, 'Urchristlicher Liebeskommunismus. Zum "Sitz im Leben" des Topos ἅπαντα κοινά in Apg 2, 44 und 4, 32', in Tornd Fornberg and David Hellholm (eds), *Texts and Contexts. Biblical Texts in Their Textual and Situational Contexts, FS Lars Hartman*, Oslo and Copenhagen: Scandinavian University Press 1995, 689–711. The criticism of Friedrich W. Horn, 'Die Gütergemeinschaft der Urgemeinde', *EvTh* 58, 1998, 370–83, has not convinced me completely. I would cite the vocabulary of the summaries as one indication (among others) that here Luke is handing on a tradition – not that this tradition is historical. That certainly cannot be proved with statistics of vocabulary. So it is not so remarkable that the reform idea of sharing possessions (localized in Jerusalem and in my view a failure) has left no traces on Mark, Matthew, Q and John. The dispute over circumcision which we can locate in Jerusalem did not leave any traces there either – although unlike the sharing of possessions it had lasting consequences. Nor do we find an echo of the Easter appearance to James (cf. I Cor. 15.7), although this Easter appearance was of great importance for the history of the Jerusalem community.

15. Louis W. Countryman, *The Rich Christian in the Church of the Early Empire. Contradictions and Accommodations*, New York and Toronto: Edward Mellen Press 1980.

16. Thus Oda Wischmeyer, 'Matthäus 6, 25–34 par. Die Spruchreihe vom Sorgen', *ZNW* 85, 1994, 1–22: the series of sayings relates to all men and women – both to disciples and to those who remain living where they are. Perhaps a distinction will help: the *Sitz im Leben* is rather different from the intended audience and this in turn is rather different from the audience that is actually addressed. I would want to keep itinerant radicalism as the *Sitz im Leben*. The freedom from care of which Matt. 6.25ff. speaks is stamped by the experiences of itinerant charismatics – namely by Jesus and his circle of disciples. There is no disputing the fact that this freedom from care is commended to all – and all men and women are

particularly meant in the two generalizing remarks in 6.27 and 6.34. But there is no contradiction between a radical way of life and a universal ethic: the itinerant Cynic philosophers embodied universal values in their marginal and radical lifestyle which were also shared by sedentary people in their culture: striving for autonomy and autarky, independence from what was only a matter of convention – in favour of what was true on the basis of the natural order.

17. I have defined the *Sitz im Leben* of the radical ethic of the Synoptic tradition as itinerant radicalism in Gerd Theissen, 'The Wandering Radicals. Light Shed by the Sociology of Literature on the Early Transmission of Jesus Sayings, Social Reality and the Early Christians', in *Theology, Ethics and the World of the New Testament*, Minneapolis: Fortress Press 1992, 33–59. The deradicalizing of sayings of Jesus in the Pauline writings is the topic of a plan which I hope to carry out with Kun Chung Wong of Hong Kong.

18. Cf. Gerd Theissen, 'Mythos und Wertrevolution im Urchristentum', in Dieter Harth and Jan Assmann (eds), *Revolution und Mythos*, Frankfurt: Fischer Verlag 1992, 62–81.

6. Dealing with Wisdom and Holiness in Primitive Christianity. Ethical Demands in the Light of the Two Basic Values: II

1. Plato, *Republic* V, 473d: 'If not, I said, either the philosophers will become kings in the states, or those who are now called kings and authorities will truly and thoroughly philosophize, and thus the authority of the state and philosophy will coincide . . . otherwise the states will make no recovery from the evil . . .'

2. Philo, *Life of Moses* II, 2f.

3. On the following section, for a comprehensive account of wisdom traditions see Max Küchler, *Frühjüdische Weisheitstraditionen*, OBO 26, Freiburg CH: Universitätsverlag and Göttingen: Vandenhoeck & Ruprecht 1979; Hermann von Lips, *Weisheitliche Traditionen im Neuen Testament*, WMANT 64, Neukirchen-Vluyn: Neukirchener Verlag 1990. For the thesis of the following section in particular see Gerd Theissen, 'Weisheit als Mittel sozialer Abgrenzung und Öffnung. Beobachtungen zur sozialen Funktion frühjüdischer und urchristlicher Weisheit', in Aleida Assmann (ed.), *Weisheit. Archäologie der literarischen Kommunikation* III, Munich: Fink 1991, 193–204.

4. For the double logion with man/woman perspectives cf. Martin Ebner, *Jesus – ein Weisheitslehrer? Synoptische Weisheitslogien im Traditionsprozess,* HBSt 15, Freiburg, Basel and Vienna: Herder 1998; Gerd Theissen, *Frauen im Umkreis Jesu, Sexauer Gemeindepreis für Theologie 1993,* Sexau 1993.

5. Michael Wolters, 'Verborgene Weisheit und Heil der Heiden. Zur Traditionsgeschichte und Intention des "Revelationsschemas"', *ZThK* 84, 1987, 297–319.

6. For the wisdom motifs in the Gospel of John cf. Martin Scott, *Sophia and Johannine Jesus*, JSNT.S 71, Sheffield: JSOT Press 1992. For the ongoing motive of the 'wisdom meal' cf. Karl-Gustav Sandelin, *Wisdom as Nourisher: A Study of an*

Old Testament Theme, its Development within Early Judaism and its Impact on Early Christianity, AAAbo 64, 3, Aabo Akademi 1986.

7. For the categories of 'holiness' and 'cleanness' cf. David P. Wright, 'Holiness (OT)', *ABD* III, 237–49; id., 'Unclean and Clean (OT)', *ABD* VI, 728–41; Robert Hodgson Jr, 'Holiness (NT)', *ABD* III, 249–54; Hans Hübner, 'Unclean and Clean (NT)', *ABD* VI, 741–5.

8. Other interpretations of the four women in Matthew's genealogy are possible: 1. There is the idea of the irregularity of divine action, which takes extraordinary courses. That also applies to the interpretation considered above. 2. The thought is of women who are sinners. That would apply only to Ruth. Gentile women are also to make clear the Messiah's claim on Gentiles. But no connection to Mary can be made here. For the different interpretations see Ulrich Luz, *Das Evangelium nach Matthäus*, EKK I, 1, Zurich: Benziger Verlag and Neukirchen-Vluyn: Neukirchener Verlag 1985, 93f.

9. There is good evidence, both literary and archaeological, for the prohibition against Gentiles entering the inner precincts of the temple. The warning inscriptions are mentioned directly in Josephus, *Antt.*15, 417; *BJ* 5, 194; 6, 124–126. Two examples have been found. Cf. also Philo, *LegGai.* 212; Acts 21.27f.; *Antt.*2, 102–104; *BJ* 2, 341; 5, 402.

7. The Origin of the Primitive Christian Sacraments from Symbolic Actions

1. Cf. Bernhard Lang, 'Ritual/Ritus', *HRWG* IV, 1998, 442–58: '"Ritual" is a covering term for religious actions which are performed in the same way on particular occasions, the course of which is fixed by tradition or precept, and which may consist of gestures, words and the use of objects' (442f.).

2. Because of this function of warding off anxiety, Sigmund Freud, 'Obsessive Actions and Religious Practices', in *Origins of Religion*, Penguin Freud Library 13, Harmondsworth: Penguin Books 1985, 27–42, has compared obsessive actions with religious rituals, but by no means takes a negative view of religious rituals in his treatment of them. They are not based on the repression of unconscious drives but on a deliberate renunciation of drives which are harmful to social survival. He makes only passing reference to neurotic religious rituals like some penitential actions.

3. Cf. Victor Turner, *The Ritual Process. Structure and Anti-Structure*, Chicago: Aldine Press 1969. His theory of ritual is reported in Rolf Gehlen, 'Liminalität', *HRWG* IV, 1998, 58–63. There is a fruitful application to the New Testament in Christian Strecker, *Transformation, Liminalität und Communitas bei Paulus. Kulturanthropologische Zugänge zur paulinischen Theologie*, Neuendettelsau dissertation 1995 (forthcoming in FRLANT c. 1999/2000).

4. For the following chapter I would refer, for the eucharist to Gerd Theissen and Annette Metz, *The Historical Jesus*, 405–39; for baptism to Gerd Theissen, *Die urchristliche Taufe und die soziale Konstruktion des neuen Menschen*, forthcoming Leiden: Brill 1999, 87–114; Petra von Gemünden, *Die urchristliche Taufe und der*

Umgang mit den Affekten, Leiden: Brill 1999, 115ff.

5. Cf. the definition of sacrifice in Hubert Seiwert, 'Opfer', *HRWG* IV, 1998, 268–84: sacrifice is 'a religious action which consists in the ritual disposal of a material object' (269). This disposal is the common denominator of all kinds of sacrifice – and in it lies the possibility of emphasizing the connection or the distancing created by the disposal of an object. Here there is either a connection with the gods, or this retreats into the background in favour of a connection with other human beings. For important suggestions I am indebted to Sigrid Brandt, *Opfer als Gedächtnis. Zur Kritik und Neukonturierung theologischer Rede von Opfer*, Habilitation dissertation, Heidelberg 1997.

6. Some theories of sacrifice presuppose a 'primal scene' for all kinds of sacrifice; others postulate different primal scenes for different types of sacrifice. Thus Walter Burkert, 'Opfertypen und antike Gesellschaftsstruktur', in Gunther Stephenson (ed.), *Der Religionswandel unserer Zeit im Spiegel der Religionswissenschaft,* Darmstadt: Wissenschaftliche Buchgesellschaft 1976, 168–86.

7. The thesis of the origin of baptism and the eucharist in prophetic symbolic actions has been convincingly been put forward by Morna D. Hooker, *The Signs of a Prophet. The Prophetic Actions of Jesus*, London: SCM Press and Harrisburg, Penn.: Trinity Press International 1997.

8. Later, despite the exclusive association of baptism with John the Baptist, there seems to have been a resumption of baptism – also among John's followers, cf. Acts 19.1–7. However, we could also understand this passage to mean that the disciples of John the Baptist had once been baptized by him. But their location in Ephesus tells against this possibility. So there also seems to have been a resumption of baptism among the followers of John the Baptist in parallel to the resumption of the practice of baptism in post-Easter Christianity.

9. In my view an opposition between baptism and the temple cult can also be read out of the controversy saying about the authority of Jesus at the 'cleansing of the temple' (Mark 11.27–33): by recognizing baptism (not primarily John as a person), the opponents of Jesus would be conceding that the temple was no longer completely fulfilling its function.

10. We have developed such an interpretation of Jesus' 'last supper' as opposition and an alternative to the temple cult in Gerd Theissen and Annette Merz, *The Historical Jesus*, 431–6.

11. For this see Burkhard Gladigow, 'Ritual, komplexes', *HRWG* IV, 1998, 458–60. The increasing complexity of rites is closely associated with the professionalizing of religion: it is practised by specialists in religion – and in turn it legitimates these specialists, because only they know how to perform a rite properly. However, associated with this as an independent motif is an aesthetic delight in the shaping of the cult. By contrast, a reduction of rites to basics is often associated with inner-religious reform and protest movements – e.g. with the Reformation.

12. There is still an argument over how far in his interpretation in Rom. 6 of baptism in terms of the death of Jesus Paul is taking over the language of the

mystery religions. There is no disputing the fact that an experience of death is often symbolized in the initiation into the mysteries, but this experience of death: 1. need not be understood as an imitation of the death of a mystery deity by one's own dying; often the initiates mourn the death of the deity without themselves experiencing this death in an imitative way. And 2. Such an experience of death staged in a symbolic way is not a washing. Where there is a washing, as in the Isis initiation ceremonies, it is only a preparatory act – several days before the initiation proper (cf. Apuleius, *Metamorphoses* XI 23, 1). Derivation from Jewish proselyte theology, which has often been cited as an alternative to derivation from the mystery religions, is not sufficient in itself as an alternative explanation: Asenath indeed knows that through her conversion to Judaism she has been recreated from death to life (*Joseph and Asenath* 8.10; 15.5), but being recreated from a previous permanent state of death is rather different from experiencing a dying through which one attains to a new life. The Christians certainly developed their interpretation of baptism with means of their own, but without pagan analogies it is hard to see how they reinforced elements which interpret baptism as an experience of death. The Isis initiation ceremony is celebrated 'in the image of a voluntary death and a redemption by grace' (*ipsamque traditionem ad instar voluntariae mortis et precariae salutis clebrari*)(*Metamorphoses* XI 21, 7).

13. There are good arguments against the thesis of the depiction of the death of Jesus in baptism in Eduard Stommel, '"Begraben mit Christus" (Röm 6, 4) und der Taufritus', *RQ* 49, 1954, 1–20; id., 'Christliche Taufriten und antike Badesitten', *JAC* 2, 1959, 5–14. Of course the archaeological remains (fonts and depictions) are all of a later date. But it would be difficult to imagine that had there been an original full baptism (with the immersion of the whole body), no influence of the earlier form of baptism would have been preserved in such remains. If baptism with water and with the spirit are parallel, the outpouring of the Holy Spirit must have corresponded to a 'pouring' with water.

14. Red wine was drunk in Palestine. This is indicated by the metaphor of the 'blood of the grape' (Gen. 49.11; Deut. 32.14; Sir. 39.26; 50.15). In Isa. 63.2; Rev. 14.19f., red is presupposed as the colour of wine. But since in antiquity it was also possible to speak of barley wine (Herodotus 2, 77) and palm wine (Herodotus 1, 193; 2, 86), a differentiation by the colour red would be conceivable in principle – if importance were attached to that colour.

15. We know the charge of cannibalism or the 'Thyestian' banquet from the defence made by the Apologists. Cf. Tertullian, *Apology* 7–8; Athenagoras, *Supplication* 3, 35; Justin, *Apology* I, 6. Porphyry, frag. 69 on John 6.53ff. is particularly interesting: he understands the eucharistic words in John 6, 'Unless you eat my flesh and drink my blood, you have no life in you', in a metaphorical sense, but nevertheless maintains his charge that it is worse than the story of the Thyestian banquet: Thyestes has his own children set before him as a meal by his brother Atreus. Thyestes thereupon curses Atreus.

8. The Sacrificial Interpretation of the Death of Jesus and the End of Sacrifice

1. For the criticism of sacrifice cf. Peter Gerlitz, 'Opfer I', *TRE* 25, 1995, 253–8, esp.257. He argues that we find three motives for criticism of sacrifice. 1. On the basis of the *doctrine of reincarnation*, animals are regarded as possible incarnations of former human beings. Empedocles rages over the way in which human beings feed on their own kind in the meat of sacrifices (frag.137, Diels Kranz). Buddhism rejects sacrifice for the same reason. 2. The notion of *righteousness* stands behind the prophetic criticism of sacrifice. The prophets vigorously state that immorality is incompatible with the sacrificial cult (Amos 5.21–24; Micah 6.6–8; Hos. 6.6; Isa. 1.11–17). Sacrifice would be allowed were behaviour ethical. We also find this criticism of sacrifice in Islam: 'Neither your flesh nor your blood attains to God, but your fear of God' (Surah 22.37). 3. *Creation faith* can in principle be played off against all sacrifices. Human beings cannot give God anything that they have not received. Such a fundamental criticism of sacrifice appears in Ps. 50.8–15, 23. Thanksgiving is the only sacrifice that human beings can give to God (cf. Ps. 40.4–9; 51.18f.; 69.31f.). The social criticism of the prophets is absent here.

2. The Essenes did not reject sacrifice in principle. Because of their deviant calendar and their rejection of the high priests in office they regarded the sacrifice practised at the temple as largely invalid. They could practise ritual slaughterings which were not associated with the temple and the cultic calendar, e.g. the passover and the burning of the red heifer. There is good evidence for their fundamental identification with the temple. They made dedicated offerings for the building and paid the temple tax. Cf. Hartmut Stegemann, *Die Essener, Qumran, Johannes der Täufer und Jesus*, Herder Spektrum 4128, Freiburg, Basel and Vienna: Herder 1993, 242–5.

3. The Samaritans lost their sanctuary in AD 128. It is hard to imagine that they could have continued to sacrifice on the site of their destroyed temple in the period of Hasmonaean rule. But in any case, they temporarily stopped sacrifice under compulsion. In fact the Pentateuch, which was authoritative for them, prescribed sacrifice. At the end of Hasmonaean rule they could have revived their cultic traditions. According to Shemarjahu Talmon, 'Die Samaritaner in Vergangenheit und Gegenwart', in Reinhard Pummer (ed.), *Die Samaritaner*, WdF 604, Darmstadt: Wissenschaftliche Buchgesellschaft 1992, 379–92: 387, they continued animal sacrifice and restricted this to the passover lamb only in the nineteenth century.

4. This hope is expressed in Mark 11.17 with the help of Isa. 56.7: the temple is to become a house of prayer for all Gentiles. The insinuation in Acts 21.28 that Paul brought a Gentile, Trophimus, into the temple may have been objectively false. But shortly beforehand the same Paul had written in Romans that he understood his mission as priestly service to God, to offer the Gentiles as a sacrifice (Rom. 15.16). Where else was he to offer them than in the temple? Whether or not it is historical, the charge of 'smuggling' Gentiles into the temple in Acts 21.28 could only be made against Christians (in reality, or in reports about them) because

they were known for believing that the thronging of all Gentiles to Zion was already taking place. Stephen may already have been motivated by this hope. He was accused of preaching that Jesus would (in the future!) change the customs of Moses (Acts 6.14). Perhaps with the imminent parousia he expected that the temple would be opened to all Gentiles -and thus the Torah would be abrogated on this one point.

5. If with a minority of exegetes we date Hebrews before 70, an internal independence of Christianity from the temple cult and sacrifice would already have been advocated before the real destruction of the temple. But this would not alter the thesis in principle. Composition after 70 is suggested: 1. By the fact that the letter (in 13.18–25) seeks to indicate Pauline authorship, without directly stating it in the prescript, which is absent. Since it seeks to be regarded as Pauline, all remarks about the temple must be made as if the temple were still there. 2. God declares the old covenant obsolete and near to disappearing (8.13); similarly the reference to the first tabernacle, which is a parable of the present, but disappears with the time of a better ordinance (9.8–10). Is not the destruction of the temple interpreted here as an indication of the imminent end, as a symbol of the world which is now passing away?

6. A fragment has been preserved of a writing by the Neopythagorean Apollonius of Tyana (in Eusebius, *Praeparatio Evangelii 4, 13; Demonstratio Evangelii* III 3, 11). Here he distinguishes a supreme God from the other gods. One may relate to this supreme God only through the Logos, and not through animals and plants, which are tainted with uncleanness. But one may sacrifice to the other gods. This too is no fundamental criticism of sacrifice.

7. Cf. Helmut Mödritzer, *Stigma und Charisma im Neuen Testament und seiner Umwelt. Zur Soziologie des Urchristentums*, NTOA 28, Freiburg CH: Universitätsverlag and Göttingen: Vandenhoeck & Ruprecht 1994, 95–167. He distinguishes between an ascetic self-stigmatizing in the preaching of Jesus which shows itself in a lack of possessions, home and protection; a provocative self-stigmatization, which shows itself in his understanding of cleanness and his action in the temple; and a forensic self-stigmatization, which shows itself in his deliberate risking of martyrdom.

8. There is a good survey in Gerhard Barth, *Der Tod Jesu Christi im Verständnis des Neuen Testaments*, Neukirchen-Vluyn: Neukirchener Verlag 1992. Cf. also Marie-Louise Gubler, *Die frühesten Deutungen des Todes Jesus. Eine motivgeschichtliche Darstellung aufgrund der neueren exegetischen Forschung*, OBO 15, Freiburg CH: Universitätsverlag and Göttingen: Vandenhoeck & Ruprecht 1977.

9. Odil Hannes Steck, *Israel und das gewaltsame Geschick der Propheten*, WMANT 23, Neukirchen-Vluyn: Neukirchener Verlag 1967, has shown that here Jesus is interpreted in accordance with the Deuteronomic tradition that Israel rejected its prophets and killed them violently.

10. Lothar Ruppert, *Jesus als der leidende Gerechte?*, SBS 59, Stuttgart: Katholisches Bibelwerk 1972.

11. The atoning significance of the death of Jesus has been made the centre of

the New Testament above all by the new 'Tübingen theology'. Here I shall mention only Martin Hengel, 'Der stellvertretende Sühnetod Jesu. Ein Beitrag zur Entstehung des urchristlichen Kerygmas', *IkaZ* 9, 1980, 1–25, 135–47; id., *The Atonement. A Study of the Origins of the Doctrine in the New Testament*, London: SCM Press 1981. Romans 3.25 is often interpreted here as a reference back to Lev. 16: Good Friday is a cosmic day of atonement.

12. With Werner Elert, 'Redemptio ab hostibus', *ThLZ* 72, 1947, 265–70, we should probably think of the ransoming of prisoners of war. This interpretation is more probable than that put forward by Adolf Deissmann, *Light from the Ancient East*, London: Hodder & Stoughton [2]1927, 320ff., who interprets the notion of ransom in terms of the ancient rite of freeing slaves in Delphi, in which a God appeared as the fictitious redeemer, since the slave himself had no rights and could not appear as a partner in the transaction.

13. In so far as the notion of reconciliation is associated with the death of Jesus, here we have a political metaphor: the reconciliation between parties in a conflict. Thus especially in II Cor. 5.18–20. Cf. Cilliers Breytenbach, *Versöhnung. Eine Studie zur paulinischen Soteriologie*, WMANT 60, Neukirchen-Vluyn: Neukirchener Verlag 1989.

14. Whereas Paul summarizes his doctrine of justification more in abstract reflective language in 3.21–31, in Rom. 4.1–25 he cites the example of Abraham as scriptural proof for the justification of the sinner. Between abstract thesis and vivid narrative scriptural proof, the weight shifts from the atoning death to the resurrection. In the abstract thesis only the atoning death of Christ is mentioned as the basis of salvation (Rom. 3.25). But with Abraham the basis of justification is exclusively belief in the fulfilment of the promise – namely, belief in the possibility of new life despite his dead body (i.e. a body which is no longer capable of procreation). His readiness to deliver Isaac over to death (Gen. 22.11ff.) plays no part at all. Then Paul combines both death and resurrection in the concluding summary (Rom. 4.25). In retrospect one can conjecture that Paul is already thinking of the resurrection in Rom. 3.24ff. Twice he interprets 'redemption through Christ' as a 'demonstration' of the righteousness of God: once as forgiveness of sins in the past and then as a demonstration of God's righteousness in the present. In the first 'demonstration of righteousness' Paul is certainly thinking of the death of Christ. So could he have been thinking of the resurrection in the second 'demonstration of righteousness'? Compare the formulations in Rom. 3.25f. and Rom. 4.25:

(Redemption through the death of Jesus took place):	(God raises Jesus from the dead)
1. to show God's righteousness, because in his divine forbearance he had passed over former sins (ἁμαρτήματα),	who was put to death for our transgressions (παραπτώματα)
2. it was to prove at the present time that he himself is righteous and to make	2. and raised

righteous (δικαιοῦν) him who has faith in Jesus.	for our justification (δικαίωσις).

15. Georg Fitzer, 'Der Ort der Versöhnung nach Paulus', *ThZ* 22, 1966, 161–83: 179. In the sacrificial cult the sacrificed animals remain dead. Therefore it follows for him that '. . . the resurrection has nothing to look for in the view of sacrifice. . . the whole notion of sacrifice becomes a farce if the victim rises again'.

16. The following remarks are based on Hartmut Gese, 'Die Sühne', in id., *Zur biblischen Theologie. Alttestamentliche Vorträge*, BEVTh 78, Munich: Christian Kaiser Verlag 1977. According to Gese, atonement is based on the representation by the sacrificial animal of the existence of the human being offering the sacrifice. Here atonement is not brought about by the killing but by two ritual acts bound up with the sacrifice, the laying on of hands and the blood rite. The laying on of hands shows that the sacrificial animal is dying in place of the human being. The application of the blood to the altar shows that the life which is destroyed is reunited with God, the Lord of life. An incorporation into the holy takes place.

17. Hendrik S. Versnel, 'Quid Athenis et Hierosolymis? Bemerkungen über die Herkunft von Aspekten des "Effective Death"', in Jan W. van Henten (ed.), *Die Entstehung der jüdischen Martyrologie*, StPB 38, Leiden: Brill 1989, 162–96.

18. Alcestis is the great exception which proves the rule. She is the only one who is prepared, for the sake of her husband Admetus, to undergo the death that threatens him because he has failed to perform a sacrifice. According to one version (Euripides, *Alcestis*), Heracles snatches her from Thanatos; according to the other (Plato, *Symposium* 179b-d), Persephone sends her back to earth because she is so moved by Alcestis' love for her husband.

19. Cf. Josef Drexler, *Die Illusion des Opfers. Ein wissenschaftlicher Überblick über die wichtigsten Opfertheorien ausgehend vom deleuzianischen Polyperspektivenmodell*, Münchener Ethnologische Abhandlungen 12, Munich: Akademischer Verlag 1993.

20. Cf. the account in Drexler, *Die Illusion des Opfers* (n.20); Hubert Seiwert, 'Opfer', *HRWG* IV, 1998, 271f.

21. Gerhardus van der Leeuw, 'Die do-ut-des-Formel in der Opfertheorie', *ARW* 20, 1920/1, 241–53; cf the account in Seiwert, 'Opfer' (n.21), 273. The special feature of this approach is the assumption of a neutral life-force which is set in motion by the sacrifice – and in a cycle reinforces the power both of God and the one offering the sacrifice; however, the decisive factor is the fluid character of this force.

22. Cf. the account in Drexler, *Die Illusion des Opfers* (n.20), 47f.; Seiwert, 'Opfer' (n.21), 272f. This explanation itself takes up different aspects. However, the characteristic feature is the interpretation of the sacrifice as the restoration of a contact between the world of the holy and the profane world. The act of killing brings about a release of energy which comes both to the world of the holy and to the persons involved.

23. W. Robertson Smith developed his theory of sacrifice only for Semitic reli-

gion, but it contains some elements which apply to all religions. Seiwert, 'Opfer' (n.21), 272, rightly emphasizes the abiding fertility of the notion of communion. The sacrifice establishes fellowship between human beings and between them and the deity. Cf. further the account in Drexler, *Die Illusion des Opfers* (n.20), 25f.

24. Sigmund Freud, 'Totem and Taboo', in *Origins of Religion*, Penguin Freud Library 13, Harmondsworth: Penguin Books 1985, 43–224.

25. René Girard, *Violence and the Sacred*, London: Athlone Press 1988; id., *The Scapegoat*, London: Athlone Press 1986.

26. Walter Burkert, *Homo Necans. Interpretationen altgriechischer Opferriten und Mythen*, RVV 32, Berlin and New York: de Gruyter 1972; id., *Wilder Ursprung. Opferritual und Mythos bei den Griechen*, Kleine Kulturwissenschaftliche Bibliothek 22, Berlin: Klaus Wagenbach 1990.

27. Seiwert, 'Opfer' (n.21), 280, distinguishes between two 'basic intentions' of sacrifice: 'associating and distancing'. Here these two basic intentions diverge: in the atoning sacrifice the distancing from sin becomes so clear that connection between human beings cannot be brought about by the shared consumption of the sacrificial matter which expresses the distancing from sin.

9. Primitive Christian Religion Becomes Independent of Judaism and Develops an Autonomous Sign World

1. This transformation of the messianic expectation was reinforced by the experience of the crucifixion of Jesus. The Emmaus pericope shows that the disciples expected an earthly redeemer of Israel (Luke 24.21). They had to learn as a completely new idea after Easter that the Messiah has to suffer – and thus contradicts earthly expectations of a ruler (Luke 24.26). Whereas already before Easter the term messiah has been applied to Jesus, soon after Easter he is venerated as son of God: already in the earliest letter of Paul (I Thess. 1.10) and in the Logia source (QLuke 4.3, 9; cf.10.22). The understandable hesitations about this term in Judaism are quickly overcome – probably in connection with the opening up of Christianity to Gentiles: in the Gospel of Mark it is still a Gentile who (alongside the demons) for the first time acknowledges Jesus as 'son of God' (Mark 15.39). The title Kyrios was added to the term son of God at a very early stage: it makes it possible to transfer statements about God to the exalted one (e.g. in the Philippians hymn; cf. Phil. 2.10 = Isa. 42.53 LXX).

2. Acts 10.1–48 still indicates that it was only after Easter that the fundamental relativization of cleanness and uncleanness had practical consequences. A revelation is necessary to do away with the distinction between unclean and clean food and to persuade Peter to eat unclean food.

3. The agreements at the Apostolic Council could contain a 'concealed conflict': Paul's partners in the agreement thought that the Gentile Christians could be accepted without circumcision as a preliminary stage to true Christianity – by analogy with the godfearers. Perhaps they expected that the eschatological miracle of a complete conversion to Judaism (with the acceptance of circumcision) would

also take place among them. That one does not compel Gentile Christians to be circumcised does not mean that one may not allow oneself to be circumcised voluntarily on the basis of inner conviction. But Paul saw the acceptance of Gentile Christians into the community as full membership which should not be burdened by any further impositions or expectations. In the conflict in Galatia he infers from the agreements made at the Apostolic Council that there is an obligation for Gentile Christians not to have themselves circumcised – certainly an interpretation which the others did not share.

4. The interpretation of Rom. 11.25–27 is disputed: could Paul also have been thinking of the Christ who had already appeared on earth? Were Isa. 59.20f. + Isa. 27.9 already fulfilled in his life and activity? For the earthly Jesus did not come 'from Zion' (Isa. 59.20 = Rom. 11.26) but from Galilee. The interpretation in terms of the Christ who is to come at the parousia is more probable. For in I Thess. 1.10 the 'redeemer' (with the same Greek word) means the future Christ who is to return.

5. The interpretation of QLuke 13.34–35 is disputed. Most exegetes do not think in terms of a positive welcome of the one who 'comes' at the parousia but of a 'doxology of judgment', i.e. the recognition of the judge who will begin his strict judgment. Three factors tell against this. 1. The scheme underlying the logion is of the vain quest of Wisdom for a dwelling-place, her rejection and her acceptance. We know this scheme from Sirach 25, the prologue of John and QLuke 7.31–35. Accordingly there must also be a positive acceptance at the end of QLuke 13.34–35. 2. As punishment for the rejection of God's messengers the threat is made that 'Your house will be forsaken' (Luke 13.35). The parousia then renews the presence of the deity. It is the abolition of the punishment of forsakenness. Hence the jubilation about the return of the deity. 3. The greeting 'Blessed is he who comes in the name of the Lord' (Ps. 118.26) also appears word for word at the entry into Jerusalem (Mark 11.9) – and is certainly not a doxology of judgment there.

6. The letters of Paul are not yet written with a canonical claim. Their form does not borrow from any form already present in the Old Testament canon. They present themselves as occasional writings. Only a collection of letters of Paul (already made by Paul himself?) could be 'canonical' in a quite specific sense, namely by claiming to give a normative basis of faith to a religious group (cf. David Trobisch, *Die Paulusbriefe und die Anfänge der christlichen Publizistik*, KT 135, Gütersloh: Christian Kaiser Verlag 1994).

7. The Logia source can be classified as a prophetic book or a wisdom writing. Both forms are represented in the Old Testament canon. Regardless of what place one gives to Q, Q could thus be a further writing in the Old Testament canon. By contrast, the Gospels are more clearly new in their form also. They are variants on the ancient *bios*.

8. Only later did the New Testament writings become 'canonical writings' in the sense of a binding collection of scriptures. However, they had a 'canonical claim' in a narrower sense: they had been written as an authoritative basis for

guiding the life of a religious community. However, many of the writings with such an intrinsic 'canonical claim' (e.g. the Gospel of Thomas or the Gospel of Truth) did not later become part of the external 'canon' in the sense of an authoritative and binding collection of scriptures. Liberal theology rightly rebelled against the dogma of the canon, in so far as it limited historical investigation of primitive Christianity to the canonical writings. Cf. Gustav Krüger, *Das Dogma vom neuen Testament*, Giessen 1896.

9. Cf. Richard A. Burridge, *What are the Gospels? A Comparison with Graeco-Roman Biography*, Cambridge: Cambridge University Press 1992, 240ff. He rightly suggests that a distinction should be made between 'biography' in the sense of a modern description of a life and the ancient *bios*.

10. It is unusual that there is no brief mention of his birth. Granted, in Lucian of Samosata's *Demonax* we find an ancient *bios* which is limited to the public activities of these Cynic philosophers and consists of individual pericopes which end with an account of his death (cf. Hubert Cancik, 'Bios und Logos. Formgeschichtliche Untersuchungen zu Lukians "Demonax"', in id. (ed.), *Markus-Philologie, Historische, literargeschichtliche und stilistische Untersuchungen zum zweiten Evangelium,* WUNT 33, Tübingen 1984, 115–30), but even in the *Demonax* there is mention of the descent of Demonax from a respected Cypriot family. We hear something of his teacher, his love of philosophy and his pre-occupation with poets in his earliest youth. Despite this analogy to the Gospel of Mark, the form of which is attractive in some respects, the way in which the Gospel of Mark begins with the baptism and public preaching of Jesus is unusual.

11. This structure of the Gospel of Mark, the way in which baptism, transfiguration and crucifixion belong together, was first recognized, as far as I know, by Philipp Vielhauer, 'Erwägungen zur Christologie des Markus-evangeliums' (1964), in id., *Aufsätze zum Neuen Testament,* ThB 31, Munich: Christian Kaiser 1965, 199–214. His analysis of the composition of Mark has been slightly modified above: 1. The epiphany scene corresponding to the baptism and transfiguration is the appearance of the 'angel' at the empty tomb (and not the confession of the centurion). 2. All the theophany scenes are prepared for by human confessions and statements: the messianic preaching of John the Baptist, Peter's messianic confession and the centurion's confession, so that these three 'confessions' are also to be seen together.

12. With Jesus' objection to being venerated as 'son of God' made in commands to the demons to keep silent we might compare and contrast Acts 12.20–23: Herod Agrippa, who does not object to his apotheosis by other human beings, is immediately punished by God. Paul and Barnabas object to it in exemplary fashion, but in so doing risk their lives (Acts 14.8–20). The Jesus of Mark does not allow his apotheosis as 'son of God' by other human beings, although he is objectively the son of God. He is the son of God exclusively on the basis of the divine voice. He emphatically calls himself only 'son of man', which in the Gospel of Mark can mean 'human being' (cf. Mark 2.27–28: the 'son of man' is in parallel to the 'man' mentioned there; 3.28: the 'sons of man' are human beings). Mark emphasizes that

the place of honour at the right hand of God is bestowed on Jesus solely by divine action – thus with Ps. 110.1 in Mark 12.36.

13. William Wrede, *The Messianic Secret in the Gospels* (1901), Cambridge: James Clarke 1971. For Wrede, the commands to be silent, the misunderstanding of the disciples and the parable theory are a community view of the messianic secret which was there before Mark. Later scholarship has regarded this 'messianic theory secret' as a Markan creation. Cf. the survey of research in Heikki Räisänen, *The 'Messianic Secret' in Mark's Gospel*, Edinburgh: T. & T. Clark 1990. He interprets the motif of secrecy (without the parable theory) as a Markan contradiction of the kind of picture of Christ preserved in Q, without cross and resurrection. In my view, pragmatic aspects as well as christological aspects need to be taken into consideration: the secret is a protective secret, which Jesus, like the first Christians, may deliberately keep for a while, but which one day they must disclose, in order to stand up for their own identity in public – with the risk of martyrdom. Cf. Gerd Theissen, 'Die pragmatische Bedeutung der Geheimnismotive im Markusevangelium. Ein wissenssoziologischer Versuch', in Hans G. Kippenberg and Guy G. Stroumsa, *Secrecy and Concealment. Studies in the History of Mediterranean and Near Eastern Religions*, Leiden, New York and Cologne: Brill 1995, 225–45.

14. For the ritual replacement of Judaism in Mark cf. Gerd Theissen, 'Evangelienschreibung und Gemeindeleitung. Pragmatische Motive bei der Abfassung des Markusevangeliums', in Bernd Kollmann, Wolfgang Reibold and Annette Steudel (eds), *Antikes Judentum und Frühes Christentum, FS Hartmut Stegemann*, Berlin and New York: de Gruyter 1999, 389–414.

15. The following assessment of Mark would change only a little if one thought of it as being written immediately before 70 in the expectation of the destruction of the temple, as Martin Hengel argues in 'The Gospel of Mark: Time of Origin and Situation', in id., *Studies in the Gospel of Mark*, London: SCM Press 1985, 1–30.

16. For the Gospel of Matthew cf. U. Luz, *Die Jesusgeschichte des Matthäus*, Neukirchen-Vluyn: Neukirchener Verlag 1993, in which he has summed up basic features of his major commentary on Matthew: *Das Evangelium nach Matthäus*, EKK I, 1–3, Neukirchen-Vluyn 1985, 1990, 1997.

17. There is a dispute as to whether Matt. 11.27, 'All things have been given to me by my Father, and no one knows the Son, but the Father alone . . .' (as in Matt. 28.18), is to be understood as a transfer of power or of knowledge. It does not make any difference that in 11.27 we have 'handed *over*' (παρεδόθη) and in 28.18 'given' (ἐδόθη) (cf. Luke 4.6; I Cor. 15.24). In 11.26 and 27 the communication of revelation is designated with 'reveal' (ἀποκαλύψαι). In 11.26 this revelation relates to something limited (ταῦτα or αὐτά) and thus is clearly distinguished from the comprehensive 'all things' (πάντα) in v.27, so one would expect: 'All things have been *revealed* by my Father – and (therefore) no one knows the Father but the Son and he to whom the Son wills to reveal it . . .' The continuation, 'and no one knows the Son but the Father alone' seems rather to presuppose the thought: 'All (power) has come over to me from my Father, and no one knows the Son (who has been

endowed with all power) but the Father, and no one knows the Father but the Son and he to whom the Son wills to reveal it (not 'hand it over').' Therefore Matt. 11.27 is probably to be related not to a communication of knowledge but to a transfer of power.

18. The best exegesis of the Sermon on the Mount is in Ulrich Luz, *Das Evangelium nach Matthäus*, EKK I, 1, Zurich: Benziger Verlag and Neukirchen-Vluyn: Neukirchener Verlag 1985, 183–420; William D. Davies and Dale C. Allison, *The Gospel According to Saint Matthew*, ICC, Edinburgh: T. & T. Clark 1988, 410–731.

19. For the fulfilment of a combination of pagan and Jewish expectation cf. Gerd Theissen, 'Vom Davidssohn zum Weltherrscher. Pagane und jüdische Endzeiterwartungen im Spiegel des Matthäusevangeliums', in Michael Becker and Wolfgang Fenske (eds), *Das Ende der Tage und die Gegenwart des Heils, FS Heinz W. Kuhn*, Leiden: Brill 1999, 145–64.

20. Cf. two further cases of apotheosis in Acts: Cornelius falls at Peter's feet and worships him. But Peter rejects this because he is a human being (Acts 11.25). Paul survives the bite of a poisonous snake. So he is regarded as a 'god' (Acts 28.6). Here the apostle does not repudiate this in any way: understandably, because he has not been addressed or venerated as a god. The pagans say only that he is a god.

21. Hans Conzelmann, *The Theology of St Luke*, London: Faber 1960 reissued SCM Press 1982.

22. Christoph Burchard, *Der dreizehnte Zeuge. Traditions- und kompositionsgeschichtliche Untersuchungen zu Lukas' Darstellung der Frühzeit des Paulus*, FRLANT 103, Göttingen 1970.

23. For these different phases see especially Jürgen Roloff, *Die Kirche im Neuen Testament*, GNT 10, Göttingen: Vandenhoeck & Ruprecht 1993, 192–206.

24. Luke continues the saving history of God with Israel in the history of the church, but at many points he tacitly changes the content of this saving history. It is not focussed on the political restoration of Israel but on the forgiveness of sins, without the political, earthly, expectation ever expressly being given up. Heikki Räisänen, *Marcion, Muhammad and the Mahatma*, London: SCM Press 1997, 63, rightly remarks: 'Luke does have a salvation-historical problem which is not solvable in "objectifying" terms. If God's old promises are fulfilled in Jesus, their content has been changed to such an extent as to be in effect nullified.'

10. The Gospel of John: The Internal Autonomy of the Primitive Christian Sign World is Brought to Consciousness

1. In what follows the exegesis is of the Gospel of John in its final form. What some exegetes attribute to a redactional stratum of revision is so extensive (e.g. the whole of the second farewell discourse with the high-priestly prayer, John 15–17), that Hartwig Thyen's proposal to see this supposed redactor as the real evangelist is convincing. Cf. id., 'Johannesevangelium', *TRE* 17, 1988, 200–25: 211. This final form shows traces of a successive origin of the Gospel of John, like two

conclusions to the book, two farewell discourses and so on. Time and again themes and texts are taken up again and reinterpreted. Here we have a deliberate rewriting and development of the tradition, or a re-reading of Johannine texts already in existence; the presupposition is that these have been preserved as texts for reference and are read along with the texts which interpret them. It is then a secondary question whether these interpretative texts go back to the same author or to different authors who belong to the same 'school' and speak the same language. Cf. Andreas Dettwiler, *Die Gegenwart des Erhöhten. Eine exegetische Studie zu den johanneischen Abschiedsreden (Joh 13, 31–16, 33) unter besonderer Berücksichtigung ihres Relecture-Charakters*, FRLANT 169, Göttingen: Vandenhoeck & Ruprecht 1995.

2. Nineteenth-century exegesis characterized the christology of the Gospel of John as a 'god going about on earth'. This formula was taken up again by Ernst Käsemann, *The Testament of Jesus*, London: SCM Press 1968, 9.

3. According to Rudof Bultmann, *Theology of the New Testament* 2, London: SCM Press 1952, 1955, 66, the Gospel of John says 'that as the Revealer of God Jesus *revels nothing but that he is the Revealer*' (italics in the original).

4. Cf. the very independent analysis of the sign world of the Gospel of John with system-theoretical categories in Astrid Schlüter, *Die Selbstauslegung des Wortes. Selbstreferenz und Fremdreferenzen in der Textwelt des Johannesevangeliums*, Heidelberg dissertation 1996.

5. In lectures on the Gospel of John which I gave in spring 1987 at the autonomous theological faculty at Montpellier I interpreted it as an expression of a 'hermeneutic-in-stages'. Jean Zumstein has taken up this expression and developed the basic idea in 'L'évangile johannique: une stratégie de croire', *RSC* 77, 1989, 217–32 = id., *Miettes exégétiques*, MoBi 25, Geneva: Labor et fides 1991, 237–52.

6. The usual order is believing and seeing (cf. II Cor. 5.7). John 6.40 has the reverse: 'Whoever sees the Son and believes in him . . .' This corresponds to the natural sequence: one sees a person before adopting an attitude to him or her. But if the 'seeing' relates to a supernatural reality, we also now and again find a gradation of believing and seeing elsewhere in the Gospel of John. Cf. John 1.50f.: here believing relates to the messiahship of Jesus and seeing to his unity with the heavenly world: 'You *believe* . . . you will *see* greater things.' There may be a heightening in John 12.44f.: 'He who *believes* in me *believes* not in me but in him who sent me. And he who *sees* me *sees* him who sent me.' That one sees God in Jesus (cf. 14.9) is more than believing in God through him. John 3.36: 'Whoever *believes* in the Son has eternal life; he who does not obey the Son shall not *see* life, but the wrath of God rests upon him.' In the first farewell discourse the reciprocal immanence of God and Son are primarily an object of 'faith' and then of 'sight': 'Do you not *believe* that I am in the Father and the Father in me? . . .' (14.10, cf.11). 'You will *see* me; because I live, you will live also. In that day you will know that I am in the Father, and you in me, and I in you' (14.19f.). In the high-priestly prayer the revelation is primarily focussed on the fact that the world 1. '*believes*' (17.21);

that it 2. '*knows*'; (17.23); and that Jesus' followers 3. '*see* the glory' which Jesus has from God (17.24).

7. The idea that in great things and in small the structure of the Gospel of John is largely stamped by a 'hermeneutic-in-stages' is inspired by C. H. Dodd, *The Interpretation of the Fourth Gospel*, Cambridge: Cambridge University Press 1953.

8. For the 'I am' sayings see Hartwig Thyen, 'Ich-Bin-Worte', *RAC* 17, 1994/96, 147–213. He argues that these 'I am' sayings take up the Old Testament self-revelation of God as 'I am'. The absolute 'I am' sayings in the Gospel of John (John 8.24, 28, 58; 13.19) are the key to the 'I am' sayings with predicates: both are revelation formulae in which a deity defines himself.

9. Cf. Martin Hengel, *Die Schriftauslegung des 4. Evangeliums auf dem Hintergrund der urchristlichen Exegese*, JBTh 4, Neukirchen-Vluyn: Neukirchener Verlag 1989, 249–88.

10. Peter's confession shows how the discourse about the loaves is to be understood. Peter does not say, 'Lord, to whom should we go? You have food of eternal life,' but, 'You have words of eternal life.' It accords with this that in the farewell discourses the promise of reciprocal immanence associated with the eucharist, 'He who eats my flesh and drinks my blood abides in me, and I in him' (6.56), is transferred from the food to the words of Jesus: abiding in Jesus is now associated with the abiding of the words of Jesus in the disciples (15.7; cf. 15.3f.).

11. Ralfs, Kokins, *Das Verhältnis von ζωή und ἀγάπη im Johannesevangelium. Stufenhermeneutik in der Ersten Abschiedsrede*, Heidelberg dissertation 1999, investigates this relationship between the revelation of life and love in the Gospel of John.

12. Jan –A. Bühner, *Der Gesandte und sein Weg im 4. Evangelium. Die kultur- und religionsgeschichtlichen Grundlagen der johanneischen Sendungschristologie sowie ihre traditionsgeschichtliche Entwicklung*, WUNT II/2, Tübingen: Mohr (Siebeck) 1977, has shown that the notion of the emissary from the heavenly world is not to be interpreted against the background of a Gnostic myth. It is sufficient to keep in view the general notion of the emissary which has its roots in the ancient world: the emissary is sent by someone who gives him a commission. He legitimates himself through a testimony, introduces himself, returns and gives an account of his mission. The metaphor of sending expresses the fact that the Gospel of John is about the restoration of communication. But the notion of unity transcends this metaphor of the emissary.

13. There are two diametrically opposed ways of grappling with Johannine anti-Judaism. 1. One can dissolve it into the universal and symbolic as an expression of statements about the world and human beings. The Jews are then regarded as representatives of the world in general. What the Gospel of John says about them and their religion it says about the religious person generally. That is the existential interpretation of the Gospel of John given by Rudolf Bultmann, *Theology of the New Testament* 2, 21ff. 2. The Johannine anti-Judaism can also be explained in terms of its concrete situation. It is then emphasized on the one hand that the Johannine Christians are themselves Jews and maintain their origin:

'Salvation comes from the Jews' (John 4.21). On the other hand, it is emphasized that they have experienced their exclusion from the synagogue (John 16.2) as a trauma and are being oppressed in the present time by non-Christian Jews. After Bultmann, this way has been taken by the historical interpretations of the Gospel of John: James L. Martyn, *History and Theology in the Fourth Gospel*, Nashville: Abingdon Press [2]1979; Klaus Wengst, *Bedrängte Gemeinde und verherrlichter Christus*, BThSt 5, Neukirchen-Vluyn: Neukirchener Verlag 1981 = Munich: Christian Kaiser Verlag [2]1990. My interpretation, sketched out above, attempts to combine both approaches. The 'Jews' in the Gospel of John stand for a universal human limit. However, this does not lie in the Jewish religion but in the political dependence of Judaism, which is coded in the mythical symbol of the Satan. Here the concrete reference is to the Roman empire, in which the Jews have lost their freedom. Concrete experiences with Judaism stand behind the Johannine anti-Judaism. At the same time a universal aspect shines through: political power and the lack of freedom which it brings alienate people from themselves.

14. Before the 'ruler of the world' is announced, Jesus leaves behind his peace (John 14.27). In contrasting 'his peace' with the peace which the world gives, in my view he is contrasting it with the *pax Romana*. In the background stands the Latin phrase *pacem dare* (Livy 3, 2, 2; 3, 24, 10; 5, 27, 15; Ovid, *Metamorphoses* 15, 832). Eberhard Dinkler, 'Friede', *RAC* 8, 1972, 434–505, sees this as an 'established political and legal phrase' (442).

15. Against the potential relationship that I claim between the mythical 'ruler' and the 'real ruler of the world' in the Gospel of John, it could be objected that in John 19.11 the power of Pilate is derived from God: 'You would have no power of me if it had not been given to you from above'. This statement does not derive Pilate's office (and thus part of the Roman state) from God (as is supposed by Rudolf Bultmann, *The Gospel of John: A Commentary*, Oxford: Blackwell 1971, 662). For it is only a mention of the concrete power of Pilate over Jesus (not his ἐξουσία generally but his ἐξουσία κατ' ἐμοῦ). Moreover the predicate of the conditional clause does not relate to ἐξουσία; were that the case we would have to have the feminine δεδομένην (cf. II Cor. 8.1). Rather, the neutral δεδομένον shows that the whole situation has been ordained in this way by God. As in John 3.27; 6.65, being 'given' from above means that God determines everything: Pilate is a puppet in a great game of which he does not have control. It is in keeping with this idea that the 'ruler of this world' has only apparent independence. He too is a puppet in a greater drama which is ultimately controlled by God.

16. I have interpreted the juxtaposition of the three representatives of Jesus as the sign of a tension in the Johannine community between a simple community piety (represented by Peter, the leader of the community and the pastor, whose understanding of the revelation sometimes leaves something to be desired), a sublime spiritual piety of educated classes (represented by the Paraclete), and an attempt to combine the two. This attempt has been preserved for us in the Gospel of John, which seeks to move from the simple faith of the community to a deeper understanding of Jesus (and it is represented by the Beloved Disciple, the author

of the Gospel of John). Cf. Gerd Theissen, 'Autoritätskonflikte in den johanneischen Gemeinden. Zum "Sitz im Leben" des Johannesevangeliums', in *Diakonia, Gedenkschrift B. Stogiannos*, Thessaloniki: Theologische Hochschule 1988, 243–58 = (revised) 'Conflits d'autorité dans les communautés johanniques. La question du Sitz im Leben de l'évangile de Jean', in id., *Histoire sociale du christianisme primitif. Jésus, Paul, Jean*, MoBi 33, Geneva: Labor et Fides 1996, 209–26. The relationship between the three representatives of Jesus has been interpreted in terms of different aspects of the self-organization of the Johannine text-world by Astrid Schlüter, *Die Selbstauslegung des Wortes. Selbstreferenz und Fremdreferenzen in der Textwelt des Johannesevangeliums*, Heidelberg dissertation 1996.

17. F. C. Baur interpreted the Gospel of John as the culmination of the development of primitive Christianity. He thought that the idea of the unity of the divine spirit with the human spirit which was establishing itself in primitive Christianity found its clearest expression here. Wilhelm Bousset, *Kyrios Christos. A History of the Belief in Christ from the Beginnings of Christianity to Irenaeus*, Nashville: Abingdon Press 1970, saw the Gospel of John as a culmination in the development of Christian mysticism, which has made positive use of the mysticism of its Hellenistic environment. Rudolf Bultmann, *Theology of the New Testament* 2, 3–29, sees it as a presentation of the pure primitive Christian kerygma. In these three great schemes the Gospel of John is always a culminating point. Ernst Käsemann, *The Testament of Jesus*, London: SCM Press 1968, argues against them with welcome freshness. For him the Gospel of John is the expression of a special sectarian development in primitive Chrisitanity, with a theology that is open to the suspicion of heresy. But at all events the Gospel of John towers above the usual – whether as a culmination of primitive Christian theology and religion – as pure idea, mysticism or kerygma – or as a heresy which has crept right to the centre of the canon.

11. The Crises of Primitive Christianity

1. We can be clear about the significance of ritual in denationalizing religious traditions from the fact that Paul speaks not only of Jews and Gentiles but also of 'circumcision' and 'uncircumcision' (Gal. 2.7; 6.15; I Cor. 7.19; Rom. 3.30). The dropping of this ritual demarcation means that Jews and Gentiles can now have fellowship.

2. The new primitive Christian religion became absolute by combining the claim of the absoluteness of the one and only God, rooted in Judaism, with a specific human being. The 'narrative' in which this is expressed most vividly is the 'narrative' of his exaltation over all powers – an event which is spoken of in hymns and confessions: in the Philippians and Colossians hymns, in confessional formulations like I Cor. 8.6, etc. The powers and authorities over which the exalted Christ is set are the depotentiated deities of antiquity. A human figure enters their cosmos and assumes their numinous power.

3. The break with traditional forms of life is not just a characteristic of early

itinerant radicalism. It can also be found in the epistolary literature. Although at first sight I Peter seems to advocate an ethic of assimilation to existing circumstances, it tersely emphasizes the break with previous life-style: 'You know that you were ransomed from the futile ways inherited from your fathers, not with perishable things such as silver or gold, but with the precious blood of Christ' (I Peter 1.18f.). One of the most sacred possessions of antiquity, the tradition of the fathers, is here despised: it is useless and meaningless. One has to be redeemed from it.

4. What is a crisis? In the social sphere it is the state of a society or a community which has to solve difficult problems of assimilation to a new situation, of co-ordination between its different groups and perhaps of a change of structure and the preservation of a system, all under pressure of time. The substance of this definition has been taken over from Bernhard Schäfers, 'Krise', in id. (ed.), *Grundbegriffe der Soziologie*, UTB 1416, Opladen: Leske & Budrich 1986, 167–9.

5. Within the so-called Tübingen school, in the nineteenth century all Paul's opponents were interpreted as Judaizers; in the twentieth century, in part of the Bultmann school they were interpreted as Gnostics. Thus by Walter Schmithals, *Neues Testament und Gnosis*, EdF 208, Darmstadt: Wissenschaftliche Buchgesellschaft 1984.

6. Particularly in the case of the Revelation of John, it is conceivable that its prophetic solemnity is a reaction to Gnostic-like tendencies in the communities. Cf. Elisabeth Schüssler Fiorenza, 'Apocalyptic and Gnosis in Revelation and in Paul', *JBL* 92, 1973, 565–81 = ead., *The Book of Revelation. Justice and Judgement*, Philadelphia: Fortress Press 1984, 114–32.

7. Above all E. P. Sanders, *Paul and Palestinian Judaism. A Comparison of Patterns of Religion*, London: SCM Press 1977, 442ff., interprets Pauline theology not as the answer to a problem but as a solution to which a problem has subsequently been reconstructed: 'The solution as preceding the problem' (442). This seems consistent: if Judaism was a religion of grace (and Sanders has demonstrated this convincingly), then the grace of God proclaimed in Christ cannot be a solution to problems which Judaism has because it did not know the grace of Christ.

8. The interpretation of the doctrine of justification as a reaction to Paul's Judaistic opponents can be found in William Wrede, 'Paulus', *RV* I, 5–6 = Halle: GebauerSchwenschke 1904 = Karl H. Rengstorf, *Das Paulusbild in der neueren deutschen Forschung*, WdF 24, Darmstadt: Wissenschaftliche Buchgesellschaft 1969, 1–97.

9. The investigation of the Jewish 'religious parties' has been given a tremendous boost by the Qumran discoveries, especially since it is still most likely that the inhabitants of Qumran were Essenes. In that case the Qumran writings, in so far as they come from the Qumran community itself, would be original Essene documents. There is a comprehensive account of the various religious currents in: E. P. Sanders, *Judaism. Practice and Belief 63 BCE – 66 CE*, London: SCM Press and Philadelphia: Trinity Press International 1992; Günter Stemberger, *Pharisäer, Sadduzäer, Essener*, SBS 144, Stuttgart: Katholisches Bibelwerk 1990.

10. Here the aporia touches on anthropology: either human beings are in principle capable of cooperating in fulfilling the will of God, or they are incapable, unless God chooses them to fulfil his will. Advocates of a pessimistic anthropology (and the Essenes and Paul have this tendency) must show that the high value put on their own actions by advocates of a more optimistic anthropology is an illusory human claim before God. Timo Laato, *Paulus und das Judentum. Anthropologische Erwägungen*, Aabo: Aabo Akademis förlag 1991, basing himself on H. Odeberg, makes this tension the key to his interpretation of Paul.

11. The ideal of 'zeal' (*zelos*) extended far beyond the 'Zealots'. This has been demonstrated by Martin Hengel, *The Zealots. An Investigation into the Jewish Freedom Movement in the Period from Herod I to AD 70*, Edinburgh: T. & T. Clark 1989, 146–228. Paul too was seized by it. He persecuted the community with zeal (Phil. 3.6) and was a 'zealot' for the traditions of the fathers (Gal. 2.14). He insinuated that his Galatian opponents had such 'zeal' (4.18), and he sees it as the motive for the repudiation of the gospel among the Jews; here in principle he assesses this 'zeal for God' positively (Rom. 10.2). In so doing Paul is generalizing his own Judaism – and the motives which once led him to reject the gospel.

12. Strabo's assessment of the Jews in *Geographica* 16, 2, 35ff. is generally attributed to Poseidonius; cf. the discussion in Menahem Stern, *Greek and Latin Authors on Jews and Judaism*, I, Jerusalem: Israel Academy 1976, 264ff. That does not exclude the possibility that views are contained in his work which we may presuppose in the radical reformers in Jerusalem after 175. Thus Elias Bickermann, *The God of the Maccabees: Studies on the Meaning and Origin of the Maccabean Revolt*, SJLA 32, Leiden: Brill 1979, 86f. Strabo's account is governed by the notion of decadence. This notion is also echoed by Paul. In Gal. 3.5ff., at the beginning stands the promise to Abraham. The law only came 430 years later – and only applies until the original promise is fulfilled. In Paul the contrast is not between Moses and his descendants but between Abraham and Moses. But the thought structure is comparable. If Strabo and Paul look at the history of Jewish religion with such thought models, these models must have been widespread in the Diaspora and its surroundings.

13. Wolfgang Harnisch, *Verhängnis und Verheissung der Geschichte. Untersuchungen zum Zeit- und Geschichtsverständnis im 4. Buch Esra und in der syrischen Baruchapokalypse*, FRLANT 97, Göttingen: Vandenhoeck & Ruprecht 1969, 60–7, has shown that the voice of the angel conceals the real position of the author, who rejects the voice of human scepticism. The only question is: how 'optimistic' is the judgment of this angel? Does it confirm the promise of salvation to Israel? Or does it confirm it only for those who really fulfil the commandments – despite a scepticism about the possibility of fulfilling them which is recognized as justified? If Israel is not to be saved, but only a very few who were faithful to the law, who despite human inadequacy fulfil the law, then IV Ezra would no longer be a representative of 'covenantal nomism'. This conclusion is drawn by Sanders, *Paul and Palestinian Judaism* (n.7), 409–18.

14. These voices which are critical of the law accumulate in the first century

AD. Strabo of Amaseia (64 BC to the 20s of the first century AD) wrote his *Geographica* at the beginning of the first century. The sources from which he draws his picture of Judaism are much older. Philo (c.15/10 BC to the 40s of the first century AD) was also writing in the first half of the first century. Josephus (AD 37/38 to the 90s) published his *Antiquities* in the 90s. IV Ezra was similarly written around 30 years after the destruction of Jerusalem – towards the end of the first century AD.

15. Cf. Gerd Theissen, *Psychological Aspects of Pauline Theology*, Edinburgh: T. & T. Clark 1987, 228ff. Gerd Lüdemann, 'Die Bekehrung des Paulus und die Wende des Petrus in tiefenpsychologischer Perspektive', in Friedrich W. Horn (ed.), *Bilanz und Perspektiven gegenwärtiger Auslegung des Neuen Testaments, FS Georg Strecker*, Berlin and New York: de Gruyter, 91–111, goes one step further. He thinks that he can establish not only an unconscious conflict with the law but also an unconscious attraction to Christ. At all events, we may presupposes that the pre-Christian Paul was intensely preoccupied with the figure of Christ. He will consciously have seen him as an accursed figure (according to Deut. 21.23: 'Cursed is anyone who hangs on the tree' = Gal. 3.13).

16. Since Werner G. Kümmel, *Römer 7 und das Bild des Menschen im Neuen Testament*, ThB 53, München: Christian Kaiser Verlag 1974, the 'I' in Rom. 7 has often been seen as a rhetorical fictitious 'I'. But here too a rhetorically stylized 'I' can be spoken of with personal involvement – and to this degree be capable of psychological evaluation. When Paul is defending his apostolate he is utterly involved, and automatically says much about himself, making use of the whole repertoire of his rhetorical capabilities. Hans Dieter Betz has with good reason used rhetorical criticism to achieve a breakthrough in the analysis of Pauline texts in which for Paul his whole existence is at stake. Cf. id., *Der Apostel Paulus und die sokratische Tradition*, BHTh 45, Tübingen: Mohr (Siebeck) 1972; *Galatians. A Commentary on Paul's Letter to the Churches in Galatia,* Hermeneia, Philadelphia: Fortress Press 1979.

17. In his pioneering works, Krister Stendahl, 'The Apostle Paul and the Introspective Conscience of the West', *HThR* 56, 1963, 199–215; id., *Paul among Jews and Gentiles and Other Essays*, Philadelphia: Fortress Press 1976, has disputed that Paul had a bad conscience over his activity as a persecutor. According to Stendahl he had a 'robust conscience'. It is correct that he speaks from the standpoint of the redeemed. How could the one who had been redeemed, called and commissioned as an apostle show remorse! But Paul was aware how monstrous his persecution of Christians was, and so in I Cor 15.9 he calls himself an 'abortion', not worthy to hold the office of apostle. In I Thess. 2.16 he says that the way in which Jews prevent the spread of the gospel is a sin, which makes up 'the measure of sins'. He is not including himself here as a perpetrator (in view of his past), but is describing himself as a sacrifice (with an eye to the present) for the sake of the Thessalonians, because these are likewise the victims of persecutions. But in principle he has no doubt that the persecution of the Christians was and is a sin. When in Rom. 11.25ff. he describes the eschatological redemption of all Israel, his

own fate is in the background: just as he was an enemy of the gospel, so too the unbelieving Israelites are enemies of the gospel. And just as he was converted by an appearance directly from heaven, so too will they be saved at the parousia by an appearance which comes from heaven. But this Christ will bring forgiveness for sins (Rom. 11.27 = Jer. 31.33f. and Isa. 27.9). Krister Stendahl has one correct insight: the doctrine of justification is related to a social problem, namely the integration of Gentile Christians into the people of God. But that does not exclude the possibility that it arose out of a personal association and has an individual meaning. For according to Paul, all, both Jews and Gentiles, need justification, because of the immoral acts which both commit (Rom. 1.18–3.20). If it were only a question of accepting Gentiles, Paul could have been content with developing a doctrine of justification especially for Gentiles (which is perhaps what he did to begin with). However, in the letters that we have, the doctrine of justification applies to all. Cf. Gerd Theissen, 'Judentum und Christentum bei Paulus. Sozialgeschichtliche Überlegungen zu einem beginnenden Schisma', in Martin Hengel and Ulrich Heckel (eds), *Paulus. Missionar und Theologe und das antike Judentum*, WUNT 58, Tübingen 1991, 331–56.

18. In order to argue for a late origin of the doctrine of justication, reference is made above all to the earliest of Paul's letters, I Thessalonians, in which the doctrine of justification does not yet appear. But in this letter to the community which he has just founded, Paul makes no mention of baptism (far less of the eucharist)! May we then conclude that he did not baptize or allow anyone to baptize in Thessaloniki? Hardly! A distinguishing feature of I Thessalonians is that its introduction takes up half the letter (I Thess. 1.1–3.13), an effect which Paul achieves by doubling the motifs which it contains (cf. 1.2; 2.13). But the introduction serves to establish good relations between the author and those whom he is addressing. It is here that we are to see the main purpose of the letter; the teaching comes second.

19. The following evidence can be produced for supposing that Paul had to work out the theological content of his Damascus experience conceptually in a long process. Paul refers back to his Damascus experience three times in his letters. Only in Phil. 3.4ff. does he interpret it as an individual conversion and connect it (in Phil. 3.10) with the doctrine of justification. In Gal. 1.15ff., as in I Cor. 15.9f., he interprets it as a call to be an apostle – in Gal. 1 combined with the revelation of God's son, in I Cor. 15 with the Easter witness. The doctrine of justification does not appear in either context. But both passages are agreed in emphasizing that the call to be an apostle is a sign of the grace (χάρις) of God: 'But by the *grace* of God I am what I am. And his *grace* was not in vain in me . . .' (I Cor. 15.10). 'but when it pleased God who had set me apart form my mother's womb and had called me though his *grace* . . .' (Gal. 1.15). Paul was certain from the start that his call or conversion was an expression of sheer grace. That he worked out his understanding of the grace of God as the justification of the godless is the result of a theological development.

20. Cf. the comprehensive investigation of the Nabataean mission and Paul's

early period in general in Martin Hengel and Anna M. Schwemer, *Paul Between Damascus and Antioch. The Unknown Years*, London: SCM Press 1997, 106–26.

21. Heikki Räisänen, 'Paul's Theological Difficulties with the Law', in id., *The Torah and Christ. Essays in German and English on the Problem of the Law in Early Christianity*, SESJ 45, Helsinki: Kirjappaino Raamattutalo 1986, 3–24; id., 'The "Hellenists"- a Bridge Between Jesus and Paul?', in ibid., 242–306, has reckoned with a spiritualizing understanding of the law in the first phase of the Pauline mission – and a radicalizing of this understanding so that it became a more fundamental repudiation of the Torah on the basis of the Judaizing counter-mission.

22. David Alvarez, *Die Religionspolitik des Kaisers Claudius und die paulinische Mission*, HBS 19, Freiburg and Vienna: Herder 1999.

23. Cf. Peter Pilhofer, *Philippi Bd I. Die erste christliche Gemeinde Europas*, WUNT 87, Tübingen: Mohr (Siebeck) 1995.

24. What for us is the arbitrary allegorical interpretation of the name Hagar has either been occasioned by a place Hegra on the east side of the Dead Sea in Arabia (thus Hartmut Gese, 'Τὸ δὲ Ἁγὰρ ὄρος ἐστὶν ἐν τῇ Ἀραβίᾳ (Gal 4, 25)', in id., *Vom Sinai zum Zion*, BEvTh 64, Munich: Christian Kaiser Verlag 1974, 49–62, and Hengel and Schwemer, *Paul Between Damascus and Antioch* [n.20], 113f.). Or there is a word-play on the Arabic word *hadjar* (= rock), a designation for Mount Sinai (thus Betz, *Galatians*, 244f.). The first interpretation better fits the general tendency in Galatians to connect Jewish traditions either directly or indirectly (though connotations) with pagan traditions.

25. The order of Galatians and II Corinthians is disputed. Galatians is often put immediately before Romans, as it is by Udo Schnelle, *The History and Theology of the New Testament Writings*, Minneapolis: Fortress Press and London: SCM Press 1998, who interprets I Cor. 16.1 as if Paul's authority were still unchallenged in Galatia – as if we were still in the time before the Galatian conflict. But this argument is not sound: even if Paul's authority were already disputed, he would hardly report this to the Corinthian community where he was fighting to maintain his authority. And the Galatian conflict could already have been long resolved. Compare Romans: there Paul sends greetings from the whole Corinthian community (Rom. 16.23). There is no trace whatsoever of the deep-seated conflicts which he had had with the community, and which were now in the recent past. Nor can one argue from a comparable structure in the making to a chronological proximity to the time of origin. Romans refers not only to Galatians but also to I Corinthians (cf. the themes of Adam and Christ, body of Christ, strength and weakness). Galatians could have been written as near to or as far from Romans as I Corinthians. It seems to me that in Galatians Paul adopts an enthusiastic position which he corrects in Romans. One explanation of this correction could be that in the meanwhile he had learned from the conflict with the Corinthian enthusiasts.

26. Cf. Petra von Gemünden and Gerd Theissen, 'Metaphorische Logik im Römerbrief. Beobachtungen zu dessen Bildsemantik und Aufbau', in Reinhold Bernhardt and Ulrike Link-Wieczorek (eds), *Metapher und Wirklichkeit. Die Logik*

der Bildhaftigkeit im Reden von Gott, Mensch und Natur, FS Dietrich Ritschl, Göttingen: Vandenhoeck & Ruprecht 1999, 108 – 31.

27. Cf. e.g. the definition of freedom in Epictetus, *Diss.* IV 1, 1: 'That man is free who lives as he wills, who can neither be compelled to do anything nor be prevented from doing it, to whom one can do no violence, whose will cannot be constrained, whose desire attains its goal, whose repudiation does not turn into the opposite.'

28. The suggested definition which was worked out at a congress on 'The Origins of Gnosticism' in Messina in 1966 is still the starting point for clarifications (Ugo Bianchi [ed.], *Le Origini dello Gnosticismo. Colloquio di Messina 13–18 Aprile 1966. Testi e Discussioni*, SHR 12, Leiden: Brill 1967, [2]1970, xxff.). According to this, 'gnosis' is a widespread phenomenon, 'the knowledge of divine mysteries which is reseved for an elite'. By contrast, 'Gnosticism' is the historical phenomenon of Gnostic systems in the second and third centuries which presuppose the presence of a divine spark in human beings and its origin and redemption through 'gnosis'. While the distinction between a type of redemptive knowledge that can be described by the phenomenology of religion and the concrete form of ancient Gnostic systems has become established, this is not completely true of the terminological relationship. The term 'gnosis' is bound up with specific phenomena in late antiquity and cannot be detached from these. However, it is also possible in the perspective of the context in antiquity to distinguish between gnosis in the broadest sense as an understanding based on redemptive knowledge and Gnosticism as the systems which build on this and which had their heyday in the second century. Five characteristics of both the 'gnosis' and the 'Gnosticism' of the second century have been agreed on. These are given in R. McL. Wilson, 'Gnosis/Gnostizismus II', *TRE* 13, 1984, 535–50: 1. A radical cosmic dualism; 2. The distinction between a transcendent God and a demiurge; 3. Belief in a spark of divine light in human beings; 4. A myth which explains the present state of human beings by a fall before the beginning of the world, and 5. The conviction of a saving 'gnosis' which brings about redemption through knowledge of the unity of this spark of light in human beings with the divine world. Josef Klauck, *Die religiöse Umwelt des Urchristentums* II, Stuttgart, Berlin and Cologne: Kohlhammer 1996, 145–98, offers an instructive survey of Gnosticism.

29. On the question of the historical origin of Gnosticism it always has to be noted that: 1. The conditions for the origin of Gnosticism need not be identical with the conditions which guaranteed its dissemination. Primitive Christianity, too, arose as a renewal movement within Judaism located in Jewish Palestine, but spread in quite different conditions – and in a transformed form. 2. There need not have been a historical place of origin for Gnosticism. Just as it could 'nest' in various existing religions, so too it could have come into being in the context of different religions. Cf. the survey of theories of origins in Hendrik J. W. Drijvers, 'The Origins of Gnosticism as a Religious and Historical Problem', *NedThT* 22, 1967/8, 321–51 = Kurt Rudolph (ed.), *Gnosis und Gnostizismus*, WdF 262, Darmstadt: Wissenschaftliche Buchgesellschaft 1975, 798–841.

30. Simon Magus is regarded as the origin of Gnosticism for the first time in Irenaeus, *Haer.* I, 23, 2. Remarkably, conservative New Testament scholars often regard Irenaeus's statements about the origin of the Gospels as credible, but mistrust him completely over the origin of Gnosticism. And conversely, critical New Testament scholars tend to mistrust his statements about the Gospels fundamentally, but to put all too much trust in what he says about Simon (and thus about an early origin of Gnosticism before AD 70).

31. Research into Simon Magus is confronted with the great alternative posed by Kurt Rudolph in the title of his account of this research: was he a magician or a Gnostic? Id., 'Simon-Magus oder Gnosticus? Zum Stand der Debatte', *ThR* 42, 1978, 279–359. Karlmann Beyschlag, *Simon Magus und die christliche Gnosis*, WUNT 16, Tübingen: Mohr (Siebeck) 1975, disputes vigorously that the historical Simon was a Gnostic. He is opposed with good arugments by Kurt Rudolph, *Gnosis: The Nature and History of Gnosticism*, Edinburgh: T. & T. Clark 1983, 294–8; Gerd Lüdemann, *Untersuchungen zur simonianischen Gnosis*, GTA 1, Göttingen: Vandenhoeck & Ruprecht 1975; id., 'The Acts of the Apostles and the Beginnings of Simonian Gnosis', *NTS* 33, 1987, 279–359. Robert F. Stoops, 'Simon. 13', *ABD* VI, 1992, 29–31, gives an informative survey.

32. The sketchy reconstruction of the 'historical Simon' which follows is largely based on such information in the sources as: 1. is conceivable on the basis of historical analogies in Palestine and Samaria in the 30s and 40s of the first century; 2. makes possible a coherent overall interpretation; and 3. explains a mythicization and divinization of the historical Simon after his death – in analogy to the rise of primitive Christian christology.

33. Primitive Christian itinerant charismatics also probably practised a kind of *hieros gamos.* In Didache 11.11 the communities are instructed to tolerate itinerant charismatics when they practise the 'earthly mystery of the church', as long as they do not teach it to others. The 'mystery' is probably the same as in Eph. 5.32: the union of Christ and the church, depicted in sexual relations between man and woman. The itinerant charismatics lived with female partners – in analogy to the syzygy of Christ and the church.

34. According to their own tradition the Samaritans could also understand themselves as 'Sidonians', cf. Josephus, *Antt.*11, 344; 12, 257–264. Probably there was a colony of Phoenicians in Samaria. So the link between Samaria and Phoenicia in the Simonian myth (but probably already attached to the historical Simon) presents a basic social problem of the Samaritans: the relationship between the indigenous population and Phoenicians.

35. Cf. I Macc. 6.2. By contrast, in Josephus, *Antt.* 12, 261, 263, the Samaritan temple is dedicated to 'Zeus Hellenios'. The two dedications need not be exclusive. There are two arguments which suggest that 'Xenios' could have been an epithet for the God worshipped on Gerizim. 1. In 'Gerizim' we could hear an echo of *ger* (Hebrew = stranger). 2. In Ps. Eupolemus (= Eusebius, *Praeparatio Evangelii* IX 17, 21–9), a tradition has been preserved which probably was also regarded as a foundation legend for the Samaritan sanctuary. According to this, Abraham had

lived in Phoenicia (in the text probably originally a name for the whole of Palestine), had freed prisoners, and had released enemies who had fallen into his hands. Consequently he was hospitably received in the sanctuary on Gerizim by Melchizedek, who was the priest there. The verb ξενιεθῆναι which occurs in this report directly recalls Ζεὺς ξένιος.

36. For what follows see above all the analysis of Gnosticism by Hans G. Kippenberg, *Die vorderasiatischen Erlösungsreligionen in ihrem Zusammenhang mit der antiken Stadtherrschaft*, stw 917, Frankfurt: Suhrkamp 1991, 369ff.

37. Cf. ibid., 384–8.

38. One must be careful to differentiate the attitude of the Gnostics to martyrdom. Cf. Klaus Koschorke, *Die Polemik der Gnostiker gegen das kirchliche Christentum,* NHS 12, Leiden: Brill 1978. Cf. also Elaine Pagels, *The Gnostic Gospels*, New York: Random House 1979, 70–101.

39. Above all Koschorke, *Polemik* (n.38), 220ff., has shown that by their understanding of themselves the Gnostics wanted to fit into the communities: as an inner circle in the community or as Christians of a higher order.

40. Christoph Markschies, *Valentinus Gnosticus? Untersuchungen zur valentianischen Gnosis mit einem neuen Kommentar zu den Fragmenten Valentins*, WUNT 65, Tübingen: Mohr (Siebeck) 1992.

41. Winrich A. Löhr, *Basilides und seine Schule*, WUNT 83, Tübingen: Mohr (Siebeck) 1996.

42. Carl Andresen and Adolf M. Ritter, 'Die Anfänge der christlichen Lehrentwicklung', in *HDThG* 1, Göttingen: Vandenhoeck & Ruprecht [2]1999.

43. Cf. Gerd Theissen, 'The Wandering Radicals. Light Shed by the Sociology of Literature on the Early Transmission of Jesus Sayings, Social Reality and the Early Christians', in *Theology, Ethics and the World of the New Testament*, Minneapolis: Fortress Press 1992, 33–59. For a critical discussion of this thesis cf. Thomas Schmeller, *Brechungen. Urchristliche Wandercharismatiker im Prisma soziologisch orientierter Exegese*, SBS 136, Stuttgart: Katholisches Bibelwerk 1989.

44. Cf. Wayne A. Meeks, *The Origins of Christian Morality. The First Two Centuries*, New Haven: Yale University Press 1993, 36. He distinguishes two ways of understanding conversion, 'as individual moral reform or as a countercultural formation of "the new human"'. Sometimes they lead to competing movements and sometimes they combine dialectically in social institutions and theological ideas. But their opposition remains: '. . . the mind of the sect and the mind of the church struggle on in the history of Christian moral thought and practice'.

45. Christopher Tuckett, *Q and the History of Early Christianity*, Edinburgh: T. & T. Clark 1996, esp. 355–91; Risto Uro (ed.), *Symbols and Strata. Essays on the Saying Gospel Q*, SESJ 65, Göttingen: Vandenhoeck & Ruprecht 1996.

46. Elisabeth Schüssler Fiorenza, *The Book of Revelation. Justice and Judgement*, Philadelphia: Fortress Press 1984; ead., *Revelation. Vision of a Just World*, Proclamation Commentary, Minneapolis: Fortress Press 1991; Christopher Rowland, *Revelation*, Epworth Commentaries, London: Epworth Press 1993.

47. Hans-Josef Klauck, 'Das Sendschreiben nach Pergamon und der Kaiserkult in der Johannesoffenbarung', *Bib* 73, 1992, 153–82 = in *Alte Welt und neuer Glaube. Beiträge zur Religionsgeschichte, Forschungsgeschichte und Theologie des Neuen Testaments,* NTOA 29, Freiburg CH: Universitätsverlag and Göttingen: Vandenhoeck & Ruprecht 1994, 115–43, distinguishes between hard and soft emperor cults (141f.). The hard emperor cult requires sacrifice before the image of the emperor and cursing of Jesus Christ, but was rare – basically only after denunciations by the population which in legal processes led to Christians being 'tested' by the hard emperor cult. By contrast, the soft emperor cult arose on the basis of social ties: participation in association meals, in legal proceedings, oaths and making contracts.

48. Ulrich B. Müller, *Zur frühchristlichen Theologiegeschichte. Judenchristentum und Paulinismus in Kleinasien an der Wende vom ersten zum zweiten Jahrhundert n.Chr.*, Gütersloh: Mohn 1976, 35, 37f., 46–50, and Jürgen Roloff, *Die Kirche im Neuen Testament*, GNT 10, Göttingen: Vandenhoeck & Ruprecht 1993, 168f., 189, see the author of Revelation as a primitive Christian itinerant prophet who comes from the Jewish Christianity of Syria-Palestine and is active in different communities of Asia Minor with the charismatic authority of a prophet – independently of the community structures already existing there. The idea of discipleship was as alive in this circle of prophets (Rev. 18.4) as the original ethical rigorism.

49. Klauck, 'Sendschreiben' (n.47), 137–9, sees the author's main concern in the invitation to exodus in Rev. 18.4.

50. Peter Lampe, *Die stadtrömischen Christen in den ersten beiden Jahrhunderten*, WUNT II, 18, Tübingen: Mohr (Siebeck) 1987, 71–8.

51. Cf. Christine Trevett, *Montanism. Gender, Authority and the New Prophecy*, Cambridge: Cambridge University Press 1996; Anne Jensen, *Gottes selbstbewusste Töchter*, Freiburg, Basel and Vienna: Herder 1992. For survey articles cf. Ronald E. Heine, 'Montanus, Montanism', *ABD* IV, 1992, 898–902; William H. C. Frend, 'Montanismus', *TRE* 23, 1994, 371–9; and Adolf Martin Ritter, in Carl Andresen and Adolf M. Ritter, *Handbuch der Dogmen- und Theologiegeschichte* 1, Göttingen: Vandenhoeck & Ruprecht [2]1999, 69–72.

52. Barbara Aland, 'Marcion', *TRE* 22, 1992, 89–101.

12. Plurality and Unity in Primitive Christianity and the Origin of the Canon

1. Two distinguished schemes of the history of the theology of primitive Christianity have worked out this multiplicity. Helmut Köster, *Einführung in das Neue Testament im Rahmen der Religionsgeschichte und Kulturgeschichte der hellenistischen und römischen Zeit*, Berlin and New York: de Gruyter 1980, describes primitive Christianity by regional differences and lines of historical development. Klaus Berger, *Theologiegeschichte des Urchristentums*, Tübingen and Basel: Francke Verlag [2]1995, compares it with a trunk with forking branches; here the linking of different notions and traditions indicates a common origin. The sketch here cannot engage in a detailed discussion of these schemes.

2. Ferdinand Christian Baur (1792–1860) developed this so-called 'Tübingen historical picture' in many publications. Here I mention only his brief account, *Das Christenthum und die christliche Kirche der drei ersten Jahrhunderte*, Tübingen : Fues 1853. His contribution is often seen as the discovery of a variety of parties. In reality the awareness of this multiplicity was already there before him. He succeeded in understanding it as a unity developing dialectically. Thus Stefan Alkier, *Urchristentum. Zur Geschichte und Theologie einer exegetischen Disziplin*, BHTh 83, Tübingen 1993.

3. Walter Bauer, *Orthodoxy and Heresy in Earliest Christianity*, Philadelphia: Fortress Press 1971 and London: SCM Press 1972, is basic for an understanding of so-called 'orthodoxy' and so-called 'heresy'. According to Bauer, even in the second century in many places – above all in Syria and Egypt – a Gnostic Christianity was more original than 'orthodoxy'. The latter was initially just one current among others and established itself through Rome. To exaggerate: 'orthodoxy' was the 'heresy' which established itself in the end.

4. Bernhard Lang, 'Kanon', *HRWG* III, 1993, 332–5, differentiates on the basis of the foundation of the authority of holy scriptures: in accordance with Max Weber's typology of a basis in rule and authority this is traditional, charismatic or legal. The traditional basis of holy scriptures is as the 'classical texts' of a religion which is unquestioningly presupposed in them. They have charismatic authority through the spontaneous recognition of people who hear in them a message of more than normal origin. For them the holy scriptures are 'the word of God'. Their authority is legal when an institution makes them 'canonical writings' with binding legal authority. The term 'canon' used above is not limited to this legal aspect. If it were, it would not fit early Christianity at all: the canon was not created in a legal act. Later synods always already presupposed its existence and simply struggled to demarcate the already existing canon and give it legal recognition. In what follows the term 'canon' covers all three forms of authority. The New Testament writings had 'canonical' quality from the start by participating in the charism of their authors (real or fictitious). Traditional authority accrued to them in a continuous process over the course of a century. They attained legal authority only at a secondary stage through conciliar decisions about the extent of the canon.

5. Cf. Roger T. Beckwith, *The Old Testament Canon of the New Testament Church and its Background in Early Judaism*, London: SPCK 1985; id., 'Formation of the Hebrew Bible', in Jan M. Mulder (ed.), *Mikra. Text, Translation and Interpretation of the Hebrew Bible in Ancient Judaism and Early Christianity*, Assen: Van Gorcum and Philadelphia: Fortress Press 1988, 39–86.

6. It should not be disputed that the Acts of the Apostles is religious historiography. Cf. Martin Hengel, *Acts and the History of Earliest Christianity*, London: SCM Press 1979. Of course that does not mean that its statements are 'historical'. But Acts does contain valuable historical reports: because of the many contradictions with the letters of Paul it cannot be derived from the letters of Paul, even if it may have known individual letters of Paul. It is based on independent traditions which can be evaluated historically.

7. The dispute between Hellenists and Hebrews has only been handed down in Acts, but no one regards it as unhistorical. For this dispute and the expulsion of the Hellenists that followed is an intermediate link between primitive Christianity and Paul (which we need for a historical understanding). The dispute arose as a result of different languages and different cultural shaping. Cf. Martin Hengel, 'Between Jesus and Paulus. The "Hellenists", the "Seven" and Stephen (Acts 6.1–15; 7.54–8.3)', in id., *Between Jesus and Paul,* London: SCM Press 1983, 1–29. The dispute need not necessarily have led to the founding of two primitive communities meeting in different places. A group of seven orientated on the local community in Jerusalem and a group of twelve orientated on all Israel could have existed side by side in the same community – and precisely this association in one and the same community could have led to tensions. Cf. Gerd Theissen, 'Hellenisten und Hebräer (Apg 6, 1–6). Gab es eine Spaltung der Urgemeinde?', in Hermann Lichtenberger (ed.), *Geschichte – Tradition -Reflexion, Bd III. Frühes Christentum, FS Martin Hengel*, Tübingen 1996, 323–43.

8. The Apostolic Council is documented by two texts, Gal. 2.1ff. and Acts 15.1ff. The minor contradictions between them guarantee their independence, and the agreements make it possible to asses them historically. In Gal. 2.7 Paul singles out himself and Peter as the two key figures – but in Gal. 2.9 puts Peter with the leading group in Jerusalem, and himself in the delegation from Antioch. There is a certain tension between the two 'versions' which cannot be resolved by supposing that v.7 describes the historical situation and v.9 the shift of power which has taken place before the composition of the letter. Thus Günter Klein, 'Galater 2, 6–9 und die Geschichte der Jerusalemer Urgemeinde', *ZThK* 57, 1960, 275–95 = id., *Rekonstruktion und Interpretation; Gesammelte Aufsätze zum Neuen Testament*, BEvTh 50, Munich: Christian Kaiser Verlag 1969, 99–118 + 118–28. Probably v.7 reflects Paul's view, which is guided by his interest, and v.9 more the historical situation. For v.7 elevates Paul to be the second authority in Christian beginnings. Paul on the one hand needs such a position of authority towards the Galatians, but on the other, by concentrating on Peter and himself he can silence the influential James – whose authority in any case he has to attack in connection with the conflict in Antioch.

9. The conflict in Antioch is connected with the 'Apostolic Decree' (Acts 15.20, 29), which defines minimal requirements for Gentile Christians: no sacrifice to idols, no immorality, no eating of flesh which has been strangled and of blood! Either the delegates from James brought these requirements with them to Antioch (thus Jürgen Roloff, *Einführung in das Neue Testament*, Stuttgart: Reclam 1995, 87), or the requirements of the Apostolic Decree were formulated after the conflict in Antioch in order to make it possible for Jewish and Gentile Christians to live together in the same community (thus the majority of exegetes). Here the question is one of the requirements for aliens (*gerim*) in Lev. 17 and 18, but only those requirements which are accompanied by a threat of extermination (Lev. 17.7; 18.6–29; 17.13f.; 17.10). This has been worked out by Matthias Klinghardt, *Gesetz und Volk Gottes. Das lukanische Verständnis des Gesetzes nach Herkunft, Funktion*

und seinem Ort in der Geschichte des Urchristentums, WUNT II, 32, Tübingen: Mohr (Siebeck) 1988, 181ff. It could be inferred from this 'threat of extermination' that the Apostolic Decree once was an answer to fundamentalist currents in Judaism which were putting pressure on Christians in Palestine. So perhaps the fear of 'those of the circumcision' is to be connected with (non-Christian) Jews.

10. This 'left-wing' Paulinism has very conservative features, as is shown particularly by Colossians. It is closely connected with the Letter to Philemon (through the list of names that they share). In building up the paraenesis about slaves in particular in the household code, Colossians is perhaps deliberately correcting Philemon. Nevertheless, in some features it still stands close to the original Paul. Colossians still knows the principle of equality (Col. 3.11) and a charismatic community order in which each admonishes the other – without special offices being provided for this (Col. 3.16).

11. Josephus, *Antt.* 20, 200, reports the execution of James the brother of the Lord. He singles him out from a group of anonymous men who were executed at that time, namely at a previous date. The reason for his importance and his reputation is that Jewish groups (probably Pharisees) protested against his execution. For his great significance see Martin Hengel, 'Jakobus der Herrenbruder – der erste "Papst"?', in Ernst Grässer and Otto Merk (eds), *Glaube und Eschatologie, FS Werner Georg Kümm*el, Tübingen: Mohr (Siebeck) 1985, 71–104.

12. In the Gospel of the Nazaraeans Jesus heals the man with the withered hand so that he can work again as a bricklayer and not suffer contempt for having to beg (frag.10). The rich young man is made into two rich young men. Jesus does not believe that one has fulfilled the law and the prophets as long as there are poor people in Israel (frag.16). The parable of the talents is told with more of a sense of justice: the only one to be punished is a servant who has squandered the talent entrusted to him on prostitutes and flute-players – not the one who has hidden it (frag. 18). Cf. Paul Vielhauer and Georg Strecker, 'Jewish-Christian Gospels', in Wilhelm Schneemelcher and R. McL. Wilson, *New Testament Apocrypha I. Gospels and Related Writings*, Cambridge: James Clarke and Louisville: Westminster John Knox Press 1991, 134–78 (on the Gospel of the Nazaraeans, 154–65).

13. At the latest in the middle of the second century Papias attributes the Gospel of Mark to one Mark, a companion of Peter who as Peter's translator wrote down his reminiscences (Eusebius, *HE* III 39, 14f.). A sharp-witted person in the second century could have inferred that from the New Testament. There are some scenes to which only Jesus' three closest disciples are witnesses. We can infer from Mark 10.38 that of these, the two sons of Zebedee have died. Only Peter can hand down these events (as also his denial). Now according to II Peter 1.13, 15, (Ps.-) Peter wants to ensure that the truth can be remembered even after his departure. That can be understood as the indication of the fixing of his testimony to Jesus in writing, which took place either during his lifetime or after his death. Who could have handed this testimony down? Only Mark. For according to I Peter 5.13, Mark is with him in Rome (= Babylon) before the death of Peter. Moreover the Gospel

of Mark contains some Aramaic words which have been translated (Mark 5.41; 7.11, 34; 15.22; 15.34). Could it not then be the work of a translator? It is understandable that even today critical exegetes reckon with the possibility that this intelligent inference is the historical truth. At all events, it is probable that the attribution of the Gospel of Mark to Mark took place in a milieu in which Peter and Mark were held in high respect – and that was that middle current in primitive Christianity which wavered between Paul and James in the conflict in Antioch.

14. Oscar Cullmann, *The Johannine Circle*, London: SCM Press 1976, also sees a connection between the Gospel of John and Samaria. Köster, *Einfuhrung* (n.1), 602, conjectures that the Johannine tradition was formed 'in the region of Palestinian Judaism, but developed outside territories controlled by the Jerusalem Sanhedrin, thus in Samaria'. In addition to the indications given, it can be pointed out that Samaria was a favourable area for a special development in primitive Christianity, since some circles of Synoptic Christianity deliberately avoided this region (cf. Matt. 10.5). The Gospel of John shares with the Samaritans an opposition to the Jerusalem temple: the cleansing of the temple in the Gospel of John introduces the public activity of Jesus. Moreover in the first century Samaria was a favourable area for forms of religion close to Gnosticism, as the origin of the Simonians and Dositheans shows. In so far as sometimes in the Gospel of John 'Jews' means 'Judaeans' (John 11.54 etc.), this could be a piece of local perspective.

15. The apostle Philip (in the Gospel of John) and the evangelist Philip (in Acts 6.5; 8.5–20; 21.8) could be the same person – and in the second century are identified with one another by Papias and Polycrates (Eusebius, *HE* III 39, 8–10; III 31, 3). For Luke, one belongs to the Twelve, the other to the Seven. It would be inconceivable for him to identify them with each other, since in Acts 6.1ff. he assumes a division of labour between the Twelve and the Seven. But why should Philip not have belonged to both circles, especially if the Seven were founded to settle the dispute? It would have been sensible to put a representative of the Hellenists, Stephen, and a representative of the Hebrews, Philip, at their head.

16. For the origin of the canon cf. Bruce Metzger, *The Canon of the New Testament*, Oxford: Oxford University Press 1987; Harry Y. Gamble, 'Canon, New Testament', *ABD* I, 1992, 852–61.

17. That letters could be regarded as testimonies of a prophetic spirit is shown by the letters to the churches in Revelation (2.1–3.22), and the framework of this book as a whole as a letter. Cf. Martin Karrer, *Die Johannesoffenbarung als Brief*, FRLANT 140, Göttingen: Vandenhoeck & Ruprecht 1985.

18. The classic work on Marcion is still Adolf von Harnack, *Markion. Das Evangelium vom fremden Gott. Eine Monographie zur Geschichte der Grundlegung der katholischen Kirche,* Leipzig: Hinrichs 1924. Adolf Martin Ritter offers an account of Marcion in the present state of scholarship in *Handbuch der Dogmen- und Theologiegeschichte* 1, Göttingen: Vandenhoeck & Ruprecht [2]1999, 65–9.

19. Marcion's distancing of himself from the Jewish religion is not an antisemitic repudiation of the Jewish people but a theological criticism of the creator God who has a covenant with this people – often with the result that the Jewish

people is exonerated. By contrast Marcion's opponents wanted to defend the Old Testament God – and to attribute all that Marcion attributed to the Jewish God to the misunderstanding of the Jews. Therefore Heikki Räisänen, *Marcion, Muhammad and the Mahatma*, London: SCM Press 1997, 64–80, is right to argue that Marcion should be acquitted of the charge of hostility to the Jews. With modern categories one could say that Marcion was not anti-semitic but a theological anti-Judaist. In so far as the chronological background of the third Jewish War played a role, we might suppose him more to feel compassion for the Jewish people who had been led into this catastrophe by their God. Marcion shares the messianic hopes for a turning point in the oppression of the Jewish people and regards them as valid and legitimate.

20. Cf. Harnack, *Marcion* (n.18), 256–313.

21. Thus above all, Hans von Campenhausen, *The Formation of the Christian Bible*, London: A. & C. Black 1968, who works out two motives in the formation of the canon: individual writings gradually become established on the basis of their content and the church is suddenly confronted with Marcion's canon. Cf. Adolf Martin Ritter, *HThD* 1, 79–84. Even if Marcion was not the first to create the idea of an authoritative collection of scriptures, he did serve as a catalyst to accelerate the formation of the canon.

22. Cf. David Trobisch, *Die Endredaktion des Neuen Testaments*, NTOA 31, Freiburg CH: Universitätsverlag and Göttingen: Vandenhoeck & Ruprecht 1996, who regards these abbreviations as an indication of the final redaction.

23. Martin Hengel, *The Johannine Question,* London: SCM Press and Philadelphia: Trinity Press International 1989, demonstrates that the Gospel of John and the Johannine letters had a particularly strong influence in Asia Minor.

24. In Didache 8.2; 11.3 a particular Gospel is being quoted, probably that of Matthew; thus Klaus Wengst, *Didache (Apostellehre), Barnabasbrief, Zweiter Klemnesbrief, Schrift an Diognet,* SUC II, Darmstadt: Wissenschaftliche Buchgesellschaft 1984, 25ff.

25. Jerome, *De vir.inl.*3, and Epiphanius, *Haer.* 29, 7, 3, attest the dissemination of the Gospel of the Nazaraeans in Beroaea (cf. Schneemelcher-Wilson, *NT Apocrypha* 1, 160, 158).

26. Graham N. Stanton, 'The Fourfold Gospel', *NTS* 43, 1997, 317–46, demonstrates that Justin already presupposes the four-Gospel canon. For the passage quoted above see ibid., 330f.

27. Ulrich H. Körtner, *Papias von Hierapolis. Ein Beitrag zur Geschichte des frühen Christentums*, FRLANT 133, Göttingen: Vandenhoeck & Ruprecht 1983, 167ff., 173ff., is sceptical whether Papias knows the four Gospels.

28. Folker Siegert, 'Unbekannte Papiaszitate bei armenischen Schriftstellern', *NTS* 2, 1981, 605–14.

29. When the Gospel of Mark speaks of 'this gospel' of course it means the content of its writing and not this writing itself. 'Gospel' is still exclusively a kerygmatic and not yet a literary term.

30. David Trobisch, *Die Entstehung der Paulusbriefsammlung*, NTOA 10,

Freiburg CH: Universitätsverlag and Göttingen: Vandenhoeck & Ruprecht 1989; id., *Die Paulusbriefe und die Anfänge der christlichen Publizistik*, KT 135, Gütersloh: Christian Kaiser Verlag 1994, 80ff., has in my view rightly seen that the letters of Paul in the most common order are arranged by length, but that this principle is interrupted twice. The first four letters – Romans, I Corinthians, II Corinthians and Galatians – follow one another and make up 18.4%, 17.5%, 11.9% and 5.9% respectively of the overall extent of the letters of Paul. Ephesians is recognizably longer than Galatians. A second series begins with it: Ephesians (6.4%), Philippians (4.3%), I Thessalonians (4.0%) and II Thessalonians (2.2%). The ordering principle begins a third time with the Pastorals: I Timothy (4.7%), II Timothy (3.5%), Titus (2.0%) and Philemon (0.8%). Hebrews with 14.1% remains outside this order and is inserted at different places in the collections. There is much to suggest that an original collection of letters of Paul comprised Romans, I and II Corinthians and Galatians. It was successively enlarged by two appendixes: first a collection of Ephesians, Colossians, I and II Thessalonians and Philemon, and secondly by a collection with the Pastoral Epistles.

13. Conclusion: The Construction and Plausibility of the Primitive Christian Sign World

1. Cf. Gerd Theissen, 'L'hérméneutique biblique et la recherche de la vérité religieuse', *RThPh* 122, 1990, 485–503.

2. This evolutionary interpretation of the primtiive Christian understanding of the world continues ideas which I developed for the first time in Gerd Theissen, *Biblical Faith. An Evolutionary Approach*, London: SCM Press 1984 and Philadelphia: Fortress Press 1985.

3. Richard Schaeffler, *Fähigkeit zur Erfahrung. Zur transzendentalen Hermeneutik des Sprechens von Gott*, QD 94, Freiburg, Basel and Vienna: Herder 1982, is an example of a transcendental philosophy of religion. This scheme is particularly impressive because no inferences are made from transcendental presuppositions in the consciousness to God. Rather, the argument is based on the shaking of such transcendental presuppositions in historically contingent situations: all experience is first made possible by the collapse of the world of experience which is constituted by them.

4. Anders Nygren, *Die Gültigkeit der religiösen Erfahrung*, Gütersloh: Bertelsmann 1922, emphasized the eternal as the transcendental basic category of the religious. A transcendental category says only that we must necessarily have the notion of something 'eternal'. But precisely because we develop this notion arbitrarily and as a necessity, we are uncertain whether there is a corresponding objective reality and of what nature it is. A sense of the 'eternal' is still no argument for the existence of the 'eternal' in a particular sense, but without a quite formal meaning for 'eternal', the schemes of which the 'eternal' is the content could not arise in the religious imagination and find faith. To put it in more concrete terms: the insight into the 'eternity' of logical structures is not a basis for religious

experience. But without the sense of the eternal expressed in it, there would be no additional religious experience of the eternal.

5. Rudolf Malter, 'Kant', *TRE* 17, 1988, 570–81: 576f.

6. The Gnostic intuitive experience of the self as a phenomenon akin to divine being is a variant of mystical experiences. In connection with it, attention has rightly been drawn to the great significance of the de-automation of perception and the assimilation of impressions. Cf. Nils G. Holm, *Einführung in die Religionspsychologie*, Munich: Reinhardt Verlag 1990, 72–5.

7. Cf. Adolf M. Ritter, *HDTh* I, 49f.

8. The image of the cathedral has a limitation: it suggests a static quality which is not present in a living system. In the New Testament, time and again this image of the building is interwoven with an organic image of the body: the church building grows with all its members (Eph. 2.21; cf. 4.12). But the image of the organism is perhaps still too harmonious: with it the deep conflicts and crises could appear only as 'sicknesses' which are to be understood as disruptions. But that is not what they were: primitive Christianity was first formed through them. Canonical Christianity owes its form to its controversies with a world which often rejected it and with bold 'heretical' currents.

Index of References to the Bible and Other Ancient Texts

2. Early Jewish literature

(b) Extracanonical literature

4. Graeco-Roman literature

5. Christian literature

General Index